Elise C. Otté

How to Learn Danish

A Manual for Students of Danish (Dano-Norwegian)

Elise C. Otté

How to Learn Danish
A Manual for Students of Danish (Dano-Norwegian)

ISBN/EAN: 9783337085902

Printed in Europe, USA, Canada, Australia, Japan

Cover: Foto ©Paul-Georg Meister /pixelio.de

More available books at **www.hansebooks.com**

HOW TO LEARN DANISH
(DANO-NORWEGIAN).

A MANUAL

FOR

STUDENTS OF DANISH
(DANO-NORWEGIAN).

Based upon the Ollendorffian System of Teaching Languages, and adapted for Self-Instruction.

BY

E. C. OTTÉ.

LONDON:
TRÜBNER & CO., LUDGATE HILL.

1879.

LONDON:
J. S. LEVIN, STEAM PRINTER, 2, MARK LANE SQUARE,
GREAT TOWER STREET, E.C.

CONTENTS.

	PAGE
INTRODUCTION	ix
FIRST LESSON.—On the Indefinite Article	1
SECOND LESSON.—On the Definite Article	4
THIRD LESSON.—On the Definite Article (*continued*) ...	8
FOURTH LESSON.—On Nouns	12
FIFTH LESSON.—On the Gender of Nouns	15
SIXTH LESSON.—On the Formation of the Plural of Nouns... ...	19
Conjugation of the Verb *at have* (= to have)	23
Conjugation of the Verb *at være* (= to be)	24
SEVENTH LESSON.—On Adjectives	25
EIGHTH LESSON.—On Adjectives (*continued*)	29
The Danish Cardinal Numbers	30
NINTH LESSON.—On Numerals	32
The Days of the Week	33
The Months of the Year	33
TENTH LESSON.—On certain Terms of Quantity, etc.	36
ELEVENTH LESSON.—On the Comparison of Adjectives	39
TWELFTH LESSON.—On Irregular Adjectives	43
Conjugation of the Auxiliary Verbs *at få* (= to get, to obtain), and *at blive* (= to become, to be, to remain)	47
Conjugation of the Auxiliary Verbs *at skulle*, to be obliged, ought (= shall, should), and *at ville*, to be willing (= will, would)	49
THIRTEENTH LESSON.—On Pronouns	51
FOURTEENTH LESSON.—On the Demonstrative Pronouns, etc. ...	55
FIFTEENTH LESSON.—On Pronouns (*continued*)	60
SIXTEENTH LESSON.—On the Regular Verbs	64
SEVENTEENTH LESSON.—On Adverbs	69

	PAGE
EIGHTEENTH LESSON.—Comparison of Adverbs, etc....	73
Examples of Verbs belonging to Class I.	78
Examples of Verbs belonging to Class II.	78
Verbs conjugated both in accordance with Conjugations I. and II.	79
NINETEENTH LESSON.—Prepositions	79
TWENTIETH LESSON.—Conjunctions, Interjections	83
TWENTY-FIRST LESSON.—Passive Verbs, etc.	87
Paradigms of Passive Form of Verbs	89
TWENTY-SECOND LESSON.—On Irregular Verbs	92
Examples of Irregular Verbs	93
TWENTY-THIRD LESSON.—On the Composition of Verbs	97
TWENTY-FOURTH LESSON.—On Irregular and other Verbs	101
List of Titles, Tradesmen's Callings, etc.	105
TWENTY-FIFTH LESSON.—Examples of Irregular Verbs	106
TWENTY-SIXTH LESSON.—On the Plural of Nouns	111
TWENTY-SEVENTH LESSON.—Examples of Nouns which make their Plural in *er*	116
TWENTY-EIGHTH LESSON.—Examples of Nouns which remain the same in the Plural as in the Singular	119
TWENTY-NINTH LESSON.—Examples of Words, the meanings of which differ in accordance with difference of Gender	123
THIRTIETH LESSON.—On Compound Verbs	126
List of Geographical and other Terms	130

PART II.

THIRTY-FIRST LESSON.—On the Formation of Words	131
THIRTY-SECOND LESSON.—On the Formation of Words (*continued*)— Nouns	135
THIRTY-THIRD LESSON.—On the Formation of Words (*continued*)— Adjectives	139
THIRTY-FOURTH LESSON.—On the Formation of Words (*continued*)— Verbs	143
THIRTY-FIFTH LESSON.—On the Formation of Words (*continued*)— Adverbs and Prepositions	147
THIRTY-SIXTH LESSON.—On Compound Words	150

	PAGE
THIRTY-SEVENTH LESSON.—Syntax.—On the use of the Indefinite Article	155
THIRTY-EIGHTH LESSON.—On the use of the Definite Article	160
THIRTY-NINTH LESSON.—On the Articles (*continued*)	164
FORTIETH LESSON.—On Nouns	168
FORTY-FIRST LESSON.—On Nouns (*continued*)	172
FORTY-SECOND LESSON.—On Adjectives	177
Names of Animals, etc.	182
FORTY-THIRD LESSON.—On Pronouns	183
FORTY-FOURTH LESSON.—On Pronouns (*continued*)	188
FORTY-FIFTH LESSON.—On Verbs	193
FORTY-SIXTH LESSON.—On the Auxiliary Verbs, etc.	197
FORTY-SEVENTH LESSON.—On Adverbs, etc.	202
FORTY-EIGHTH LESSON.—On Prepositions	206
List of Geographical and other Terms	210
FORTY-NINTH LESSON.—On Prepositions (*continued*)	211
FIFTIETH LESSON.—On the use of certain Prepositions and Conjunctions	216
FIFTY-FIRST LESSON.—On the use of certain Conjunctions	219
FIFTY-SECOND LESSON.—On the use of certain Conjunctions (*continued*)	223
FIFTY-THIRD LESSON.—On the use of some of the Auxiliaries	227
FIFTY-FOURTH LESSON.—On the use of the Participles	231
Names of Minerals, etc.	235
FIFTY-FIFTH LESSON.—On the different Forms of Verbs	236
FIFTY-SIXTH LESSON.—On the Distinctive Characteristics of Irregular Verbs	240
First Class	241
FIFTY-SEVENTH LESSON.—On the Irregular Verbs (*continued*)—	
Second Class	245
Third and Fourth Classes	246
FIFTY-EIGHTH LESSON.—On the Irregular Verbs (*continued*)—Fifth and Sixth Classes	250
Seventh, Eighth, Ninth, and Tenth Classes	251
FIFTY-NINTH LESSON.—On Passive and Deponent Verbs	255
SIXTIETH LESSON.—On the use of the Auxiliaries *at vare* and *at have*	259

	PAGE
SIXTY-FIRST LESSON.—On the use of the Potential Mood, etc. ...	263
SIXTY-SECOND LESSON.—On the Position of Words in a Sentence, etc.	266
SIXTY-THIRD LESSON.—On the Apposition of Words...	271
APPENDIX I.—Examples of the use of Danish Prepositions... ...	275
Danish Idioms in common use	277
Abbreviations of Common Occurrence	286
APPENDIX II.—The Alphabet	287
On the use of the Letters	289
On Accentuation	291
On the Division of Syllables	292
On Spelling and Mode of Writing	293
APPENDIX III.—Recapitulation of Grammatical Rules	296
Etymology	296
The Indefinite Article	296
The Definite Articles	297
The Noun	298
The Declination of Nouns	301
Adjectives	303
On the Comparison of Adjectives...	305
Adverbs	308
On the Comparison of Adverbs	309
Pronouns	310
Verbs...	312
Regular Verbs	313
Passive Verbs	313
Deponent Verbs	314
Irregular Verbs	315
On the Moods and Tenses of Verbs	320
Prepositions	322
Conjunctions	325
Interjections	326
On the Formation of Words	326
Composition of Words	328
Construction of Sentences	329

INTRODUCTION.

THE term "Dano-Norwegian" has been used throughout the present work to avoid the constant repetition of the words *Danish* and *Norwegian*, both being, in point of fact, one and the same language.

Of late years a desire has been shown by certain patriotic Norwegians to secure for their native land a special mother-tongue, distinct from that which has for ages been common to the natives of Denmark and Norway. But the attempt to revive the language spoken by Norwegians before the union of their country with Denmark, at the close of the fourteenth century, would seem as impracticable and undesirable in our times, as if Englishmen were to insist upon incorporating in their written language the various remnants of Old English, which still survive in the local dialects of Cumberland, Dorset, and Somerset.

Since the Reformation, Norwegians and Danes have had the same Bible and Psalter, and have studied from the same school-books, while the same national ballads, songs, and proverbs have been common to both. The illiterate classes of Norway have, indeed, used Old Northern words, and spoken with a special provincial accent, but the peasants of Jutland, Fyen, and Sealand have done the same. The educated classes, on the other hand, have long spoken and written the same form of Danish, whether they were natives of Norway or of Denmark. In every branch of Danish literature Norwegians have added their full share to the common national treasury of learning, while in some departments it is not too much to say, that their country may challenge comparison with the most highly cultivated nations of Europe. In proof of this we need only point to that "Admirable Crichton" of Norway, Ludvig Holberg (born at Bergen, 1684, died in 1754), in whom

Scandinavians justly pride themselves in having a second Molière. The numerous works with which Holberg enriched his Danish mother-tongue include learned treatises on Scandinavian and European History, Biography, Statistics, Geography, Jurisprudence, Metaphysics, and Philosophy. But great as were the merits of some of these, they have been eclipsed by the more brilliant light of his inimitable comedies, the broad humour and sparkling wit of which are still as keenly appreciated by every class of Danes as they were a century and a half ago, when Holberg's plays were first acted in the theatres of Copenhagen.

Such a common heritage of language, which has grown with the growth of the literary and social culture of the two nations, is not to be cancelled at the will of one generation. Nor is there reason to fear, that any attempt to rehabilitate the Norwegian of past ages will have other results than that of preserving, for Scandinavians, the many relics of provincial dialects, which have been transmitted by word of mouth, from one generation to another, among the peasants of the Bergen, Hardanger, Nordland, Telemark, and other districts of Norway. Every effort, made for the preservation of these important heirlooms of the past condition of the language, merits the gratitude of all who are interested in the study of the Scandinavian tongues; and, happily for the fate of some of the old Norwegian dialects, several glossaries of provincial words have, during the last two centuries, been compiled by natives of the several districts in which they were current. The earliest of these compilations that deserve notice is a work, printed at Copenhagen, in 1646, and entitled *Den norske Dictionarium eller Glosebog*. And here it is curious to note that the author, Christian Jensen, pastor of Askevold in the Söndfjord, deems it necessary to crave the indulgence of the learned for his attempt to preserve a record of words, used only by illiterate persons; although he expresses a faint hope, that his dictionary may be found serviceable to those who desire to become better acquainted with their own mother-tongue. A century later, the learned historian and naturalist, Erik Pontoppidan, bishop of Bergen, brought out his *Glossarium Norvagicum, eller Samling af rare norske Ord*, (Bergen, 1749), which, small as it is, contains much interesting matter that had escaped Jensen's notice. From these and other materials, augmented by the results of numerous local glossaries, compiled since Pontoppidan's time, Herr Ivar Aasen has, in our own day, successfully constructed a complete dictionary of popular Norwegian words. This exhaustive work, which appeared at Christiania in 1873, under the title of *Norsk Ordbog, med dansk Forklaring*, "Norwegian Dictionary, with explanations in Danish," makes no pretensions to be a school class-book, or to serve as a guide to the literary written language of the country, but simply claims to be a depository of all genuine northern words, with the numerous variants and differences of meaning belonging to them in different districts. In this respect it would be difficult to overrate the value of Herr Aasen's compilation, not merely for Scandinavians, but also for English students, who will find that his explanations of the strictly local meanings of many nearly obsolete Norwegian words, not unfrequently, throw considerable light on obscure etymologies in their own language.

The choice of the system of spelling and writing Danish, which should be adopted in the present work, has not been unattended by some degree of doubt and difficulty, since Danish orthography has not yet fully emerged from that condition of uncertainty and confusion, which is inseparable from the period of transition, which must intervene between the breaking away with an old state of things, and the acceptance of that which is new. Danish spelling has in fact, within the last ten years, been passing through a radical revolution, in which the objects principally aimed at have been: to arrest the further progress of the marked degeneration into which the language had fallen through contact with foreign elements; and to fix the rules for spelling upon sound phonetic principles, having respect to the Old Northern, and to the existing usages of the other Scandinavian people. This movement, which derived its origin from Rask, and some of the earlier Danish grammarians, who had long been sensible of the absolute need of instituting a complete change in the spelling of their mother-tongue, owes its present successful development to the Orthographical Congress, which met at Stockholm, in the summer of 1869.

The objects set forth at this meeting were: to deliberate upon the best means of removing the differences that existed in the written languages of the Scandinavian peoples, in order to bring them more closely into harmony with the rules of the Old Northern, from which Swedish (*Svensk*) and Danish (*Dansk-Norsk*) have derived their common origin.

The Resolutions passed by the Congress, which was composed half of Swedes, and half of Danes and Norwegians, have been so cordially received in all three countries, that they have achieved, within the limited period of one decennium, nearly all the results for which grammarians had been unsuccessfully striving during more than two hundred years. The system of spelling, advocated by the Congress of 1869, although practically in its infancy, owes its existence to long-standing requirements, since the necessity for introducing a radical change in Danish orthography had been recognised, alike by Danes and Norwegians, from the moment that scholars began to turn their attention to the study of their native tongue. One of the earliest and most zealous advocates for a reform in the spelling and writing of Danish was the accomplished and genial Peder Syv (born in 1631, died in 1702), who specially distinguished himself by the practical good sense and sound learning, with which he demonstrated the evils, resulting from the practice of his times, in using letters and modes of construction which were wholly foreign to the Old Northern. He waged special war against the inelegant practice, that had crept into the language, of doubling the consonants; but neither precept nor ridicule could cure his countrymen of the taste for indulging in such verbal superfluity as that, for instance, of using *ffu* to represent the sound of *v*, as in *haffue* (*have*, to have). Yet, no man had a better claim than Peder Syv to command a hearing in regard to grammatical or linguistic questions, for while his great work, entitled *Grammatica danica* (Kjöbenhavn, 1685) had earned for him the appellation of *Philologus regius lingræ danicæ*, his various collections of Danish Proverbs, and his edition of the old *Kæmpeviser*, or national ballads, had made him known to his countrymen as a zealous and proficient student of their common national literature.

It is difficult to say whether Peder Syv effected any improvement in the vicious spelling of his times, but he was soon followed by an able disciple, J. K. Rosenqvist Höjsgård, (born 1698, died in 1773), who, taking up another weak point in his native language, assailed the cumbrous practice of doubling the vowels, as for example, in writing *Steen*, (*Sten*) stone; *Viin* (*Vin*) wine; *Noord* (*Nord*) north; *Huus* (*Hus*) house, etc. It is to Höjsgård, moreover, to whom we are indebted for the earliest suggestion that the double a (aa), which has not the same sound as simple *a*, should be represented by the character å, which is found in early Danish and Norwegian MSS., and had been used in Swedish from the middle of the sixteenth century. The vowel-sounds received special attention from Höjsgård, who, in addition to two learned treatises, known as *Förste og anden Pröve af dansk Ortographie* (Kjöbenhavn, 1743) "First and Second Examination of Danish Orthography," wrote a comprehensive work, entitled *Accentueret og raisonneret Grammatica, som viser det danske Sprog i sin naturlige Skikkelse*, 1747, "An Accentuated and Systematic Grammar, showing the Danish language in its natural forms."

If these works, like Peder Syv's, failed to bring about any radical amendment in the spoken and written language of their day, they had, at all events, the distinguished merit of being accepted by the great philologer, Rasmus Kristian Rask, as the basis of that system of orthography, which has become identified with his name, and which he first made popularly known in a paper, which appeared in the *Tidskrift for nordisk Oldkyndighed*, entitled *Forsög til en videnskabelig dansk Retskrivningslære med Hensyn til Stamsproget og Nabosproget* (Khvn., 1825), "An Attempt towards a Scientific Danish Orthography, having reference to the derivative mother-tongue (Old Northern), and to the language of our neighbours (Swedish)."

Rask's system, although advocated by some of the ablest northern scholars of his time, as N. M. Petersen and others, was neglected, if not ridiculed, by the majority of his countrymen, who regarded it as at once impracticable and pedantic. It has, however, outlived neglect and ridicule, and, with some few modifications and amendments, is now embodied in the Resolutions passed by the Stockholm Congress, through which it seems destined to exert a lasting influence on the character and future development of Swedish and Danish. In doing honour to the original founders of the new system of Danish orthography, and to those who have so ably reduced to a practical form the suggestions of Syv, Höjsgård, Rask, and Petersen, it would be unjust were we to omit to record the fact, that it is mainly due to the exertions of one man, Professor Då, of Christiania, that the meeting at Stockholm was called together, and consequently that to him his Scandinavian brethren are indebted for the great benefits which their mother-tongue has derived from the deliberations of the Congress of 1869.

Professor Då had long been sensible of the important practical advantage which the Scandinavian peoples would secure for themselves by a more uniform method of spelling and writing their respective languages; the differences in which were often exaggerated, and even in some cases created, by the absence of fixed rules of orthography. Actuated by the desire to bring about such a result, Professor Då visited Copenhagen in the summer of 1868, and by his strenuous endeavours secured the cooperation of the leading Danish university professors and teachers, who willingly entered into his suggestion, that the question of Scandinavian spelling should be submitted to the consideration of a mixed Commission of Swedes, and of Danes and Norwegians. In this scheme the Swedish and Norwegian universities concurred, and, after some discussion, it was finally decided that each of these bodies should choose its appointed number of representatives, in accordance with its own special rules for the election of delegates. In Copenhagen, the university authorities invited writers, publishers, printers, and other sections of the community interested in the question, to take part, through representatives, in the election of the Danish members of the Congress, which, it was agreed, should hold its meetings at Stockholm, during the last week of July, 1869. The mixed Commission consisted of 18 members (including in the Dano-Norwegian half, the poet Ibsen, Professor Då, and the able Danish lexiographer Svend Grundtvig), and was under the presidency of Professor Malmström, of the university of Upsala.

Full reports of the proceedings **were** drawn up **at** the close of the meeting, by the respective secretaries, and were written and printed in strict conformity with the resolutions that had been unanimously accepted by each section. In 1870, Herr Svend Grundtvig, in conjunction with Herr A. J. Block and K. J. Lyngby, Secretary of the *Dansk-Norsk* (Dano-Norwegian) section of the Congress, brought out, at Copenhagen, a Danish dictionary, *Dansk Retskrivnings-Ordbog*, which had been compiled in exact accordance with the rules laid down at the meeting. This dictionary, which gives only words that are genuinely Danish, either through origin or long-established adoption, has been selected as the standard for spelling in the present work from the conviction, which, we think, can scarcely fail to be shared by all who are following the progress of Danish and Norwegian literature, that this new and scientifically well-based system of orthography will rapidly supersede the older and less exact modes of spelling. The benefits derived from the new forms of spelling and writing are not limited to appearance, or to the convenience arising from the rejection of superfluous characters; nor are they restricted to natives, for the changes, which the Stockholm Congress advocates, have the important advantage that they very materially lessen the apparent differences between Dano-Norwegian (*Dansk-Norsk*) and Swedish (*Svensk*), and thus supply foreigners, who have studied one of these forms of Scandinavian, with a key to the comprehension of the sister-tongue.

Having thus traced the progress of the changes in Danish orthography from their earliest development, we will briefly enumerate the principal features of the new system, which are as follows:—

 1. To use *æ* and *ä* in both languages, wherever the sound of these letters is etymologically warranted: discarding in Swedish the use of the character *ä*, and in Dano-Norwegian that of *e* or *o*, often erroneously made use of to represent the sounds of *æ* and *ä*:

 2. To substitute in both languages *t* for *th*:

 3. To replace in both *q* by *k*;

 4. To eliminate *x*, and replace it by *ks*:

 5. To avoid, as far as practicable, to write as one compound any associated group of words, which belong

to different parts of speech (as *igåraftes*, which should be written *i Går Aftes*, last evening);
6. To substitute Latin characters in writing and printing for the Gothic, or German;
7. To discard *e* in all cases where it is mute;
8. To discard the use of double vowels;
9. To substitute the character *å* for *aa*;
10. To use *j*, instead of *i*, in the so-called diphthongs *ej*, *öj*;
11. To discard *j* after *g* and *k*, followed by a soft vowel, as *æ*, *e*, *ö*;
12. To change *vt* into *ft*;
13. To discard mute *d* before *sk*, and *ns*, and wherever else it may occur, unless its presence is required on etymological grounds (as in *vidste*, knew, from *at vide*, to know);
14. To avoid doubling a consonant, except for the purpose of marking the plural of a noun ending in a short syllable;
15. To discard the use of capital initial letters for common nouns, unless they begin a sentence.*
16. To use an accent to distinguish words of different meanings, which are spelt the same; as: *let* (light), *lét* (laughed); this distinctive mark should, however, only be employed where the context fails to show the sense.

We have excluded from the above summary as irrelevant several points which refer exclusively to Swedish. It ought, however, to be observed that in the majority of cases, where the two languages differed, the *Dansk-Norsk* was generally found to have deviated much more widely than the *Svensk* from the rules and usage of the Old Northern. The Swedes have kept their mother-tongue much purer from admixture with foreign elements than their neighbours, and this is, undoubtedly, in a great measure due to the geographical position of Sweden, and to her long immunity from foreign

---

* In this particular instance we have not followed the rules laid down in S. Grundtvig's *Dansk Retskrivnings-Ordbog*. This deviation from the regulations of the new system was made, however, solely with a view of giving the student some help in recognising nouns as distinct from the other parts of speech.

domination. Denmark, on the other hand, from her close contiguity to Germany, the incorporation of German-speaking populations with her own people, and the presence of a long line of rulers, who, with few exceptions, never forgot that they were Germans by origin, has for ages been exposed to Germanising influences, which could not fail to affect the genuine Scandinavian character of her language. This is shown, amongst many other points, in the presence of numerous alien particles, and of certain modes of grammatical construction, not met with in Swedish; while the spoken language of the Danes betrays, in its less strongly-marked Northern intonation, its subjection to influences which have not acted on Norwegians with equal force, and have had comparatively little power over the Swedes.

In conclusion, it would seem almost superfluous to remind the reader, that, through the acquisition of the living Scandinavian languages, the English student will open for himself an easy road towards the attainment of Icelandic, or Old Northern, the sister-tongue of Anglo-Saxon, and a most efficient interpreter of the derivations of his own language. Even modern Danish, in spite of its numerous adventitious foreign ingredients, will be found able to show the English student the significance of numerous expressions, whose etymological meaning has been lost by the disappearance from his mother-tongue of certain derivatives, which still survive in the language of Denmark and Norway. In proof of this we will only select a few words, taken at random, as in the following list, which might easily have een extended to much greater dimensions:—

DANISH.

to ban	*at bande*	to curse
barm	*Bærme*	dregs
bast	*Bast*	a straw band
a beck	*Bæk*	a stream
to blazen	*at bløse*	to blow
to bleach, blight	*bleg*	pale
to box	*at baske*	to strike
bracken	*Bregne*	a fern
brackish	*brak*	flat
to brag	*at brage*	to crash
brocade	*broget*	variegated

b

buckwheat	*Boghvede**	*Bog*, beech / *Hvede*, wheat
bye-law	*Bylov*	town-law
to clap	*at klappe*	to strike
clout	*Klud*	a rag
hay-cock	*Kok*	a heap
costermonger	*Kost*	a broom
to cow	*at kue*	to intimidate
to cram	*at kramme*	to crush
a crate	*Krate*	copse, undergrowth
crockery	*Krug*	a jug
to cruise	*at krydse*	to cross
deal, dole	*Del*	a part
dowdy	*doven*	lazy
to drill	*at drille*	to make a hole
to egg on	*at egge*	to stir, urge
a fell	*Fjæld* (Norw.)	mountain-side
a fellow	*fælles*	mutual
flask	*Flaske*	a bottle
flagstone	*Flag*	a flake, cutting
a flint	*at flise*	to split
gammon (slang)	*Gammen*	mirth
garden	*Gård* / *Gærde*	yard / enclosure
to harrow	*at hærje*	to ravage
rose hip	*Hybe*	seed-vessel of a rose
husband	*Hus* / *Bonde*	house / peasant owner / house master
jolly boat	*Jolle*	little boat
to nag	*at nage*	to gnaw
neighbour	*nær* / *Bo*	near / dwelling
queen, quean	*Kvinde*	woman
ransack	*Ran* / *Sag*	robbery / action
rowan	*Rön*	mountain ash
to score	*at skære*	to cut
scurf	*Skorpe*	a crust
scrubwood	*skrubbet*	rough, rugged
smuggle	*Smug*	underhand
tarn	*Tjærn*	small lake
twine, twist	*tvende*	two
ware, aware	*var* / *at blive var*	watchful / to perceive
wont	*Vane*	custom
wrist	*Håndvrist* / *Fodvrist*	wrist / ancle,

(the joints on which the hand and foot turn [*at vriste*, to turn]).

* So called from the resemblance of the grain to a beech-nut.

It now only remains for us to state, that the object aimed at in the present grammar has been to enable the learner to be his own teacher, should circumstances not allow him to secure the help of an efficient master. With this end in view, the Ollendorffian system has been followed in its main principles of repetition and retrogression; each lesson being worked out by means of some additional words, or new rules, together with those already learnt in previous lessons. Whilst this method of progress by retrogression has been followed throughout, provision has also been made for the requirements of students, who may desire to combine with it a study of the Danish grammar in a more abstract form. We have accordingly devoted the last 50 pages of the work to a complete summary of all the grammatical rules given in the lessons, including remarks on the alphabet, accentuation, spelling, construction of sentences, etc.

By this double method of recapitulation, we have endeavoured to meet the wants of all learners, and to afford the self-taught student the means of acquiring, with facility, a practical, yet thorough knowledge of the Danish language.

London, 1879.

E. C. OTTÉ.

FIRST LESSON.

ON THE INDEFINITE ARTICLE.

Det ubestemte Kendeord.

The indefinite article in Danish must agree in gender with the noun which it precedes.

The Danish language recognises two distinct genders, viz.:

I. The *common gender*, including all masculines and feminines, which is known in Danish as *Fælleskön*, from *fælles*, common, mutual, and *Kön*, gender or sex.

II. The *neuter gender*, which is known as *Intetkön*, from *intet*, nothing, and *Kön*, gender or sex.

The Indefinite Article (*det ubestemte Kendeord* [= *Artikkel*]) is:—

COMMON GENDER.	NEUTER GENDER.
En, a.	Et, a.

This article precedes in an independent form the noun to which it refers, precisely in the same manner as the indefinite article is used in English.

All nouns are either of the common, or of the neuter gender.

EXAMPLES of nouns of both genders:—

COMMON GENDER.	NEUTER GENDER.
en *Mand*, a man (husband)	et *Barn*, a child
en *Kone*, a woman (wife)	et *Hus*, a house
en *Pige*, a girl	et *Værelse*, a room
en *Dreng*, a boy	et *Vindue*, a window
en *Ven*, a friend	et *Skib*, a ship
en *Bog*, a book	et *Brev*, a letter
en *Skov*, a wood	et *Æble*, an apple
en *Kniv*, a knife	et *Lys*, a light
en *Stol*, a chair	et *Bord*, a table
en *Snor*, a string, cord.	et *Glas*, a glass.

The following words are given for the formation of sentences in connection with these nouns :—

ja, yes	*At have*, to have.
nej, no	PRESENT INDICATIVE.
men, but	*Singular.*
og, and	
også, also	*jeg har*, I have
ikke, not	*du har*, thou hast
eller, or	*han har*, he has
nu, now	*hun har*, she has
med, with.	*De har*, you have.

It will be observed that all persons in the singular, and *De*, answering to our "you," take the same form of the verb, viz., *har*. This is in conformity with the ordinary mode of conjugating Danish verbs, which, with few exceptions, to which attention will be drawn in the lessons on the irregular verbs, take an *r* in the present tense of the indicative mood for all persons of the singular, (including *De*, You).

COMMON.	NEUTER.		*At være*, to be.		
god,	*godt*,	good	PRESENT INDICATIVE.	*her*, here
stor,	*stort*,	large	*Singular.*	*der*, there
kort,	*kort*,	short	*jeg er*,	I am	*hvor*, where
lang,	*langt*,	long	*du er*,	thou art	*på*, on
min,	*mit*,	my	*han, hun er*,	he, she is	*i*, in
Deres,	*Deres*,	your.	*De er*,	you are.	*ud*, out.

SIMPLE PHRASES.

To illustrate the use of the words already given.

Jeg har et godt Værelse i mit Hus.	I have a good room in my house.
Er Du der?	Art thou there?
Ja, her er jeg.	Yes, here am I.
Hvor er Deres Kone?	Where is your wife?
Hun er med mit Barn.	She is with my child.
En Dreng er i Deres Skov.	A boy is in your wood.
Har ikke min Ven et stort Hus?	Has not my friend a large house?
Han har en stor Stol og en lang Kniv.	He has a large chair and a long knife.
Der er en kort Snor og et stort Bord.	There is a short string and a large table.
Hvor er min Ven?	Where is my friend?
Han er i Deres Skib.	He is in your ship.
Hun har et godt Æble med.	She has a good apple (with her).

Der er et Lys på et Bord.	There is a light upon a table.
Mit Værelse har et Lys.	My room has a light.
Der er et Vindue her.	There is a window here.
Du er også på mit Skib.	Thou art also onboard my ship.
En Dreng eller en Pige, men ikke en Mand eller en Kone.	A boy or a girl, but not a man or a woman.
Nu! hvor er Du?	Now (then)! where art thou?
Jeg er her, og hun er også her i Deres Hus.	I am here, and she is also here in your house.
Er hun en god Pige?	Is she a good girl.
Nej, en god Pige er hun ikke.	No, she is not a good girl.
Min Mand har et langt Brev.	My husband has a long letter.

FIRST EXERCISE.

A woman has a house and a wood. I have a knife and a string. Have you a knife? Yes, I have a knife. Have you a husband? No, I have not a husband. Has a boy a ship? No, a man has a ship. A house has a room. A room has a table and a chair also. A window has glass. Has a girl a book, or has he a book? No, now I have a book and a letter. A room has a light. A woman has a glass. Have you a friend? Yes, I have a friend, a wife, and a child. A boy has an apple, but not a knife or a string. A man has a candle. Has a girl or a boy a house and a wood? No, now she has not a house or a wood; but he has a house. A boy has a table and a chair, and a child has an apple and a book. Has a girl a friend? No, she has not a friend. Have you a letter? Yes, I have a letter.

Translate into English.

En Mand gav[1] en Pige et Æble. Jeg har et Hus med et Værelse og et stort Vindue. Har De et godt Værelse? Nej, men min Ven har et godt Værelse, og et godt Hus også. En Dreng gav min Kone en Kniv og en Bog med en Snor. Har min Kone et Brev? Nej, hun har ikke et Brev, men hun har en Bog. Mit

[1] Gav, gave; from give, to give.

Hus har et Værelse med et Vindue, et Bord og en Stol. Har Deres Ven et Skib? Ja, min Ven har et Skib og også en Skov, men nu har han ikke et Hus eller et Værelse. Har De min Stol eller mit Bord? Nej, jeg har ikke Deres Stol eller Deres Bord. Hun gav et Barn et Æble, og jeg gav en Pige et Lys og et Glas. Har De mit Glas eller mit Lys? Nej, jeg har ikke Deres Lys eller Deres Glas. Hun har en god Skov, men ikke et godt Hus. Har Deres Mand ikke en god Skov? Nej, han har ikke en god Skov, men han har et godt Hus.

SECOND LESSON.

ON THE DEFINITE ARTICLE.

Det bestemte Kendeord (=Artikkel).

The definite article in Danish is used under two forms:—

I. The *substantive form*, which is expressed by an affix.

II. The *adjective form*, which is used as an independent word.

In either case the definite article (*den bestemte Artikkel*) must agree in gender and number with the noun which it defines.

I.—THE SUBSTANTIVE FORM (*Substantivernes Artikkel*).

This is used to designate the noun, but only in cases where the latter is *not* preceded by an adjective, pronoun, or other qualifying part of speech.

This form of the article is expressed by the following affixes:—

Singular.
COMMON GENDER.   NEUTER GENDER.
en or *n*.   *et* or *t*.

Plural.
BOTH GENDERS.—*ene* or *ne*.

The following examples will show how these affixes are incorporated with the noun, forming when thus appended one sole word, which expresses the noun and its corresponding article:—

en Mand, a man		Manden, the man	
en Kone, a woman		Konen, the woman	
et Barn, a child		Barnet, the child	
et Værelse, a room		Værelset, the room	
Mænd, plural of Mand, man		Mændene, the men	
Koner	„	Kone, woman	Konerne, the women
Børn	„	Barn, child	Børnene, the children
Værelser	„	Værelse, room	Værelserne, the rooms.

It will be observed that where the noun ends in *e*, as *Kone*, it only takes an *n*, instead of *en*, as in *Mand*, to designate the common gender of the definite article. Similarly in neuter nouns, ending in *e*, as *Værelse*, the definite article is expressed by the addition of *t* only, as *Værelset*, and not of *et*, as in *Barn, Barnet*.

By the above examples it will be seen that the definite article, in its simple indicative character, combines with the noun, and forms one word with it.

In this peculiarity of the Danish article (which will be more fully considered in Part II.) we have a remnant of an old northern mode of construction, which is still common to all the Scandinavian dialects.

N.B.—As the use of this article-affix presents special difficulties to foreigners, it is desirable that the student should thoroughly familiarise himself with it before he passes on to the consideration of the other parts of speech.

en Pære, a pear.	pl.	Pærer, pears		grå, grey
en Blomme, a plum	„	Blommer, plums		hvid, white
en Kake, a cloak	„	Kaker, cloaks		rød, red
en Hat, a hat	„	Hatte, hats		grøn, green
en Stok, a stick	„	Stokke, sticks		blå, blue
en Pen, a pen	„	Penne, pens		gul, yellow
en Ryg, a back	„	Rygge, backs.		sort, black
Kan jeg få? can I obtain (get)?				

COMMON.	NEUTER.			
smuk,	smukt,	pretty	hans, his	fra, from
lille,	lille,	little	hendes, her, hers	til, to (prep.)
bred,	bredt,	broad	indi, within	at, to (conj.)
smal,	smalt,	narrow	udi, without	af, of (prep.)
kær,	kært,	dear	oppe i, up in	ud af, out of

¹ Words of one syllable ending in a consonant, as *k, n, t, s, t*, in which the vowel is short and unaccented, as *Ryg, Hat, Top, Stok*, &c., double the final consonant, when modified by the definite article *en, et*, as *Ryggen, Hatten, Toppen, Stokken, Glasset.*

SIMPLE PHRASES.

To illustrate the use of the words given in this, and the preceding Lesson.

Hvor er Manden, og hvor er Drengen?	Where is the man, and where is the boy.
Pigen er her, men ikke Konen.	The girl is here, but not the woman.
Vennen har et lille Barn.	The friend has a little child.
Barnet er inde i Huset.	The child is inside the house.
Værelset har et smukt Vindue.	The room has a pretty window.
Her er Pigen med Stolen.	Here is the girl with the chair.
Der er Bordet med Lyset.	There is the table with the light.
Jeg har et Lys, min Ven, men Lyset er ikke paa Bordet.	I have a light, my friend, but the light is not on the table.
Hvor er Pennen og hvor er Brevet?	Where is the pen, and where is the letter?
Han har Hatten på.	He has his (the) hat on.
Hun har Stokken med.	She has the stick (with her).
Konen har Æbler, Blommer og Pærer.	The woman has apples, plums, and pears.
Manden har Börn.	The man has children.
Barnet er ude i Skovene.	The child is out in the woods.
Her er Brevet fra Vennen.	Here is the letter from the friend.
Hans Kone gav Kåben til Pigen.	His wife gave the cloak to the girl.
Kan jeg få hendes sorte Stok?	Can I get her black stick?
Stokken er på Stolen inde i Værelset.	The stick is on the chair in the room.
Nej, hendes Kåbe kan De ikke få.	No, you cannot have her cloak.
Barnet har en smal Ryg.	The child has a narrow back.
Ryggen på Stolen er ikke smal.	The back of the chair is not narrow.

SECOND EXERCISE.

I have the knife and the string. Have you a husband? Yes, I have a husband. Has the woman a child? Yes, she has a boy. Has the friend a ship? No, he has the house. The wife has the wood, but the husband has the house. The letters, the tables, the ships, the knives, and the strings. The boy has a letter, a pear, and an apple. The room has a table. The house has a room. Has the boy the table and the knife? No, but he has the ship and the string. Have you a boy? Yes, I have a boy. Has the friend a wife? No, but he has a house. The child has the knife, but the woman has the table. The man, the woman, and the child. The friend and the boy. The house, the room, and a ship. The woman has the letter, and the boy has the apples, the pears, and the plums. The child has the apple, the knife, and the string; but the man has the ship, a house, and the woods. She has the letter and the table. I have the stick, the hat, and the cloak. Can you get a white chair? Can I obtain a green, yellow, blue, or red string?

Translate into English.

Han har Skibet, men hun har Huset. Mændene og Manden. Jeg har en Dreng. Drengen har Skibe, Æbler, Pærer og Borde. Konen har Breve. De har Husene og Skovene, men Vennen har Skibene. Barnet har Æblet. Brevet har en grön Snor. Værelset har et Bord. Manden har Knivene, og Drengen har Snoren og Stokken. Konen har Værelserne. Drengen har Knivene og Snorene. Har De Skibet? Nej, min Mand har Skibet. Har Drengen Hatten, Stokken, Snoren, Kåben og Brevet? Drengen har en sort Hat, en god Stok, en grå Kåbe, en grön og röd Snor, en hvid Hat og en sort Kniv. Kan jeg få et rödt Æble? Jeg har ikke et rödt Æble eller en gul Blomme. Hatten har en blå og röd Snor. Stokken har en gul og hvid Snor. Kniven har Snoren. Min Pige har Kåben, Hatten, Stokken, Lyset, Æblet, Blommen, Pæren og Kniven. Hatten har Snoren. En Hat har en Snor. Jeg har et Hus. Huset har et Værelse. Værelset har et Lys. Lyset har et Glas. Glasset har en Snor

THIRD LESSON.

ON THE DEFINITE ARTICLE.
(*Continued.*)

II.—The Adjective Form (= *Adjectivernes Artikkel*).

The definite article, when standing before an adjective, as "*the good* man," is used in Danish in its separate and independent form, as "*den gode* Mand," and is then designated the "adjective article."

This form of the article is expressed as follows:—

Singular.

COMMON GENDER.   NEUTER GENDER.
den, the.   *det*, the.

Plural.

BOTH GENDERS.—*de*, the.

Examples of its mode of application:—

Singular.	Plural.
den gode Mand, the good man	*de gode Mænd*, the good men
den lange Kniv, the long knife	*de lange Knive*, the long knives
det smukke Barn, the pretty child	*de smukke Börn*, the pretty children
det sorte Skib, the black ship	*de sorte Skibe*, the black ships.

A. The adjective, as will be seen by the above examples, ends in *e* in both genders and numbers, when following the definite article.

B. The adjective, when qualifying a noun of common gender, as *Mand*, man, *Kone*, woman, *Skov*, wood, etc., and when preceded by the indefinite article *en*, does not take an *e*, as in the above case; but remains unchanged from its primary abstract form, as for example: "*en god* Mand, *en god* Kone, *en god* Skov;" *god*, good, being the abstract form of the adjective.

C. An adjective qualifying a noun of neuter gender, as *Barn*, child, *Værelse*, room, *Skib*, ship, etc., and preceded by the indefinite article *et*, takes a final *t*, except in cases to which attention will be drawn in subsequent lessons, as for example: *et godt Barn, et stort Værelse, et langt Skib*, etc.

D. Adjectives, when preceded by possessive pronouns, take an *e* for both genders and numbers, in the same manner as when they are preceded by the definite independent article, *den, det, de,* as for example: *min gode Mand,* my good husband; *hans kære Kone,* his dear wife; *Dit smukke Barn,* your handsome child; *hendes store Værelse,* her large room, etc.

E. In expressions such as *den Gode, det Store, de Smukke,* the adjective is used to express a noun, which is understood as in *den Gode,* the good (the word *man* is understood), in *det Store,* the great (*thing* is understood), in *de Smukke,* the handsome (the word *persons* is understood). Where the adjective is thus used with the definite independent article it is written with a capital initial letter, to indicate that it represents a noun; nouns or their representatives being thus distinguished in Danish from other parts of speech.

min, c., *mit,* N.; pl. *mine,* my
vor, c., *vort,* N.; pl. *vore,* our
Din, c., *Dit,* N.; pl. *Dine,* thy
deres, c., N., and pl. *their*
det er, it is
vi, we; *vi have,* we have
I, ye; *I have,* ye have
de, they; *de have,* they have
jeg[1] *önsker,* I wish
Du kommer, thou comest
han, hun kan, he, she can
idag, to-day, *igår,* yesterday
Farvel, farewell, good-bye
en Fader, a father
en Moder, a mother
en Bedstefader, a grandfather
en Bedstemoder, a grandmother
en Søn, a son
en Datter, a daughter
min Herre,[2] Sir; *Hr.,* Mr.
min Frue,[2] Madam; *Fru,* Mrs.
min Frøken,[2] Miss
en Dag, a day
God Dag, good day
en Morgen, a morning
God Morgen, good morning
en Aften, an evening
God Aften, good evening
en Nat, a night
God Nat, good night.

[1] *Jeg,* I, is usually written with a small *j,* when it does not begin a sentence. *De,* you, is always written with a capital initial to distinguish it from *de,* they, while *Du,* thou, and *I,* ye, are occasionally printed and written with small initial letters. *De,* you, is used in ordinary conversation; *I,* ye, only where numbers are addressed, and *Du,* thou, as in German, between parents and children, or intimate friends, in prayer, special appeals, etc.

[2] These titular forms of address are not often used by Danes or Norwegians in ordinary conversation; but in speaking to strangers, or where a deferential tone is adopted, the third person may be employed, as for example: *Kan Herren sige mig?* will you tell me, literally: can the gentleman tell me? *Kommer Fruen?* Are you coming? literally: is the lady coming? Oldfashioned politeness exacted the use of the titular *Herr* (*Hr.*), *Fru, Frøken,* in referring to the relatives of the person addressed, as for example: *Hvor er Deres Fru Moder?* where is your mother? *Her er Deres Herr Fader,* here is your father.

PHRASES.

To illustrate the use of the words given in this and the preceding Lessons.

Nej, idag kan jeg ikke få min smukke, lange hvide Kåbe.	No, I cannot get my handsome, long, white cloak to-day.
Hvor er Deres kære Bedstemoder?	Where is your dear grandmother?
Hun er i Skoven med Deres Datter, Fru Hansen.	She is in the wood with your daughter, Mrs. Hansen.
Kan hun få et Brev i Aften?	Can she get a letter this evening?
God Dag, kære Moder.	Good day, my dear mother.
Farvel, min Kære.	Good-bye, my dear.
Hvor er den lille Stol idag?	Where is the little chair to-day?
Her er det store Bord, min Dreng.	Here is the large table, my boy.
Deres smukke Bog er på det sorte Bord.	Your pretty book is on the black table.
Vi have den lange Kniv.	We have the long knife.
Idag har Manden den gode Bog.	The man has the good book to-day.
God Nat, min Fader.	Good night, father.
Kommer Herren til Moder idag?	Are you coming to (my) mother to-day, Sir?
Nej, min Dreng; idag kommer jeg ikke.	No, my boy; I shall not come to-day.
Det er en smuk Kone.	That is a pretty woman.
Ja, det er hun.	Yes, she is.
Nu kommer den kære Ven med den smukke Lille.	Now the dear friend is coming with the pretty little one.
God Aften, min Frøken.	Good evening (Miss, Madam).
Har Frøkenen den hvide Kåbe?	Have you the white cloak? (Miss, Madam).

THIRD EXERCISE.

Where is thy mother? My good mother is not here. The woman has thy table. She has the black table. The large house has not a large room. The pretty boy has a black cord. Where has the knife a black string? My wife has a large table. His son has the ship, but not the knife. The green woods and the large houses.

Where have I his white knife? Have you her black knife? No, I have not her knife or her strings. Have you the good apples here to-day? No, but my child has good apples, pears, and plums to-day. My good friend has your black table and the book. This child has a black chair. The woman has a good husband, and a good father also. Where have you a house? Have you not houses and woods there, Sir? My husband has beautiful (*smukke*) woods here, and her father has a large ship. The child has large apples. She has a good room to-day. The man has good boys there. The woman has my large hats there. This large house has not large rooms. Has the girl a letter to-day? Yes, to-day she has a letter. Has the knife a white string? The knife is not here. Where is your husband to-day, Madam? My husband is not here. Where is thy child? Good evening my son.

Translate into English.

Her har min Fader vort smukke Bord, Stolen, Glasset og de hvide Knive. Har Du mit Brev min Datter? Nej, kære Moder, men jeg har Din smukke, store Bog, og Hr. Jansen har Brevet. Hvor er Bordet og den sorte Stol? Bordet er i det hvide Værelse, men Stolen er ikke der idag. Min kære Mand har en stor Skov og et Hus, men Huset er ikke stort. Deres Hr. Fader er i Skoven med min kære Datter. Kommer Fruen og den gode Kone med Barnet i Skoven idag? Nej, idag kommer jeg ikke i Skoven med Konen og det kære Barn. Det er godt; kan jeg få Æbler, Blommer, Pærer og en Kniv. Nej, her i Huset har jeg ikke Æblerne eller Blommerne, men Pærerne har jeg i det gule Værelse. Ønsker Frökenen at få en blå Hat idag? Nej, idag önsker jeg at få Kåben og Stokken. Hvor er min grå Kåbe? Kan jeg få et smukt Værelse med et stort Bord og en god Stol. Nej, her i Huset kan De ikke få et smukt Værelse.

FOURTH LESSON.

ON NOUNS (= *Navneord*).

All nouns in Danish belong either to the common gender, *Fælleskön*, including masculines and feminines, or to the neuter gender, *Intetkön*.

General Rules.

I. To the *common gender* belong nouns which express a masculine or a feminine being, as for example: *en Fader*, a father; *en Moder*, a mother; *en Tjenestepige*, a servant-girl; *en Tjener*, a man-servant; *en Hane*, a cock; *en Höne*, a hen; *en Sanger* (fem. *Sangerinde*), a singer; *en Slægtning*, a relation; *en Laps*, a dandy; *en Tolk*, an interpreter.

II. To the *neuter gender* belong the names of countries, cities, metals, letters, etc., as for example: *det lille Danmark*, little Denmark; *det folkerige London* (*et Folk*, people; *rige*, rich), the populous London; *det gule Guld*, the yellow gold; *det hvide Sölv*, the white silver; *det store A*, the big A, etc.

To the neuter gender also belong—with many exceptions—nouns in which the precise sex is not specified, and which are taken to indicate a class, as well as an individual, as for example: *et Barn*, a child; *et Væsen*, a being; *et Menneske*, a person (human being); *et Dyr*, an animal; *et Lam*, a lamb; *et Får*, a sheep; *Kvæget*, cattle; *et Bæst*, a beast, brute; *et Æsel*, a donkey; *et Svin*, a pig.

As exceptions to this general rule we may instance *en Fugl*, a bird; *en Fisk*, a fish; *en Hest*, a horse; *en Hund*, a dog.

styg, ugly, disagreeable	*kun*, *blot*, only	*meget*, much, very
söd, sweet	*for*, for	*ganske*, quite
sur, sour	*uden*, without	*temmelig*, tolerably
glat, smooth	*fra*, from	*vi ere*, we are
rå, raw	*endnu*, yet, still	*I ere*, ye are
tro. trofast, faithful	*med*, with	*de ere*, they are
utro, unfaithful	*om*, about	*at komme*, to come
fuld, full	*nok*, yet, enough	*at give*, to give
tom empty.	*dog*, though, yet	*at önske*, to wish.

et *Land*, a country, ... *Landsmand*, compatriot
England, England, *engelsk*, English, { *en Engænder*, an Englishman
en Englænderinde, an Englishwoman
Tyskland, Germany, *tysk*, German, *en Tysker*, a German
Finland, Finland, *finsk*, Finish, *en Fin, Finlap*, a Finlander
Holland, Holland, *hollandsk*, Dutch, *en Hollænder*, a Dutchman
Rusland, Russia, *russisk*, Russian, *en Russer*, a Russian
Preussen, Prussia, *preussisk*, Prussian, *en Preusser*, a Prussian
Danmark, Denmark, *dansk*, Danish, *en Dansk*, a Dane
Sverrig, Sweden, *svensk*, Swedish, *en Svensker* (pl.*Svenske*), a Swede
Norge, Norway, *norsk*, Norwegian, *en Normand*, a Norwegian.

PHRASES.

To illustrate the use of some of the words given in this and the preceding Lessons.

Er Deres Datter i Tyskland eller i Rusland?	Is your daughter in Germany or in Russia?
Hun er med min Fader i Holland.	She is with my father in Holland.
Hvor er den preussiske Fröken?	Where is the Prussian young lady?
Hun er endnu i Sverrig.	She is still in Sweden.
Min Ven, Englænderen, har en meget trofast norsk Tjæner.	My friend, the Englishman, has a very faithful Norwegian servant.
Hvor er det stygge Menneske?	Where is that disagreeable person?
Han er endnu i Norge.	He is still in Norway.
I ere Svenske.	Ye (you) are Swedes.
Nej, min Herre, vi ere fra det kære Danmark.	No, Sir, we are from (belong to our) dear Denmark.
Hunden og Fåret ere med min lille Pige og min Vens Sön.	The dog and the sheep are with my little girl and with my friend's son.
Det er godt.	That is well.
Nu har De det godt her i Norge.	Now you are well off (you have it well) here in Norway.
Huset er fuldt af Mennesker.	The house is full of people.
Hendes Hat er ganske glat.	Her hat is quite smooth.
Hun gav Barnet et temmelig stort Æble.	She gave the child a tolerable large apple.
Hvor kan jeg få en lille Hund?	Where can I get a little dog?

[1] Adjectives expressing nationality are written with a small initial letter, as :—*den engelske Pige, det svenske Barn.*

Den smukke engelske Hund kan De ikke få, men her er en meget smuk Hund fra Sverrig.	You cannot have the pretty English dog, but here is a very nice Swedish dog.
Min Fader gav Sangerinden en Fugl idag.	My father gave the singer a bird to-day.

FOURTH EXERCISE.

The bird is very yellow, but not very pretty. I am only a little child. His daughter is a singer, and his son is a very good interpreter. Her dear mother has a black hen, and a very large cock. The cattle are (is) in the woods. My English man-servant and my boy have also long black knives. Is her relation here or in Sweden. No, she is still in Denmark. Where is your dear mother, and where is your good father? She is in Sweden, but he is in Denmark. There is an animal in the room. Where is the ugly little animal? On the yellow chair. His father is a great dandy, and also a very disagreeable person. Her grandmother is my relation. The little *a* and the big *b*. He is in populous London with her relation, the singer (*fem.*). Here is my large, black horse. Where is the fish? The fish is on the table. The animal is in the wood. The country is very pretty. Good morning, Sir. Where is your dear wife to-day? She is in the house. My child is in the room with his father. His son is in Norway, and my daughter is in (on) the ship. The cock is in the wood, and the hen is still in the house. I have the horse here, but where are (is) the cattle? She has the bird, and his friend has the fish. The singer is with her son in Norway. The short string is on the table. The child is with the woman in the room. The sweet apple is on the large table. The people are (is) in the wood. There is not a creature in the house.

Translate into English.

Min söde lille Datter er her med min Fader og med Tolken fra Norge. Det gode Menneske er på Landet.

Det er blot et lille Vindue, men Vinduet i dit Værelse har meget godt Glas. Lyset er stygt her i Huset. Er Pigen med Barnet i Skoven? Nej, Deres trofaste Tjæner har den lille Dreng i det gule Værelse. Norge, Sverrig og Danmark ere ikke folkerige Lande, men England er et meget folkerigt Land. Guldet er et gult Metal. Der er godt Sölv i Norge og i Sverrig, men ikke i Danmark. Engllænderinden har et tomt Hus. Det svenske Skib er kort, smalt og stygt. Min danske Tjænestepige er ikke trofast. Er Tjæneren her i Huset? Nej, den engelske Tjæner er ikke her, men den danske Tjænestepige er her med min Kone. Kvæget er i Skovene, men Svinet er ikke der. Min Mand har en hvid Hest, et gråt Æsel og et hvidt Lam. Lammet og Fåret ere i Skoven. Hvor er Fisken? Fisken er på det sorte Bord inde i Huset. Min kære Moder gav min Mand en stor Hest. Hvor er Hesten? Hesten er i det tomme Hus. Pigen har en Hane og en Höne og den store sorte Fugl. Min norske Tolk er en stor Laps. Tolken er her. Han gav Æblet, Blommen og Pæren til min Moder, og Fisken og Fuglen til det lille Barn.

FIFTH LESSON.

ON THE GENDERS OF NOUNS.

To the *common gender* belong generally:—

I. Words ending in *dom*, *hed*, *skab*, which indicate a quality or character, as for example: *Barndom*, childhood; *Stolthed*, pride; *Troskab*, fidelity.

II. Words ending in *de* and *e*, as for example: *Længde*, length; *Brede*, breadth.

III. Words derived from verbs, as for example: *Læsning*, reading, from *at læse*, to read; *Vækst*, growth, from *at vokse*, to grow.

The feminine of titles or personal designations is formed by adding *inde* to the masculine, as for example : *en Danser*, fem., *en Danserinde*, a dancer; or, in a few cases, by adding *ske* or *ning*, as : *en Lögner*, fem., *en Lögnerske*, a liar; *en Dronning*, a queen (from the disused old word *Drot*, a ruler).

In designations of nationality the masculine and feminine forms are either identical, as: *en Dansk*, a Dane; or the feminine is formed by adding *inde* to the masculine, as: *en Englænder*, an Englishman, *en Englænderinde*, an Englishwoman.

Distinctions of sex are sometimes expressed by the help of another noun or pronoun, having a special sexual character, as for example: *Bonde*, a peasant, fem., *Bondekone*, a peasant woman; *Enke*, a widow, masc., *Enkemand*, a widower; *Barn*, child; *Pigebarn*, a girl-child; *en Kat*, a cat; *Hankat*, Tomcat, *Hunkat*, she-cat; *Kanariehan*, canary-cock, *Kanariehun*, canary-hen.

Many names of animals differ, as in English, in the masculine and feminine, as for example: *en Tyr*, a bull; *en Ko*, a cow; *en Vædder*, a ram; *en Får*, a ewe.

Feminine proper names are variously formed, by adding to the masculine *a, e, ine*, etc., as for example: *Theodor*, fem. *Theodora; Frederik*, fem. *Frederikke*; *Hans*, fem. *Hansine*.

To the *neuter gender* belong :—

I. Words ending in *at, et, eri, ti*, as: *Kvadrat*, a square; *Kabinet*, a closet; *Krammeri*, trumpery; *Politi*, police.

II. Some words of one syllable formed from verbs, as: *et Skrig*, a scream, from *at skrige*, to cry out; *et Digt*, a poem, from *at digte*, to compose verses.

udmærket, remarkable, excellently	*en Kirke*, a church	*snart*, soon
dejlig, beautiful	*en Stemme*, a voice	*straks*, directly
stolt, proud	*en Vogn*, a carriage	*næsten*, nearly
venlig, friendly	*en Stald*, a stall, stable	*hende*, her
hæslig, plain, ugly	*en Farve*, a colour	*ham*, him
lykkelig, happy	*en Saks*, scissors	*mig*, me
farlig, dangerous	*en Kage*, a cake	*os*, us
flittig, industrious	*en Flid*, industry	*Dem*, you (obj. case)
sand, true	*et Stykke*, a piece	*dem*, them
betydelig, considerable	(*et*) *Köd*, flesh, meat	*sin*, his, her own
	(*et*) *Bröd*, bread	*alt*, all, quite

at elske, to love	at köbe, to buy	alle (pl.), all
at bringe, to bring	jeg kan köbe, I can buy	slet ikke, not at all.
at tage, to take	(en) Dejlighed, beauty	ofte, often
at få, to get, procure	et Stykke, a piece	efter, after
at se, to see	en Familie, a family	för, before
jeg ser, I see	et Bur, a cage	sig (refl. pron.), him-
at gå, to go	et Skur, a shed, outhouse	self, herself
han går, he goes	at tage på Landet, to go into the country.	

SIMPLE PHRASES.

Min sorte Ko er i min store Kostald. — My black cow is in my large cow-shed.

Hvor er Deres kære Bedstemoder? — Where is your dear grandmother?
Hun er i Kirke med Bedstefader. — She is in church with (my) grandfather.

Hendes Venskab for Danserinden er mig meget kært. — Her friendship for the dancer pleases me greatly (is very dear to me).

Min Veninde Leopoldine er i Vognen med den lykkelige Englænderinde. — My friend, Leopoldine, is in the carriage with the fortunate Englishwoman.
Det er Længden af Skibet. — That is the length of the ship.
Er det Farven af Din Hat og Din Kåbe? — Is it the colour of thy hat and thy cloak?
Er den dejlige Dronning stolt? — Is the lovely queen proud?
Ja, hendes Stolthed er mærkværdig. — Yes, her pride is remarkable.
Bondekonen bringer mig en Fugl og et Fuglebur. — The peasant-woman is bringing me a bird and a bird-cage.
Jeg giver Dem mit Ur og min Saks. — I give you my watch and my scissors.

Kan Pigebarnet få Kagen og Brödet? — Can the little girl have the cake and the loaf?
En Dansk gav os den hæslige Hankat. — A Dane gave us the ugly Tom-cat.
Min Sön köber sig snart en stor Vogn. — My son will soon buy (himself) a large carriage.
Kan min Mand ikke straks få Hesten? — Cannot my husband have the horse directly?
Snart er Hesten her; den er i Stalden og kommer straks. — The horse will soon be here; it is in the stable, and will come immediately.

C

FIFTH EXERCISE.

I do not love pride, but I love fidelity. The length and breadth of the church. The singer has a remarkably fine voice. The Englishman is in the carriage with the queen. Here is a closet in the room. The bull is in the wood, but the cow is in the shed, and the horse, the ewe, the cock, and the hen are also in the wood. The cat is in the large room, where the cock and hen-canary are in the cage. The peasant and the pretty peasant-woman are in the church. A Dane is in the house. The widow is remarkably handsome and friendly. I see the horse and the boy in the stable. The police are (is) not here to-day. The dancer (*fem.*) is very proud, and remarkably beautiful. Where is her friendship? The breadth is considerable. I have a long poem. She goes immediately to her mother. I love my friend, the singer, but I do not see him (see him not). Now the young girl is in the house. The carriage has a window, with a square of glass. A liar is an ugly creature. She sees the man. I love my father. He is going into the country. His friendship is not very great. I see a beautiful church. My watch does not go. Where is the child's cake?

Translate into English.

Der er kun Krammeri i Kabinettet. Hun er en udmærket god Sangerinde; hendes Stemme er dejlig; og er hun ikke et venligt Menneske. Min Datter elsker hans lille Pige. Jeg ser Koen i Stalden, Fisken på Bordet, Fåren (*or* Fåret) med Tyren og Kvæget i Skoven, og Bondepigen i Huset med Hanen og Hönen. Hvor er mit smukke Fuglebur? Deres Bur er på den lille Stol. Går De i Kirke idag? Nej, jeg tager på Landet med min Bedstefader og Bedstemoder. Nu er det dejligt på Landet. Hun går straks. Min Datter elsker den smukke Veninde. Han gav mig en stor Hund. Deres Sön er meget stolt. Nej, det er han ikke; han er venlig nok.

Hvor er Deres flittige Veninde, Enken? Hun er på Skibet med min lille Pige. Hvor er Politiet idag? Jeg ser Mændene i en Vogn. Jeg elsker min Bedstefader, men ikke min Bedstemoder. Han gav mig et Digt at læse. Der er et Skrig ude i Skovene. Ser De det hæslige Dyr.

SIXTH LESSON.

ON THE FORMATION OF THE PLURAL OF NOUNS (= *Navneord*), etc.

The plural of Danish nouns is formed as follows:—

I. In **e**.—In words of one syllable, as *Hus*, house, pl. *Huse*: *Lov*, leave, law, pl. *Love*; in words ending in unaccented *er* and *dom*, as *Ridder*, knight, cavalry-man, pl. *Ryttere*: *Sygdom*, illness, pl. *Sygdomme*.

II. In **er**.—In words ending in a *y*, as *By*, town, pl. *Byer*; and in words of foreign origin, ending in *al, in, ent, ar, er, et, ir, or*, etc; as, for example, *en General*, a general, pl. *Generaler*: *et Gardin*, a curtain, pl. *Gardiner*: *en Husar*, a hussar, pl. *Husarer*: *en Karakter*, a character, pl. *Karakterer*: *en Student*, a student, pl. *Studenter*.

III. Some plurals are formed irregularly, and must be learned by a simple effort of memory:—

Examples:—

en *Mand*, a man,	pl. *Mænd*	en *Hand*, a hand,	pl. *Hænder*
en *Fader*, a father,	,, *Fædre*	en *And*, a duck,	,, *Ænder*
en *Moder*, a mother,	,, *Mødre*	et *Barn*, a child,	,, *Børn*
en *Datter*, a daughter,	,, *Døttre*	en *Himmel*, heaven, sky,	,, *Himle*
en *Søster*, a sister,	,, *Søstre*	en *Engel*, an angel,	,, *Engle*
en *Broder*, a brother,	,, *Brødre*	en *Frøken*, unmarried lady,	,, *Frøkener*
en *Gås*, a goose,	,, *Gæs*	et *Øre*, an ear,	,, *Øren*
en *Fod*, a foot,	,, *Fødder*	et *Øje*, an eye,	,, *Øjne*.

Some nouns are used only in the plural, as *Forældre*, parents; *Søskende*, brothers and sisters; *Penge*, money; *Klæder*, clothes;

Sæder, custom, usage. Some are used only in the singular, as *Bröd*, bread; *Hår*, hair; *Får*, sheep; *Dyr*, animal; *Ære*, honour; *Haab*, hope; *Uld*, wool; *Fruentimmer*, woman.

As in English, nouns are not modified by any case, except the genitive, which is formed by the addition of *s*, or *es*, according to the termination of the word; as, for example :—

SINGULAR.—Nom., Dat., Obj.

et *Skib*, a ship,	*Skibet*, the ship,	det store *Skib*, the large ship.
en *Ko*, a cow,	*Koen*, the cow,	den store *Ko*, the large cow.

Genitive.

et *Skibs*, of a ship,	*Skibets*, of the ship,	det store *Skibs*, of the large ship.
en *Koes*, of a cow,	*Koens*, of the cow,	den store *Koes*, of the large cow.

PLURAL.—Nom., Dat., Obj.

Skibe, ships,	*Skibene*, the ships,	de store *Skibe*, the large ships.
Köer, cows,	*Köerne*, the cows,	de store *Köer*, the large cows.

Genitive.

Skibes, of ships,	*Skibenes*, of the ships,	de store *Skibes*, of the large ships.
Köers, of cows,	*Köernes*, of the cows,	de store *Köers*, of the large cows.

The genitive *es* occurs as a rule in words ending in the vowels *a, i, u, y, æ, o*, and in *s* or *sk*; as, for example: *en By*, a town, gen. *Byes*: *en Tjavs*, a rag, gen. *Tjavses*: *en Saks*, scissors, gen. *Sakses*.

As in English, the genitive case may be indicated by the use of the preposition *of* (Danish *af*); as, for example: *Mælken af Koen*, the milk of the cow; *en Ven af mig*, a friend of mine.

at *leve*, to live	et *Öjeblik*, a moment
at *takke*, to thank	(en) *Tak*, thanks
at *hilse*, to greet	et *Hjærte*, a heart
at *tale*, to talk	et *Ord*, a word
at *bevare*, to preserve	(en) *Gud*, God
at *velsigne*, to bless	(en) *Skyld*, fault, guilt
at *vænte*, to wait	et *Hjem*, a home
at *finde*, to find	(en) *Klokke*, clock
at *blive*, to remain, become	*hos*,[1] at, at the house of
at *håbe*, to hope	*velkommen!* welcome
at *forlade*, to remit, to forgive	(en) *Forladelse*, forgiveness.

[1] *Hos* corresponds to the French *chez*, but it does not admit of being used in a reflective sense, unless in some cases where *hjemme* is associated with it; thus, for instance, such sentences as: "Madame est chez elle," "Monsieur, est-il chez lui?" &c., are inadmissible in Danish, and must be

SIMPLE PHRASES.

Hvorledes lever De?	How are you? *lit:* How live you?
Mange Tak!	Many thanks.
Tak skal De have.	Thank you. *lit:* Thanks shall you have.
Tak!	Thank you. *lit:* Thanks.
Det går mig godt.	I am well. *lit:* It goes well with me.
Hils Deres Moder.	Remember me to your mother. *lit:* Greet your mother.
Hjærtelig Velkommen.	You are heartily welcome.
Gud velsigne Dem!	God bless you.
Gud bevare os!	God preserve us.
Vænt et Öjeblik.	Wait a moment.
Kun et Ord.	Only one word.
Tak for Sidst.	Thanks for the last time (of entertainment).
Nu straks! på Öjeblikket	Now immediately. In a moment.
Om Forladelse!	Forgive me (excuse me). *lit:* for forgiveness.
Vær så god.	Please (I beg). *lit:* Be so good.
Det er min Skyld.	It is my fault.
Hvis Skyld var det?	Whose fault was it?
Alt forladt!	Pray, do not mention it. *lit:* all forgiven.
Hvorlænge bliver De her?	How long do you remain here?
Jeg véd det ikke.	I do not know.
Er De færdig?	Are you ready?
Jeg bliver hjemme til efter Klokken fire.	I shall remain at home till after four o'clock.
De vil ikke finde ham hjemme för Klokken fem.	You will not find him at home before five o'clock.
Jeg tror det.	I believe so. *lit:* I believe it.
Jeg véd det.	I know it.

expressed as follows: either, *Fruen er hjemme hos sig*, or better thus: *Fruen er hjemme; er Herren hjemme hos sig?* or better, *er Herren hjemme?* The distinctive applicability of *hos* and *hjemme* corresponds, therefore, very closely with the sense conveyed by the expressions "at." "at the house of," and "at home" in English, as for example: I was at Jansen's, *Jeg var hos Jansens.* Is Mr. Turner at home to-day? *Er Herr Turner hjemme idag?* No, he is not at home, he is at the house of his brother. *Nej, han er ikke hjemme, han er hos sin Broder.*

Jeg håber det.	I hope so (it).
Kommer De hos mig idag?	Are you coming to me to-day? (my house).
Nej, jeg skal hos dem idag.	No, I am going to them to-day. (their house).
Han var hos os igår.	He was with us (at our house). yesterday.

SIXTH EXERCISE.

The peasant-woman has ducks and geese, and her daughter, the pretty peasant-girl, has a cock and a hen. The angels in heaven. The heavens. The father has money, and the mother has clothes. My children, my parents, and my brothers and sisters are in the country. The Danish laws. The law of Sweden. The woman's sickness. The window has curtains. I see the cavalry-man, the hussar, and a general. The child's hands, ears, and eyes. The young lady has very pretty hands. Here is my hand. My daughters have the wool. The ducks are in the wood. I have bread and milk. Is the general here to-day? No, he is with the hussars in the town. A man's honour. My grandfather's character. The houses of the town. England is a charming country. The Swede is a general. The English lady has brothers and sisters in Denmark. The book is in your hands. The young lady is in the house. She has houses in the town. My husband's sickness. Where is your husband now? He is in the country with my parents. The student is my relation.

Translate into English.

Er Fru Generalinden i Huset, min lille Pige? Nej, Fruen er i Byen med Frøkenen. Forældrene have Pengene. Børnene ere på Landet med Bedstefaderen. Har jeg den Ære at se Herr Generalen? Sygdommen er slet ikke farlig. Skibsmanden er ikke på Skibet. Hvor ere Ænderne, Gæssene, Hanerne og Hönerne? De ere med Bondekonen i Skovene. Bondepigerne ere i

Værelset. Har Husaren Lov til at tage paa Landet? Nej, det har han ikke; han er endnu i Faderens Hus i Byen. Frökenen har dejlige Hænder og Öjne, men Örene ere ikke udmærket smukke. Hans Hår er sort. Hvor ere Deres Söskende? De ere endnu i Sverrig, men mine Forældre ere i Norge. Hun har blå Öjne, men hendes Söskendes Öjne ere sorte. Det er Lov i Danmark, men ikke i Norge. Mit Håb er at Fru Nielsen får ikke den Sygdom. Er Sygdommen i hendes Broders Hus? Hvor er Deres Datter? Hun er pa Landet med min Sön, Studenten. Er Deres Broder General? Nej, endnu er han kun Major, men snart bliver han General. En af mine Söskende bringer mig Gæs, Ænder og Mælk fra Landet, og Broderen gav mig igår Uld og Klæder for Bondebörnene.

CONJUGATION OF THE VERB *at have* (= to have).

INDICATIVE.

PRESENT.
(*I have*.)
jeg har
du har
han har
vi have
I have
de have.

PAST.
(*I had*.)
jeg havde
du havde
han havde
vi havde
I havde
de havde.

PERFECT.
(*I have had*.)
jeg har haft
du har haft
han har haft
vi have haft
I have haft
de have haft.

PLUPERFECT.
(*I had had*.)
jeg havde haft
du havde haft
han havde haft
vi havde haft
I havde haft
de havde haft.

FUTURE.
(*I shall have*.)
jeg skal have
du skal have
han skal have
vi skulle have
I skulle have
de skulle have.

FUTURE-PERFECT.
(*I should have had*.)
jeg får haft
du får haft
han får haft
vi få haft
I få haft
de få haft.

POTENTIAL.

PRESENT.	PAST.
(*I may have.*)	(*I may have had.*)
jeg have!	jeg have haft!
du have!	du have haft!
han have!	han have haft!
vi have!	vi have haft!
I have!	I have haft!
de have!	de have haft!

IMPERATIVE.
PRESENT.

hav du (*have thou*)   haver I (*have, have ye*)
han have (*let him have*).   de have (*let them have*).

INFINITIVE.

PRESENT.	PAST.
at have (*to have*).	at have haft (*to have had*).

FUTURE.
at skulle have (*to be obliged to have*).

PARTICIPLES.

PRESENT.	PAST.
havende (*having*).	haft (*had*).

CONJUGATION OF THE VERB *at være* (= to be).

INDICATIVE.

PRESENT.	PAST.
(*I am*).	(*I was*).
jeg er	jeg var
du er	du var
han er	han var
vi ere	vi vare
I ere	I vare
de ere.	de vare.

PERFECT.	PLUPERFECT.
(*I have been*).	(*I had been.*)
jeg har været	jeg havde været
du har været	du havde været
han har været	han havde været
vi have været	vi havde været
I have været	I havde været
de have været.	de havde været.

POTENTIAL.

PRESENT.
(*I may be.*)
jeg være
du være
han være
vi være
I være
de være.

PAST.
(*I may have been.*)
jeg have været
du have været
han have været
vi have været
I have været
de have været.

IMPERATIVE.

PRESENT.

vær du (*be thou*)
han være (*let him be*).

være I (*be, be ye*)
de være (*let them be*).

INFINITIVE.

PRESENT.
at være (*to be*).

PAST.
at have været (*to have been*).

FUTURE.
at skulle være (*to be obliged to be*).

PARTICIPLES.

PRESENT.
værende (*being*).

PAST.
været (*been*).

SEVENTH LESSON.

ON ADJECTIVES, etc.

(= *Tillægsord, o.s.v.*[1])

I. Adjectives retain their abstract form when they stand between the indefinite article *en*, a (common gender), and the nouns which they qualify, as for example:—

en god Dreng,   a good boy
en sort Hat,   a black hat.

But when an adjective stands between the indefinite article *et*, a (neuter gender), and the noun which it qualifies, it cannot, (except in cases to which reference will be made), be left

---

[1] *o.s.v.*: the abbreviation of *og* (and), *så* (so), *videre* (further) = *etcetera*.

POTENTIAL.

PRESENT.	PAST.
(*I may have.*)	(*I may have had.*)
jeg have!	jeg have haft!
du have!	du have haft!
han have!	han have haft!
vi have!	vi have haft!
I have!	I have haft!
de have!	de have haft!

IMPERATIVE.
PRESENT.

hav du (*have thou*)   haver I (*have, have ye*)
han have (*let him have*).   de have (*let them have*).

INFINITIVE.

PRESENT.	PAST.
at have (*to have*).	at have haft (*to have had*).

FUTURE.
at skulle have (*to be obliged to have*).

PARTICIPLES.

PRESENT.	PAST.
havende (*having*).	haft (*had*).

CONJUGATION OF THE VERB *at være* (= to be).

INDICATIVE.

PRESENT.	PAST.
(*I am*).	(*I was*).
jeg er	jeg var
du er	du var
han er	han var
vi ere	vi vare
I ere	I vare
de ere.	de vare.

PERFECT.	PLUPERFECT.
(*I have been*).	(*I had been.*)
jeg har været	jeg havde været
du har været	du havde været
han har været	han havde været
vi have været	vi havde været
I have været	I havde været
de have været.	de havde været.

POTENTIAL.

PRESENT.	PAST.
(I may be.)	*(I may have been.)*
jeg være	jeg have været
du være	du have været
han være	han have været
vi være	vi have været
I være	I have været
de være.	de have været.

IMPERATIVE.
PRESENT.

vær du *(be thou)*	værer I *(be, be ye)*
han være *(let him be).*	de være *(let them be).*

INFINITIVE.

PRESENT.	PAST.
at være *(to be).*	at have været *(to have been).*

FUTURE.
at skulle være *(to be obliged to be).*

PARTICIPLES.

PRESENT.	PAST.
værende *(being).*	været *(been).*

SEVENTH LESSON.

ON ADJECTIVES, etc.
(= *Tillægsord, o.s.v.*[1])

I. Adjectives retain their abstract form when they stand between the indefinite article *en*, a (common gender), and the nouns which they qualify, as for example:—

en god Dreng,	a good boy
en sort Hat,	a black hat.

But when an adjective stands between the indefinite article *et*, a (neuter gender), and the noun which it qualifies, it cannot, (except in cases to which reference will be made), be left

---

[1] *o.s.v.*: the abbreviation of *og* (and), *så* (so), *videre* (further) = *etcetera*.

SEVENTH EXERCISE.

That is a good and faithful animal. My dear mother was very healthy and well, but my poor father is very ill, and he is also very peevish. My parents were rich, and I could wish that my dear husband was also rich. The cow's milk is very sweet, but the peasant-woman's bread is sour. The poor woman has a dangerous illness. He is quite sober to-day. I wish to have good fields. I was in the white house yesterday. My good wife is coming on foot to-morrow. We had sour apples and sweet pears. The southern fields and the northern woods. I see my dear little daughter and my rich sister's son. We were in a beautiful country this year. The good general comes by sea. I (shall) come by sea, but my rich son is coming on foot. It was unfortunate (bad) that she had clothes, but not money. My parents were not rich people. The child is obedient, and has a good heart. I wish to procure a comfortable Norwegian house. The nice Swedish lady has an English horse. The man had a light task, but he was ill. That is a very shy and childish young lady. My dear sister is timid and cross. Thy good mother is ill in my house in town. The illness is fortunately not dangerous. It is difficult. He was cross and angry.

Translate into English.

Jeg ser, at hun önsker at få rige Venner. Generalen og Generalinden komme med Börnene tilsös på min Faders store, sorte Skib. Jeg kommer til Byen imorgen; igår var min kære Broder også der, men idag er han hos Deres Söster. Lev vel, min kære, gode Frue. Mit Hjærte var ikke let. Det stakkels Fruentimmer er meget flittig; hun önsker at få et let Arbejde. Iår ere Husarerne i Norge med den svenske General og det norske Kavalleri. Et godt Ord er kært. Imorgen kan jeg ikke få Breve fra min Familie i Sverrig. Min gode

Ven, Herr Sörenson, önsker at få en engelsk Tjener. Skibet kommer fra Syden og går til Norden. Er Vinden sydlig eller nordlig? Min gode Moder har en udmærket god Helbred, men min stakkels Söster er i Fare for at få en hæslig Sygdom. Er det norske Barn vranten, eller kun bly? Hun er slet ikke vranten, men igår var hun ikke rask. Vrantenhed er hæslig. Heldigvis er Faren ikke stor.

EIGHTH LESSON.

ON ADJECTIVES (– Tillægsord).
(Continued.)

Adjectives ending in *el*, *en*, or *er* lose the *e* before *l*, *n*, *r* when they are preceded by the definite, independent article *den*, *det*, *de*, or when they are used as nouns; thus for example:—

ædel, noble,	changes to	adle,	den adle Mand, the noble man
moden, ripe,	,,	modne,	den modne Pære, the ripe pear
mager, meagre, thin,	,,	magre,	den magre Hest, the thin horse
gammel, old,	,,	gamle,	det gamle Hus, the old house
vågen, wakeful,	,,	vågne,	det vågne Barn, the wakeful child
vakker, pretty, nice	,,	vakre,	de vakre Piger, the pretty girls
bunden, bound,	,,	bundne,	de bundne Dyr, the chained animals
doven, idle,	,,	dovne,	de dovne Börn, the idle children.

Adjectives of one syllable, or those in which the last syllable is short, double the final consonant; as for example:—

| slem | bad | slemme | fornem, distinguished, fornemme |
| slet | | slette. | let, light, easy, lette. |

en slem Sag, a bad case, den slemme Sag, the bad case.

Adjectives follow the same rules, in regard to cases, as nouns, undergoing no change except in the genitive, where they take *es* or *s*, according to the terminal letter of the word.

Examples:—

Singular.	Plural.
Nom.—en Rig, a rich man	Nom.—Rige, rich men
Gen. —en Rigs, of a rich man.	Gen. —Riges, of rich men.
Nom.—den Gode, the good man	Nom.—de Gode, the good men
Gen. —den Godes, of the good man.	Gen. —de Godes, of the good men.

The Danish Cardinal Numbers are:—

én	1	elleve	11	tredive	30
to	2	tolv	12	fyrretyve	40
tre	3	tretten	13	halvtreds, or halvtredsindstyve	50
fire	4	fjorten	14	tredsindstyve	60
fem	5	femten	15	halvfjærds, or halvfjærdsindstyve	70
seks	6	seksten[1]	16	firsindstyve	80
syv	7	sytten	17	halvfems, or halvfemsindstyve	90
åtte (otte)	8	atten	18	hundrede (et Hundrede)	100
ni	9	nitten	19	tusinde (et Tusinde)	1000
ti	10	tyve	20	en Million	1,000,000

Up to one hundred the lesser numeral precedes the greater; after one hundred it goes after it, as for example: *én og tyve, to og tredive, tre og fyrretyve*, etc., 21, 32, 43; *hundrede og én, tusinde og to*, etc., 101, 1002. When the numeral is not followed by a noun or adjective, the termination *sindstyve* may be omitted, as for example: *Har han firsindstyve Kavalerister?* has he 80 horsemen? *Nej, han har kun halvtreds*, no, he has only 50.

at sælge, to sell
at tro, to believe
at koste, to cost
jeg véd, I know
at binde, to bind
bunden, bound
omtrent, about

ti, fordi, because
hvor meget, how much
engang, once
ikke engang, not even
et Pund, a pound
et Bind, a volume
et Værk, a work

en Bogbinder, a bookbinder
en Boghandler, a bookseller
mere end, more than
allerede, already
aldrig, never.

SIMPLE PHRASES.

Hvor mange Bind har dette Værk? — How many volumes has this book?
Det har fem Bind, men jeg har dem ikke alle. — It has five volumes, but I have not got all of them.
Ser De de fire Skibe? — Do you see the four ships?
Jeg ser kun tre. — I only see three.
Min Fader har mer end tolv Heste, men Englænderen har kun syv. — My father has more than twelve horses, but the Englishman has only seven.
Har den franske Herre mer end én Tjener? — Has the French gentleman more than one servant?
Ja, han har mer end én, men jeg véd ikke hvormange. — Yes, he has more than one, but I do not know how many.
Kan Bondekonen sælge mig to hundrede Æbler? — Can the peasant-woman sell me 200 apples?

[1] Pronounced *seisten*.

Hun har kun omtrent tredsindstyve, fordi Fru Generalinde Holk har köbt dem næsten alle.	She has only about sixty, because Mrs. (General) Holk has bought almost all.
Hvor gammel er Deres Mands Bedstefader?	How old is your husband's grandfather?
Han er næsten halvfems.	He is nearly ninety.
Hvor meget koster dette Ur?	How much does this watch cost?
Det koster, tror jeg, omtrent atten Pund Sterling.	It costs, I think, about £18.
Hvor mange Værelser har De i Huset?	How many rooms have you in the house?
To og tyve.	Two-and-twenty.
Det er et stort Hus; jeg har kun femten Værelser i mit.	That is a large house; I have only fifteen rooms in mine.

EIGHTH EXERCISE.

The old man is awake. The pretty girl is very idle. Rich people are not always noble. My dear mother is forty-seven years old. The black horse is tied up in the large stable. She has ten children, six sons and four daughters. My rich brother has four menservants in the house. The noble Englishwoman is very rich. The boy has thirteen pears, seventeen apples, and thirty-three plums. Now we are in eighteen hundred and seventy-eight. She has a million of money. The general has five hundred and ninety-nine cavalry. The rich man's wife is fifty-three. How old is your pretty daughter? She is seventeen years old, but my son is twenty-one. My friend's house has sixty-eight windows. His cowhouse, where the white cow is, has only one window. The peasant woman has forty geese, sixty ducks, nineteen cocks, and thirty-six hens. The young lady has seven cloaks, and four hats. It is not easy to be rich. The noble general is in town to-day. Where is my old friend? He is with the rich girl in the large house. That is a very bad child.

Translate into English.

Er den rige Mand en af Deres Slægtninge? Nej; men han er en Ven af mine kære Forældre og af min gamle Bedstemoder. Hans nette lille Pige er med den norske Veninde i Sverrig. Generalindens smukke Döttre have mange Penge og dejlige Klæder. Min Broder, Kavalleristen, har åtte Börn, fem Sönner og tre Döttre. Han er halvtreds, og hans Kone er kun fyrretyve År gammel. Er Deres Bedstefader halvfems? Nej, den kære Gamle er kun firsindstyve År. Farvel, du Gode. Hvor hun er doven idag! Der er kun tretten Höner og fem Haner i Skoven. Det gode Fruentimmer har to Köer, en Får og fjorten Får. Hvor gammel er Deres Broder? Han er kun ni og tyve, men min Söster, Sangerinden, er allerede syv og tredive År gammel. Han er fem og halvfjærds. Bonden har ikke et halvt hundrede Gæs iår, men ifjor var der fem hundrede Gæs og Ænder på hans gode Marker. Hvor mange Heste ere idag i Stalden? Næsten fyrretyve, tror jeg. Det er slemt at være vågen om (*English:* at) Natten. Hvormange Penne har De på Bordet? Jeg har omtrent tyve eller fem og tyve. Har hendes Broder mange Börn? Han har fem, men Börnene ere alle i England med deres Moders Söster, Fru Bell. De to Franskmænd have mange Skibe.

NINTH LESSON.

ON NUMERALS (= *Talord*), **etc.**
(*Continued*).

The ordinal numbers (*de ordnende Talord*) are formed by adding *te*, *nde*, *ende*, or *er* to the cardinal number, excepting *förste*, first; *anden*, second; *tredje*, third; *fjærde*, fourth; *sjætte*, sixth.

den første	1st	den ellevte	11th	den tredivte	30th
„ anden	2nd	„ tolvte	12th	„ fyrretyvende	40th
„ tredje	3rd	„ trettende	13th	„ halvtredsindstyvende	50th
„ fjærde	4th	„ fjortende	14th	„ tredsindstyvende	60th
„ femte	5th	„ femtende	15th	„ halvfjerdsindstyvende	70th
„ sjætte	6th	„ sekstende	16th	„ firsindstyvende	80th
„ syvende	7th	„ syttende	17th	„ halvfemsindstyvende	90th
„ åttende	8th	„ attende	18th	„ hundrede	100th
„ niende	9th	„ nittende	19th	„ tusinde	1000th
„ tiende	10th	„ tyvende	20th		

The only ordinal number which is modified by gender, is *anden*, which makes *andet* in the neuter.

As in English, it is only the second of two composite numbers that is declined, as for example: *den én og tyvende*, the one and twentieth; *den syv og tredivte*, the seven and thirtieth.

The Days of the Week.
(*Dagene af Ugen.*)

Söndag,	Sunday
Mandag,	Monday
Tirsdag,	Tuesday
Onsdag,	Wednesday
Torsdag,	Thursday
Fredag,	Friday
Lördag,	Saturday.

The Months of the Year.
(*Månederne af Året.*)

Januar	Juli
Februar	August
Marts	September
April	Oktober
Maj	November
Juni	December.[1]

en *Dag*, a day
en *Uge*, a week
en *Måned*, a month
et *År*, a year
et *Halvår*, a half-year
et *Skudår*, a leap year.

at *skrive*, to write
jeg *skriver*, I write
at *komme*, to come
at *sige*, to say
at *kalde*, to call
han *kalder*, he calls
at *mangle*, to want, need [needs
han *mangler*, he wants,
at *rejse*, to travel
De *rejser*, you travel
en *Bro*, a bridge

stor, large
större, larger
hvad, what
når, when
hjem, at home
måske, perhaps
hvilken, which
hver, each
silde, late
tidlig, early
altid, always
halvfem, half-past four

et *Minut*, a minute
et *Sekund*, a second
en *Time*, an hour
en *Halvtime*, half an hour [an hour
et *Kvarter*, a quarter of
et *Datum*, a date
et *Selskab*, a company
en *Klokke*, a clock
en *Indbydelse*, an invitation
en *Gade*, a street.

[1] The Danes frequently say *Majmåned, Julimåned,* etc., where we should simply say "May," "July," etc.

SIMPLE PHRASES.

Klokken er fire.	It is four o'clock.
Når kommer Deres lille Broder hjem?	When does your little brother come home?
Han kommer altid hjem Klokken halv fem.	He always comes home at half-past four.
Klokken er et Kvarter til fem.	It is a quarter past four.
Klokken er tre Kvarter til syv.	It is a quarter to seven.
Klokken mangler tyve Minutter i ti.	It is twenty minutes to ten.
Klokken er ti Minutter over ti.	It is ten minutes past ten.
Han kalder på mig Klokken seks.	He calls me at six o'clock.
Hvad er Klokken?	What time is it?
Hvert fjærde År kaldes et Skudår.	Every fourth year is called a leap-year.
Hvor meget er én, og tre, og fem, og ni, og elleve?	How much is 1, 3, 5, 9, and 11?
Ni og tyve.	Nine-and-twenty.
Jeg kommer den förste Februar.	I will come on the first of February.
De ser ham måske Torsdagen den syvende August.	You will (or shall) see him perhaps on Thursday, the seventh of August.
Nu ere vi snart i atten hundrede og ni og halvfjærds.	Now we shall soon be in 1879.
Hvad skriver man idag?	What date is it? *Lit:* what writes one to-day.
Idag skrive vi den tolvte Juni.	It is the twelfth of June to-day.
Jeg rejser den niende April.	I shall start (travel) the ninth of April.
Hun har en Indbydelse til den tredje Juli.	She has an invitation for the third of July.
Han skal i Aftenselskab Mandagen den femte Marts.	He is going to an evening entertainment on Monday, the fifth of March.
Höjgade Nummer fire, Torsdag Eftermiddag.	No. 4, High street, Thursday afternoon.
Igår skrev vi den trettende Maj.	Yesterday was (we wrote) the thirteenth of May.
Hvad Dato er det imorgen?	What date will it be to-morrow?

NINTH EXERCISE.

Will he come on the eighteenth of January? My dear wife was in England in May, 1867. Is it the thirteenth to-day? Will you be so good as to tell me what date it was yesterday? Yesterday, my dear boy, was the sixteenth of March. I was in Norway with my children in 1870. My grandfather and my son were in Sweden with Mr. Paulsen's brother and sister in 1869. You will perhaps see him on the thirteenth of July. The beautiful singer will come into town on the nineteenth of April. To-day is the second of May, and yesterday was the first of the month. A week has seven days: Sunday, Monday, Tuesday, Wednesday, Thursday, Friday, Saturday. A month has four weeks. A year has twelve months: January, February, March, April, May, June, July, August, September, October, November, December. A half-year has six months. The first month of the year has thirty-one days. The third month has also thirty-one days, but the fourth month has only thirty days. Sunday is the first, and Saturday the seventh day of the week. He will come on Friday, the eleventh of November. Tuesday is the third day of the week. His friend was in Denmark in the month of May, 1839. My son was there in 1868. Good-bye till the twelfth.

Translate into English.

Herr og Fru Hansen komme til Byen den trettende Juli atten hundrede og ni og halvfjerds. Imorgen er det den sekstende Juli atten hundrede og åtte og halvfjerds. I Junimåned kommer jeg til Norge. Vil De være så god, min kære Fru Martensen, at sige mig hvad Dato det er idag? Han kommer måske om et halvt År. Ser De Deres Mand og Deres prægtige Börn imorgen eller idag? Jeg ser dem snart på Landet. Det er mit förste År i Byen. Hvad skrive vi idag? Hvad Dato var det i Torsdags? Hvormange Minutter er der i en Time? Tredsindstyve. Hvormange Sekunder er der i et Minut? Også tredsindstyve. Hvilken Måned har åtte og tyve Dage? Den anden, (2den) Februar. Er Klokken allerede fem? Den er endnu ikke fem; den er tre Kvarter til fem. Kommer hun hjem den nittende (19de)? Nej, hun kommer först den to og tyvende (22de). Han er aldrig i Byen i Julimåned. Han kommer hjem hver Aften Klokken syv. Min kære Mand kommer til Danmark den syttende (17de) April. Torsdag den femte (5te) kommer jeg til Byen. Klokken elleve er meget sildig. Er Klokken ni tidlig nok? Ja, det er tidlig nok. Söndag kommer jeg ikke med Börnene.

TENTH LESSON.

ON CERTAIN TERMS OF QUANTITY, etc.

The ancient practice of counting quantities, and selling small articles (as fruits, vegetables, eggs, etc.) by the score, is still prevalent in Denmark and the other Scandinavian lands.

en *Snés* (pl. *Snese*), a score	*snesevis*, scorewise, by the score
en halv *Snés*, half a score	i *Snesetal*, scorewise, in twenties.

En Snés is sometimes used to express a number generally and approximately, as for example: *jeg så en Snés Mennesker i Stuen*, I saw a number of people (about a score) in the room; *Bondepigen havde måske en halv Snés Kyllinger i Kurven*, the peasant-girl had perhaps half a score (ten or a dozen) chickens in her basket.

et *Dusin* (pl. *Dusiner*), a dozen.	*dusinvis*, by dozens.

This form of enumeration is rapidly superseding the score in all the larger towns of Scandinavia.

en *Ske*, a spoon	et *halvt Pund*, half a pound
en *Kop*, a cup	et *Lod*, an ounce
et *Par*, a pair, a couple	et *halvt Lod*, half an ounce
en *Flaske*, a bottle	en *halv Flaske*, a small bottle.

The above words are all used without the intervention of a preposition between them and the noun to which they refer, as for example:—

et Pund Kød,	N.G.,	a pound (of) meat
et Stykke Ost,	C.G.,	a piece (of) cheese
et Par Æg,	N.G.,	a couple (of) eggs
en Flaske Øl,	N.G.,	a bottle (of) ale
et halvt Pund Flæsk,	N.G.,	half a pound (of) salt pork
et Lod Kaffe,	C.G.,	an ounce (of) coffee
et halvt Lod Te	C.G.,	half an ounce (of) tea
en halv Flaske Vin,	C.G.,	half a bottle (of) wine
et Glas Vand,	N.G.,	a glass (of) water
en Kop Chokolade,	C.G.,	a cup (of) chocolate
en Skefuld Brændevin,	C.G.,	a spoonful (of) brandy
fem Pund Smör,	N.G.,	five pounds (of) butter.

at betale, to pay	billig, billigt, cheap	saa, so
at sælge, to sell	en Krone, a crown	han vil ikke, he will not
solgt, sold	en Alen, an ell	dette, this
at ske, to happen	Hundreder, hundreds	igen, again
noget, something	Tusinder, thousands	kan være, it may be
intet, nothing	dobbelt, double	en Mil, a mile
en Forretning, a business	en Fjerding, a quarter	en Del, a part
en Pris, a price	en Fjerdingsmil, ¼ of a mile	en Vej, a way, road
dyr, dyrt, dear	halvanden, one and a [half	et Fjerdingår, quarter of a year.

SIMPLE PHRASES.

Hvormeget betaler De for et Hundrede af deres Cigarer?	What do you pay a hundred for your cigars?
Jeg köber dem ikke i Hundreder, men kun i Dusiner.	I do not buy them by the hundred, but only by the dozen.
Hvad betaler Herr Thomsen for det store Hus i Byen?	How much is Mr. Thomson to pay for the large house in town?
Han betaler ti tusind Kroner.	He is to pay 10,000 crowns.
Hvor meget er det i engelske Penge?	How much is that in English money?
En dansk Krone er omtrent en engelsk Shilling og halvanden Penny.	A Danish crown is about 1s. and 1½d.
Han har en stor Forretning, men han er ikke meget rig.	He has a large business, but he is not very rich.
Har De ikke noget at betale Bonden?	Have you nothing to pay the peasant?
Nej, jeg har intet at betale.	No, I have nothing to pay.
Hun har solgt Smörret for halvtredsindstyve Kroner pr. Centner.	She has sold the butter for fifty crowns the cwt.

Jeg önsker at köbe halvandet Dusin Flasker fransk Vin.	I want to buy a dozen and a half bottles of French wine.
Hvormange Pund Köd har Deres Mand at sælge idag?	How many pounds of meat has your husband to sell to-day?
Han har måske et Par Centner.	He may perhaps have two cwt.
Prisen er ikke billig nok for mig.	The price is not low enough for me.

TENTH EXERCISE.

I wish to buy a bottle of wine, half a bottle of brandy, and seven bottles of ale. Where is my glass, and the water? The peasant-girl has four score of eggs to sell, and half a score of ducks and geese. What does an ounce of tea cost? The servant-maid is coming immediately with a cup of tea, a couple of eggs, bread, butter, and cheese. What do you wish (to have)? I wish to buy three pounds of meat, half a pound of salt pork, and a piece of old Norwegian cheese. We have not got that. What have you? We have Swedish cheese, Danish butter, and eight small bottles of English ale. Give me a piece of bread with half a score of apples, or sweet pears, or yellow plums. How much does an ounce of coffee cost? It does not cost much. Where is my spoon? It is in the cup. The boy will soon bring a couple of chickens. Is the butter not good? The peasant wishes to buy half a pound of meat, but he never has money. How much does half an ounce of chocolate cost? Give me a spoonful of wine. Is the meat always so dear? No, it is often very cheap.

Translate into English.

Vil De sælge mig en halv Snés Kyllinger. Idag er Torsdag, og på den Dag af Ugen har jeg næsten aldrig Kyllinger at sælge. Mandagmorgen kommer jeg igen med Æg, Bröd, Smör og Ost, og måske bringer jeg også Kyllinger, eller et Par Ænder og en Gås Hvormeget koster en Flaske svensk Brændevin? Den koster måske næsten fire Kroner. Hvad har Pigen i

Kurven? Hun har et stort Stykke Flæsk og tre eller fire Snese Æg. Jeg önsker at sælge mine Æbler, Pærer og Æg snesevis. Jeg har Brændevin, Öl, Kaffe og Te i Huset. Hans Ven har et Par Köer og næsten et halvt hundrede Får at sælge. Bring mig en Kop Te og et Stykke Bröd med Smör og Ost. Hvormeget koster det? Hvad er Prisen på denne Hat? Han er en rig Mand og sælger sine Hatte hundredevis. Bondekonen sælger sine Æbler, ikke i Hundreder, men i Tusinder. Jeg köber mit Hus meget billigt. Jeg önsker at få halvandet Dusin Pærer og omtrent et Par Snese Blommer.

ELEVENTH LESSON.

ON THE COMPARISON OF ADJECTIVES
(= *Tillægsordenes Gradforhöjelse.*)

In Dano-Norwegian the comparative of the adjective is formed by adding *ere* to the positive, except when the word ends in *e*, in which case it takes only *re*; while the superlative is formed by adding *est* to the positive, except when the word ends in *e*, *ig*, or *som*, in which cases it takes only *st*, as for example:—

Positive.	Comparative.	Superlative.
blöd, soft	blödere	blödest
grov, coarse	grovere	grovest
bred, broad	bredere	bredest
stille, quiet	stillere	stillest
gruelig, horrible	grueligere	grueligst
virksom, active	virksommere	virksomst.

It will be observed that in the last example the *m* is doubled in the comparative; this is done because the last syllable *som* in *virksom* is unaccentuated, and the doubling of the final consonant is required in the comparative and superlative of words consisting of one short, unaccentuated syllable, as for example:—

grön, green	grönnere	grönnest
tör, dry	törrere	törrest
let, light (easy)	lettere	lettest
smuk, pretty	smukkere	smukkest.

Adjectives ending in *el, en, er*, drop the *e* in the Comparative and Superlative; as for example:—

ædel, noble	ædlere	ædlest
simpel, simple, foolish	simplere	simplest
doven, idle	dovnere	dovnest
sikker, certain	sikrere	sikrest
mager, lean, meagre	magrere	magrest.

As in English, the Comparative and Superlative may be expressed by the adverbs *mér*, mere, more, and *mest*, most; as for example:—

våd, wet	mér våd,	mest våd
fattig, poor	mér fattig	mest fattig.

The use of *mér* and *mest* is imperative:—

1. For adjectives, derived from the participles of verbs.

2. For adjectives compounded of a noun and another adjective.

3. For adjectives ending in unaccentuated *et, ed, s, sk*; as for example:—

ophidset, excited	mér ophidset	mest ophidset
skævhalset, wry-necked	mér skævhalset	mest skævhalset
broget, variegated	mér broget	mest broget
fremmed, strange	mér fremmed	mest fremmed
fælles, mutual, common	mér fælles	mest fælles
malerisk, picturesque	mér malerisk	mest malerisk

The Comparative and Superlative of the diminutive degree is expressed by *mindre*, less, and *mindst*, least.

The Superlative may be made additionally forcible by the use of the word *aller*, all, most of all, as for example: *det allergrönneste Træ*, the greenest tree of all.

End, than, is used as in English to characterise a Comparative; as for example:—

min Pære er södere end hendes, my pear is sweeter than hers.

hun er mindre ophidset end min Broder, she is less excited than my brother.

at tro, to believe	så...som, as...as	at, that, (to)
jeg tror, I believe	ligeså...som, just as...as	en Jurist, a lawyer
at skulle, to be obliged	imod, against	en Kurv, a basket
man siger, one says, they say, it is said	vist, certainly, assuredly	en Rose, a rose
	vistnok, no doubt	Onkel, uncle
disse, these	hvilken, who, which	Tante, aunt

Fætter (masc.), cousin	*en Gang*, once, one time	*en Have*, a garden
Kousine (fem.), cousin	*tre Gange*, three times	(*en*) *Vinter*, winter
Kjöbmand, merchant	*på en Gang*, at once	(*en*) *Sommer*, summer.

SIMPLE PHRASES.

Vor fælles Ven, Juristen, kommer vistnok en Gang igen.	Our mutual friend, the lawyer, will certainly come once again.
Man siger, at den fremmede Herre her i Huset er meget ophidset imod Generalen.	It is said that the foreign gentleman, who lives in this house, is much excited against the general.
Min Bedstefader er den rigeste Kjöbmand i Danmark.	My grandfather is the richest merchant in Denmark.
Vor Have er smukkere end Deres om Sommeren.	Our garden is prettier than yours in the summer.
Hvor mange Gange har De været i min Onkels Have?	How many times have you been in my uncle's garden?
Kun to Gange, og det var om Vinteren.	Only twice, and that was in the winter.
Han er den flittigste af alle mine Börn.	He is the most diligent of all my children.
Er min Stok så lang som Deres?	Is my stick as long as yours?
Er min Datters Kåbe ligeså billig som hendes?	Is my daughter's cloak as cheap as hers?
Min Hat er ligeså dyr som Deres.	My hat is just as dear as yours.
Hvor mange Döttre har Deres Tante?	How many daughters has your aunt?
Hun har to Döttre mer end jeg.	She has two daughters more than I have.
Min Onkels Sön er dovnere end Bondedrengen.	My uncle's son is more idle than the peasant-boy.
Er Deres Hest ligeså stor som vor?	Is your horse as large as ours?
Hvilken af de tre Drenge er den dovneste?	Which of the three boys is the most idle?
Deres Fætter Vilhelm.	Your cousin William.
Ere disse Penne gode?	Are these pens good?
De ere de mindst gode jeg har köbt i Byen iår.	They are the least good pens I have bought in town this year.

ELEVENTH EXERCISE.

The woman is more active than her husband. The water is calmer to-night. He is the laziest creature in the house. The woods are greener in May. She is prettier than I am. She was more excited than the husband. Our mutual friends, the general and his wife, have more active servants than my parents. The boy's hands were the wettest. My house is more picturesque than my brother's. The chair is softer than the table. The canary-bird is greener and yellower than the cock. Her cloak is prettier than her hat. The peasant-woman's basket is lighter than my servant-maid's. The fields are less wet than they were yesterday. I wish to have twenty sweeter pears. She wants seven broader and redder strings. The woods are green in May, greener in June, and greenest, perhaps, in July. The fields are scarcely ever dry in February. The green room is wetter than the white room. My unhappy friend is poorer than your father. The tree is least green in January.

Translate into English.

Hun var mér ophidset end hun skulde have været. Mit stakkels Barn er mér skævhalset iår, end hun var i åtten hundrede og syv og treds. Den ellevte Gang var gruligere end den förste. Hans Hjærte er blödere end mit. Din Stok er vådere end min. Mine Piger ere dovnere end mine Drenge. Den danske Sangerinde er mér fremmed her i Danmark end den svenske Dame. Hun önsker lettere Arbejde, men hun er gammel og syg. Hvormeget koster den grönne Hat. Hatten er broget og styg. Skovene ere mest maleriske i Junimåned. Tolken er den virksomste Mand i den lille norske By. Pigen er smukkere end Deres Datter. De Rige ere ikke altid lykkeligere end de Fattige. Roserne ere de hvideste og smukkeste jeg har. Her er det störste

Værelse i mit lille Hus. Hans Marker ere de grönneste i Landet. Hvor er min bedste Ven? Her er jeg, kæreste Fru Blom. Min Datter er altid god, men rask er hun ikke altid. Det er stort og godt af Manden. Mit Bord er bredere end min Søsters. Mine Drenge ere ikke skævhalsede; det er stygt af Dem at sige det. Pigerne ere ikke lykkelige hjemme. Jeg tror at Bondepigen er endnu lykkeligere.

TWELFTH LESSON.

ON IRREGULAR ADJECTIVES

(= Uregelrette Tillægsord).

Numerous adjectives form their Comparatives and Superlatives irregularly. Of this class the following are the most conspicuous examples:—

Positive.	Comparative.	Superlative.
god, good	*bedre*	*bedst*
ond, bad	*værre*	*værst*
stor, large	*större*	*störst*
liden, lidet,[1] little	*mindre*	*mindst*
megen, meget,[2] much	*mér*	*mest*
få, few	*færre*	*færrest*
lang, long	*længer*	*længst*
mange, many	*flere*, several	*flest*
gammel, old	*ældre*	*ældst*
ung, young	*yngre*	*yngst*
nær, near	*nærmere*	*nærmest* or *næst*.

[1] The plural of *lille, liden, lidt* (neuter) is *små*, as for example: *et lille Barn*, a small child; *små Börn*, small children. *Små* is used in combination with other words to form singular nouns, as *en Småhed*, a littleness; *en Småhandler*, a petty trader.

[2] The plural of *megen, meget*, is *mange*. The old forms *mangen, mangt* are used in the same manner as the English "many a," as for example: *Mangen en Gang har jeg sét det*, many a time have I seen it; *mangt et Menneske glæder sig idag*, many a man is rejoicing to-day.

Some adjectives are defective, and do not admit of being used in more than one or two degrees of comparison; as for example:—

Positive.	Comparative.	Superlative.	Derived from:—
egen, eget, own	....	....	*egen,* own
	indre, inner	*inderst*	*inde,* within
	ydre, without	*yderst*	*ud, ude,* out, out of
	övre, upper	*överst*	*over,* over
	nedre, lower	*nederst*	*ned,* below, down
	nærmere, nearer	*nærmest* or *næst*	*nær,* near
		bagest,	*bag,* behind
		eneste	*ene,* alone
		forrest	*foran,* in front
		först	*för,* before
		midterst ⎫ mid-	*midt,* in the middle
		mellemst ⎭ most	*mellem,* between
		sidst	*siden,* afterwards, since.

Adjectives of time, which in English end in "ly," occur, as a rule, in Danish with the termination *lig,* as *ärlig,* yearly; *halvärlig,* half-yearly; *månedlig,* monthly; *ugentlig,* weekly; *daglig,* daily; *natlig,* nightly.

at få, to get, obtain
jeg får, I get, obtain
at göre, to make, do
han gör, he makes, does
at göre ondt, to hurt
at begynde, to begin
det begynder, it begins
at köre, to drive
du körer, thou drivest
at koste, to cost
det koster, it costs
at se, to see
hun ser, she sees
at kunne, to be able

en Læge, a doctor
en Præst, a clergyman
en Officer, an officer
en Soldat, a soldier
en Professor, a professor
et Önske, a wish
en Sö, a lake, sea
en Klasse, a class
en Dör, a door
en Godsvogn, a goods van
en Jærnbane, a railway
en Plads, a place
Bagage, luggage

en Omnibus, an omnibus
en Sporvogn, a tramway carriage
en Billet, a ticket
et Tog, a train
en Sal, a room
næppe, scarcely
begge to, both
forbi, past
da, when, as
vel, well, truly
altfor, too
precis, precisely

SIMPLE PHRASES.

Jeg tror det næsten. — I almost think so.
Det gör ondt. — That hurts (does harm).
Det er altfor sildigt. — It is too late.
Det er næppe tidlig nok. — It is scarcely soon enough.
Hvor er Juristen? — Where is the lawyer?

Han körer med Lægen.	He is driving with the doctor.
Ser De Præsten i Vognen?	Do you see the clergyman in the carriage?
Jeg ser kun Officeren med en Soldat.	I only see the officer with a soldier.
Professoren önsker at give min Onkel en norsk Bog.	The professor wishes to give my uncle a Norwegian book.
Hvormeget koster en förste Klasses Billet?	How much does a first class ticket cost?
Det koster slet ikke meget.	It does not cost much.
En anden Klasses Billet til Stockholm er meget billig.	A second class ticket to Stockholm is very moderate.
Når får De Roser i Deres Have?	When will you have roses in your garden?
Roserne ere alle forbi i min Have.	The roses are all over in my garden.
..ynder det at være smukt på .andet.	Now it begins to be charming in the country.
..r det altfor sildig at få en Billet?	Is it too late to get a ticket?
Nej! her har De Billetten.	No! here is the ticket.
Når går der en Omnibus?	When does the omnibus go?
Den går Klokken ni præcis.	It goes exactly at nine.
Hvor er Lægen?	Where is the doctor?
Han er i Salen.	He is in the room.
Går De med Toget?	Are you going by the train?
Ja! jeg går med det förste Tog.	Yes! I am going by the first train.

TWELFTH EXERCISE.

The clergyman was ill, but now he is better. My best friend, the Swedish doctor, is older than I am. My youngest daughter is in Norway with her oldest brother, the professor. The nearest town has seven churches. He has the worst carriage in the town. The carriage is very old, but it is the only one. My own child was in the uppermost room of the house. The young man is much older than my son. The little girl has the largest and reddest apples. Her chair is larger, but less good than my mother's. The butter is worse than the cheese. The last time he was here. My very dear little children are daily in the large woods. That is the worst. I have fewer young chickens to-day. Shall you have more to-morrow? The old doctor is not a bad person. The woman is worse in town than she was out in the country. The outermost ship is English, the innermost one Norwegian. The hindermost horse is very old. The nearest house is the largest. My only child was down in the garden. There were only a few persons there. The officer could not at all see the soldiers when he was in the lowermost room.

Translate into English.

Mit kæreste Önske er at kunne se mine små Börn næste År. Jeg var flere Gange i Norge ifjor. Hvormange Gange var hans yngste Sön ude på Söen? Hun kommer ugentlig til min yngre Söster. De ere begge To ude i Lægens störste Vogn med et Par store sorte Heste. Præsten og hans Kone ere vel fattige Mennesker, men de ere rigere end Lægen og hans Kone. Det midterste Par röde Gardiner ere meget værre end de bageste. Det yderste Kabinet er det nærmeste til det grönne Værelse. Det er bedre at have et godt Hjærte end mange Penge. Kun få gamle Mennesker vare i den mindste Sal med de små Piger og de unge Drenge. Der var næppe en Snés Soldater med Officeren på Landet. Har De ligeså mange Værelser i Deres Hus som vi? Jeg har færre Værelser, men de ere större. Jeg tror ikke at vore Værelser ere mindre end Deres. Disse Penneknive ere de bedste, Köbmanden har at sælge. Giver De Deres Tante de bedste Böger? Nej, jeg giver min Onkel de bedste Böger, men Tanten giver jeg de smukkeste Roser i min Have. Hvilken er den nærmeste Vej til Byen? Den nærmeste Vej er ikke den mest maleriske. Er Deres ældste Broder ældre end min yngste Sön? Nej, han er kun syv År gammel. Deres Döttre ere de smukkeste Piger her i Byen.

CONJUGATION OF THE AUXILIARY VERBS (= *Hjælpeord*)
at få (= to get, to obtain), and
at blive (= to become, to be, to remain).

INDICATIVE.

PRESENT.

(*I get.*)
jeg får
du får
han får
vi få
I få
de få.

(*I become.*)
jeg bliver
du bliver
han bliver
vi blive
I blive
de blive.

PAST.

(*I did get.*)
jeg fik
du fik
han fik
vi fik
I fik
de fik.

(*I became.*)
jeg blev
du blev
han blev
vi bleve
I bleve
de bleve.

PERFECT.

(*I have got.*)
jeg har fået
du har fået
han har fået
vi have fået
I have fået
de have fået.

(*I have become.*)
jeg er bleven *or* blevet
du er bleven *or* blevet
han er bleven *or* blevet
vi ere blevne
I ere blevne
de ere blevne.

PLUPERFECT.

(*I had got.*)
jeg havde fået
du havde fået
han havde fået
vi havde fået
I havde fået
de havde fået.

(*I had become.*)
jeg var bleven *or* blevet
du var bleven *or* blevet
han var bleven *or* blevet
vi vare blevne
I vare blevne
de vare blevne.

FUTURE.

(*I shall get.*)
jeg skal få
du skal få
han skal få
vi skulle få
I skulle fa
de skulle få.

(*I shall become.*)
jeg skal blive
du skal blive
han skal blive
vi skulle blive
I skulle blive
de skulle blive.

POTENTIAL.

PRESENT.

(*I may get.*)	(*I may become.*)
jeg få	jeg blive
du få	du blive
han få	han blive
vi få	vi blive
I få	I blive
de få.	de blive.

PAST.

(*I may have got.*)	(*I may have become.*)
jeg have fået	jeg være bleven *or* blevet
du have fået	du være bleven *or* blevet
han have fået	han være bleven *or* blevet
vi have fået	vi være blevne
I have fået	I være blevne
de have fået.	de være blevne.

IMPERATIVE.

få du (*get thou*)	bliv du (*become thou*)
han få (*let him get*)	han blive (*let him become*)
får I (*get ye*)	bliver I (*become*)
de får (*let them get*).	de blive (*let them become*)

INFINITIVE.

PRESENT.

at få (*to get*).   at blive (*to become, etc.*).

PAST.

at have fået (*to have got*).   at være bleven (*to have become*).

PARTICIPLES.

fående (*getting*)	blivende (*becoming*)
fået (*got*).	bleven, blevet, *sing.* } (*become*).
	blevne, *plur.*

It will be observed that the verb *at få* is conjugated with the auxiliary *at have*, while *at blive* is conjugated with the verb *at være*, to be.

At få, when used as an auxiliary with an active verb, conveys to the latter a sense of compulsion, or necessity, and usually refers to a future period, as for example: *jeg får se*, I must see.

At blive, when used as an auxiliary with an active verb, converts the latter into a passive verb, as for example: *jeg elsker*, I love; *jeg bliver elsket*, I am (become) beloved.

CONJUGATION OF THE AUXILIARY VERBS (= *Hjælpeord*) *at skulle*, to be obliged, ought (= shall, should), and *at ville*, to be willing (= will, would).

INDICATIVE.

PRESENT.

(*I shall.*)
jeg skal
du skal
han skal
vi skulle
I skulle
de skulle.

(*I will.*)
jeg vil
du vil
han vil
vi ville
I ville
de ville.

PAST.

(*I should.*)
jeg skulde
du skulde
han skulde
vi skulde
I skulde
de skulde.

(*I would.*)
jeg vilde
du vilde
han vilde
vi vilde
I vilde
de vilde.

PERFECT.

(*I have been obliged.*)
jeg har skullet
du har skullet
han har skullet
vi have skullet
I have skullet
de have skullet.

(*I have been willing.*)
jeg har villet
du har villet
han har villet
vi have villet
I have villet
de have villet.

PLUPERFECT.

(*I had been obliged.*)
jeg havde skullet
du havde skullet
han havde skullet
vi havde skullet
I havde skullet
de havde skullet.

(*I had been willing.*)
jeg havde villet
du havde villet
han havde villet
vi havde villet
I havde villet
de havde villet.

At skulle has no future tense, as the verb itself implies the future; *at ville* can only be used in the future with the auxiliary *at skulle*, as follows:—

FUTURE.

(I shall be willing.)

jeg skal ville   vi skulle ville
du skal ville   I skulle ville
han skal ville   de skulle ville.

POTENTIAL.[1]

PRESENT.

(I should.)   *(I would.)*
jeg skulle   jeg ville
du skulle   du ville
han skulle   han ville
vi skulle   vi ville
I skulle   I ville
de skulle.   de ville.

PAST.

(I ought to have.)   *(I may have been willing.)*
jeg have skullet   jeg have villet
du have skullet   du have villet
han have skullet   han have villet
vi have skullet   vi have villet
I have skullet   I have villet
de have skullet.   de have villet.

At skulle and *at ville* have no Imperative mood, since both verbs convey a sense of obligation or necessity.

INFINITIVE.

PRESENT.

at skulle *(to be obliged, ought)*.   at ville *(to will, be willing)*.

PAST.

at have skullet *(to have been obliged)*.   at have villet *(to have willed)*.

PARTICIPLES.

PRESENT.

skullende *(being obliged)*.   villende *(being willing)*.

PAST.

skullet *(obliged, ought)*.   villet *(willed)*.

---

[1] The potential mood is so little used in Danish, that it may be regarded as nearly obsolete, more especially in the auxiliary verbs.

THIRTEENTH LESSON.

ON PRONOUNS (= *Stedord*).

The Danish personal pronouns (*Personlige Stedord*) are:—

Singular.

Nominative.	Genetive.	Objective.	Reflective.
jeg, I	. . .	*mig*	. . .
du, thou	. . .	*dig*	. . .
han, he	*hans*	*ham*	*sig*
hun, she	*hendes*	*hende*	*sig*
det, it	*dets*	*det*	. . .

Plural.

vi, we	. . .	*os*	. . .
I, ye	*Eders* or *Jeres*	*Eder* or *Jer*	. . .
de, they	*deres*	*dem*	*sig*

De, when used in the signification of "you," takes a singular verb, as already stated; as for example, *De har*, you have (has).

The possessive pronouns (= *Ejestedord*) are:—

	Singular.	Plural.
COMMON GENDER.	NEUTER GENDER.	
min, my	*mit*	*mine*
din, thy	*dit*	*dine*
hans, his	*hans*	*hans*
hendes, her	*hendes*	*hendes*
sin, his, her (their own)	*sit*	*sine*
vor, our	*vort*	*vore*
Jeres,[1] your	*Jeres*	*Jeres*
Eders,[2] your	*Eders*	*Eders*

(referring only to numbers, and used in relation to *I*, ye.)

Deres, your	*Deres*	*Deres*

(referring to one person, and used in relation to *De*, you.)

deres, their	*deres*	*deres*.

[1] Used principally by the less well-educated classes.
[2] Used in composition, in general conversation, etc.

(52)

The distinctive differences between the pronouns *sin, sit, sine,* and *hans, hendes, deres,* will be fully considered in Part II., and it will therefore suffice for the present to draw attention to the fact that, *in general,* the use of *sin, sit, sine* is imperative where, in English, the adjective " own " is used or implied. In other words, this pronoun, *sin, sit, sine,* is used in a subjective sense, in opposition to *hans, hendes, dets, deres,* which have an objective meaning. Thus, for example, by the correct use of these pronouns, all ambiguity may be avoided in Danish in a sentence such as the following: " He took his hat and went through his garden," which may be rendered thus :—

Han tog hans Hat, og gik igennem hans Have:
He took his (another man's) hat, and went through his (another man's) garden.

Han tog sin Hat, og gik igennem sin Have:
He took his (own) hat, and went through his (own) garden.

Han tog hans Hat, og gik igennem sin Have:
He took his (another's) hat, and went through his (own) garden.

Han tog sin Hat, og gik igennem hans Have:
He took his (own) hat, and went through his (another's) garden.

en Kjole, a coat, dress
en Skjorte, a shirt
et Ur, a watch
en Lomme, a pocket
Klæder (pl.), clothes
en Smag, a taste
en Mode, a fashion
et Øje, an eye
et Øjeblik, a moment
en Kusk, a coachman
et Skur, a shed
et Vognskur, a coach-house
Aviser (pl.), newspapers
et Foteral, a case
et Hattefoteral, a hat-box

at bringe, to bring
jeg bringer, I bring
at hente, to fetch
jeg henter, I fetch
at sende, to send
jeg sender, I send
at holde, to hold
at holde af, to like
jeg holder af, I like
at bryde sig om, to care for
jeg bryder mig ikke om ham, I do not care for him
han bryder sig ikke om det, he does not care about that

kold, cold
(en) Kulde, a cold
en stræng Kulde, excessive cold
varm, warm
(en) Varme, a warmth
hed, hot
ny, new
moderne, fashionable
et Sygehus, a hospital
på Moden, in the fashion
i god Smag, in good taste
efter min Smag, according to my taste.

SIMPLE PHRASES.

Fru Jansen bringer sine Börn med i Vognen, men ikke Deres.
Mrs. Jansen will bring her own children in the carriage, but not yours.

Min Mand kommer i et Öjeblik med Hr. Hansen og hans Ven, Juristen.
My husband is coming in a moment, with Mr. Hansen and his friend, the lawyer.

Lægen gav Drengen i Sygehuset sine bedste Æbler.
The doctor gave the boy in the hospital his best apples.

Er det mit Hattefoteral eller Dit?
Is that my hat-box, or yours?

Det er ikke mit, men min Faders.
It is not mine, but my father's.

Har De min Broders Aviser?
Have you my brother's papers?

Nej, han har dem i sin Vogn.
No, he has them in his carriage.

Har hun sit Ur i Lommen?
Has she her watch in her pocket?

Nu kommer Tjænestepigen med hendes Ur.
Now the maid is coming with her watch.

Min Tjæner henter min Kåbe og min Hat.
My servant is bringing me my cloak and hat.

Deres Hattefoteral er i Vognen i Vognskuret.
Your hat-box is in the carriage in the coach-house.

Jeg vil bringe Dem det i et Öjeblik.
I will bring it to you in a minute.

Er denne Kjole ganske på Moden?
Is this dress quite in the fashion?

Ja, den er ganske ny og moderne.
Yes, it is quite new and stylish.

Holder De af hendes Mands Ven, Lægen?
Do you like her husband's friend, the doctor?

Nej, jeg bryder mig ikke om ham.
No, I do not care for him.

Hendes Kjole var grå og röd.
Her dress was grey and red.

En hvid og blå Kjole er mer efter min Smag.
A white and blue dress is more to my taste.

Har hun sin varme Kåbe på?
Has she her warm cloak on?

Hvor er Deres Kusk?
Where is your coachman?

Han er på Sygehuset med min Onkel, den gamle Læge.
He is at the hospital with my uncle, the old doctor.

Min Moder sender mig tre hvide Skjorter.
My mother sends me three white shirts.

Der er ingen Lomme i min Kjole.
There is no pocket in my coat.

Hendes Klæder ere meget smukke.
Her clothes are very pretty.

THIRTEENTH EXERCISE.

Where is my little girl and her friend ? They are in your room with Mrs. Bang and her daughter. Should you not give me my son's coat ? He has his coat with him. Can you send us a pair of ducks and two or three score of eggs ? How old are you (ye) ? We are both almost ten years old. Our eldest son has his sweet little wife with him in Sweden. A good man loves his little children very dearly (highly). My garden has higher trees than yours. Will he bring me a good pair of chickens the next time he comes to town ? She had her children with her (reflective *sig*). Will your child fetch me a glass of cold water with a tea-spoonful of red wine ? I wish you to give her eldest daughter a large cup of hot milk with a piece of bread, and a little butter and cheese. She ought to send him a long letter soon. I am coming (come) immediately with her red cloak and his black hat. Our old houses are the most picturesque. Will you come with me and my son through the doctor's garden ? Where are our daughters ? Your daughters are in the wood with their husbands. It is my own carriage, but the horse is not mine. Is the garden yours ? No, the garden is not mine, but the house is mine. Has your daughter's husband a better coach-house than his brother ?

Translate into English.

Han giver sin Sön en deilig Bog. Deres egne Kåber ere våde. Det er gruelig koldt her i vort Hus. De to Mænd ville ikke se hinanden. Kan Du sige hende, om den hvide Hat er Din eller hendes ? Den er min, men Hatten på Bordet er hendes. Undertiden elsker en Kone sine Börneborn bedre end sine egne Börn. Er Dyret dit eller mit ? Er det vor Fugl eller deres ? Er det Deres Vogn, eller er det Deres Faders ? Vognen er min Faders, men det er vort Vognskur. Lægen er endnu i Sygehuset med sin Sön. Sönnen er meget syg, og hans Söster Anna er med ham. Han holder så meget af de Börn. Det er meget koldt i Deres Have idag; jeg vil hente Dem Deres Kåbe. Tak skal Du have; jeg bryder mig ikke om Kulden. Min Ven, Præsten, kommer imorgen med sine gamle Forældre og med sin Kones Fætter, Husar-Officer Langberg. Jeg bryder mig slet ikke om Husar-Officeren, men jeg holder meget af de Gamle. Har De Deres Sösters Börn med Dem? Nej, Börnene ere ikke her i Landet; de ere endnu hos deres Slægtninge i Spanien. Når kommer Sösteren til Danmark med sine Börn? Måske kommer hun næste År med sin Veninde, Englænderinden. Er hendes Mand en Englænder? Nej, han er ikke engelsk, men tysk.

FOURTEENTH LESSON.

ON THE DEMONSTRATIVE PRONOUNS, &c.

(=Påpegende Stedord, o. s. v.)

The demonstrative pronouns are:—

Singular.		Plural.	Singular.		Plural.
COMMON G.	NEUTER G.		COMMON G.	NEUTER G.	
den, that	det	de	slig, such	sligt	slige
denne, this	dette	disse	sådan, such	sådant	sådanne
hin, that	hint	hine	samme, same	samme	samme

Selv, pl. selve, self, admits, as in English, of being added to pronouns for the sake of emphasis or opposition; as for example, jeg selv, I myself; den selvsamme Mand, the self-same man; begge, both, is used directly before nouns, and before the numeral to, two, as begge Brödre, both brothers; begge to, both of them.

A. The demonstrative pronouns, *den, det, de,* are, in point of fact, the component parts of the independent definite (adjective) article used as pronouns, and distinguished, when thus employed, by a special intonation of the *e*, as *dĕt Bord, that* table; *dĕn Stol er min, that* chair is mine; *den Mand kalder jeg den sande Vise, that* man I call the true Solon!

B. *Hin, hint, hine,* that, those, used in opposition to *denne, dette, disse,* this, those, are similarly mere adaptations of the Old Northern independent definite article. (*See* Part II.)

C. *Slig, slige,* such, are used very much the same in Danish as in English. In the singular, *slig* may precede the indefinith article, as *slig en Mand,* such a man; in the plural, *slige* precedes the substantive directly; as for example, *slige Koner,* such women.

D. *Sådan, sådant, sådanne,* such, may be used both before and after the indefinite article; as for example, *en sådan Mand, sådan en Mand,* such a man.

E. *Samme,* same, is the defective form of an Old Northern demonstrative pronoun, and is used very much as its English equivalent; as for example, *den selv samme Mand,* the self-same man; *den samme Aften,* the same evening.

The RELATIVE PRONOUNS (= *Henvisende Stedord*) are :—

Singular.		Plural.
COMMON GENDER.	NEUTER GENDER.	
hvilken, which	*hvilket*	*hvilke*
som, which, that	*som*	*som*
der, which, that	*der*	*der.*

Hvem, objective of *hvo,* who, is used instead of *hvilken,* when the relative applies to a *person.*

Hvad, hvad for en, what, is used instead of *hvilket,* where the relative is taken in a general sense, and refers exclusively to a neuter singular.

Hvis, whose, which, is used as the genitive of all the above given relative pronouns.

A. *Der* is used only as a nominative; the old objective *den*, C.G., and *det*, N.G., and the dative, *dem*, have been superseded in modern Danish by *som*, and are wholly dispensed with; as for example, *Nöden, som Gud sender*, the trial that God sends; *Manden, som jeg har at takke for mit Liv*, the man to whom I owe (whom I have to thank for) my life.

at ligge, to lie	at sige, to say	en Krave, a collar
at have på, to have on	at se, to see	en Vest, a waistcoat
at klæde sig på, to dress oneself	en Stövle, a boot	en Handske, a glove
	et Par Stövler, a pair of boots	en Frakke, a coat
at höre til } at tilhöre } to belong to	et Par Benklæder, a pair of trowsers	en Skrædder, a tailor
at bestille, to order		en Handskemager, a glover
at köbe, to buy	et Par Strömper, a pair of stockings	en Krone, a crown (coin = to about 1s. 1½d.).
at agte, to esteem		
at bringe, to bring	en Sko, a shoe	

SIMPLE PHRASES.

Kan Skrædderen ikke sende mig min Frakke idag?	Cannot the tailor send me my coat to-day?
Han siger, at han kan ikke bringe den sorte Frakke, som Herren önsker, förend i Morgen.	He says that he cannot bring the black coat which you want till to-morrow.
Der ligger den sorte Vest, som jeg havde på igår; giv mig den.	There is the black waistcoat that I wore yesterday; give me that one.
Jeg önsker at bestille et Par sorte Benklæder, en hvid Vest og en sort Frakke.	I wish to order a pair of black trowsers, a white waistcoat, and a black coat.
Hvad er det for en Krave?	What collar is this?
Det er den selv samme Krave, som De havde på igår.	It is the same collar you had on yesterday.
Hvor ere mine Stövler?	Where are my boots?
Her har De dem begge to.	Here are both of them.
Hine ere ikke mine; dette Par tilhörer min Fader.	Those are not mine; this pair belongs to my father.
Disse ere de selv samme Handsker, som jeg gav min Broder.	These are the same gloves that I gave to my brother.
Jeg vil köbe mig tre Par hvide Handsker og et Par sorte Silkeströmper.	I want to buy myself three pairs of white gloves, and one pair of black silk stockings.

Barnet kan ikke klæde sig selv på.	The child cannot dress himself.
Hvis Barn er dette?	Whose child is this?
Det er min Sösters lille Barn, som önsker så meget at se Deres små Drenge.	It is my sister's little child; he wishes so very much to see your little boys.
Denne Kåbe har kun én Lomme; hvor er Urlommen?	This cloak has only one pocket; where is the watch-pocket?
Skrædderen siger at en Urlomme hörer ikke til en Kåbe.	The tailor says a watch-pocket is not needed in (does not belong to) a cloak.
Slig en Kåbe er ikke efter min Smag.	Such a cloak is not to my taste.
Sådant et Par Handsker ser man ikke her i Byen.	One does not see such a pair of gloves as these in this town.

FOURTEENTH EXERCISE.

I do not at all care for that girl, but I like her sister very much. Who was here yesterday? It is my sister who gave me a horse. The doctor who was here yesterday is coming again to-morrow to my youngest sister. Both soldiers were quite sober on that evening. It was not that lawyer, but his elder brother. It was that one who sends me money every month (monthly). Which cows are yours? Those in the little cow-house, and those which are in the fields to-day. This white house is higher than that gray one. Which house is theirs? Whose daughter is she? I send you the same large black basket again. Which basket is yours? I have not (got) his ugly basket. Is her sister not in the house? No, but the master (*Herre*) is at home with his three little sons. Is the same person in the kitchen? Yes, the boy who brings the bread daily, is there with my mother's maid-servant. My daughter can bring the newspapers at (upon) the same time. This year the cold is dreadful in Norway. There are only about a score of persons in that room, but in this one there is nearly a hundred. It is the self same man who was here with

(59)

my uncle, the clergyman, yesterday. Whose letter is that? I ought to send this letter. He has not a single crown. I can only say these few Danish words.

Translate into English.

Denne stolte Mand er ikke den jeg önsker at se. De samme små Piger vare med hine Fruentimre, og begge to havde höje Hatte. Han kalder sig Jurist, og hin Dame, som De ser i denne Sal, er hans Kone. Hans förste Kone var udmærket smuk, meget smukkere end hans anden. Jeg har mine gamle Forældre at takke for mine Penge og mine Klæder. Jeg agter disse gode Böndepiger meget höjere end hine fornemme Frökener. Denne Mands Stolthed er större end hans Höjhed. Begges Nöd er skrækkelig. Hvor ere disse Folks Heste? Jeg ser dem ikke i denne Skov. Hvis Have önsker De at se? Jeg önsker at se Juristens Have, som har de höje Træer. Er hans Får i disse eller i hine Marker? Hvor er Deres Herskab? Er dette Deres eller vort? Har De flere Penge end disse to Kroner? Hvilken Stol bringer De ind i dette Værelse? Den sorte, men den hvide hörer til hint Værelse. Har Tjæneren mine Benklæder? Nej, de ligge på hin Stol i det gule Værelse. Det er Manden, som var hos mig. Hine Piger ere ikke så smukke som disse. Hvor ere mine Knive? Jeg har dem begge to. Hvad er det som jeg ser? Det er ikke noget. Jeg selv var i Huset med denne Mand, som nu ligger syg i Sygehuset. Önsker De at tage rene Stövler på? Ja, vil De være så god at sige til Tjæneren, at han skal bringe mig et Par rene Stövler. Hvad skal De give for Deres Ur? Jeg skal give hundrede og tyve Kroner; men sig ikke til min Fader, at det koster så meget.

FIFTEENTH LESSON.

ON PRONOUNS (=*Stedord*).
(*Continued.*)

The following are used as INTERROGATIVE PRONOUNS (=*Spörgende Stedord*) as well as in the sense of RELATIVE PRONOUNS (=*Henvisende Stedord*).

Singular.   *Plural.*

COMMON GENDER.   NEUTER GENDER.
Nom.:—   *hvo*, who   *hvad*,   } what, which   *hvilke*, who, which.
Gen.:—   *hvis*, whose   *hvad for*
Obj., etc.:—*hvem*, whom

Hvo is seldom used, except in poetry, impressive appeals, &c.; *hvem* being employed both as a nominative and an objective; as for example, *hvem er det?* who is that?

The following rank in Dano-Norwegian as indefinite pronouns (*Ubestemte Stedord*):—

Man, one, they. This pronoun can only be used as a nominative singular, as, for example, *man ved det meget godt*, one knows that very well; where the objective or genitive case is required, the pronoun *en* must be substituted for *man*, as, *man söger hvad der behager en*, one seeks for what pleases one.

Det (pronounced *dé*), it; is used impersonally, as for example, *det regner, det blæser, det sner, det fryser*, it rains, it blows, it snows, it freezes; *der er*, there is, answers to the French *il y a*, as for example, *der er fremmede Folk i Stuen*, there are strange people in the room. *Der*, there, is used with a passive verb in the following manner: *der læses og skrives i Salen*, people are reading and writing in the drawing-room, lit., there is being read and written in the drawing-room.

Somme (pl.), some, is used only under certain limited conditions, but it may, in special cases, be employed as in English, as for example, *somme Tider röyer jey i Salen,* I sometimes smoke in the drawing-room.

The following indefinite pronouns are modified by gender and number:—

Singular.		Singular.		Plural.
COMMON G.	NEUTER.	COMMON G.	NEUTER.	
en, a, one	et	ingen, no one	intet	ingen
en anden, another	et andet	nogen, some, some one	noget	nogle, some
hver en } each	hvert et			few
enhver }	ethvert	mangen, many,	mangt	mange
		al, all	alt	alle.

A. When *en* and *et* are used as pronouns, the words are pronounced with a deepened intonation of the e, as, for example, *én gör ét, en anden gör et andet,* one person does one thing, another does another thing.

B. *Hver en,* and *enhver,* may be used in one and the same sense; as for example, *enhver Mand, hver en Mand,* every man; *ethvert Hus, hvert et Hus,* every house.

Hver, hvert, admit of being combined with certain ordinal numbers; as for example, *hveranden,* every second; *hver tredje Gang,* every third time.

Hverandre, one another, and *hinanden,* each other, are used in the same reciprocal sense as in English.

C. *Ingen,* no one, *nogen,* some one, and *mangen,* many, are used in Dano-Norwegian in the same manner as their English equivalents, as for example, *er der Ingen hjemme?* is there no one at home? *Jo, der er Nogen hjemme,* yes, there is some one at home; *mangen en Köbmand bliver rig,* many a merchant becomes rich; *er der mange i Kökkenet?* are there many in the kitchen?

D. *Nogle,* some, occurs only in the plural, and is frequently followed by *få,* few; as for example, *jeg har kun nogle få Böger med mig,* I have only a few books with me.

at *bo*, to dwell, live in
at *gå hen*, to go towards
jeg må, I may
at *lade*, to let (allow)
at *synes*, to think
et *Blad*, a leaf
et *Dagblad*, a daily paper
en *Flokke*, a flake
(en) *Sne*, snow
(et) *Vejr*, weather
et *Löfte*, a promise
en *Skorsten*, a chimney
en *Skomager*, a shoemaker
en *Broche*, a brooch
en *Knap*, a button
et *Törklæde*, a handkerchief
en *Manchette*, a cuff
en *Dame*, a lady
en *Herre*, a gentleman.

SIMPLE PHRASES.

Sommetider kommer Fru Nielsen hos mine Forældre.	Mrs. Nielsen sometimes comes to my parents' house.
Har De mange Par Manchetter?	Have you many pairs of cuffs?
Jeg har nogle få Par med Sölvknapper på.	I have a few pairs with silver buttons on them.
Der siges så meget usandt i Byen.	So many false things are said in town.
Vær så god at sige mig, hvor Dameskomager Holm bor.	Will you please tell me where the ladies' shoemaker Holm lives?
Han bor ikke i denne Gade.	He does not live in this street.
Hvem har mine Manchetknapper?	Who has my cuff-studs?
Hvis Knapper ere disse?	Whose buttons are these?
Sådan en Kjole köber jeg ikke.	I will not buy such a dress (as that).
Enhver Dame har en Silkekjole som denne.	Every lady has a silk dress like this.
Du må ikke gå ud, min Datter, det sner og fryser.	Thou must not go out, my daughter, it is snowing and freezing.
I sligt et Vejr går man ikke på Gaden; Vejen er glat, og hvert et Hus er hvidt, Sneflokkene ligge overalt.	In such weather as this you cannot go into the streets; the road is slippery, and every house is white, the snow-flakes are covering everything.
Det kan nok være, men jeg klæder mig varmt på; og Kulden er måske ikke så stræng som De synes.	That may be, but I am warmly dressed; and the cold is perhaps not so severe as you may think.
Jeg tror at Skorstenen ryger.	I think the chimney smokes.
Er der Ingen her i Huset, som har Aviserne for idag?	Is there any one here, who has the day's papers?
Jo, der er Nogle som have dem.	Yes, there are some persons who have them.
Vil De lade mig gå hen til Köbmanden i Vestergade for at læse Dagbladene.	Will you let me go to the merchant in Vestergade (West Street) to read the daily papers?

FIFTEENTH EXERCISE.

One man has one thing, and another man something else (another thing). Every ship has such a table. Every good man is a good man's friend. Whom do I see? You see the doctor, whose youngest daughter is ill. What have you in your basket? I have many pretty canary birds. Every house has a room, but every room has not many windows. Is there no one at home to-day, my dear boy? Yes, there are some of the children at home. There are only some few children in the sitting-room. The cold is sometimes very great in February. Will you give me this promise? Such a promise I cannot give (can I not give) you. My sister has such a beautiful picture. Whose picture is it? A psalm is being sung in the old church. There is reading and writing going on in that large hall with the black curtains. It rains and snows in the country to-day. Yesterday it was very bad weather in town. To whom do you give (give you) a crown every week? I give five crowns monthly to my sister's Swedish servant; he is such a faithful creature. They wish it in Norway, and also perhaps in Sweden, but not in Denmark. That rich merchant has many newspapers. Every kitchen does not smoke.

Translate into English.

Gud giver Mennesket mangt godt. Hun var meget ulykkelig hin Dag. Sådan en Pige kan jeg ikke elske. De höje Træer, som De ser på denne Mark, ere ældre end min egen gamle Bedstefader. Hin Præst er ingen Vismand. Den Mand holder jeg mer af end af hans Ven, Lægen, som var her igår. Enhver Dreng har sin Bog. Er Herr Jurist Thomsen hjemme idag? Nej, der er Ingen hjemme idag; en af disse Dage kommer Herren hjem med nogle Venner, som ere med ham på Landet; men jeg kan ikke sige hvilken Dag det bliver. Måske kommer han eller Fruen på Tirsdag eller Onsdag. Soldaten bringer ingen Aviser; men nogle få Böger har han. Sligt et Dyr er grueligt. Officeren, hvis Kone er syg i hendes Forældres Hus, sender en af Soldaterne for at hente den fremmede Læge, som har været nogle Uger i Byen. Ens eget er dog det bedste. Hvad er det for en Dreng? De må ikke lade sådan en Dreng blive hos Dem

SIXTEENTH LESSON.

ON THE REGULAR VERBS
(=*Regelrette Udsagnsord*).

Danish regular verbs admit of being grouped under **two** heads:—

I. Those which take *ede* in the past tense of the indicative, and *et* in the past participle.

II. Those which take *te* in the past tense of the indicative, and *t* in the past participle.

The following paradigms will show the simple **mode of** inflexion followed in both systems of declination.

Active Form.

INFINITIVE.

(I.) at elske (*to love*).   (II.) at tænke (*to think*).[1]

PARTICIPLES.

PRESENT.   PAST.
elskende (*loving*)   elsket (*loved*)
tænkende (*thinking*).   tænkt (*thought*).

---

[1] The use of the verb *at tænke* is generally limited to the expression of some definite mental process; as, for example: *jeg har tænkt over alt hvad De sagde mig,* I have been thinking over all that you said to me.

INDICATIVE.

PRESENT.[1]

(*I love.*)
jeg elsker
du elsker
han elsker
vi elske
I elske
de elske.

(*I think.*)
jeg tænker
du tænker
han tænker
vi tænke
I tænke
de tænke.

PAST.

(*I loved.*)
jeg elskede
du elskede
han elskede
vi elskede
I elskede
de elskede.

(*I thought.*)
jeg tænkte
du tænkte
han tænkte
vi tænkte
I tænkte
de tænkte.

PERFECT.

(*I have loved.*)
jeg har elsket
du har elsket
han har elsket
vi have elsket
I have elsket
de have elsket.

(*I have thought.*)
jeg har tænkt
du har tænkt
han har tænkt
vi have tænkt
I have tænkt
de have tænkt.

PLUPERFECT.

(*I had loved.*)
jeg havde elsket
du havde elsket
han havde elsket
vi havde elsket
I havde elsket
de havde elsket.

(*I had thought.*)
jeg havde tænkt
du havde tænkt
han havde tænkt
vi havde tænkt
I havde tænkt
de havde tænkt.

Where the English "think" might be rendered by "suppose," "believe", etc., the Danes use the verbs *at tro*, to believe (*tror, troede, troet*), and *at synes* (defective), to seem, to think; as for example: *jeg tror at min Sön kommer idag*, I think that my son will come to-day; *det Maleri syntes mig så dårligt*, I thought that picture so wretchedly bad.

[1] The present indicative is used in Danish not merely to convey the full meaning of the same tense in English with its auxiliaries "do," "be," as: *jeg ser*, I see, I do see, I am seeing; but it is also very commonly employed in the place of the simple future, as for example: *jeg kommer en eller anden Dag*, I shall come some day or other; *hun begynder strax*, she will begin immediately.

FUTURE.

(*I shall* or *will love.*)

jeg skal elske
du skal elske
han skal elske
vi skulle elske
I skulle elske
de skulle elske.

(*I shall* or *will think.*)

jeg skal tænke
du skal tænke
han skal tænke
vi skulle tænke
I skulle tænke
de skulle tænke.

POTENTIAL.

PRESENT.

(*I may love.*)

jeg elske
du elske
han elske
vi elske
I elske
de elske.

(*I may think.*)

jeg tænke
du tænke
han tænke
vi tænke
I tænke
de tænke.

PAST.

(*I may have loved.*)

jeg have elsket
du have elsket
han have elsket
vi have elsket
I have elsket
de have elsket.

(*I may have thought*).

jeg have tænkt
du have tænkt
han have tænkt
vi have tænkt
I have tænkt
de have tænkt.

IMPERATIVE.

elsk du! (*love thou!*)
han elske! (*let him love!*)
elsker I! (*love ye!*)
de elske! (*let them love!*)

tænk du! (*think thou!*)
han tænke! (*let him think!*)
tænker I! (*think ye!*)
de tænke! (*let them think!*)

VERBS *belonging to* CONJUGATION I.

 at arbejde, to work *(jeg arbejder,*
  I work, *jeg arbejdede,* I worked,
  jeg har arbejdet, I have worked)
 at more, to amuse
 at nægte, to deny
 at sne (defective), to snow
 at takke, to thank.

VERBS *belonging to* CONJUGATION II.

 at begynde, to begin *(jeg begynder,*
  I begin, *jeg begyndte,* I began,
  jeg har begyndt, I have begun)
 at köbe, to buy
 at köre, to drive
 at lære, to learn
 at stræbe, to strive, to try.

med *Tilladelse*, with permission, permit me
en *Tur*, a tour, journey
en *Spadseretur*, a walking tour
en *Lyst*, a pleasure
(en) *Ret*, right, law
at *have Ret*, to be right
en *Uret*, a wrong
at *have Uret*, to be wrong.
om *Forladelse*, for forgiveness, pardon me!
behagelig, pleasant
ubehagelig, unpleasant
ren, clean
smudsig, dirty
en *Dal*, a valley
en *Bygning*, a building
en *Stad*, a city.

SIMPLE PHRASES.

Det er ikke meget behageligt at være pa Landet i dårligt Vejr.

It is not very pleasant to be in the country in bad weather.

Man kan ikke nægte at somme Tider er det ubehageligt nok; men dog synes jeg, at det er altid mere behageligt at være på Landet, end at bo i en stor Stad.

One cannot deny that it is at times unpleasant enough; but yet I think that it is always pleasanter to be in the country than to live in a large city.

Jeg önsker at gå en Tur i Byen for at se Bygningerne.

I want to take a walk in the town to see the buildings.

Önsker De at tage nye Handsker på?

Do you wish to put on a pair of new gloves?

Ja, og vær så god at sige til Tjæneren at han skal bringe mig et Par rene Stövler; mine ere smudsige.

Yes, and please tell the servant to bring (that he must bring) me a clean pair of boots; mine are dirty.

Han har ikke Lyst til at tage ud på Landet idag.

He does not want to go into the country to-day?

Det er ikke behageligt at gå på Gaden når det sner.

It is not pleasant to walk in the street when it snows.

Jeg synes at det er bedre at være i Byen end på Landet i dårligt Vejr.

I think it is better to be in town than in the country in bad weather.

Hvem önsker De at tale med?

Whom do you wish to speak to?

Med Deres Sön, som skulde köre omkring i Staden med mig og min Tante.

With your son, who was to drive about the town with me and my aunt.

Hun nægtede ikke at hun elskede sin ældste Sön mer end den yngste.

She did not deny that she loved her eldest son more than the younger one.

Har jeg ikke Ret?	Am I not right?
Jeg nægter ikke at De har Ret.	I do not deny that you are right.
Hvorledes morede De Dem igår?	How did you amuse yourself yesterday?
Tak! jeg morede mig ret godt.	Thanks (thank you), I amused myself pretty well.

SIXTEENTH EXERCISE.

My brother is beginning to learn Swedish, but he has no great pleasure in learning the language. To-day it rains and blows, and yesterday it snowed out in the country, but not in town. My husband and my brother love one another. I thought she was in the house with your little children. No, that she is not; but she was there yesterday, I think. We shall always love that pretty young Swede, but her relations have never loved her. Her mother thinks that the Norwegian lawyer loves her eldest son more than his own brother. Brothers and sisters should love one another. He began to read a Danish book to his father. I amused myself greatly (much) at my doctor's. I heard my niece say that she amused herself yesterday, but she denies it to-day. They drive in the carriage with a pair of black horses every day. Do you think that (Danish, *at*) she is reading with his wife? Yes, I think so (it). She always strove to be a loving mother. Where does my dear child wish to drive to-day? To-day, dear mother, I wish (wish I) to drive out into the country with my friend (*fem.*) the Englishwoman. Her brother has (is) already driven into town, where he is amusing himself. She never thinks of her old home now that she lives in a great city.

Translate into English.

Nogle af mine Venner önske at köre i Skovene på Torsdag Aften, men måske regner eller sner det på den

Dag. Ingen kan nægte at hun har endnu en udmærket dejlig Stemme. Hvor tænker De at ga næste Ar? De må stræbe at læse danske Böger. Jeg begynder allerede at læse nogle få danske Ord. De skulde köbe Dem nogle lette danske Böger. Hvad tænker De på, min Ven! Om Forladelse, kære Frue, jeg önsker kun at sige et eneste Ord. Nu, min Ven, hvad kan det være, som De har at sige mig? Vænt et Öjeblik, Herr Læge, så kommer jeg straks med Vognen og Hestene. Jeg nægter slet ikke at min gamle Ven, Juristen, må være et ondt Menneske. Mine små Piger morede sig så udmærket hin Aften hos Fru Generalinde Rothe. Generalen körte dem hjem meget sildigt, og Klokken var næsten elleve förend de kom til Sengs. Var det Dem ikke behageligt? Har De nogle engelske Böger? Jeg har nogle, som min Onkel har givet mig.

SEVENTEENTH LESSON.

ON ADVERBS (= Biord.)

The following groups indicate the principal sources from which the Danish adverbs are derived:—

I. Some adverbs are identical with adjectives, especially where the latter end in *s*, *ig*, etc., as for example: *fælles*, mutual, mutually; *indvortes*, internal, internally; *evig*, or *evigt*, eternal, eternally; *rigtig*, right, rightly.

II. Some are identical with the neuter singular of the adjective, as for example: *smukt*, prettily (c.g. *smuk*); *vildt*, wildly (c.g. *vild*); *tyndt*, thinly (c.g. *tynd*); *godt*, well (c.g. *god*); *klogt*, cleverly (c.g. *klog*).

III. Some adverbs of time are formed by adding *lig* (identical with English "ly") to the noun from which they are derived, as for example: *ärlig*, yearly; *daglig*, daily; *ugentlig*, weekly.

IV. Some adverbs of time and place are formed by prefixing a preposition to the noun which they indicate, as for example: *iår*, this year; *tilårs*, in years; *ifjor*, last year; *imorgen*, to-morrow, etc.; *undervejs*, on the way, underway; *tilsös*, by sea; *tilfreds*, satisfied.

V. Adverbs are formed from nouns, or adjectives, by the addition of certain affixes, viz., *vis* (Engl. "wise"), *ledes*, etc., as for example: *stykkevis*, piecewise; *lykkeligvis*, happily; *sandsynligvis*, probably; *anderledes*, otherwise; *ligeledes*, likewise; *således*, suchwise.

The following list contains a number of irregularly formed adverbs, and various groups of words used adverbially.

hen, away, off	*itu*, in two, torn, broken	*uden Tvivl*, undoubtedly
op, oppe, up	*udenfra*, from outside	*af og til*, off and on
netop, precisely	*indefra*, from within	*nu og da*, now and then
bort, borte, away	*tilbage*, back	*vist*, certainly
nogenlunde, in any way	*overhoved*, over and above	*allerbedst*, best of all
særdeles, especially	*i lige Måde*, in the same way	*ilde*, badly
sjælden, seldom		*vel*, well, surely
måske } may be,		
kanske } perhaps		

A. The word *til*, to, which may be used adverbially as well as prepositionally, forms in combination with other words a very large number of adverbial groups, which, until recently, have always been written as conjoint words, as for example: *tilsös*, by sea; *tillands*, by land; but which modern writers now generally write in the originally separate forms, as: *til Sengs*, in bed; *til Fods*, on foot, etc.

at pynte (I.), to smarten	*en Snedker*, a carpenter	*et Torv*, a market
at spise (II.), to eat	*en Modehandler*, a haberdasher, milliner	(*en*) *Frokost*, breakfast
at foretrække, to prefer		(*en*) *Middag*, dinner
at möblere, to furnish	*en Nabo*, a neighbour	(*en*) *Spisetime*, dinner-hour
at fordærve, to spoil	*en Maler*, a painter	
bestemt, decidedly	*en Butik*, a shop	*virkelig*, truly, indeed.

SIMPLE PHRASES.

Idag må jeg blive hjemme til Klokken syv.	I must stay at home to-day till seven o'clock.
Min Mand er taget på Landet; men kommer han tidlig nok tilbage, spise vi til Middag Klokken seks eller halv syv.	My husband has gone into the country; if he comes home early enough, we shall dine at six or half-past six.
Hvad synes De om min nye Kjole?	How do you like my new dress?
Jeg synes særdeles godt om den.	I like it very much indeed.
Det Værelse er særdeles smukt möbleret.	This room is remarkably well furnished.
Jeg finder at hun har pyntet sit Hus altfor meget.	I think she has decorated her house too much.
Mine Værelser ere bedre möblerede end hendes.	My rooms are better furnished than hers.
Ja, det ere de ganske bestemt.	Yes, that they certainly are.
Har De en god Modehandlerinde?	Have you a good milliner?
Madame Blaue, som bor i den næste Gade, har altid særdeles smukke Klæder at sælge.	Madame Blaue, who lives in the next street, has always remarkably pretty dresses to sell.
Arbejder Maleren nogenlunde billigt?	Does the painter work tolerably cheaply?
Han arbejder betydeligt billigere end hans Nabo, Snedkeren.	He works for considerably less than his neighbour, the carpenter.
Han bor i Bredgade Nr. 23.	He lives at No. 23, Bredgade.
Hvad hedder Gaden?	What is the name of the street?
Jeg spiser Frokost Klokken ni.	I (eat) breakfast at nine o'clock.
Når spiser man til Middag?	At what time is dinner? (*lit:* when eats one at midday.)
Hvor er Læseværelset?	Where is the reading room?
Jeg går hen til Posthuset.	I am going to the post-office.
Her er Butikken.	Here is the shop.
Bonden er på Torvet.	The peasant is in the market place.

SEVENTEENTH EXERCISE.

I see very well. He was there likewise. The ship is going (goes) seawards. He sells meat piecewise. The doctor goes yearly to Sweden. My parents are both in years. The singer (*masc.*) comes daily to (into) town. I love my little children dearly. You think quite rightly. I think (believe) that (Danish, *at*) she is on the way. He is seldom away. She comes off and on to the clergyman's, and now and then she is (is she) at my grandfather's. My best hat is spoilt and my cloak is in pieces. They were, without doubt, in one of the rooms of the house. That is a lazy woman; she goes to bed at seven nearly every evening. She will probably come late to church to-day. She does not at all love her grandmother. That I can well believe (think). The poor lady is aged (in years), and she is probably somewhat cross. The old often love the young more than the young love the old. Now you must (must you) get up, and not lie in bed till ten o'clock. I wish to get up daily at seven. The officer will travel (travels) by sea, but his mother and his younger children, whom he loves so dearly, think of coming (to come) by land.

Translate into English.

Jeg önsker at rejse bort så snart som jeg får mine Penge fra Professoren. Min ældste Datter foretrækker at blive hjemme i Norge, men ifjor blev hun kun sjælden hos mig. Hendes ældste Sön har i Sinde at rejse til London, hvor han altid morer sig så udmærket godt. Når han er en Gang borte, kommer han ganske bestemt ikke så snart tilbage. Måske ikke, og det er en stor Ulykke for hans Moder, at han ikke nogenlunde kan være tilfreds her i Landet. Har De nylig set vor

Veninde, Fru Horneman? Jeg ser hende kun sjælden, men nu og da gar jeg op hos hende. Kommer hun ikke ofte her ned i Dalen til Dem? Jo, af og til kommer hun med sin Mand, og uden Tvivl ser jeg hende tidlig i Morgen. Tjænestepigen siger at alle Kopperne ere itu, og at hun ikke er i Stand til at give os Te i Aften. Måske kan hun give os noget at spise til Middag? Jo vist kan hun det; her i Huset spiser man hver Dag godt til Middag. Hvor ere alle de dovne Börn; de ligge da vel ikke endnu i Sengen? Dovne kan jeg ikke kalde dem; för Klokken syv havde de alle klædet sig på, og nu spise de allerede Frokost.

EIGHTEENTH LESSON.

COMPARISON OF ADVERBS, etc.

Danish adverbs admit, like adjectives, of various modes of comparison:—

I. By dropping the final *t*, and taking *ere* or *re* in the comparative, and *est* or *st* in the superlative, precisely the same as the corresponding adjectives, as for example:—

Positive.	Comparative.	Superlative.
klogt, cleverly	*klogere*	*klogest*
slemt, badly	*slemmere*, worse	*slemmest*
morsomt, amusingly	*morsommere*	*morsomst*
nydeligt, charmingly	*nydeligere*	*nydeligst*
ofte, often	*oftere*	*oftest*.

The comparative and superlative are the same, it will be observed, in the adverb and adjective, where the former has been derived from the latter; as for instance: *klogt* from *klog*, *slemt* from *slem*, etc.

II. Some adverbs form their comparative and superlative irregularly, both when they are derived from adjectives, and when they are of independent origin; as for example:—

Positive.	Comparative.	Superlative.
ilde, badly	*værre*, worse	*værst*
vel, well	*bedre*, better	*bedst*
tit (or *tidt*), frequently	*tiere*	*tiest*
gærne, rather, readily	*hellere*	*helst*.

III. Some adverbs are defective, and admit of being used only in one or two forms, as for example:—

Positive.	Comparative.	Superlative.
nede, below	....	*nederst*, lowest
....	*för*, before, earlier	*först*, first
oven, above	....	*överst*, uppermost
ude, outward	....	*yderst*, excessively
inde, inmost	....	*inderst*, inmost.

The superlative of an adverb may often be expressed by a superlative adjective in the neuter gender, with a preposition; as for example:—

i det Mindste, at the least; at all events
på det Bedste, for the best; in the best way
på det Behageligste, in the most pleasant manner.

Some adverbs of place indicate motion towards a spot, or repose at a spot, by the absence or the presence of a terminal *e*; as for example:—

at gå ud, to go out   *at være ude*, to be out
at gå hjem, to go home   *at være hjemme*, to be at home
at gå op ad Trappen, to go up the stairs
at være oppe på Bjærget, to be up on the mountain.

Thus it will be observed that a condition of rest is expressed by the addition of *e*.

Some adverbs are formed by the addition of an *s* to the adjective, and sometimes to a noun, and are in such cases generally used in combination with a preposition; as for example:—

(75)

tværs, på tværs, across,	from	trær, cross
skrås over for, nearly opposite	„	skrå, sloping, oblique
på skrå, aslant		
langs med, alongside with	„	lang, long
til Sengs, to bed	„	en Seng, a bed
til Fods, on foot	„	en Fod, a foot
til Stede, on the spot	„	et Sted, a spot
hjærtens, heartily	„	et Hjærte, a heart.

at betale, to pay	en Öre, Dan. coin, a 100th part of a crown.
at forlange, to demand	et Kontor, a counting house, office
at standse, to stop	et Tog, a railway train
at behage, to please	et Navn, a name
at leie, to hire	en Båd, a boat
at kalde på, to call	Bådsmænd, boatmen
at hedde, to be called, named	en Rorskarl, a rower
at hilse, to greet, salute	en Bro, a bridge
hyggeligt, comfortably	til Leje, for hire
Landsmænd, compatriots	en Kyst, a coast.

SIMPLE PHRASES.

Det er altfor slemt at man ikke kan leje en Båd her idag; jeg vilde så gærne sejle langs med Kysten.

It is too bad that one cannot hire a boat here to-day; I should so much like to sail along the coast.

Og jeg vilde hellere gå til Lands.

And I would much rather go by land.

Går De altid til Hest eller til Vogns?

Do you always go on horseback or in a carriage.

Jeg rejser allerhelst på Jernbanen; men om det behager Dem bedst at gå til Sös, kommer jeg med.

I prefer travelling by railway; but if you like best to go by water, I will accompany you.

Er der en Båd her til Leje?

Is there a boat here for hire?

Der nede, langs med Broen, finde vi vist Bådsmændene.

We shall most likely find the boatmen down by the bridge.

Vil De kalde på Bådsmand Hansen; han kommer netop ud af sit Hus.

Will you call the boatman Hansen; he is just coming out of his house.

De forlanger vel ikke mer end fem Kroner?

I suppose you do not ask more than five crowns?

Jo, jeg forlanger i det mindste seks Kroner.

Yes, indeed, I require at the least six crowns.

Undertiden betaler man mig syv Kroner, men tiere får jeg seks Kroner og halvtredsindstyve Öre.	Sometimes I am paid seven crowns, but I oftener get six crowns and 50 öre.
Nu, da! bring en sikker Båd, og kom ikke for silde; vi betale Dem, hvad De forlanger.	Very well! bring us a safe boat, and come in good time. We will give you the money you ask.
Her er Jernbanestationen, Kontoret og Væntesalen.	Here is the station, the booking office and the waiting room.
Det er yderst morsomt at se så mange Fremmede; jeg ser kun få af vore egne Landsmænd.	It is extremely amusing to see so many foreigners; I see hardly any of our own countrymen.
Nu standser Toget! har De Deres Billetter og Penge hos Dem?	Now the train is stopping! have you your tickets and money with you?
Hvad hedder Herren, som hilste Dem?	What is the name of the gentleman who bowed to you?
Han hedder Thomsen; i sit danske Hjem kalde de ham Hans Thomsen, men på Engelsk er hans Navn "John."	His name is Thomsen; in his Danish home he is called Hans Thomsen, but in English his Christian name is John.

EIGHTEENTH EXERCISE.

It would have been better, if (Danish, *om*) they had thought more frequently of (upon) their little children. I will readily go there, but I (should more readily) should prefer to go to the doctor's. She comes more frequently (oftener) to my brother, the lawyer's. The table is aslant. The professor is going alongside with (even with) the water. She dresses herself charmingly, but no one can dress themselves worse than her younger sisters. At all events, he loves his eldest sister better than that sister who is at home with her parents. He wishes me to go out this evening, but I would rather remain at home. My husband is out, and my younger son is gone up on the mountain. The old peasant woman is going up the stairs. I would rather have a long than a short bed. Is there no one about (on the spot) on the farm?

All the men are up on the mountains. I feel worse (it goes worse with me) to-day than yesterday. I am oftener ill than well. That is unfortunate, but it would be worse if you had not so many heartily-loved friends. Now my little boys are going home and to bed. Is the master on the spot? No; he is seldom here before eleven o'clock.

Translate into English.

Jeg er så ofte syg, at jeg næsten ikke kan gå op ad Trappen. Kan man ikke få noget morsommere at læse her i Huset? Lægens smukke Kone, Englænderinden, er næsten klogere end sin Mand. Hvorledes befinder Deres Broder sig i den store engelske By? Tak skal De have, det går ham godt der, men han vilde hellere være hjemme hos os end så langt borte iblandt Fremmede. Nu, det kan man let forstå; hils ham fra mig og sig ham, at jeg önsker så tit at se ham igen. Han har det ikke ilde der i Udlandet, og her i Hjemmet kunde det gå værre for ham. Hvorledes går det hjemme? Mange Tak, kære Frue, det går fortræffeligt; det kunde ikke gå bedre. Om Forladelse! Hendes Barn er næsten altid vrantent. Hans Hænder ere endnu vadere end hendes. Hvor gærne vilde jeg ikke gå til Fods med Dem op på Bjærget! Min Broder går også gærne med til Fods, men hans Kone kører helst i sin Vogn med sine små Börn. Hvorledes går det Deres Broders Börn? Tak, det går dem på det allerbedste. Ere de tit hos Dem? De komme i det mindste engang hver Uge hos mig; men endnu tiere ere de hos min yngste Söster, som bor der nede skrås over Vandet. Hvor det er morsomt her i Vinduet at se ud på Folk, som morer sig der nede på Torvet. Det er dog hyggeligere her inde i Stuen end der nede på Gaden. Jeg forlanger intet bedre, men jeg ser dog så gærne at Andre ere i Stand til at more sig som de synes bedst.

(78)

Examples of Verbs, belonging to Class I., which are conjugated like *at elske*, to love.

INDICATIVE.			PAST PARTICIPLE.	PRESENT INFINITIVE.	
PRESENT.		PAST.			
Sing.	Plur.	Sing. and Plur.			
jeg, du, han, De	vi, I, de	jeg, du, han, vi, I, de			
agter	agte	agtede	agtet	at agte	to intend, esteem.
erfarer	erfare	erfarede	erfaret	at erfare	to learn, experience.
handler	handle	handlede	handlet	at handle	to act, handle.
henter	hente	hentede	hentet	at hente	to fetch.
lever	leve	levede	levet	at leve	to live.
samler	samle	samlede	samlet	at samle	to collect.
tröster	tröste	tröstede	tröstet	at tröste	to comfort.
vander	vande	vandede	vandet	at vande	to water.
venter	vente	ventede	ventet	at vente	to wait, expect.

Examples of Verbs, belonging to Class II., which are conjugated like *at tænke*, to think.

bruger	bruge	brugte	brugt	at bruge	to use, employ
forlanger	forlange	forlangte	forlangt	at forlange	to require.
föler	föle	földe	fölt	at föle	to feel.
förer	före	förte	fört	at före	to lead, guide
hörer	höre	hörte	hört	at höre	to hear.
kalder	kalde	kaldte	kaldt	at kalde	to call.
kender	kende	kendte	kendt	at kende	to know.
klæder	klæde	klædte	klædt	at klæde	to dress.
köber	köbe	köbte	köbt	at köbe	to buy.
körer	köre	körte	kört	at köre	to drive.
låner	låne	lånte	lånt	at låne	to lend.
låner af	låne af	lånte af	lånt af	at låne af	to borrow.
læser	læse	læste	læst	at læse	to read.
löser	löse	löste	löst	at löse	to loosen.
möder	möde	mödte	mödt	at möde	to meet.
rejser	rejse	rejste	rejst	at rejse	to travel.
sender	sende	sendte	sendt	at sende	to send.
spiser	spise	spiste	spist	at spise	to eat.
stræber	stræbe	stræbte	stræbt	at stræbe	to strive.
vender	vende	vendte	vendt	at vende	to turn.
viser	vise	viste	vist	at vise	to show.

(79)

Some verbs admit of being conjugated both in accordance with Conjugations I. and II., as for example:—

INDICATIVE			PAST PARTICIPLE.	PRESENT INFINITIVE.	
PRESENT.		PAST.			
Sing.	Plur.	Sing. and Plur.			
jeg, du, han, De	vi, I, de	jeg, du, han, vi, I, de			
taler	tale	talede or talte	talet or talt	at tale	to speak.
praler	prale	pralede or pralte	pralet or pralt	at prale	to boast.
nævner	nævne	nævnede or nævnte	nævnet or nævnt	at nævne	to name.

NINETEENTH LESSON.

PREPOSITIONS (= *Forholdsord*).

Prepositions in Danish admit of being grouped under two heads:—

I. As primary and simple.

ad, to, at
af, of, from
bag, behind
blandt, among (implying surroundings of the same kind)
efter, after
for, for, before (space)
fra, from
för, before (time)
gennem, through
hos, at the house of, with
i, inde i, inden i, in
med, with

mellem, between, in the midst (implying different surroundings)
mod, against
om, about
over, over
på, on
samt, together with
siden, beside, since
til, to
trods, in spite of
uden, without
under, under
ved, by, at, near.

II. As compound.

bagefter, after
bagved, behind
foran, before, beyond
formedelst, by means of
iblandt, amongst
igennem, through

imellem, between
imod, against
istedetfor, instead of
omkring, round about
ovenpå, on the top of
udenfor, outside of.

A. The difference between *blandt* and *mellem* will be seen in the following example: *Klinten vokser mellem Stene blandt Hveden*, the corn-cockle grows in the midst of stones among the wheat.

B. Differences in respect to periods of time admit of being indicated by the use of *i, på*, and *om;* the first implying the past, the second the future, and the third some recurring interval; as for example: *jeg var der i Tirsdags; jeg skal dér igen på Torsdag, men jeg er dér ellers altid om Söndagen*, I was there on Tuesday, I shall be there again on Thursday, but I am otherwise always there on Sundays.

Onkel, uncle
Tante, aunt
Fætter, cousin
Kousine, fem. cousin
Nevøu, nephew
Niece, niece
Svigerfader, father-in-law
Svigermoder, mother-in-law
Svoger, brother-in-law

Svigerinde, sister-in-law
Stedfader, step-father
Stedmoder, step-mother
Kone, Hustru, wife
Mand, Ægtemand, husband
Ægtefælle, spouse
Farbroder, Morbroder, uncle
Faster, father's sister
Moster, mother's sister.

Spanien, Spain,   *spansk*, Spanish,   en *Spanier*, a Spaniard
Italien, Italy,   *italiensk*, Italian,   en *Italiener* (fem. *Italienerinde*), an Italian
Frankrig, France,   *fransk*, French,   en *Franskmand*, a Frenchman
Österrige, Austria, *österrigsk*, Austrian, en *Österriger*, an Austrian
Tyrkiet, Turkey,   *tyrkisk*, Turkish,   en *Tyrk*, a Turk.

SIMPLE PHRASES.

Showing the manner in which various prepositions are used in Danish.

Det var af ham jeg köbte mit Ur.	It was of him I bought my watch.
Jeg gav Börnene et af hans Malerier til Eksempel.	I gave the children one of his pictures as an example.
Hun vilde jo ikke tale om sig selv, men om sin Steddatter.	She was not intending to speak of herself, but of her step-daughter.
Han er ikke en Ven af mig.	He is not a friend of mine.
Soldaten tillader ikke at mere end tre ad Gangen gå over Broen.	The soldier will not allow more than three at a time to go over the bridge.
Hvad er der bleven af Spanieren?	What has become of the Spaniard?
Hvad fik De til Middag?	What did you have (get) for dinner?
Hvad holder De mest af?	What do you like best?
Jeg holder mest af at spadsere för Frokosten.	I like best to go out walking before breakfast.
Hun holder mest af ham, tror jeg.	She likes him best, I think.
Tag den De synes bedst om.	Take the one you like the best.
Jeg synes godt om Huset.	I am pleased with (like) the house.
Hold op! lad mig være!	Have done! let me be!
Se efter min Hat.	Look for (after) my hat.
Jeg er ikke vred på ham.	I am not angry with him.
Hvad er der i Vejen med ham?	What is the matter (in the way) with him?
For fjorten Dage siden.	A fortnight ago (since).
De har ikke Ret til at gå der.	You have no right to go there.
Jeg har ikke Lyst til at spadsere.	I have no inclination for walking.
Han var vred over at hun ikke skrev til ham.	He was angry because she did not write to him.
Hvorledes kommer De på det?	How did that occur to you?
Hun tvivlede på at få Hjælp.	She was doubtful of getting help.
Han arbejder på at erhverve sig en god Plads.	He is striving to secure himself a good situation.
Jeg forlader mig på Dem.	I depend upon you.
Jeg var overrasket ved at se ham.	I was astonished at seeing him.
Hun har aldrig brudt sig om sin Onkel.	She has never cared for her uncle.

De har godt ved at le.	You may laugh if you will.
Hun förte Barnet ved Hånden.	She led the child by the hand.
Hun går med Briller på.	She wears spectacles.
Han gik med en tyk Frakke.	He wore (went with) a thick coat.
Jeg beder om Forladelse.	I beg pardon.
Har De set Dem om i Byen?	Have you looked about you in the town.

NINETEENTH EXERCISE.

The Norwegian child gets up too late. My nephews and nieces get up at six in the summer, and at half-past seven in the winter. My Italian cousin and her eldest son read German, French, English, and Dutch. He heard yesterday that his Russian uncle was in Copenhagen on Thursday, the 15th of March. What do you call him in (on) Danish? We call him Carl in (on) Danish, but his parents, brothers and sisters, and relations call him Charles in English. Will you fetch me my Spanish hat and my Russian cloak. Her aunt and uncle expect her and her stepson on Monday. Your brother and sister in-law have bought my step-father's large carriage and the white horses. I always meet the doctor on Thursdays at our good old clergyman's. My mother-in-law cares nothing at all for her German cousins; she thinks them (that they are) proud, and wishes that they had remained in Germany. My nephew, Mr. Larsen, is a Dane, but his relations are nearly all Dutch, or Spanish, and his young wife is a Russian. I was in London on Wednesday, and I expect to be in France on Friday. My dear wife is not at all well to-day; she has heard that her brother-in-law, the English lawyer, is dead, and now her sister will not be able to come to Denmark to see her.

Translate into English.

Hun forlanger af Svigerfaderen, at han skal köbe hende et Hus. Den norske Tolk förte min gamle engelske Ven op på Bjærgene, og lige på samme Tid begyndte det at sne og blæse; begge to tabte deres Hat og Stok; om Aftenen mödte de en Bondemand, som viste dem Vejen, og sildig om Natten körte de hjem igen i en Vogn, som var lånt dem af den gode Gamle. Vil De spise hos mig idag? jeg venter kun nogle få Venner, som agte at rejse imorgen, eller måske ikke för iovermorgen. Hun har mistet sin Mand, og nu forlanger hun, at hendes ældste Sön, som er hos en Köbmand i Rusland, skal komme tilbage til Danmark. Den stakkels Kone, hvor hun er ung til at være Enke! hvor jeg vilde önske at kunne få hende at se! Hvad kalder man den röde Vin, som De köbte af Hollænderen i Foråret? den smager meget bedre end den spanske Vin, min Svoger sendte mig fra Madrid. Penge forlanger jeg ikke; jeg önsker kun at få Ret.

TWENTIETH LESSON.

CONJUNCTIONS (= *Bindeord*).—**INTERJECTIONS** (= *Udråbsord*).

I.—Copulative Conjunctions, etc.

at, that, to
både...og, both...and
da, as, since (past time)
dels...dels, in part
dernæst, in the next place
dersom, in case that, if
fordi, because
fremdeles, moreover, besides
först, first
hvis, if, in case that

ifald, in case
når, when, if (present and fut. time)
nemlig, for instance
om, if, whether, about, for
og, også, and, also
samt, together with
siden, since
som, as
såvel...som, as well...as.

II.—Disjunctive, Compound Conjunctions, etc.

allerede, already	*ligeså,* just as
alligevel, all the same	*medens,* whilst
derimod, against, on the contrary	*men, sämen,* but, indeed
efter, after, according	*nok så mange,* ever so many
efterdi, whereas	*nok så snart,* ever so soon
eftersom, in accordance with	*om ikke,* if not
eller, ellers, or, otherwise	*sköndt (endsköndt)* notwithstanding,
enddog, although	*så,* so, then
for at, in order that	*så godt som,* as good as, as well as
följelig, consequently	*uagtet,* notwithstanding.
hverken...eller, neither...nor	

A. *At,* to, is used to indicate the infinitive of the verb, as in English.

B. *Om,* if, about, admits of being used as in English in the following manner: *At se sig om,* to look (see oneself) about one. *Han ser sig om efter en Plads,* he is looking about for a place.—*Om* is used in the sense of "if," in the following manner: *Jeg må se, om han arbejder,* I must see if he is working.

C. *Ligeså...som,* as...as, are used to express a comparative degree, as for example: *Min Broder er ligeså stor som jeg,* my brother is just as tall as I am.

D. *Jo...jo, jo...desto* express a relative proportion, as for example: *Jo længere jo værre,* the longer the worse; *jo större Besværlighed, desto större Fortjæneste,* the greater the difficulty, the greater the merit.

The Danish Interjections are derived from the imperative of verbs (I.), or are merely imitative sounds (II.), as for instance:—

(I.) *Tak!* thanks!   from *at takke,* to thank
     Tys! silence!   „   *at tysse,* to be silent
     Bi! wait!   „   *at bie,* to wait
     Hör! listen!   „   *at höre,* to hear.

(II.) *Knak! Puf! Plump! Hej! Vips! Visvas!*

Surprise is expressed by such ejaculations as: *Hm! Haha! O-nej-da!*
Sorrow   „   „   „   *Ak! Ve! Ve!*
Joy   „   „   „   *Hej Hej! Hejsa-hopsa! O!*

at *forbyde* (I.), to forbid
at *pibe* (I.), to whistle
at *beholde* (II.), to keep
at *indskrive*, to book, to write down
at *leve* (II.), to live
at *rose* (II.), to praise
(en) *Ros*, praise

(en) *Födsel*, birth
(et) *Födested*, place of birth
et *Rab*, a cry, call
en *Klasse*, a class
en *Port*, a gate
et *Lokomotiv*, an engine.

SIMPLE PHRASES.

Siden jeg kom til London har jeg set Dronningen flere Gange.	Since I came to London I have seen the Queen a great number of times.
Er London Deres Födested?	Is London your native place?
Nej, jeg er Dansk ligesåvel som min Mand; men vi have været så længe her i Landet, at vi ere begge To næsten så godt som Englændere.	No! I am a Dane as well as my husband; but we have been here so long, that we are both of us nearly English?
Han önsker at se sig lidt om i Byen.	He wishes to see a little of the town.
Han vil snart se at denne By er ligeså stor og smuk som hans Födeby.	He will soon see that this town is quite as large and handsome as his native town.
Når rejser De til England?	When are you going to England?
Dersom min Mand önsker det, rejser jeg med ham efter Jul.	If my husband should wish it, I shall go with him after Christmas.
Jeg takker Dem for Deres Brev, samt Bogen.	I am obliged to you both for your letter and the book.
Idag kommer jeg ikke til Köbenhavn, fordi det sidste Tog er gået.	I shall not get to Copenhagen to-day because the last train is gone.
Det Tog, som afgår Kl. 8, går helt igennem uden at standse.	The train which leaves at 8 o'clock goes right through without stopping.
Det ringer jo allerede tredje Gang.	They have already rung the third time.
Vi have jo ingen Billetter.	Why! we have no tickets!
Hvor er Billetkontoret? hvis jeg bare vidste, om vi ere i Tide.	Where is the booking-office? I only knew if we were still time.

Skynd Dem! Lokomotivet piber allerede.	Make haste! the engine is whistling already.
Betjænten lukker Dörene i.	The guard is locking the doors.
De må ikke lukke Dören op.	You must not open the door.
Det er forbudt at röge i förste Klasses Vogne.	It is forbidden to smoke in first-class carriages.
Foretrækker De at sidde med Ryggen mod Lokomotivet?	Do you prefer to sit with your back to the engine?
Jeg vil beholde min Plads, for at se ud af Vinduet.	I will keep my place that I many look out of the window.

TWENTIETH EXERCISE.

She comes to me when she wishes to see my daughters. If she comes home soon, then I shall go together with my sister to France. She talked about something else last evening. In case you wish it I will fetch my children to-morrow. He is coming from Holland together with his sisters-in-law. I paid the peasant-boy partly in crowns, and partly in Dutch money. My aunt is looking out for a house in the country. Although my French cousin is so ill that she cannot stand on (upon) her feet, she goes to church all the same every day. His eldest daughter is nearly as tall as my step-son. When is she going (to travel)? In case her mother should be (is) better, she will go (travel) next week. According to what I hear from her doctor she will soon be better. The Italian maid-servant is coming as well as the French man-servant. Whilst the peasant-woman was here, she fetched water to water my garden. Both my wife and I wish it. Be silent my child! thy sister is still in bed, because she is ill.

Translate into English.

Ifald min Fætter rejser til Rusland i År, går jeg med, fordi jeg önsker så meget at se hvorledes Russerne leve i deres eget Land. Mine Forældre ere ligesä rige som Deres Slægtninge, men alligevel ere de ikke så fornemme Hör, min Dreng! ifald min Mand kommer hjem förend jeg har været hos Lægen, må Du sige ham, at jeg venter at kunne köre tilbage med min Svoger, som skal være med Lægen, eller hans Sön, i Sygehuset. Den tyske Tjæner önsker at höre om hans Broder har fået en Plads her i Byen. Det er et meget dygtigt Menneske. Ja! det kan nok være. Er min Broder hjemme? Om De vil være så god at vente et lille Öjeblik, skal jeg straks hente Deres Herr Broder. Hvis han ikke er hjemme endnu, kommer han vist snart tilbage. Hör engang hvor det blæser ude i Skoveue og oppe på Bjærgene inat! Vil De ikke köre med mig imorgen tidlig? Jeg har intet derimod, men medens min Hustru er på Landet, går jeg ikke gærne ind til Byen. Min Svigermoder, samt mine Söstre, rejse i År til Italien med vor Slægtning, Italieneren. Tys! jeg hörte et Råb fra Skoven. Bi lidt! nu kommer Kusken.

TWENTY-FIRST LESSON.

PASSIVE VERBS, etc. (= *Udsagnsord; den lidende Form.*)

The Danish language possesses a characteristic feature in its mode of forming the passive by the simple addition to the active voice of the letter *s*.[1] Thus, for example, the passive of *at elske*, past indicative *elskede*, is *at elskes, elskedes*, and of *at tænke, tænkte, at tænkes, tænktes*.

[1] *See* Part II.

The passive may also be expressed by the help of the auxiliaries *at være, at blive*, to be, to become (remain); as for example : *at være* or *at blive elsket*, to be loved; *jeg var* or *jeg blev elsket*, I was beloved; *at være* or *at blive tænkt*, to be thought; *jeg var* or *jeg blev tænkt*, I was thought.

When the auxiliary *at få*, to get, must be, is used either with the passive or the active, it implies future necessity or an unavoidable contigency, as for example : *jeg får elskes*, I must be loved; *det får tænkes*, it must be thought; *jeg får elske*, I must love; *han får tænke*, he must think.

Passive Impersonals may be formed from active personal verbs, as for example : *det bruges*, it is used, it is customary, from *at bruge*, to use, wear; *det siges*, it is said (corresponding to the French *on dit*), from *at sige*, to say; *der köres*, there drives, or there is being driven, from *at köre*, to drive; *der tales, der læses, der gåes*, there is being spoken ; read ; is going; from *at tale*, to speak; *at læse*, to read; *at gå*, to go. *Der synes*, it seems, is derived from the defective deponent *at synes*, to appear, to think; *der tales, der læses*, etc., may be best rendered by paraphrases, such as: it is being said, there is a talk of, reading is going on, one reads, etc.

Some *passive impersonals* belong to defective verbs, having generally only a passive form, as for example : *det dages*, it dawns, from *at dages*, defective passive, to become day ; *det lykkes*, it succeeds, from *at lykkes*, defect. passive, to be lucky. This verb admits, however, of being used in an active as well as a passive impersonal sense, as for example : *det lykkede ham at löbe bort*, he succeeded (or : it fell out luckily for him) in running away ; *det lykkede hende denne Gang*, it proved successful for her (she has succeeded) this time.

By the use of the passive form in Danish a reciprocal action may be expressed, as for example :—

at mödes, to meet one another,   active : *at möde*, to meet
at slås, to fight together   „   *at slå*, to strike
at kysses, to kiss one another   „   *at kysse*, to kiss
at ses, to see one another (to meet) „   *at se*, to see
at giftes, to marry each other   „   *at gifte*, to marry
at mundhugges, to bicker (no active form),
            derived from *et Mundhuggeri*, a scolding
at kappes, to vie with (no active form).

(89)

The following paradigms show the manner in which regular verbs belonging to Class I. (as *at elske*, to love), and Class II. (as *at tænke*, to think) are conjugated in the passive voice (=*Lideformen*).

INDICATIVE.

PRESENT.

I am loved.) (*I am thought*).
jeg elskes jeg tænkes
du elskes du tænkes
han elskes han tænkes
vi elskes vi tænkes
I elskes I tænkes
de elskes. de tænkes.

PAST.

(*I was loved.*) (*I was thought.*)
jeg elskedes jeg tænktes
du elskedes du tænktes
han elskedes han tænktes
vi elskedes vi tænktes
I elskedes I tænktes
de elskedes. de tænktes.

There is no true potential or imperative mood in the simple passive form of the verb.

INFINITIVE.

at elskes (*to be loved*).   at tænkes (*to be thought*)

PARTICIPLE PAST.

Singular.	Plural.	Singular.	Plural.
(beloved)		(thought)	
at blive elsket	at blive elskede	at blive tænkt	at blive tænkte.

at afgå, to depart | *en Fart*, a tour, journey | *i lige Måde*, in the same way
at nå, to reach | *et Sæde*, a seat | (*et*) *Hastværk*, haste
at sidde, to sit | *en Seddel*, a ticket, label | *gift*, married
at veje, to weigh | *en Side*, a side | *ugift*, single.

SIMPLE PHRASES.

Det glæder mig at vi træffes idag; men jeg har så stort Hastværk, at jeg må bort om et Öjeblik.	I am very glad that we have met to-day, but I am in such haste that I must be off at once.
Er der noget usædvanligt på Færde?	Is there anything unusual going on?
Paa ingen Måde; men mine to ugifte Söstre vænte på mig hos deres Veninde, Fru Larsen.	Not at all; but my two unmarried sisters are waiting for me at their friend, Mrs. Larsen.
Farvel! vi ses dog snart igen.	Good-bye! I daresay we shall soon meet again.
Jeg kommer til Dem om tre Dage.	I will come to you in three days.
Vil De gå med mig til Jernbanestationen?	Will you go with me to the station?
Det lykkes os vel ikke at nå Stationen, förend Toget går.	We shall scarcely succeed in reaching the station before the train starts.
Her gives dog Sedler for Bagagen?	One can get receipts for the luggage here (I suppose)?
Lad den först blive vejet.	Let it first be weighed.
Alle disse Småting tages ikke med ind i Voguen.	All these small things cannot be taken into the carriage.
Der lægges intet her under Sædet.	Nothing must be laid here under the seat.
Det lykkedes mig den sidste Gang jeg rejste at få Plads i Koupéen; men idag siges det, at der ingen Koupéer er at finde.	The last time I was travelling I was fortunate enough to get a place in the coupée; but to-day they say that there is no coupée to be found.
Hvor langt rejse vi sammen?	How far shall we travel together?
Kun til næste Station på Sidebanen.	Only as far as the next station at the branch line.
Farvel! jeg önsker Dem Lykke på Rejsen.	Good-bye! I wish you a prosperous (pleasant) journey.
I lige Måde!	The same to you!
Konduktör! vil De lukke Dören op?	Guard! will you open the door?
Hvad hedder denne Station?	What is the name of this station?
Den hedder det Hvide Hus.	It is called the White House.

TWENTY-FIRST EXERCISE.

It is said that the French dancer (*fem.*) is going to Russia next year. She is to be married to (with) her German cousin, the professor, who is travelling in France. It is seldom that we meet (see one another). They vie with one another for the honour. He was so lucky as to get a great deal of (many *pl.*) money. There is reading and talking going on every day in that house. I am compelled to think of (on) what is said in the town. It is not customary (the custom) now in the country. I am dearly loved by (of) my brother, but we seldom meet. How she is beloved by her old parents! It seems (to me to be) very cold to-day. Meat is not to be bought this week. It grows light (dawns) early up on the mountains. I think I never could be happy if I were not beloved by (of) my parents and my brothers and sisters. She succeeded in getting the letter to read. The general is not named, but it is said that he will be (*bliver*) sent to Russia in June. I was fetched by (of) the Swedish clergyman. What is he to be called? He is to be called Henry; he is called John in English, and Hans in Danish. One may dine here on Thursday.

Translate into English.

Man siger, at her i Huset holdes ikke længere Restauration. Det er sandt, her holdes ikke Restauration efter September, men om De önsker det, skal jeg give Dem en Kop Te og lidt Smör, Bröd og Ost. Tak skal De have; men jeg synes det vilde være bedre, om jeg gik til den næste Landsby, hvor, som det siges, man altid kan få noget at spise. De må göre hvad De synes bedst; det kan vel lykkes Dem at möde Bondevognen, som köres af en god gammel Soldat, der ifjor rejste i Rusland med Generalen. Jeg er nödt til at gå på Öjeblikket, men jeg vænter ikke at vi mödes. Kan sådant et Menneske elskes af sine Slægtninge? Der sendtes et langt Brev hver Morgen til Broderen. Vær så god at sige mig hvad der forlanges. Herren forlanger Intet; men han synes at Vognen skulde sendes lidt tidligere, fordi han önsker at Frökenen skal hentes fra Stationen Klokken fem precis. Det kan nok være, men her i Byen siges det at Toget går ikke om Söndagen. Jeg önsker at vi kunne rejse sammen lige til Köbenhavn.

TWENTY-SECOND LESSON.

ON IRREGULAR VERBS (= *Uregelrette Udsagnsord*).

The irregularities of the Danish verbs admit of being classed under distinct heads, as will be seen in the following groups, which give the first person of the present indicative, the past of the indicative, the past participle, and the present of the infinitive.

As in regular verbs, the singular of the present indicative ends in *r* in all persons, while the plural has the termination *e* in all its persons, as for example in the present indicative of the verb *at falde*, to fall :— .

SINGULAR.	PLURAL.
jeg falder, I fall	*vi falde*, we fall
du falder, thou fallest	*I falde*, ye fall
han, hun falder, he, she falls	*de falde*, they fall.
De falder, you fall.	

In the past tense of the indicative, as *faldt, græd*, etc., no change is made in the plural.

I. Verbs in which the past of the indicative undergoes no change in its radical vowel, and is of one syllable only :—

INDICATIVE.		PARTICIPLE.	INFINITIVE.	
PRESENT.	PAST.	PAST.		
Sing.	Sing. and Plur.			
jeg	jeg, vi			
falder	faldt	c.g., falden n.g., faldet pl., faldne	at falde	to fall
græder	græd	grædt	at græde	to cry
hedder	hed	hedt	at hedde	to be named
holder	holdt	holdt	at holde	to hold
kommer	kom	c.g., kommen n.g., kommet pl., komne	at komme	to come
löber	löb	c.g., löben n.g., löbet pl., löbne	at löbe	to run
sover	sov	sovet	at sove	to sleep.

II. Verbs which change the radical vowel in the past indicative tense and the past participle; the alteration being generally from *i* to *e*, as for example:—

INDICATIVE.		PARTICIPLE.	INFINITIVE.	
PRESENT.	PAST.	PAST.		
Sing.	Sing. and Plur.			
jeg	jeg, vi			
driver	drev	drevet	at drive	to drive on, urge
glider	gled	c.g., gleden n.g., gledet pl., gledne	at glide	to glide, slide
griber	greb	grebet pl., grebne	at gribe	to seize, grip
kniber	kneb	knebet	at knibe	to pinch
skriver	skrev	skrevet	at skrive	to write
stiger	steg	c.g., stegen n.g., steget pl., stegne	at stige	to mount
vrider	vred	vredet	at vride	to wring, twist.

III. Verbs which change the radical vowel in the past tense only, as for example:—

INDICATIVE.		PARTICIPLE.	INFINITIVE.
PRESENT.	PAST.	PAST.	
Sing.	Sing. and Plur.		
jeg	jeg, vi		
bider	bed	bidt	at bide	to *bite*
lider	led	lidt	at lide	to *suffer*
strider	stred	stridt	at stride	to *struggle.*

IV. Verbs which not only change the radical vowel, but which take a different vowel in the past tense and the past participle, as for example:—

binder	bandt	bundet	at binde	to *bind*
drikker	drak	drukket	at drikke	to *drink*
finder	fandt	fundet	at finde	to *find*
slipper	slap	c.g., sluppen n.g., sluppet *pl.*, slupne	at slippe	to *slip*
springer	sprang	c.g., sprungen n.g., sprunget *pl.*, sprungne	at springe	to *spring, leap*
synger	sang	sunget	at synge	to *sing*
tvinger	tvang	tvunget	at tvinge	to *force*
vinder	vandt	vundet	at vinde	to *wind,* also to *win.*

Some grammarians have attempted to establish a very great number of groups for the irregular verbs, but the above examples will suffice, for the present, to show the leading characteristics of the changes which such verbs undergo in Danish. For further information the student is directed to the lists of irregular verbs.

  at *besöge* (II.), to visit   en *Sag*, a cause, thing
  at *tage*, to take   en *Bevægelse*, a movement
  at *modtage*, to receive   en *Lærke*, a lark
  at *bevæge* (II.), to move   en *Nattergal*, a nightingale
  at *gå*, to go, walk   en *Droske*, a cab
  at *spörge*, to ask   (en) *Damp*, steam
  Töj, stuff, luggage   en *Fuglerede*, a bird's nest.

SIMPLE PHRASES.

Min Svoger skrev mig igår, at han kom iforgårs tilbage til Byen; måske besöger han Dem idag eller imorgen.	My brother-in-law wrote to me yesterday, that he had come back to town the day before; perhaps he will come to call on you to-day or to-morrow.
Det vil glæde mig at komme sammen med ham nok en Gang.	It will give me great pleasure to meet him once more.
Vi spiste til Middag i Torsdags hos Grev Brandt, og vi sad til Bords fra Klokken seks til Klokken ni.	We dined on Thursday at Count Brandt's, and we sat at table from 6 till 9 o'clock.
Bondedrengen har fundet en Fuglerede med flere Lærkeæg i.	The peasant-boy has found a nest with several larks' eggs in it.
Det var næsten Midnat förend jeg tog ud på Landet.	It was almost midnight before I went out into the country.
Hvorfor gik De ud af Byen så sildig på Natten?	Why did you go out of town so late at night?
Fordi jeg skulde besöge en Syg.	Because I was to visit a patient.
Han tog Bogen fra mig og gav den til min Söster.	He took the book from me and gave it to my sister.
Jeg modtog to Breve fra min Kusine.	I received two letters from my cousin.
Min Onkel blev syg på Rejsen.	My uncle fell (became) ill on the journey.
Da jeg kom til Stationen, var Toget allerede i Bevægelse.	When I came to the station the train was already in motion (moving).
Idag kom Toget noget for sent.	To-day the train was a little after time (too late).
Jeg tror at de lade Dampen gå ud.	I believe they are letting off steam.
Hvor skal jeg få mit Töj?	Where must I go to get my luggage?
Spörg denne Mand.	Ask that man.
Vil De ikke have en Droske?	Will you have a cab?
Jeg vil gå; jeg gik igår, og jeg fandt at Hotellet er ikke langt fra Stationen.	I will walk; I walked yesterday and I found that the hotel is not far from the station.
Bring mig nu Alt ordentlig til mit Hotel iaften.	Be sure to bring me everything quite right to my hotel this evening.

TWENTY-SECOND EXERCISE.

I wrote five long letters this morning to my children in Holland. Why does the child cry. He has run too fast, and he fell down. Are all my children come from the wood with their little friends? No; they are still running (about) in the woods, where they are singing with loud voices. That is a remarkably bad boy; he punishes his pretty little sister, and twists her hands. Where is that ugly animal? It slipped from my hands, bit me, and sprang up the tree. The next time the animal comes into the garden, you must (must you) bind it better. I forced it yesterday to drink a little water, and after that I seized (gripped) my stick, and drove it into the empty cow-stall. She wrote a long letter yesterday to her brother-in-law. What is his name (he named)? He is named Charles John William Henry. The general found his wife very ill; she has not slept for (in) three nights. The doctor came very late last night to see several patients.

Translate into English.

Bondedrengen kunde hverken holde eller binde den sorte Hest; den slap fra hans Hænder og löb bort. Det er slemt med de Mennesker; de stride med hinanden fra Morgen til Aften. Bondepigen sang så smukt igår, medens hun arbejdede i Markerne. Det onde Menneske kom lige ind i Kökkenet, hvor han så sig om, greb det Förste det Bedste, som kom ham i Hænderne, og löb bort. Har De fundet Kurven, hvori jeg lagde mine Æbler og Pærer? Et Æble er faldet ned, men de andre er Barnet löbet bort med. Min stakkels gamle Bedstemoder er gleden i Aften på et Stykke Glas, som er faldet ned fra et höjt Vindue, og nu lider hun så meget i Ryggen. Min Svoger greb Brevet, förend min Svigerinde kunde skrive halvt hvad hun önskede at sige til sine Söskende i Frankrig. Soldaten er sprungen op i Træet, hvor han fandt en Fuglerede med flere små grönne og hvide Æg. Jeg holder så meget af de små Sangfugle; når det dages tidlig om Sommeren er det så dejligt at höre på deres Stemmer. Vi have så mange Lærker og Nattergale i vor Have.

TWENTY-THIRD LESSON.

ON THE COMPOSITION OF VERBS.

I. Many verbs are formed by the addition of a prefix to a simple verb. The principal prefixes in Danish are: *be, er, for, mis, over, ud, under, ved*, from which such verbs as the following are formed:—

at begribe, to comprehend,	from at gribe, to catch
at erkende, to recognize	,, at kende, to know
at fortjæne, to deserve	,, at tjæne, to serve
at mishandle, to ill-treat	,, at handle, to act, trade, treat of
at overstå, to overcome	,, at stå, to stand
at udföre, to accomplish, carry out	,, at före, to carry, lead
at underholde, to maintain	,, at holde, to hold
at vedblive, to persevere	,, at blive, to remain, become.

II. Compound verbs are often formed by the addition of a noun, adjective, preposition, etc., to another verb, as for example:—

at korsfæste, to crucify,	from Kors, a cross, and at fæste, to fasten
at fuldstændiggöre, to complete	,, fuldstændig, perfect, and at göre, to make
at omtale, to report	,, om, about, and at tale, to speak
at påtage, to assume	,, på, upon, and at tage, to take
at påtage sig, to take upon oneself	

H

III. Some compound verbs retain the same meaning after decomposition as before it; thus, for example, we may say:—

at sammenregne, and *at regne sammen*, to reckon together
at istandsætte ,, *at sætte istand*, to put in order
at ihjelslå ,, *at slå ihjel*, to strike dead, to kill.

IV. Some verbs, as in English, have a different sense in accordance with the position of the preposition associated with them, as for example:—

at blive ude, to remain out
at drage op, to pull up
at se over, to look across
at skride over, to step over
at sætte over, to convey over, across
at rælde over, to pour over, upset

at udeblive, to fail to appear
at opdrage, to educate
at overse, to overlook
at overskride, to overstep
at oversætte, to translate
at overvælde, to overpower.

IV. The prefix *for* (short *o*), and the preposition *for* (long *o*) or *fore*, before, impart widely different meanings to the verbs with which they are associated; as for example:—

at forgå, to perish
at forholde, to keep
at forholde sig, to behave
at forstå, to understand

at foregå, to precede
} *at foreholde*, to remonstrate
at forestå, to superintend, to stand at the [head of.

at tilgive, to forgive
at holde for, to wait outside (as a carriage)
at tillade, to permit

en Tilgivelse, a forgiveness
om Forladelse, pardon me
en Tilladelse, a permission
med Tilladelse, allow me

højre, right
til højre, on the right
venstre, left
til venstre, on the left

SIMPLE PHRASES.

Vil De tillade mig at tage Plads på denne Stol?
De fortjæner ikke at jeg skulde lade Dem sidde ved Siden af mig; det er så længe siden De var hos os.
Tilgiv mig denne Gang.
Hvor bor Deres Tante?
Hun bor i (bebor) et stort Hus på St. Hans Plads.

Will you allow me to take this chair?
You do not deserve that I should let you sit down by me; it is so long since you came to see us!
Forgive me this once!
Where is your aunt living?
She is living in a large house in St. John's Place.

Bliver Englænderen her i Köbenhavn.	Will the Englishman remain in Copenhagen?
Jeg tror at han kun vil opholde sig her nogle få Måneder.	I think he will only stay here (for) a few months.
Han holder meget af sine Börnebörn.	He is very fond of his grandchildren.
Han holdt hende ved Hånden.	He held her by the hand.
Jeg forsikrer Dem, at Barnet er ikke her i Huset.	I assure you that the child is not in the house.
Det kan man være sikker på.	That one may be sure of.
Giv mig min Söns nye Skjorter.	Give me my son's new shirts.
Om Forladelse! jeg hörte ikke hvad De sagde.	Pardon me! I did not hear what you said.
Denne Skjorte tilhörer ikke min Sön.	This shirt does not belong to my son.
Denne Handske er til den venstre Hånd.	This glove belongs to the left hand.
Drosken holder for Dören.	The cab is standing at the door.
Juristen påstår at han har Ret.	The lawyer insists upon it that he is right.
Det gör intet til Sagen.	That is no matter (that does nothing to prove the case).
Hun tilintetgör alle mine Planer for min Datters Velvære.	She frustrates all my plans for my daughter's well-being.
Hvorledes tilbringer De Tiden?	How do you spend your time?
Jeg oversætter et tysk Værk på Dansk.	I am translating a German work into Danish.

TWENTY-THIRD EXERCISE.

The English doctor does not educate his younger children as well as the elder ones. That old peasant behaved very badly yesterday. The clergyman takes too much upon himself. The German lawyer wishes to translate a Danish poem into German. My French nephew will complete (*p. t. ind.*) his work on Swedish law this year. That peasant is always so industrious; she deserves to get money. It is said in the town that your sister-in-law ill-uses your pretty little niece. The

Russian soldier is pulling the boat up from the water. I do not at all understand the Dutch singer when she talks Danish. She does not comprehend that there are parents who do not love their children. We do not understand a single Norwegian word. Her father-in-law superintends the work. Be so good as to take us over the lake. My brother does not deserve that from so old a friend. Forgive me if I say that your younger brother behaves very badly.

Translate into English.

Soldaten slog sin Kaptain ihjel oppe på Bjærgene. Min Svigerinde væltede Mælken over Bordet, men nu har hun bragt alting i Orden igen, fordi hun vænter sine tyske Venner om et Öjeblik. Jeg begriber ikke, hvorledes hun har kunnet gifte sig med sådan en Laps. Det stakkels Fruentimmer var så ulykkelig hjemme; hendes Söskende mishandlede hende hvert År værre og værre. Vi erkende alle, at han havde Ret i hvad han sagde til den svenske Jurist. Min Neveu, med Konen og Börnene, bliver ude på Landet til September. Soldaterne udeblive ikke denne Gang. Deres Svigermoder önsker gærne at fuldstændiggöre Arbejdet förend hun tager til Byen næste Forår. Regner jeg mine Penge sammen, så finder jeg at jeg har tabt hundrede og halvfemsindstyve Kroner på Vejen. Generalen vodbliver at påtage sig alt for meget. Man kan ikke begribe, at han skal kunne få Lov til at mishandle Bönderne her i Landet. Han overskrider vel ikke Landets Lov? Det kan nok være, men dog udförer han alt som det synes ham bedst. Er det ikke alt for slet? Er der en Bådsmand, som kan sætte os over Vandet i Aften?

TWENTY-FOURTH LESSON.

ON IRREGULAR AND OTHER VERBS.

Some verbs are both etymologically and grammatically irregular; of these the principal are the auxiliaries (= *Hjælpeord*), as for example:—

INDICATIVE.		PARTICIPLE.	INFINITIVE.	
PRESENT.	PAST.	PAST.		
Sing.	Sing. and Plur.			
jeg	jeg, vi			
er	var	været	at være	to be
har	havde	haft	at have	to have
kan	kunde	kunnet	at kunne	to be able, can
må	måtte	måttet	at måtte	to be allowed, may
skal	skulde	skullet	at skulle	to be obliged, shall
vil	vilde	villet	at ville	to be willing, will.

Besides these, the following verbs are similarly irregular:—

bör	burde	burdet	at burde	to be obliged, ought
dör	döde	(er) död	at dö	to die
gör	gjorde	gjort	at göre	to do, make
tör	turde	turdet	at turde	to dare, ought
ved	vidste	vidst	at vide	to know.

Active and transitive verbs may be used reflectively, as for example:—

jeg bader, I bathe   *jeg bader mig*, I bathe myself
vi tillade, we permit   *vi tillade os*, we permit ourselves.

Some verbs are used only in a reflective sense, as for example:—

at beflitte sig, to busy oneself
at forsyne sig, to provide oneself with
at betakke sig, to beg to be excused.

These and similar verbs require that the object referred to shall be preceded by a preposition; as for example: —

han beflitter sig på så meget, he busies himself with many things
han benytter sig af Leiligheden, he avails himself of the opportunity
han forsyner sig med Böger, he provides himself with books.

Some transitive and intransitive verbs present, as in English, considerable resemblance to one another in some of their modifications; thus, for example, we have:—

INDICATIVE.		PARTICIPLE.	INFINITIVE.	
PRESENT.	PAST.	PAST.		
Sing.	Sing. and Plur.			
jeg	jeg, vi			
lægger	lagde	(har) lagt	at lægge	to *lay* (trans.)
ligger	lå	ligget	at ligge	to *lie* (intr.)
sænker	sænkte	(har) sænket	at sænke	to *sink* (tr.)
synker	sank	sunket	at synke	to *sink* (intr.)
vækker	vækkede	vækket	at vække	to *wake* (tr.)
vågner	vågnede	vågnet	at vågne	to *wake, be awake.*

at *lægge Mærke til*, to notice
at *være bange for*, to be afraid
at *göre ondt*, to hurt
at *skænke* (II.), to pour out
at *tordne* (I.), to thunder
at *ledsage* (II.), to accompany
at *spise* (II.), to eat

at *foretrække*, to prefer
en *Frygt*, a fear
frygtsom, timid
frygtelig, horrible
en *Besiddelse*, a possession
en *Ulejlighed*, an inconvenience
en *Undskyldning*, an excuse

en *Spisesal, Spisestue*, a dining-room
(en) *Torden*, thunder
(et) *Vejr*, a weather
et *Uvejr*, a bad weather
en *Storm*, a storm
et *Mærke*, a mark
en *Time*, an hour
(en) *Ende*, an end
(en) *Tid*, a time.

SIMPLE PHRASES.

Vilde De göre Dem den Ulejlighed at ledsage min lille Pige på Vejen? hun er bange for at gå alene.

Would you take the trouble to accompany my little girl; she is afraid of going alone.

Det vilde ikke göre mig nogen Ulejlighed; men jeg er bange for at vi få en stærk Storm inden en Times Tid.

It would not give me any trouble; but I fear we shall have a **great** storm within an hour's time.

Jeg har ikke lagt Mærke til Vejret.	I have not noticed the weather.
Det gör mig ondt at den Lille må blive hjemme, men hun bör ikke gå ud i sådant dårligt Vejr.	I am sorry that the little girl must remain at home, but she ought not to go out in such bad weather.
Hör! det tordner allerede; lad os forlade Haven og gå tilbage til Huset.	Listen! it is thundering already; let us leave the garden, and return to the house.
Tör jeg bede Dem gå ind i Spisestuen.	May I beg you to go into the dining-room.
Er De så god at tage Plads ved den överste Ende af Bordet.	Will you be so good as to take a seat at the upper end of the table.
Herr Johnson, vil De sidde her eller ved Siden af min Söster.	Mr. Johnson, will you sit here or by my sister?
Mine Damer, tör jeg bede Dem tage Plads.	Ladies, may I beg you to take your seats (to sit down).
De burde ikke göre Dem så stor Ulejlighed.	You should not give yourself so much trouble.
Må jeg skænke Dem et Glas Rhinskvin?	May I pour you out a glass of Rhenish wine?
Her er Buffetten (Skænkebordet); jeg beder Dem sörge for Dem selv.	Here is the sideboard; I beg you will help yourself.
Hvad Slags Vin synes De bedst om?	What kind of wine do you like best?
Jeg foretrækker Portvin.	I prefer Port.
De Fraværendes Skål!	A health to the absent!
Det vilde glæde mig, hvis jeg kunde ledsage Dem til Dampskibet.	I should be glad if I could accompany you to the steamer.
Jeg er bange for Vejret.	I am afraid of the weather.
Tror De, det bliver Tordenvejr?	Do you think we shall have thunder?
Jeg frygter vi få Uvejr.	I am afraid we shall have a storm.
De burde ikke være så frygtsom.	You ought (should) not to be so timid.
Jeg ved nok, at man ikke burde lægge Mærke til hver Småting.[1]	I know very well one ought not to pay attention to every trifle (little thing).

---

[1] *Småting* is used elliptically for a little thing.

TWENTY-FOURTH EXERCISE.

Your cloak is lying on the table; I do not know who laid it there. Did the clergyman die in 1857, or in 1859? Did you not know that the good old man died only last year? No, that I did not know. You ought not to do that. Here is a bull in the field; I dare not fetch the peasant, who is coming through the wood; the animal may perhaps do me some mischief. You must not be so timid, the bull is not in the field. The poor little girl had sunk before her father could cross the water. My aunt is ill, and lying in bed; I think she is sleeping, and I dare not wake her. He laid his sister's letter on the table, but he did not know if he should (ought to) let it lie there, because she was not at home. My eldest son bathes in the sea every morning at seven o'clock, about an hour after my English man-servant has roused him. It seems to me very early to get up at six o'clock. You ought not to lie in bed till ten. The king died last night, but the people do not yet know that he is dead. I woke the coachman at six o'clock, but he is still lying in bed.

Translate into English.

Jeg lagde ikke Mærke til Manden, men jeg synes han må være Soldat. Han burde bestemt ikke sætte sig i Besiddelse af Skibet? Det gjorde han heller ikke, men man siger, at Skibet skulde gives ham af hans Fader. Han beflitter sig på at få en Plads under Generalen, men han tör ikke lade sin Broder vide, at han önsker noget sådant, fordi Broderen vil at han skal blive her i Landet hos sin egen Familie. Hesten bed mig igår i Hånden, og den smerter mig næsten så meget idag som den gjorde iaftes. Ved De, om man tör gå igennem denne Skov? Nej, det ved jeg ikke. Juristen vidste ikke hvad han skulde sige til Bondepigen, som græd så hæftigt fordi den gamle Bedstefader var död. Det gjorde mig så ondt at måtte sige hende, at Skibet **var** sunket. Hvor sank det? Det ved jeg ikke.

List of Titles, Tradesmen's Callings, etc., etc.

en Konge, a king	en Dronning, a queen	kongelig, royal
en Prins, a prince	en Prinsesse, a princess	prinselig, princely
en Hertug, a duke	en Hertuginde, a duchess	et Hertugdømme, duchy
en Greve, a count	en Grevinde, a countess	et Grevskab, a county, count's dignity
en Baron, a baron	en Baronesse, a baroness	et Baroni, a barony
en Admiral, an admiral	en Admiralinde, wife of an admiral	et Admiralitet, an admiralty
en Oberst, a colonel	en Lieutenant, a lieutenant	en Hær, an army
en Major, a major	en Søofficer, a naval officer	en Flåde, a fleet
en Kaptain, a captain	en Dampfregat, a steam frigate	et Tårn, a tower

en Bager, a baker — et Bagværk, pastry, baked cakes
en Brygger, a brewer — et Bryggeri, a brewery
en Bygmester, a builder — en Bygning, a building
en Embedsmand, a man in office — et Embede, an office
en Fisker, a fisherman — et Fiskeri, a fishery
en Hattemager, a hatter — en Hatteskygge, a hat-brim
en Hjulmager, a wheelwright — et Hjul, a wheel
en Krœmmer, a retail trader — et Krambod, a retail shop
en Kulhandler, a coal merchant — en Kulmine, a coal mine
en Lods, a pilot — en Lodsbåd, a pilot boat
en Låssmed, Kleinsmed, a locksmith — en Låsfjœder, a spring of a lock
en Møller, a miller — en Mølle, a mill
en Papirhandler, a stationer — Papirpenge, pl., paper-money
en Skibskaptain, a captain, skipper — en Skibsfart, a ship's way, navigation
en Skomager, a shoemaker — en Skobørste, a shoebrush
en Skolelærer, a schoolmaster — en Skolekammerat, a school fellow
en Skrœdder, a tailor — en Skrœddersvend, a journeyman tailor
en Slagter, a butcher — et Slagtertorv, a meat market
en Smed, a smith — en Smedje, a smithy
en Sømand, a seaman — en Indsø, a lake
en Tigger, a beggar — en Tiggermunk, a mendicant friar
en Torvebonde, a peasant who brings farm produce to market — en Torvebod, a market-booth
en Tømmermand, a carpenter — en Tømmerflåde, a timber-raft
en Urtekrœmmer, a grocer — en Urtehave, a vegetable garden
en Vinhandler, a wine merchant — en Vingård, a vineyard
en Vognmand, a coachmaster — et Vognhjul, a carriage-wheel
en Vægter, a watchman — en Vægterpibe, a watchman's rattle
en Væver, a weaver — en Vævning, a weaving.

TWENTY-FIFTH LESSON.

IRREGULAR VERBS (= *Uregelrette Udsagnsord.*)

In the following list of irregular verbs, we have given the first person singular of the present of the indicative; the past of the indicative, which is the same for all persons; the past participle, and the present of the infinitive. All parts of the verbs which are not given, follow the regular modes of conjugation.

INDICATIVE.		PAST PARTICIPLE.	INFINITIVE.	
PRESENT.	PAST.			
Sing.	*Sing. and Plur.*			
jeg	jeg, vi	har, er		
beder	bad	bedt *pl.*, bedte	at bede	*to beg, pray.*
binder	bandt	bundet	at binde	*to bind.*
brister	brast	brustet *or* bristet	at briste	*to burst.*
drager	drog	draget	at drage	*to drag.*
drager bort	drog bort	draget bort	at drage bort	*to drag, go away.*
drikker	drak	drukket	at drikke	*to drink.*
erfarer	erfarede *or* erfor	erfaret	at erfare	*to experience, learn.*
farer	for	faret	at fare	*to travel, go.*
fortryder	fortrød	fortrudt	at fortryde	*to repent, regret.*
går	gik	gået	at gå	*to go.*
giver	gav	c.d., given N.d., givet *pl.*, givne	at give	*to give.*
gælder	gjalt	gældt	at gælde	*to be worth.*
hænger	hang, *intr.* hængte, *tr.*	hængt	at hænge	*to hang.*
hjælper	hjalp	hjulpen	at hjælpe	*to help.*
jager	jog *or* jagede	jaget	at jage	*to hunt.*

INDICATIVE.		PAST PARTICIPLE.	INFINITIVE.	
PRESENT. *Sing.*	PAST. *Sing. and Plur.*			
jeg kryber	jeg, vi kröb	har, er c.g., kröben N.G., kröbet *pl.*, kröbne	at krybe	to creep.
ler	lo	lét	at le	to laugh.
lyder	löd	lydt	at lyde	to sound.
lyver	löj	löjet	at lyve	to tell a lie.
nyder	nöd	nydt	at nyde	to enjoy.
rider	red	redet	at ride	to ride.
river	rev	c.g., reven N.G., revet *pl.*, revne	at rive	to tear.
ryger	rög	röget	at ryge	to smoke.
sker (det) (*impers.*)	skete	sket	at ske	to happen.
skyder	sköd	skudt	at skyde	to shoot.
skærer or skær	skar	skaren skaret	at skære	to cut.
står	stod	stået	at stå	to stand.
stjæler	stjal	stjalet	at stjæle	to steal.
stryger	strög	ströget	at stryge	to rub clothes, iron.
synger	sang	sunget	at synge	to sing.
tager	tog	taget	at tage	to take.
tier	tav	tiet	at tie	to be silent.
træffer	traf	truffet	at træffe	to hit, meet.
trækker	trak	trukket	at trække	to draw, drag.
foretrækker	foretrak	foretrukket	at foretrække	to prefer.
viger	veg	c.g., vegen N.G., veget *pl.*, vegne	at vige	to give up, make way.
æder	åd	ædt	at æde	to eat (as animals).

det gælder ikke, it is not worth, it does not refer to, affect
det ærgrer mig, it annoys me
det går ikke an, that will not do
at have Lyst til, to like, take pleasure in
at hugge ned, to cut down
at spænde, to draw out
at spænde Hanen, to cock, pull a trigger

at spænde Heste, to harness horses
at pleje, to be accustomed
at fange, to catch
at fornöje, to please
(en) Fornöjelse, pleasure
at tåle, to endure
tålmodig, patient
en Tålmodighed, patience
at formode, to suppose
formodentlig, probably

heldig, lucky
snu, cunning
et Fjæld (Norw.), a fell, mountain-side
et Bjærg, a mountain
en Mose (Dan.) } a moor, moss
en Myr (Norw.)
Myrebær, moor-berries
en Elv (Norw.), a river
et Slags, sort, kind

en Flok, a flock
en Ren } a reindeer
et Rensdyr
en Buk, a buck
(en) Jagt, hunt, hunting
(et) Brænde, firewood
en Riffel, a rifle
en Bøsse, a gun
en Birk, a birch-tree
en Kæde, a chain

SIMPLE PHRASES.

Jeg har Lyst til at gå på Jagt.

I should like (have a mind) to go out hunting.

Hvad Slags Jagt er her?

What kind of animals does one find here for hunting?

Når man er heldig kan man finde Rensdyr.

If one is fortunate, one may meet with reindeer.

Jeg har aldrig endnu skudt en Rén.

I have never yet shot a reindeer.

Engang ifjor traf jeg en Flok Rener; men förend jeg kunde spænde Hanen fór de alle over Mosen.

I fell in with a flock of reindeer once last year; but before I could draw the trigger they had all gone off over the moor.

Man må krybe på alle fire, når man vil træffe en Rénbuk.

One must creep upon all fours, if one wants to hit a buck.

Ja, jeg ved at Bukkene ere udmærket snu Dyr.

Yes, I know that the bucks are extremely cunning animals.

Holder De meget af Jagt?

Are you very partial to hunting.

Jeg foretrækker at fiske.

I prefer fishing.

Det gör min Broder også; han kan stå den hele Dag ganske tålmodig ved Elven, uden at fange en eneste Fisk.

It is the same with my brother; he will stand quite patiently all day long by the side of the stream, without catching a single fish.

Det går ikke an at gå på Jagt når man er halv syg, og ikke i Stand til at nyde det frie Liv på Fjældene.

It does not do to go out on a hunting expedition when one is half ill, and not able to enjoy the free life on the Fjelds.

Hvor er Englænderen, som plejer at fiske i Elven?

Where is the Englishman, who fishes in the stream.

Han er oppe på Bjœrgene idag.	He is up on the mountains to-day.
Vi spise idag hos Præsten.	We are going to dine to-day at the clergyman's.
Kan De sige mig hvad Rénerne æde?	Can you tell me what the reindeer eat?
De æde Mos på Mosen (*Dan.*), Myren (*Norw.*).	They eat moss on the moors.

TWENTY-FIFTH EXERCISE.

This affair does not affect his life but his honour. The admiral met the young prince on board his large ship. Is the admiral's ship a steam vessel? Yes, it is a steam frigate which belongs to the Danish fleet. It would please me very much if my son could go into the navy (become a naval officer). Where is the English pilot? he is in the pilot boat with the Swedish lieutenant and the captain of the Norwegian frigate. The admiral's wife has ascertained that the carpenter, the smith, and the ship's baker, with three of the sailors, have never drunk any thing but water or tea or coffee, since they were all so ill in the Russian hospital. The schoolmaster took the book in his hand, and sang charmingly. The brewer, Hansen, and the builder, Evaldsen, with his wife the miller's daughter were standing just outside the large window of the dining room, and they all were silent whilst the good old schoolmaster was singing. Whom did you see at the market? I saw the butcher, and the greengrocer, Thomsen, who has a large vegetable garden in the neighbourhood of the royal woods. I know the woods; the King and Duke William, with Count Holk, Baron Falsen, Colonel Brand, and my brother-in-law, Major Collin, hunted there the day before yesterday. The duke shot a stag, and the king begged him to take the animal home with him in order that the duchess and Princess Mary might see it.

Translate into English.

Jeg kan ikke ride den sorte Hest, fordi min kære Moder har i Sinde at köre til Indsöen idag. Han stod i Dören og rög, da jeg kom ridende forbi Huset. Jeg traf ham förste Gang på Jagt, og det fortryder mig, at jeg lod Lejligheden slippe til at spörge ham, hvor hans Svigerinde var gået hen. Hvis Tyven siger, at han ikke stjal min Hund og min Kalv, lyver han. Jeg gav Tiggeren Lov til at forsyne sig med Brænde i min Birkeskov; men ikke at hugge store Træer ned og drage dem bort. Hun har nydt Lykken at se alle sine Börn i Sommer. Det gælder ikke om at give de Fattige Penge, men om at göre sine Medmennesker godt. Jeg fortryder aldrig, at jeg hjalp den stakkels syge Skomager. Jeg traf Tiggeren på Vejen til Kirken; han stjal mit Ur og kröb bort, medens jeg talte med min Ven, Vinhandler Paulsen. Min Tjæner, Tyskeren, löb efter ham, men til ingen Nytte: mit Ur var stjålet; og nu har Tiggeren formodentlig den Fornöjelse at kunne sige hvor mange Klokken er. Det ærgrer mig, at jeg ikke bandt Kæden fastere, fordi Hunden löb bort, medens jeg var ude på Söen i Båden. Jeg viger ikke af Stedet, indtil De giver mig Pengene igen, som De tog igår fra min Söster. Han har skudt to Renbukke på Fjældene, den ene beholder han selv, men den anden har han i Sinde at sende med et Par små Fugle til sin Svoger, Embedsmanden, som bor i Dalen ved Elven. Hvorlænge har De i Sinde at blive ude på Fjældene? Jeg vilde gærne blive der ude endnu et Par Uger, men bliver Vejret slemt, tager jeg ind til Byen så snart som mulig. Plejer De at tage på Jagt hvert År? Det gör jeg altid, ifald jeg ikke går på en eller anden lang Rejse i Udlandet.

TWENTY-SIXTH LESSON.

ON THE PLURAL OF NOUNS (=Navneordenes Flertal).

Nouns in Danish may be classed under three heads:—

I. Those which form the plural by the addition of *e* to the singular.

II. Those which form the plural by the addition of *er* to the singular.

III. Those which remain unchanged, and are the same in the plural as in the singular.

These different modes of termination do not admit of being brought under any definite rule, and must, therefore, be mastered by memory. Most of the words contained in the first class were originally masculine, but many, as will be seen below, now belong to the neuter gender. The asterisk indicates that the final consonant is doubled, as for example: *en Flok*, a flock; *Flokken*, the flock.

I. Nouns which take an *e* in the plural from usage, rather than in accordance with any definite rule:—

en Arm (pl. Arme), an arm
en Bad, a boat
et Bad, a bath
et Bed, a flower-bed
en Birk, a birch
et Bjærg, a mountain
en Björn, a bear
et Blad, a leaf
en Bold, a round ball
en Bolt, a bolt
en Bom,* a bar
et Bord, a table
en Borg, a castle
en Brand, a fire, brand
et Brev, a letter
en Brud, a bride
en Bråd,* a sting
en Brönd, a well

en Buk,* a buck
en Busk, a bush
en Bæk,* a brook
en Bænk, a bench
en Bög, a beech
en Bör, a barrow
en Dag, a day
en Dal, a dale
en Dam,* a dam
en Damp, a vapour, steam
en Dans, a dance
en Del, a quantity, part, deal
et Digt, a poem
en Disk, a counter, desk
en Dolk, a dagger
en Dom,* a judgment
en Dram,* a dram
en Dreng, a boy

en Drik,* a drink
en Dröm,* a dream
en Dværg, a dwarf
en Dör, a door
en Eg (long e), an oak
en Eg* (short e), an edge of a blade, selvage
en Egn, a district, spot
en Elv (Norw.), a river
en Eng, a narrow valley
et Fad, a dish
en Favn, a fathom
en Fil, a file
en Fjord, a frith, Fjord
en Flig, a flap, lappet
en Flok,* a flock
en Fold,[1] a fold, pen
en Fork,[2] a pitch-fork
en Fugl, a bird
en Gang, a turn, walk
en Gård, a farm-yard, court
en Gavl, a gable
en Grav, a grave, pit
en Gren, a branch, twig
en Gris, a pig
en Grund, a ground, bottom of sea
et Gulv, a floor
en Hals, a neck
en Hank, a handle
et Hav, an ocean, sea
en Havn, a haven
en Heks, a witch
en Helt, a hero
en Hest, a horse
en Hjælm, a helmet
en Hjord, a hearth
en Hjort, a stag
en Hob, a heap, crowd
en Holm, a small island
en Hov, a hoof
en Hund, a dog
en Hvalp, a puppy
en Hæl, a heel
en Hær, an army

en Höj, a height
en Kalv, a calf
en Kam,* a comb
en Karl, a fellow
en Kat,* a cat
en Klud, a clout, rag
en Kniv, a knife
en Kok,* a cook
en Kost, a broom
en Krans, a wreath
en Kreds, a circle
en Krig, a war
en Krog, a corner
en Krop,* a trunk of body
en Kurv, a basket
en Kusk, a coachman
et Land, a land
en Lås, a lock (of door)
en Leg, a game (of play)
en Lem,* a trap-door
en Lov, a law, permission
en Lund, a grove
en Lögn, a lie
en Mund, a mouth
en Munk, a monk
en Nar,* a fool
en Nattergal, a nightingale
et Navn, a name
en Negl, a nail (of finger)
en Orm, a worm
en Ost, a cheese
en Ovn, an oven, stove
en Pen,* a pen
en Pisk, a whip
en Plov, a plough
en Port, a gate
en Pult, a desk
en Pung, a purse
en Pæl, a pile
en Pös, a bucket
en Rand, an edge
en Ravn, a raven
en Rem,* a strap
en Ring, a ring
en Ryg,* a back

[1] *Fold* takes *er* in pl., when meaning "plait."

[2] "Table-fork" is rendered in Danish by the word *Gaffel*, pl. *Gafler*, which also signifies a gaff-sail.

en Ræv, a fox
en Saks, scissors
en Sal, a drawing-room, hall
(et) Salt, n salt
en Sang, a song
en Seng, a bed
en Sjæl, a soul
en Skat,* a treasure
et Skib, a ship
en Skik,* a custom
en Skovl, a shovel
et Skrin, a cupboard
en Skurk, a rogue, rascal
et Slot,* a palace
en Smed, a smith
en Snegl, a snail
en Snor, a string
et Sogn, a see, parish
en Spand, a bucket
et Spejl, a mirror
en Stak,* a stack
en Stald, a stall
en Stav, a staff
en Steg, a roast joint
en Sten, a stone
en Stil, an exercise
en Stilk, a stalk
en Stok,* a stick
en Stol, a chair
en Stork, a stork

en Storm, a storm
en Straf,* a punishment
en Strand, a strand
en Streng, a string (of instr.)
en Ström,* a stream
en Sump, a swamp
en Svamp, a sponge
en Svend, a boy, workman
et Sværd, a sword
en Svarm, a swarm
en Sæk,* a sack
en Söm, a seam
et Tag, a roof
et Tårn, a tower
et Telt, a tent
en Tolk, an interpreter
en Top,* a top
en Torn, a thorn
et Torv, a market
en Tråd, a thread
en Trold, a goblin
en Tyv, a thief
en Ulv, a wolf
et Ur, a watch
en Vej, a way
en Vest, a waistcoat
en Vin, a wine
en Vold, a rampart
en Væg,* a wall
en Örn, an eagle.

The following words undergo a vowel-change in the plural viz.:—

en Broder, a brother, pl. Brödre
en Datter, a daughter, pl. Döttre (en Dotter, in early Danish)
en Fader, a father, pl. Fædre
en Moder, a mother, pl. Mödre.

at låne, to lend, borrow
at tænde, to set light to
at slukke Ilden, to put out the fire
en Rype, a ptarmigan, red grouse
en Edderfugl, an eider-duck
en Agerhöne, a partridge
en Dragt, a dress, dressing, load
en Dragt Prygl, a sound thrashing

et Lån, a loan
et Fyr, a light
en Ild, a fire
(et) Svovl, sulphur
en Stikke } a match
en Svovlstikke }
(en) Tobak, tobacco
en Tobakspung, a tobacco-pouch

I

SIMPLE PHRASES.

Kan De låne mig Deres Tobakspung?	Can you lend me your tobacco-pouch?
Jeg lod den falde ud af Båden.	I let it fall from the boat.
Lad mig tænde min Cigar.	Let me light my cigar.
Har Dé set min Pibe?	Have you seen my pipe?
Det er forbudt at ryge her i Teltene.	Smoking is forbidden in the tents.
Kan jeg ikke tænde min Pibe i Kökkenet?	Can I not light my pipe in the kitchen?
Der er ikke Ild i Kökkenovnen.	There is no fire in the kitchen-stove.
Her har De Svovlstikker.	Here are matches.
Tak! Mange Tak!	Many thanks!
Vil De pröve en af mine Cigarer?	Will you try one of my cigars?
Det stormer på Bjærgene, og jeg tror næppe at vi komme over Sumpene og Strömmene.	There is a storm on the mountains, and I hardly think we can get over the swamps and streams.
Så få vi vel sætte over Vandet i Fiskerbåden.	Then we shall have to cross the water in the fishing boat.
Hvor mange Favne dyb er Söen?	How many fathoms deep is the lake?
Den er omtrent femten Favne dyb.	It is about fifteen fathoms deep.
Jeg vilde gærne skyde nogle Vandfugle på Vejen; eller et Par Ryper eller Agerhöns.	I should like to shoot some water-fowls on the way; or a brace of grouse or partridges.
Iaftes så jeg en Flok Fjældryper nær ved Brönden; men der var ingen Vandfugl at se.	Last night I saw a flock of (mountain) ptarmigans near the well; but there was no water-fowl to be seen.

TWENTY-SIXTH EXERCISE.

The miller's-boy crossed the fjord in a boat. The water from the well near the castle is not wholesome to drink. The floors of the rooms are as smooth as a mirror. The doors of the house are just under the gables. My brother's cook has brought the bucket and the steam-kettle. Shall we have a dance at the palace this evening? No, there will be no dance at Princess Wilhelmina's, because the prince is hunting bears in Norway. The coachman is sitting on the bench under the large beeches. Your purse is lying on my daughter's desk. I have lost two letters, a great deal of string, three pens and a knife. The peasant-woman is standing in the stable with the little calves. Where is the white calf? It is in the corner of the stable. Will you be so good as to lend me two baskets, a sack, and some brooms? You are welcome to take the sack and the brooms, but the baskets are not mine. The locks of the old oak-cupboard are broken. You must send for the smith. There is not a smith in this valley; but you may, perhaps, find one at the farm on the river. I saw a large flock of birds on the edge of the brook. There are snails on the leaves, and on all the twigs and stalks. The peasant took a whip and gave his ploughboys a sound whipping.

Translate into English.

Soldaternes Sværde hænge på Husvæggene. Min norske Tolk siger at der er Ulve og Ræve nær ved Fjorden, og at mange Ravne sidde på Taget af hans Hus i Dalen. Er der Ege i denne Egn? Ja, der er Ege, Birke, Böge og Hyldebuske på Höjene på Söholmen. Iaften og igår hörte jeg en Nattergal i Skovene. Min Sön så tre Storke og nogle små grå Fugle på Grenene af den store Bög i den gamle Slotsgård. Deres Grave ere ikke langt fra Havet. Manden havde tre Dolke, et Sværd og et Par Örne i sin Vogn. Disse Strömme rive uhyre store Stene med sig. Alle Lande have deres Skikke. Disse Karle have ikke Lov til at piske Hundene.

TWENTY-SEVENTH LESSON.

II. Nouns which make their plural in *er* from usage rather than in accordance with any definite rule :—

en *Ånd*, a spirit
en *Akt*, an act
et *Amt*, an office
en *Art*, a kind
et *Bal*,* a ball (dance)
en *Bank*, a bank
en *Bisp*, a bishop
en *Blomst*, a flower, blossom
en *Bod*, a booth
en *Bord*, a border
en *Brig*,* a brig
en *Brink*, a brink
et *Bryst*, a breast
en *Brök*, a fraction
en *Bugt*, a bay
en *Byld*, a tumour
en *Bylt*, a bundle
en *Bön*,* a prayer
en *Dragt*, a dress
en *Dunst*, a vapour, mist
en *Dyd*, a virtue
en *Flod*, a river
en *Fragt*, a freight
en *Frugt*, a fruit
en *Ged*, a goat
en *Gæst*, a guest
en *Glöd*, a glow
en *Gnist*, a spark
et *Gods*, an estate
en *Grad*, a degree
en *Gröft*, a ditch
en *Gud*, a god
et *Hof*,* a royal court
en *Hud*, a skin
en *Jagt*, a hunt
(en) *Jord*, an earth
en *Kant*, an edge, margin
en *Kind*, a check
en *Klap*,* a clap, flap

en *Klint*, a cliff
en *Klods*, a stump
en *Klöft*, a chasm
en *Knap*,* a button
en *Knop*,* a knob, bud
en *Kop*,* a cup
en *Kyst*, a coast
en *Lap*,* a rag
et *Lem*,* a limb
et *Lod*,* the lead, an ounce[1]
en *Lods*, a pilote
et *Loft*, a loft, ceiling
en *Lygte*, a lamp, lamp-post
en *Lyst*, a desire, pleasure
en *Last*, a cargo, load
en *Magt*, a power
en *Mark*, a field
en *Mast*, a mast
en *Mynt*, a coin
en *Nöd*,* a nut
et *Pant*, a pledge
en *Park*, a park
en *Pjalt*, a rag, tatter
en *Plan*, a plain, plan
en *Plet*,* a stain, spot
en *Pligt*, a duty
en *Post*, a post
en *Prik*,* a dot
en *Prins*, a prince
en *Præst*, a priest, clergyman
en *Pynt*, a point (of land)
en *Råd*, a member of a council
en *Rad*, a row, series
en *Rén*, a reindeer
en *Rest*, a remnant, rest
en *Ret*,* court of justice
en *Rift*, a rift, crevice
en *Röst*, a voice
en *Saft*, a juice

* The asterisk indicates that the final consonant is doubled when the definite article is affixed to it; as for example : *et Bal, Ballet.*

[1] *Et Lod*, meaning an ounce, is unaltered in the plural.

(117)

en *Sag*, a cause, matter, case
en *Sans*, a sense
en *Skål*, a health, toast
et *Skaft*, a shaft
en *Skal*,* a shell
en *Skank*, a shank
en *Skat*,* a tax, rate
en *Skælm*, a rogue
en *Skjorte*, a shirt
en *Slægt*, species, race
en *Sorg*, a grief, mourning
en *Spids*, a point
en *Stat*, a state, realm
et *Sted*, a place

en *Streg*, a trick, stroke, streak
en *Stump*, a stump
en *Sum*,* a sum
en *Synd*, a sin
en *Søn*,* a son
en *Tak*,* an antler
en *Tid*, a time
en *Toft*, an enclosed field
en *Tut*,* a cornet
en *Vagt*, a watchman
en *Vægt*, a weight
et *Værk*, a work
en *Vært*, a landlord
en *Æsp*, an aspen.

at *undersøge*, to examine
at *underrette*, to inform
(en) *Underretning*, information
at *forskaffe*, to procure
at *råde*, to advise
at *komme i Kost*, to board with
lav, low
skøn, beautiful

en *Told*, a tax
en *Toldbod*, a custom-house
en *Værdi*, a value, price
en *Kost*, a food, board
et *Besvær*, a trouble
en *Lighed*, a likeness
en *Lethed*, a facility
fornöden, sufficient.

SIMPLE PHRASES.

Kan De give mig lidt Underretning om en Rejse til Norge?

Jeg råder Dem til at gå med Dampskibet fra Hull direkte til Kristiania.

Jeg er istand til at give Dem fornöden Underretning om Jernbanerne og Landevejene.

De vil komme til at sejle opad Kristiania Fjorden, og De vil få at se mange skönne Træer på Markerne, og dybe Klöfter i Bjærgene.

Blive Kufferterne undersögte af Toldbetjæntene?

Det ville de rigtignok; men det vil ikke forårsage Dem noget Besvær.

Can you give me any information in regard to going to Norway?

I recommend you to go in the steamer direct from Hull to Christiania.

I am able to give you all requisite information concerning the railways and the highroads.

You will sail up the Christiania Fjord, and you will see many fine trees in the fields, and deep chasms in the clefts of the mountains.

Will the trunks be examined by the custom-house officials?

That they undoubtedly will; but that will not occasion you any trouble.

Råder De mig til at gå i Kost hos Præsten, som taler Engelsk?	Do you advise me to board with the clergyman, who speaks English?
Ja; jeg finder at hans Selskab vil være af stor Værdi for Dem. Hans Familje taler Sproget med megen Lethed.	Yes; I think his society would prove of great value to you. His family speak the language with great facility.
Mange Tak; nu er det Tid at hente mine Penge og forskaffe mig et Kreditbrev.	Many thanks! now it is time for me to fetch my money, and procure a letter of credit.

TWENTY-SEVENTH EXERCISE.

The bishops of the land had more power in the old times than they have in our times. Country-clergymen have many duties to perform. The taxes of the State are not large, and the prince has no great estates. Do you see the buds and the blossoms in the flower-beds? The cargoes and freights of the brigs. The rogues had large bundles of rags on their backs. Those landlords give bad weight. The juices of the fruits are sweet. The shafts and shanks of the carriages are English. The coasts and fields, and nearly all places in Denmark are low. The glow and sparks went right up to the ceiling. My senses left me. One might hear the voices of the councillors (barristers) far from the court. The points of the knobs and buttons are green, but the edges are white. The prince's virtues are not great. Are those rogues Danes or Swedes. The English pilot let the lead drop in 15 fathoms. I saw ditches on the plains, and chasms on the cliffs. Goats have brown skins. He gave the coins as pledges. All men commit sins, and endure sorrows.

Translate into English.

Han faldt i en af de dybeste Kløfter på Klinterne, og Ingen hörte hans Röst da han råbte om Hjælp.

Der er en hvid Plet på alle Lygterne. Jeg tog mine uldne Skjorter med, da jeg gik på Jagt. Når det er koldt, gör det godt at se de hede, röde Gnister stige op af Ilden. Denne Tigger er klædt i lutter Pjalter og Lapper. Det er en af Skurkens Streger. Præsterne kom i Stedet for Bispen. Hendes Bönner blev uopfyldte. Mine unge svenske Gæster ere i Huset med mine Sönner. Idag have vi to Graders Frost, og jeg har slet ikke Lyst til at gå på Jagt. Borderne på Kjolerne vare sorte og grönne med gule og röde Prikker. Safterne af disse Frugter ere rigtignok sure. Han er kommen i Kost hos en Rådmands Enke.

TWENTY-EIGHTH LESSON.

III. Nouns which remain the same in the plural as in the singular:—

et År, a year
et Aks, an ear of corn
en Alen, an ell
et Ar, a scar
et Bånd, a band
et Ben, a bone, leg
et Besög, a visit
et Bid, a bite
et Blik,* a glance
et Blus,* a blaze
et Brud,* a rupture
et Bryn, an eyebrow
et Bröd, a loaf
et Bud,* a message, order
et Buk,* a bow, bend (of body)
et Drön, a din
et Dyb, a depth
et Dyr, an animal
et Dæk,* a deck
et Får, a sheep

et Fag, a vocation
et Fald, a fall, case
en Fejl, a fault
et Flag, a flag
et Folk, a people
et Forhold, a condition, relation
et Forhæng, a curtain
et Forsög, an attempt
et Garn, a thread
et Glas,* a glass
et Gran, a grain
et Greb, a handle, grip
et Hår, a hair
et Hegn, a hedge
et Hjul, a wheel
et Hop,* a jump, hop
et Kald, a calling, living
et Kid,* a kid
et Kön,* a gender
et Knæk,* a crack, blow

* The asterisk indicates that the final consonant is doubled when the definite article is affixed to the word, as for example: Blik, Blikket.

et *Kors*, a cross
et *Kort*, a card, map
et *Kryb*, a reptile, vermin
et *Kys*,* a kiss
et *Låg*, a cover
et *Lån*, a loan
en *Laks*, a salmon
et *Lam*,* a lamb
et *Led*, a joint, small gate
en *Lyd*, a sound
et *Løb*, a running
et *Løg*, an onion, bulb
et *Løv*, a foliage
et *Mord*, a murder
en *Myg*,* a fly
et *Møl*, a moth
et *Neg*, a sheaf
et *Næb*, a nib
et *Næs*,* a point of land
et *Oprør*, an uproar
et *Ord*, a word
et *Par*,* a couple, pair
et *Præg*, an impression, stamp
et *Puds*, a trick
et *Puf*,* a puff
et *Pund*, a pound
et *Råb*, a call, cry
et *Råd*, a council, plan
et *Rap*,* a rap
et *Ribs*, a white or red currant
et *Ror*, a rudder
et *Sagn*, a tradition
et *Sår*, a sore
et *Savn*, a loss
et *Segl*, a seal, signet
et *Sejl*, a sail
en *Sild*, a herring
et *Sind*, mind, intention
et *Skar*, a cut
et *Skin*,* a glare
et *Skind*, a skin
et *Skæg*,* a beard
et *Sköd*, a lap
et *Skrål*, a scream
et *Skridt*, a step
et *Skud*, a shot, shoot
et *Slag*, a blow
en (or et) *Slags*, species, kind
et *Slör*, a veil
et *Smil*, a smile
en *Snært*, a lash
et *Spand*, a span
et *Spid*,* a spit
et *Spor*, a trace
et *Spring*, a jump
et *Sprog*, a language
et *Stik*,* a prick, thrust
et *Sting*, a stitch, pain
et *Strå*, a straw
et *Stöd*, a thrust
et *Svar*, an answer
et *Sving*, a swing
et *Söm*,* an iron nail
et *Tab*, a loss
et *Tegn*, a sign
et *Tilfælde*, an accident
en *Ting*, a thing
et *Tog*, a train
en *Torsk*, a cod
et *Trin*, a step
et *Træk*,* a feature
en *Tvivl*, a doubt
et *Våben*, a weapon, arms
et *Vår*, a pillow-case
et *Vers*, a verse
et *Vink*, a wink
et *Vrag*, a wreck
et *Æg*, an egg
en *Østers*, an oyster.

It must be borne in mind that Danish compound words always follow the gender and number of the last of the two or more words of which they are composed; as for example: *Piskeskaftet*, the whip-handle; *Saltvandsfisken*, the salt-water fish.

* The asterisk indicates that the final consonant is doubled.

at tage Fejl, to make a mistake
at bruge, to use, employ
at skydse (Norw.), to convey travellers
at skifte, to change
at spille Kort, to play cards

at lege, to play, sport
en Fejl, a mistake
en Skive, a target, disk
en Kariol (Norw.), a cariiole
en Kariolsæle, a carriole harness
en Skydsgut (Norw.), a post-boy.

SIMPLE PHRASES.

De tager Fejl, det er ikke min Båd. — You make a mistake, that is not my boat.

Har Deres Båd et eller to Sejl? — Has your boat one or two sails?
Det har et lille og to store Sejl. — It has one little and two large sails.
Hörte De det Skud? — Did you hear that shot?
Det er min Fætter Hans, som skyder til Skive. — It is my cousin John, who is shooting at a target.
Nu kommer Turen til mig. — Now it is my turn.
Har De set min Sösters Hund? — Have you seen my sister's dog?
Den sidder ved Hegnet. — It is sitting by the hedge.
Dyret hörer en eller anden Lyd. — The animal hears some sound or other.

Hvad Slags Hund er det? — What kind of dog is it?
Det skal være en Rénhund. — It is said to be a dog for hunting reindeer.

Det er uden Tvivl en god Hund til at gå på Fjældene. — It is, without doubt, a good dog to have with one on the fjælds.
Er det Hunden som hviner? — Is it the dog which is whining?
Der kommer en Dame körende i en Kariol med to Skydsheste. — Here comes a lady driving in a carriole with two post-horses.
Hun bruger Piskesnærten altfor meget. — She uses the lash of her whip too much.
Hun gör Forsög på at standse, men Hesten vil ikke standse indtil den har nået Skydsskiftestedet. — She is trying to draw up, but the horse will not stop until he comes to the place for changing carriages.

Hun har ladet sit Slör ligge i Kariolen, og Handskerne også. — She has let her veil remain in the carriole, and her gloves also.
Hvor er Skydsgutten? — Where is the carriole post-boy?

TWENTY-EIGHTH EXERCISE.

I bought two bands, three ells longs, and a quarter of an ell broad. The woman gave her child a kiss on the mouth and cheeks. He got a bad bite on his right leg. Was it not the left leg? I saw the English flags on the masts. The Danish people do not often make an uproar. He made an attempt to see you. I wish to say a few (couple of) words to the Englishman. I wish to buy two lambs, and a calf. The pilot has two salmon, three herrings, two large cod, a score of oysters, and a basket of eggs. Did you hear the cry in the woods? No, I did not hear a call or any sound; but yesterday I heard a scream on the coast, and I had a mind to go out into the woods. I see no traces of footsteps. How many wheels has this carriage? Two wheels.

Translate into English.

Jeg ser et stort hvidt Möl og to Myg på Forhænget af min Seng. Barnet sidder på sin Moders Sköd, og leger med nogle Kort. Datterens Træk ligne hendes Faders, men Sönnens Træk, både Munden, Kinderne og Brynene, have större Lighed med Moderens. Det er ikke en Soldats Fag at sidde ved Pulten, og det er ikke Juristens Kald at bære Våben. Han vilde gærne være Præst, men hans Fader siger at det er ikke hans Kald. Hans Ord gör intet Indtryk på Sönnen, og Forholdet imellem Fader og Sön er ikke af det bedste. Lodsen bragte mig Bud fra den svenske Admiral, og rådede mig til at rejse med det förste Tog iaften. Har De fået Svar på Deres Breve? Masterne på de russiske Brigger ere altfor höje. Jeg så de store Pletter på Bordet. Min Skjorte er i Pjalter. Jeg fandt Skallerne på Klinterne og på Kysten af Bugten. Bondedragterne i Norge ere skönne i nogle Dele af Landet. Bjærgklöfterne ere dybe. Dunsterne ere farlige på Kysterne.

TWENTY-NINTH LESSON.

List of words, the meanings of which differ in accordance with difference of gender:—

COMMON GENDER.	NEUTER GENDER.
en *Ark*, Noah's ark	et *Ark*, a sheet of paper
en *Bid*, a bite, bit of food	et *Bid*, a bite, edge, bit for horses
en *Birk*, a birch	et *Birk*, an administrative division of land
en *Bord*, a border	et *Bord*, a table
en *Borg*, a castle	et *Borg*, a pledge taken in pawn
en *Buk*,* a buck	et *Buk*,* a bow, salutation
en *Flor*, an abundance	et *Flor*, a gauze, crape
en *Frö*, a frog	et *Frö*, a seed
en *Fyr*, a dandy	et *Fyr*, a sea-light, light-house
en *Gran*, a pine-tree	et *Gran*, a grain
en *Led*, an incline, side	et *Led*, a link, joint
en *Leje*, payment of rent, etc.	et *Leje*, a bed, layer
en *Lem*,* a trapdoor	et *Lem*,* a limb
en *Læg*,* a calf of a leg	et *Læg*, a fold, plait
en *Mor*, a Moor	et *Mor*, a moiré, brocade
en *Nögle*, a key	et *Nögle*, a tangle
en *Råd*, a councillor	et *Råd*, a counsel
(en) *Ris*, rice (a grain of)	et *Ris*, a birch-rod, a ream of paper
en *Segl*, a sickle	et *Segl*, a seal of letter
en *Skrift*, a piece of writing	et *Skrift*, a book, work
en *Snært*, a lash on a whip	et *Snært*, a lash with the whip
en *Spand*, a bucket	et *Spand*, a span (of horses)
en *Stift*, a pin, nail	et *Stift*, a see, diocese
en *Söm*,* a seam (of sewing)	et *Söm*,* an iron nail
en *Ting*, a thing	et *Ting*, legislative assembly
	Storting, legislative assembly of Norway
(en) *Tryk*,* a print	et *Tryk*,* a pressure

* The asterisk indicates that the final consonant is doubled.

COMMON GENDER.

en *Vår*, a spring-time (poet.)
en *Værge*, a guardian
en *Værk*, a spasm, ache
en *Æg*,* an edge of a knife
en *Æsel*, a donkey (as a term of reproach)
en *Öre*, a coin, a hundreth part of a crown

NEUTER GENDER.

et *Vår*, a pillow-case
et *Værge*, a weapon
et *Værk*, a work
et *Æg*,* an egg
et *Æsel*, an ass (animal)
et *Öre*, an ear.

at *så*, to sow
at *sy*, to sew
en *Syerske* ⎱
en *Syjomfru* ⎰ a workwoman
en *Symaskine*, a sewing machine
at *leje*, to let, hire
at *forlange*, to require
at *trykke*, to print
at *regne*, to rain, reckon
at *flytte*, to move
(et) *Frökorn*, corn, grain

en *Jomfru*, a maid, girl
et *Kammer*, a little room
en *Sal*, a drawing-room
en *Lejlighed* ⎱ rooms,
en *Huslejlighed* ⎰ lodgings
en *Paraply*, an umbrella
en *Parasol*, a parasol
et *Stöv*, a dust
et *Pas*, a pass
en *Regning*, an account
en *Advokat*, a lawyer.

SIMPLE PHRASES.

Vi få vist Regn; De må bringe mig min engelske Paraply, min lange Kåbe og den gamle Parasol.

I think we shall certainly have rain; you must bring me my English umbrella, my long cloak, and the old parasol.

Har De Værelser til Leje?
Lejen er altfor stor.
På hvilken Sal ere Værelserne?
Der er en Lejlighed på förste Sal.

Have you rooms to let?
The rent is too high.
On which floor are the rooms?
There is a set of rooms on the first floor.

Jeg önsker fire Værelser og et Kammer til en Tjæner.
Hvad er Prisen for sådan en Lejlighed?
Når Værelserne ere möblerede, forlange vi to Pund om Ugen, eller omtrent seks og tredive Kroner og nogle Öre.
Når kunne vi flytte ind?

I want four best rooms, and one room for a servant.
What is the price of such a set of rooms?
If the rooms are furnished we require £2 a week, or about 36 crowns and some öre.
When can we move in?

Iovermorgen, om De önsker.	The day after to-morrow, if you like.
Hvor er min Jomfru?	Where is my maid?
Hun sidder og syr paa en lang Söm.	She is sitting sewing a long seam.
Igår kunde hun ikke sy fordi hun fik et Söm i Haanden.	Yesterday she could not work because she got a nail into her hand.
Mit Rejsepas, min Paraply og mine Nögler ere alle paa Bordet.	My passport, my umbrella, and my keys are all on the table.
Her har De alle Deres Smaating.	Here are all your little things.
Forlanger De noget?	Do you require anything?
Hvor er min Bagageseddel?	Where is the ticket for my luggage?

TWENTY-NINTH EXERCISE.

Can you lend me a sheet of paper and a seal. Here is paper, ink, a pen, and a seal. What is the fashion now? The fashion for ladies' dresses is not pretty in these days. The printing of this book is very good. That man is a donkey; yet he has written a poem. That must be a wretched work! His last work was just as bad as the first. Who is that gentleman? He is a lawyer, and a member of the Norwegian legislative assembly. There is not a single pillow-case on my bed. Where are my keys? Your keys are in the door of the white room. Will you go with me to the pine wood? There is nothing more pleasant in the spring. There is a yellow fog in London. There is dust on the road to the castle. The bishop is in his diocese, and his son the councillor is with him.

Translate into English.

Om Foråret er det dejligt i Granskovene. Bonden siger, at han har intet Frö at så i sine Marker. Den Dreng er så uartig, han burde få Riset. Jeg önsker ikke så meget som et Ris Papir, jeg har nok med tre Ark.

Moret, som jeg köbte for min Moders Kjole, var dyrt. Moret er ikke i Mode i År, og derfor har jeg bestilt mig en Kjole af Flor. Flor er nydeligt for unge Damer, men ikke for gamle. Manden havde et Segl, som han gav Konen i Hænderne. Kan De give mig halvtredsindstyve Öre for en halv Krone? Jeg har ikke en eneste Öre. Hun giver de små Fugle nogle Riskorn. Risen synes mig altfor kostbar for Fuglene. Det er en doven Pige; hun har ikke syet en Söm. De burde sende hende til en Syskole. Næste År rejser hun til England med mig.

THIRTIETH LESSON.

Some verbs, which are composed of an affix and another word, do not admit of the separation of these two compound parts, which remain under all conditions as integral and inseparable syllables of the word, as in the following:—

at beklage (I.), to deplore, lament	at samtale (II.), to converse
at beskylde (II.), to accuse of	at samvirke (I.), to co-operate
at bedömme (II.), to judge	at undgå, to avoid
at erhverve (I.), to gain, earn	at undskylde (II.), to excuse
at erfare (I.), to learn	at undslippe, to escape
at erstatte (I.), to replace	at undvige, to evade, avoid
at forestille (I.), to represent	at vanhellige (I.), to desecrate
at foreskrive, to prescribe	at vanære (I.), to dishonour
at foreslå, to propose	at vederfares, to happen, befall
at mishandle (I.), to ill-use	at vederkvæge (I.), to refresh, recruit
at mistyde (I.), to misinterpret	at vederlægge, to indemnify.

Some of these verbs take the auxiliary *at blive*, to become, to be, in forming the passive voice, as for example: *det blev foreslået*, it was proposed; *hun blev beskyldt*, she was blamed; *Drengen blev mishandlet*, the boy was ill-treated.

At blive, when used as an active verb, may be translated by the English verb "to remain," taken in its fullest sense; as for example: *jeg blev i Paris*, I stayed in Paris; *mange Mand blev på Pladsen*, many men were left (lay dead) on the field; *bliv mig fra Livet*, stand off.

The auxiliary verb *at få*, to get, to have, must, etc., admits of being used in a large number of variously modified combinations; as for example:—

at få Nogen til at tie, to make any one keep silence.
at få Nogen vred, to make any one angry.
Du får mig ikke til at gå, thou wilt not make me go.
hun fik ham til at gå, she got him to go.
De får Bogen læst iaften, you will get the book read to-night.
han får tale, he will be forced to speak.
han har fået Lov, he has got permission.
jeg fik gjort alt hvad jeg önskede, I got everything done that I wished.
hun får göre det med alle sine Kræfter, she will have to do it with all her might.
min Sön har fået en Tand trukket ud, my son has had a tooth drawn.
hun fik det kun engang at höre, she only heard it once.
Konen påstår at hun får intet at sige i den Handling, the woman insists that she will not be allowed to have a voice in that matter.
han fik en ung Pige til Ægte, he married a young girl.

at pröve, to try, test	*en Tale*, a speech
at tale, to talk	*et Mål*, a measure
at måle, to measure	*en Klods*, a lump, log
at passe, to suit, fit	*Klodset*, clumsy
at fortjæne, to earn	(en) Sundhed, Helbred, health
at kvittere, to acquit	*en Håndvrist*, a wrist
at være frisk og sund, to be hale	*en Fodvrist*, an instep
at göre færdig, to finish	*en Höne*, a hen (pl. *Höns*), fowls
færdig, finished, ready	*en Såi*, a sole
travl, busy	(et) Såleläder, sole-leather
snæver, narrow	*en Last*, a lust
tyk, thick	*en Skyld*, a fault
tynd, thin	*en Skade*, an injury
en Pröve, a trial, rehearsal	*det er Skade*, it is a pity.

SIMPLE PHRASES.

Er De færdig med mine Böger?	Have you done with my books?
Nej, jeg havde så travlt; jeg kunde ikke få dem læst.	No, I was so busy; I could not read them.
Her er Skomageren.	Here is the shoemaker.
Han önsker at få Dem i Tale.	He wishes to speak to you.
Han er kommen her idag for at tage Mål af Dem til et Par Stövler.	He has come to-day to take your measure for a pair of boots.
Kan De få dem færdige til på Lördag?	Can you have them ready by Saturday?
Jeg har meget travlt, men jeg skal se at få dem færdige til den Dag.	I am very busy, but I will see if I can get them ready by that day.
Jeg må absolut have dem, da jeg skal rejse til London Lördag Aften.	I must positively have them, because I am going to start for London on Saturday night.
Vil De have Sålerne tykke eller tynde?	Will you have the soles thick or thin?
Stærke, men ikke klodsede.	Strong, but not clumsy.
Vil De pröve de nye Stövler?	Will you try on the new boots?
Jeg er bange for at de ere for små.	I am afraid they are too small.
Disse Stövler passe mig ikke; de ere for snævre over Vristen.	These boots do not fit me; they are too narrow over the instep.
Så får jeg sætte dem på Læsten og blokke dem lidt ud.	Then I must put them on the last, and stretch them out a little.
Nu passe de mig godt.	Now they will do very well.
Har De Regningen med?	Have you your account with you?
Vær så god at kvittere den.	Be so good as to receipt it.

THIRTIETH EXERCISE.

The tailor illtreats his wife and children. My cousin Anne always misinterprets what one says to her. What can that poor creature earn by his work? He earns perhaps about 12 crowns a week. One ought not to condemn the woman. He proposes to replace the money. That he must do if he wishes to be happy.

She laments that she has had a tooth drawn, because she thinks that the tooth was quite sound. The doctor prescribes a long journey for my poor little boy. I wish he would prescribe the same for my sister's eldest daughter. The soldier has not dishonoured his name, no one can accuse him of that. I cannot learn what has become of the old shoemaker, who lived in St. Peter's Street. My son has got leave from the general to remain in the country a little longer, and now he will have the opportunity of recruiting his health and his strength.

Translate into English.

Det er en besynderlig Pige, og jeg er bange for at hendes Forældre aldrig få nogen Ære af denne Datter. Når hendes Fader erfarer hvad hun havde i Sinde bliver han vist vred. Fru Justitsrådinde Paulsen mishandler sine Tjænestepiger, men hun forestiller sig at hun vil undgå Følgerne af sine Mishandlinger. Er det ikke muligt at få den Dreng til at tie? Lad ham være! han får nok Prygl af sin Fader iaften. Jeg får se hvor mange Æg Bondepigen har i sin Kurv. Hun beklager, at hun næsten ingen Æg får af Hönsene iår. Hun giver sin Svoger Skylden for den Ulykke, og påstår at han aldrig kan erstatte denne store Skade. Hun skulde ikke mistyde alt hvad hun hörer. Sådan en Kone får vel Lov til at sige hvad hun vil. Vi få ingen Tid til at nyde Noget her; dette er Stedet, hvor vi skulle sætte over Vandet i Lodsbåden. Det stormer altfor stærkt i Aften til at sætte over Elven i en åben Båd. Jeg foretrækker at gå med Toget.

K

LIST OF WORDS.

(en) *Jord*, an earth
(en) *Himmel*, a heaven
(et) *Himmerige*, the kingdom of heaven
en *Luft*, an air
et *Vand*, a water
en *Sky*, a cloud
en *skyfuld Himmel*, a cloudy sky
en *Torden*, a thunder
et *Lyn*, a lightning
en *Ild*, a fire
en *Lynild*, a flash of lightning
et *Lys*, a light
et *Mörke*, a darkness
i *Mörke*, in the dark
en *Sol*, a sun
et *Solbillede*, a sun picture, (a photograph)
en *Måne*, a moon
en *Nymåne*, a new moon
et *Skudår*, a leap-year
en *Stjærne*, a star
en *Planet*, a planet
en *Sö*, a sea
en *Indsö*, a lake
et *Hav*, an ocean
en *Flod* } a river, stream
en *Elv* (Norw.) }
en *Kam*,* a crest of a hill
en *Pöl*, a pool
Pölvand, ditchwater
et *Vindpust*, a puff of wind
et *Stålbad*, a chalybeate, (mineral) bath

et *Vandfald*, a water-fall
en *Kilde*, a spring
en *Regn* } a rain
et *Regnvejr* }
et *Vejr*, a weather
en *Dal*, a valley
en *Höjde*, a height
en *Strækning*, a stretch, range
et *Græs*,* a grass
en *Plet*,* a spot
en *Afstand*, a distance
(en) *Sne*, a snow
en *Snebold*, a snow-ball
en *Frost* } a frost
et *Frostvejr* }
(en) *Is*, ice
en *Bræ* } (Norw.), glacier
en *Isbræ* }
en *Hede*, a heath
en *Lyng*, a heath, heather
en *Sæter* (Norw.), a summer-pasture
en *Höyde* (Norw.), a height
en *Hagel*, a hail
en *Plaskregn*, a sharp shower
en *Top*,* a top, summit
et *Tövejr*, a thaw
et *Törvejr*, dry weather
et *Stöv*, a dust
et *Bad*, a bath
et *Badested*, a bathing place
en *Badeanstalt*, a bathing establishment
en *Vandhvirvel*, a whirlpool.

* The asterisk denotes that the final consonant is doubled.

PART II.

THIRTY-FIRST LESSON.

ON THE FORMATION OF WORDS (= *Orddannelsen*).

I. Nouns are formed by adding to an adjective one of the following affixes: *de, dom, e, hed, me, skab*, as for example:—

en *Højde*, a height,	from	*høj*, high
en *Rigdom*, riches	,,	*rig*, rich
en *Vrede*, an anger	,,	*vred*, angry
en *Godhed*, a goodness	,,	*god*, good
en *Fedme*, a fatness	,,	*fed*, fat
en *Retskaffenhed*, an uprightness	,,	*retskaffen*, upright
en *Dybde*, a depth	,,	*dyb*, deep
en *Sygdom*, a sickness	,,	*syg*, sick, ill
en *Skævhed*, a crookedness	,,	*skæv*, crooked
en *Rødme*, a redness	,,	*rød*, red
en *Galskab*, a madness	,,	*gal*, mad.

A. Some nouns have been formed by adding the affix *skab* to another noun; as for example:—

et *Herskab*, a dominion,	from	en *Herre*, a master
et *Venskab*, a friendship	,,	en *Ven*, a friend
et *Fjendskab*, an enmity	,,	en *Fjende*, an enemy.

The terminations *hed* and *skab* originally constituted distinct words; the former representing the German *heit*, signifying a property, and the latter the Old Northern *skap*, mind, disposition. The same distinctive meanings still adhere to these affixes; words ending in *hed*, expressing an attribute, or property, as for example: en *Kærlighed*, a love; en *Slethed*, a badness, while *skab* conveys the sense of condition, as for example: *en Vildskab*, a wildness; *et Broderskab*, a brotherhood.

B. *dom*, originally an independent word (*dóm-r*, O.N., an important thing) is used to express a property, or quality; as for example: *Ungdom*, youth; while *dömme* indicates the exercise of power, as for example: *Kongedömme*, kingdom; *Fyrstendömme*, principality.

II. Nouns which express an action, and a few which indicate a property, or condition, often end in *else* or *sel*, *ing* or *ning*, *en*, and *eri*, as for example:—

en Bevægelse, a motion,	from	*at bevæge*, to move
et Fængsel, a prison	,,	*at fænge*, or *at fange*, to capture
en Handling, an action	,,	*at handle*, to act, trade
en Tænkning, a thinking	,,	*at tænke*, to think
en Gnaven, a gnawing	,,	*at gnave*, to gnaw
et Bryderi, a worry, disturbance	,,	*at bryde*, to care for, annoy
et Maleri, a painting	,,	*at male*, to paint.

The termination *eri* in most cases conveys a disparaging sense, somewhat similar to that implied in English by the affix "ling;" as for instance:—

et Skriveri, a piece of scribbling,	from	*at skrive*, to write
et Skænderi, a brawling	,,	*at skænde på*, to scold
et Vrövleri, a twaddling	,,	*et Vrövl*, nonsense.

III. Personal nouns, especially when they convey a sense of diminution or inferiority, are often formed by adding *ling* to the adjective, or other part of speech from which they are derived; while they take *er* to indicate the agent generally; as for example:—

en Lærling, a learner,	from	*at lære*, to learn, teach
en Yngling, a youth	,,	*ung*, young
en Kælling (or more correctly *Kærling*), an old crone	,,	*en Karl*, a fellow
en Dommer, a judge	,,	*en Dom*, a judgment
en Lærer, a teacher	,,	*at lære*, to teach
en Tysker, a German	,,	*tysk*, German.

IV. Various meanings are conveyed to the same verbal

root by the addition of different affixes, or particles; as for example:—

en *Egenhed*, a peculiarity
en *Egenskab*, a property, quality
en *Manddom*, a manhood
et *Mandskab*, a troop of men, soldiers, crew
en *Frihed*, a liberty
en *Frist*, a respite

en *Hellighed*, a holiness
en *Helligdom*, a sanctuary
en *Vildhed*, a ferocity
et *Vildskab*, a wildness
en *Vildelse*, an error, aberration
en *Vildsomhed*, an intricacy

at *tage sig i Agt*, to beware
at *agte*, to esteem, intend
at *lide*, to suffer
at *tage* (or *få*) *fat på*, to get hold of
at *pådrage sig*, to draw upon oneself
at *löse*, to loosen
at *bare*, to bear, endure
at *ældes*, to grow old
at *udskælde*, to abuse
at *tage Del i*, to take part in

en *Agtelse*, an esteem
et *Palads* (*Palai*), palace
en *Lidelse*, a suffering
en *Nabo*, a neighbour
en *Jul*, a Christmas, Yule
en *Alder*, an age
en *Juvel*, a jewel
lös, loose
vanvittig, insane
dum, stupid.

DIALOGUES.

Det gör mig ondt at höre fra min Nabo, Lægen, at Deres Svoger er syg nu i Julen.

I am sorry to hear from my neighbour, the doctor, that your brother-in-law is ill this Christmas.

Han lider meget, men han bærer sine Lidelser med stor Tålmodighed.

He suffers very much, but he bears his sufferings with great patience.

De må tage Dem i Agt ikke at lade Födderne slippe når De går op ad de höje Bjærge.

You must take care not to let your feet slip when you are going up the high mountains.

Man kan ikke altid få fat på noget til at standse sit Fald.

One cannot always catch at anything to stop one's fall.

I min Alder vilde det virkelig være dumt, om jeg ikke kunde stå på mine Födder.

At my age it would really be stupid not to be able to keep myself up on my legs.

Hvor ung og rask man end er, kan man dog let komme på en Fjældside, hvor der er stygge, löse Stene.

However young and strong one may be, one may easily come upon a hillside, where there are ugly, loose stones.

Stene eller ingen Stene; nu går jeg til Sæteren nærved Elstad.

Stones or no stones, I am off to the Sætter-hut, near Elstad.

READING.

To translate into English.

En Mand havde to Sönner, af hvilke den ene holdt af[1] at sove længe om Morgenen, og den anden var meget flittig[2] og stod altid meget tidlig op. Da den Sidstnævnte[3] en Dag var gäet ud meget tidlig, fandt han en Pung[4] med Penge. Han löb hen til sin Broder for at underrette[5] ham om sin gode Lykke,[6] og sagde til ham: "Se, Henrik, hvad man får ved at stå tidlig op." — "Men," svarede Broderen, "dersom den, hvem Pungen tilhörer,[7] ikke var stået tidligere op end jeg, vilde han ikke have tabt[8] den."

FARVEREN[9] OG DOMMEREN.[10]

En Farver, som skulde aflægge en Ed,[11] og hvis Hånd var ganske sort, blev befalet[12] at række denne i Vejret.[13] — "Tag Deres Handsker af, min Ven," sagde Dommeren til ham. — "Tag Deres Briller[14] på,[15] min Herre," svarede Farveren.

THIRTY-FIRST EXERCISE.

How high are the masts of the English brig? I cannot tell you their height. My neighbour, the old doctor, is a good friend of mine; I esteem his friendship very highly. That is a man whose enmity I should not like to have; he does not care for anything but riches; his pride is something unbearable. The general does not think much of the king's actions and modes of thought. It is a peculiarity of my sister-in-law, that she is never

[1] to like	[7] to belong to	[12] ordered
[2] diligent	[8] to lose	[13] *række i Vejret*,
[3] last-named	[9] dyer	to hold up
[4] purse	[10] judge	[14] spectacles
[5] inform	[11] *aflægge en Ed*, take	[15] *tage på*, put on.
[6] fortune	an oath	

happy when she cannot scold her servants. The thief is no longer in prison, he has recovered (got) his freedom since Christmas. The queen has a German lady-reader. It is said that the queen is angry because this lady, who does not read well, is always making a disturbance among the German servants in the palace. Do you see where the animal has gnawed right through the door of the Sætter-hut? What animal is it? It is a wild animal which runs about on the high mountains. How fat and red that boy is. Fatness and redness belong to a little child of his age. I think my neighbour, the judge, must be mad; his judgment is pure madness. Have you read the last work by the young German who was here yesterday? It is a stupid piece of writing. She is so crooked, every movement pains her. Poor thing! has she never any respite from her sufferings? Not often, she is nearly always ill. How cold it is to-day. The cold was greater yesterday. There will probably be much illness amongst old people and little children.

THIRTY-SECOND LESSON.

ON THE FORMATION OF WORDS.—(Continued).

NOUNS (= Navneord).

A large number of nouns are formed in the Danish language by placing a prefix before another noun, or before a word derived from some other part of speech.

These prefixes may be divided into two classes: (I.) the positive; and (II.) the negative.

I. The positive prefixes are: *an*, *be*, *bi*, *er*, and *sam*, the four first of which have been borrowed from the German, **and** are identical with their German analogues, whilst the last named, derived from *samme*, same, corresponds with the English particles *con*, *sym*, *syn*; as for example :—

et Ansigt, a face,	from	*at ansé*, to regard (*sé*, see; *an*, on)
et Begreb, a conception	,,	*at gribe*, to grasp (*at begribe*, to understand)
et Bidrag, a contribution	,,	*at bidrage*, to tend to
en Erfaring, an experience	,,	*at erfare*, to learn
en Samlyd, a symphony	,,	*en Lyd*, a sound
et Samtykke, a consent	,,	*et Tykke*, an opinion.

A. *An* and *bi*, although not independent words, admit of being used as such in certain phrases, borrowed from the German; as for example :—

det går an, that will do (German: das geht an)
at stå En bi, to stand by one
at ligge bi, to lay by (nautical).

II. The negative particles are *for*, *mis*, *u*, *und*, *van*, and *veder*; as, for example :—

en Foragt, a contempt	from	*en Agt*, a consideration, esteem
en Mistanke, a suspicion	,,	*en Tanke*, a thought (*at tænke*, to think)
en Udyd, a vice	,,	*en Dyd*, a virtue
en Undskyldning, an excuse, pardon	,,	*en Skyld*, a blame
en Vanart, degeneracy	,,	*en Art*, a nature, kind
et Vederlag, a compensation	,,	*et Lag*, a layer, firm, association

A. The particle *for* in such words as *Foragt*, *at foragte*, to despise, etc., is unaccentuated, to distinguish it from the preposition *for*, before; thus, in the word *at forklæde*, to dress up, the *o* in *for* is short, while in *et Forklæde*, an apron, (compounded of *for*, before, and *et Klæde*, a cloth), the *o* in *for* is marked by a long accent (= *Tonehold*).

at eje, to own	*en Ejer*, an owner
at benytte, to make use of	*en Nytte*, a use
at betinge, to bargain for	*en Fiskegrund*, a fishing ground
at fiske, to fish	*et Beløb*, an amount
at opholde sig, to stay, sojourn	(*et*) *Fuglevildt*, wild fowl, game
med Hensyn til, in respect to	*i så Fald*, in that case.

DIALOGUES.

Jeg har ingen stor Erfaring med Hensyn til Vejret i Fjældene, men dog tror jeg at vi få Regn og koldt Vejr iaften.	I have no great experience of the weather on the fjælds, but yet I think we shall have rain and cold weather this evening.
Herr Svendsen har i Sinde at opholde sig her på Rype- og Renjagt en fjorten Dages Tid i August.	Mr. Svendsen intends to stay here about a fortnight in August, to shoot ptarmigans and reindeer.
Han skulde först betinge sig Log hos Fiskegrundens Ejer, tilligemed Tilladelse til at fiske.	He should first secure a lodging with the owner of the fishing ground, and at the same time get permission to fish.
Uden Mandens Samtykke kunde De ikke benytte Dem af hans Både.	Without the man's consent you could not use any of his boats.
Det går ikke an at fiske uden Ejerens Tilladelse, men Rype- og Renjagten er endnu tilladt enhver Normand.	It will not do to fish without the owner's permission, but every Norwegian is still at liberty to shoot ptarmigans and reindeer.
Imorgen gör jeg en Prövetur på Vandet, medens min Broder går tilfjælds for at skyde Fuglevildt.	I shall make a trial expedition on the water to-morrow, whilst my brother goes on the fjælds to shoot wild fowl.

READING.

To translate into English.

RÆVEN[1] OG VINDRUERNE.[2]

En Ræv kom til et Sted, hvor der var nogle smukke modne[3] Druer,[4] men de hang så höjt, at den ikke kunde nå[5] dem. Den sprang til den var ganske udmattet,[6] og anstrængte[7] sig af alle Kræfter, men det hjalp ikke. Tilsidst, da den så, at den på ingen Måde kunde komme til dem, sagde den: "Å, det er kun nogle grönne, sure Ting; derfor

[1] fox, [2] grapes, [3] ripe, [4] grapes, [5] reach, [6] to tire out, [7] to exert,

vil jeg ikke göre flere Forsög,[1] men lade dem hænge, hvor de ere."

DEN GAMLE KONE OG RAVNEN.[2]

En gammel Kone köbte en ung Ravn. Hendes Naboerske[3] spurgte hende, hvad hun vilde med det hæslige[4] Dyr. — "Jeg vil pröve," svarede hun, "om det er sandt, at en sådan Fugl kan leve i 200 År."

THIRTY-SECOND EXERCISE.

I despise the Spanish colonel, and therefore I will not stand by him. She had no suspicion of her neighbour, the old miller. Now she learns that this man who looks so respectable is a very vicious person. I must beg you to pardon (excuse) me, the fault is mine. How can you esteem a man who consents to take part in such a vicious action. The children were to dress themselves up on Christmas Eve; the youngest boy was to wear his sister's black silk dress and his mother's white apron. Do you believe that the brothers will get compensation? No, I do not. With your permission I will make use of the opportunity to fish in the river. If your father consents, you may bring your youngest brother with you. I will try to get his consent. You shall be at liberty to fish from morning till evening, if you will only allow my old fisherman to go in the boat with you. My cousin, Captain Hansen, is coming to shoot reindeer in the first fortnight of July. It will be of no use; he will probably not see a single animal. In that case he must betake himself to something else. I despise men who only think of acquiring riches. What use is it to be rich if one is not happy. How long will you stay in London? For about a fortnight, and

[1] attempts, [2] raven, [3] fem. of *Nabo:* neighbour, [4] ugly.

then I shall make a short journey in England and in France with my eldest sister. Have you any great experience in travelling? No, I have never yet had an opportunity of travelling; but that has not been my fault. I am still young, and my father insisted always that I ought to think of earning some money before I made travelling-tours.

THIRTY-THIRD LESSON.

ON THE FORMATION OF WORDS.—(Continued).

ADJECTIVES (=Tillægsord).

I. Adjectives, expressing a material quality, often end in *en* or *ern*, as for example:—

gylden (pl. gyldne), gold, golden, from (et) Guld, gold
sölvern, silver, silvery (poet.)   ,,   (et) Sölv, silver.

A. In poetry the older form *sölver* is also still used; as for example: *sölverhvid*, silvery-white; *sölverklar*, silvery-pure (clear).

B. In ordinary phraseology the substance of which an object is made is not expressed by using an adjective, as in the phrase "a wooden spoon," but by combining into one word both the object, and the substance of which it is made; as: *en Træske*, a wood-spoon; *et Guldlommeur*, a gold pocket-watch; *en Silkekjole*, a silk dress; *en Saltvandsfisk*, a salt-water fish.

II. Adjectives, expressive of form or appearance, often end in *et*; as for example:—

blåöjet, blue-eyed,   from *blå*, blue; *et Öje*, an eye
buget, curved, bulging   ,,   *en Bug*, a bulge
hornet, horned   ,,   *et Horn*, a horn
firkantet, four-cornered   ,,   *fire*, four; *en Kant*, an edge
sorthåret, black-haired   ,,   *sort*, black; *et Hår*, a hair.

III. The termination *laden* diminishes the force of the quality expressed by the adjective to which it is joined; as in :—

 grønladen, greenish, inclining to green, *grøn*
 sortladen, blackish ,, ,, black, *sort*.

IV. The termination *haftig*, having, and the more rarely used affixes *vorn*, and *el*, have a qualitative signification, which is generally analogous with the English termination "ly;" as for example:—

 mandhaftig, manly, from *en Mand*, a man
 tossevorn, silly ,, *en Tosse*, a simpleton
 vammel, sickly ,, *at vamle*, to loathe

V. Some adjectives are formed by adding to nouns or other adjectives the following affixes: *agtig* (neuter *agtigt*), *bar* (*bart*) *ig* (*igt*), *lig* (*ligt*), *som* (*somt*), and *sk;* as for example:—

 barnagtig, childish,   from *et Barn*, a child
 bondeagtig, peasant-like ,, *en Bonde*, a peasant
 frugtbar, fruitful   ,, *en Frugt*, a fruit
 kostbar, costly   ,, *en Kost*, a cost
 skriftlig, written   ,, *et Skrift*, a writing
 ensom, lonely   ,, *en*, one
 politisk, political   ,, *en Politik*, a policy.

A. Many national adjectives, as already shown, terminate in *sk*; as for instance:—

tysk, German	*fransk*, French	*græsk*, Greek
polsk, Polish	*russisk*, Russian	*hebræisk*, Hebrew
norsk, Norwegian	*svensk*, Swedish	*finlandsk*, Finnish.

These adjectives, as already mentioned (*in Lesson* IV.), are written in Danish with small initial letters like all other adjectives. An exception to this rule may be made where the adjective is used to indicate a special language; as for example :—

 den svenske Dame taler Russisk, the Swedish lady talks Russian.
 min engelske Ven finder at Spansk er ikke så vanskeligt som Portugisisk, my English friend thinks that Spanish is not so difficult as Portuguese.

en *Födsel*, a birth
at *forære*, to make presents
en *Foraring*, a gift
at *bebo*, to inhabit
at *tilbyde*, to offer
indfödt, native
en *Knipling*, a lace
et *Skind*, a skin
et *Lin*, a linen
gammeldags, old-fashioned

en *Krave*, a collar
en *Hals*, a neck
et *Halsbånd*, a necklace
(et) *Elfenben*, ivory
en *Vifte*, a fan
en *Ring*, a ring
(en) *Olje*, oil
en *Bistand*, an assistance
en *Omgang*, an intercourse
dannet, cultivated.

DIALOGUES.

Er det sandt, at Deres Broder befinder sig i en ubehagelig Stilling, fordi han mangler hundrede Pund?

Is it true that your brother is placed in an unpleasant position for want of a hundred pounds?

Det er kun altfor sandt.

It is only too true!

Det gör mig ondt at höre, men dog glæder det mig at have en Lejlighed til at tilbyde ham min Bistand, som jeg ofte har lovet ham.

I am sorry to hear that, but in the meantime I am glad to find an opportunity of offering him my assistance, as I have often promised.

Jeg har altid været overbevist om, at De vilde være ligesá beredt til at holde som til at love.

I have always been convinced that you would be as ready to perform as to promise.

Gör mig den Tjæneste at besörge dette Brev til ham; vedlagt vil han finde Belöbet, og han kan selv bestemme, når han vil tilbagebetale det.

Do me the favour to forward this letter to him; enclosed he will find the amount, and he may name his own time for payment.

READING.

To translate into English.

PEN OG BLÆKHUS.[1]

I.

Der blev sagt i en Digters Stue,[2] idet man så på hans Blækhus, der stod på Bordet: "Det er mærkeligt, Alt hvad der dog kan komme op af det Blækhus! Hvad mon[3] nu det Næste bliver? Ja, det er mærkeligt!"

[1] ink-stand [2] a poet's room [3] what, I wonder!

"Det er det!" sagde Blækhuset. "Det er ubegribeligt! det er det, jeg altid siger!" sagde det til Pennefjæderen,[1] og til hvad Andet, der på Bordet kunde höre det. "Det er mærkeligt, Alt hvad der kan komme fra mig! Ja, det er næsten utroligt! og jeg ved virkelig ikke selv, hvad det Næste bliver, når Mennesket begynder at öse[2] af mig. Én Dråbe[3] af mig, den er nok til en halv Side Papir, og hvad kan der ikke stå på den! Jeg er noget ganske mærkeligt! fra mig udgår alle Digterens Værker! disse levende Mennesker, som Folk tro at kende, disse underlige Fölelser,[4] dette gode Humör,[5] disse yndige[6] Skildringer[7] af Naturen;— jeg begriber det ikke selv, for jeg kender ikke Naturen, men det er nu engang i mig! fra mig udgik og udgår denne Hærskare[8] svævende,[9] yndige Piger, kække[10] Riddere på fnysende Gangere![11] oh, ja, jeg ved det ikke selv! eg forsikrer Dem, jeg tænker ikke ved det!"

THIRTY-THIRD EXERCISE.

This is a silver spoon, that is not what I want. Give me a wooden-spoon. The wooden spoon is in the kitchen, but here is a horn-spoon. Has the child light, or dark hair? It is a charming blue-eyed, black-haired little girl. It is my niece's birthday to-day, and I must therefore make her some pretty present. What are you intending to give her? I am giving her a brown silk dress, a lace veil, a pair of black silk stockings, two pairs of French kid gloves, a fine linen collar, and a pair of linen cuffs with gold studs in them. Her mother gives her a four-cornered silver case (casket) with some jewels in it, and from her father she receives a gold watch, a gold chain, a heavy silver bracelet, two dozen (dress) gloves, a costly necklace, several rings, and an ivory fan.

[1] quill-pen
[2] to bale; at öse af, to draw up or from
[3] drop
[4] feeling
[5] humour
[6] charming
[7] description
[8] host
[9] gliding, fluttering
[10] brave
[11] snorting steeds.

THIRTY-FOURTH LESSON.

ON THE FORMATION OF WORDS.—*(Continued).*

VERBS (= *Udsagnsord*).

I. Verbs are formed directly from nouns, as for example:—

at agte, to esteem, intend, from en Agt, a consideration, intention
at smage, to taste „ en Smag, a taste, flavour
at lyde, to sound „ en Lyd, a sound
at hæfte, to fasten „ et Hæfte, a fastening.

A. In some cases the radical vowel of the noun is changed in the verb, as for example:—

at mægte, to master, from en Magt, a power
at hænde, to happen, come to hand „ en Hånd, a hand
at virke, bevirke, to effect „ et Værk, a work
at skyde, to shoot „ et Skud, a shot, discharge.

II. Many verbs, which are derived from nouns and adjectives, end in *ge, ige, le, re, ske, me, ne, se te*; as for example:—

at spörge, to inquire, from et Spor, a trace, foot-print
at bemægtige sig, to take possession of „ en Magt, a power, force
at smugle, to smuggle „ i Smug, clandestinely
at gnistre, to sparkle „ en Gnist, a spark
at åbenbare, to reveal „ åben, open; at åbne, to open
at herske, to rule „ en Herre, a master
at rödme, to blush „ röd, red
at hvidne, to turn white „ hvid, white
at rense, to rinse „ ren, clean
at smægte, to pine „ en Smag, a taste.

III. Many verbs convey elliptically the meaning of the roots from which they have been derived; as for example:—

at gifte, to marry, from at give i Ægteskab, to give in marriage
at nægte, to deny „ at sige nej, to say no
at opdage, to discover „ at bringe noget op til Dagen (= Lyset), to bring something to the light of day.

IV. Some verbs are simply imitative sounds, as for example:—

at *brumle*, to buzz, grumble
at *mumle*, to mumble
at *pikke*, to tap, tick

at *kvidre*, to twitter
at *pible*, to bubble
at *tude*, to howl (like a dog).

V. Verbs derived from Greek and Latin roots, and those which long have been, or still are being introduced from foreign sources, may be incorporated in the Danish language by adding *ere* to the original word; as, for example:—

at *diktere*, to dictate
at *identificere*, to identify

at *protestere*, to protest
at *reformere*, to reform.

A. This facile mode of verbal adoption was carried to its greatest height in the latter part of the eighteenth century, when custom and fashion threatened to reduce the Danish language to the condition of a mere polyglot mongrel tongue. The efforts of Rask and later writers to restore the use of genuine Danish words, have so far succeeded in arresting this process of verbal fabrication, that the writings of the best living authors of Norway and Denmark present few, if any, instances of this kind of word-coining.

VI. Many verbs are formed by placing before another verb one of the following prefixes: *be, er, for, fore, und, veder, mis, over*; as for example:—

at *begribe*, to comprehend,   from   at *gribe*, to seize
at *erkende*, to acknowledge, own   ,,   at *kende*, to know
at *forsætte*, to misplace   ,,   at *sætte*, to set
at *forestille*, to present   ,,   at *stille*, to place
at *undgå*, to avoid   ,,   at *gå*, to go
at *vederkvæge*, to recuit strength   ,,   at *kvæge*, to refresh
at *misforstå*, to misunderstand   ,,   at *forstå*, to understand
at *overleve*, to outlive   ,,   at *leve*, to live.

A. The affixes *be* and *er* must be considered as genuine German particles. *For* is usually the representative of the German *ver*, but *ore*, although occasionally representing the German *vor*, are more frequently to be referred to the Old Northern words *for, fyrir*, for, before. *Und* is the German *ent* and Old N. *undan*, without; *veder* represents the German *wider*,

Old N. *við, viðr*, with; *mis* is Old N. *Mis*, deviation, fault; while *over* is equivalent to the German *über* and Old N. *yfir*, over.

It should be observed that the prefixes *u* and *van*, which occur in a few verbs, and in numerous nouns and adjectives, are both borrowed from Old Northern, in which the former conveyed the sense of negation, and the latter that of deficiency, as well as negation, as they still do in Dano-Norwegian; as for example: *sand*, true; *usand*, untrue; *at skabe*, to form, create; *vanskabt*, deformed.

VII. Intransitive verbs acquire an active, transitive sense by a change in the radical vowel; as for example:—

at *brage*, to crack	at *brække*, to break
at *falde*, to fall	at *fælde*, to fell
at *fare*, to go, drive	at *føre*, to lead
at *knage*, to creak	at *knække*, to crack
at *ligge*, to lie	at *lægge*, to lay
at *ryge*, to smoke	at *røge*, to smoke (meat, etc.)
at *sidde*, to sit	at *sætte*, to set

DIALOGUES.

Man mærker, at Dagene begynde at tage af (tage til).	One perceives that the days begin to shorten (to lengthen).
Det er Tegn til, at de smukke Dage snart ville være forbi.	It is a sign that the fine days will be soon at an end.
Ikke altid; vi have undertiden Sommervejr om Efteråret, og Vinter om Foråret.	Not always; we sometimes have summer-weather in autumn, and winter in spring.
Agter De at tilbringe Vinteren i London?	Do you intend to spend the winter in London?
Nej, jeg skal ledsage min Fætter til det sydlige Frankrig.	No, I shall go with my cousin to the South of France.
Det er et af de skönneste Klimater i Europa; De har vel Venner der?	It is one of the finest climates in Europe; I suppose you have friends there?
Ja, min Onkel bor dér bestandig for sin Sundheds Skyld, og han har indbudt os til at tilbringe Vintertiden hos ham.	Yes, my uncle resides there constantly on account of his health, and he has sent us an invitation to spend the winter with him.
Det vil være særdeles behageligt; jeg önsker Dem en lykkelig Rejse.	That will be charming; I wish you a pleasant journey.

READING

to translate into English.

PEN OG BLÆKHUS.—(Continued.)

II.

"Det har De Ret i!" sagde Pennefjæderen; "De tænker slet ikke; for tænkte De, da vilde De forstå,[1] at De kun giver Væde![2] De giver Væde, så at jeg kan udtale og synliggöre[3] på Papiret det jeg har i mig, det jeg skriver med. Pennen er det som skriver! derom tvivler[4] intet Menneske; og de fleste Mennesker have da ligeså god Indsigt[5] i Poesien, som et gammelt Blækhus!

"De har kun lidt Erfaring,"[6] sagde Blækhuset. "De er jo knap[7] en Uge i Tjænesten, og allerede halvt opslidt.[8] Bilder De Dem ind,[9] at De er Digteren! De er kun Tyende,[10] og mange af den Slags har jeg haft för De kom, og det både af Gåsefamiljen og af engelsk Fabrik;[11] jeg kender både Fjæderpen og Stålpen![12] Der er Mange jeg har haft i Tjæneste, og jeg vil få Mange endnu, når han, Mennesket, som gör Bevægelserne[13] for mig, kommer og skriver ned, hvad han får ud af mit Indvendige.[14] Jeg gad nu nok vide,[15] hvad det Förste bliver, han löfter[16] ud af mig!"

"Blækbötte!"[17] sagde Pennen.

THIRTY-FOURTH EXERCISE.

Will you be so kind as to wash this glass for me? The wine does not taste well. The fastening of my fan is broken, I must make enquiries if I can have it repaired here in town. I think it possible that the silversmith, Jansen, who lives in Östergade, might put it to rights

[1] to understand
[2] wet, moisture
[3] make visible
[4] to doubt
[5] insight
[6] experience
[7] scarcely
[8] to wear out
[9] to imagine
[10] servants
[11] manufacture
[12] steel-pen
[13] movement
[14] inside
[15] should like to know
[16] to lift
[17] ink-tub.

again. My maid has not fastened my cloak. How could she fasten it, when there is no fastening to be seen? Do you see how she blushes because her brother asked her if she had read the French book? Yes, and now she is growing pale just as quickly. The sailor cannot deny that he smuggles something or other each time he comes back from a voyage. In case he does this often, the captain will certainly find it out.

THIRTY-FIFTH LESSON

ON THE FORMATION OF WORDS.—(*Continued*).

ADVERBS AND PREPOSITIONS (*Biord og Forholdsord*).

The addition of *e* changes the sense of some adverbs from that of motion to that of rest, as for example:—

han står ude på Gaden, og Konen kommer straks ud, he is standing out in the street, and the woman is coming out immediately.
Soldaten gik bort igår, men nu må han være hjemme, the soldier went away yesterday, but he must be at home now.
Soldaten er borte, han rejser hjem idag, the soldier is away, he is going home to-day.

The terminations *en* and *er* convey a sense of direction, or of motion whether suspended or active, as for example:—

Østen for, to the east of (*Øst*, east)   *en Østenvind*, an easterly wind
Vesten fra, from the west (*Vest*, west)   *en Vestenvind*, a westerly wind
Vinden er Norden (*Norden fra*), the wind is northerly.

Øster, east, eastward   *atter*, once again
Vester, west, westward   *efter*, after.

III. Some adverbs are formed by adding to nouns or adjectives the terminations *igen, elig, lig, ligen* (analogous to English *y* and *ly*), as for example:—

kraftigen } strongly, forcibly { from *en Kraft*, a strength
kraftelig }   „   *kraftig*, strong
hjærtelig, heartily   „   *et Hjærte*, a heart.

IV. Some adverbs have been formed directly from the neuter of the corresponding adjectives, as for example:—

bredt, broadly, from *bred, t*, broad
vidt, widely, far ,, *vid, t*, wide
skælmsk, roguishly ,, *skælmsk*, roguish (unchanged in neuter).

V. Some adverbs, which are formed by the combination of a preposition and a noun, or of an adverb and some other part of speech, usually have the termination *s*, or *es*, or simply *e*; as, for example:—

påtværs, across, aslant, from *på*, on, *tværs*, askew, across
allesteds, everywhere ,, *alle*, all, *et Sted*, a place
medrette, rightly ,, *med*, with, *en Ret*, a right
undervejs, on the way ,, *under*, under, *en Vej*, a way
tilvogns, by carriage ,, *til*, to, *en Vogn*, a carriage.

A. These and many similarly composed words admit of being used either in their compound or disintegrated form; as for example:—

tilskibs, til Skibs, by ship
tilsengs, til Sengs, to bed
igåraftes, igår Aftes, last evening
itide, i Tid., i Tide, in time
indenfor, inden for, within
tilligemed, tillige med, together with
ovenikøbet, oven i Købet, besides
tilsyneladende, til Syne ladende, seemingly

indenlands, ind i Landet, inland
udenbys, ude af Byen, outside the town
tilarbejds, til Arbejde, at work
tildörs, til Dörs, to the door
tiltaffels, til Taffels, at table (in reference to State dinners, etc.)
tilbords, til Bords, at table (ordinary occasions).

READING

to translate into English.

PEN OG BLÆKHUS.—(*Continued.*)

III.

Sent[1] på Aftenen kom Digteren hjem; han havde været i Konsert, hört en udmærket Violinspiller[2] og var ganske opfyldt[3] og betagen[4] af dennes magelöse Spil.[5] Det havde

[1] late
[2] violin-player
[3] to be impressed by
[4] overwhelmed
[5] matchless play

været et forbavsende[1] Væld[2] af Toner, han havde fået ud af Instrumentet; snart löd[3] det som klingende[4] Vanddråber,[5] Perle på Perle,[6] snart som kvidrende[7] Fugle i Kor,[8] som bruste[9] Stormen igennem en Granskov;[10] han troede at höre sit eget Hjærte græde,[11] men i Melodi, som det kan höres i en Kvindes[12] dejlige Röst.[13] Det havde været som om ikke blot Violinens Strænge[14] klang;[15] men Strængestolen,[16] ja Skruer[17] og Sangbund![18] det var overordentligt! og svært havde det været, men sét ud som en Leg,[19] som om Buen[20] kun löb frem og tilbage hen over Strængene, man skulde tro, at Enhver kunde göre det efter. Violinen klang af sig selv, Buen spillede af sig selv, de to var det, som gjorde det Hele, man glemte Mesteren,[21] der förte[22] dem, gav dem Liv og Sjæl. Mesteren glemte man: men på ham tænkte Digteren, ham nævnede han, og nedskrev sin Tanke derved!

DIALOGUES.

Det vilde glæde mig, om en Lejlighed vilde tilbyde sig for mig at rejse til London.

I should be glad, if I could find an opportunity of going to London.

Og det vilde glæde mig meget, hvis jeg kunde ledsage Dem.

And I should be very glad, if I could accompany you.

Det vilde også være mig til megen Nytte, da De er bekendt med de forskællige Måder at rejse på; i ethvert Tilfælde vil jeg takke Dem for et godt Råd desangående.

It would also be of great use to me, as you are acquainted with the different ways of travelling; at all events I shall be very much obliged to you for good advice on the subject?

I hvilken Del af Byen tror De det vilde være bekvemmest for mig at bo? De kunde måske også give mig et Begreb om, hvormeget Rejsen vil koste?

In what part of the town do you think it most convenient for me to stay? Perhaps you could give me an idea how much the journey will cost?

[1] to overpower
[2] rush
[3] to sound
[4] resounding
[5] drops
[6] bead, drop
[7] twittering
[8] chorus
[9] to roar
[10] a pine-wood
[11] to weep
[12] woman
[13] voice
[14] string
[15] sound
[16] bridge of violin
[17] screw
[18] body of instrument
[19] play, sport
[20] bow
[21] master
[22] to lead.

Blandt Andet råder jeg Dem til at forsyne Dem med engelske Penge før Afrejsen.	Among other things I advise you to procure English money before you start.
Kan jeg udføre nogen Kommission for Dem?	Can I do anything for you?
Jeg kunde have Lyst til at sende nogle ubetydelige Foræringer til nogle Bekendte i London.	I should like to send a few trifling presents to some friends in London.

THIRTY-FIFTH EXERCISE.

I shall be heartily glad to see my husband's old friend, the French lawyer. Is he already in Denmark, or is he still on the way? He is in Germany, and we do not know if he will come by the inland route or by ship. Last night the children went to bed in time for their mother to drive out to see her friend, the admiral's wife, who lives out of town. That little boy goes to work together with his father in time to see the sun rise (stand up). The king and the queen go to dinner (to table) at six o'clock. That is rather early; in England the queen does not dine (go to table) before eight o'clock. We were sitting at table when the officer came into the room. Will your son be at home on Thursday evening?

THIRTY-SIXTH LESSON.

ON COMPOUND WORDS (*Ordsammensætning*).

The Danish language possesses an inexhaustible source of richness and variety in its capacity for forming compounds. The very facility, however, with which polysyllabic combinations may be created, exposes the language to the danger of being vitiated by the incorporation of numerous incongruous elements with its native structure. Modern writers of authority have shown themselves sensible of this danger, and, accordingly, we find that multiple compounds are being more and more rarely used among living Danish and Norwegian authors, although simple dual compounds are freely employed by the best writers.

As this verbal plasticity, which is a characteristic, common in different degrees to all languages of Northern and Teutonic origin, gives rise in Danish to combinations, which are often very puzzling, the English student should devote special attention to the manner in which the several parts of such compounds are brought together.

I. As a rule, the last member of a compound verbal group expresses the dominant idea of the whole, and on that assumption it always regulates the gender and number; as for example:—

 et Sövandspattedyr, a marine mammal, from *Sö*, sea, *Vand*, water,
  at patte, to suck, *Dyr*, animal, *Pattedyr*, mammal
 en Kirkeklokkedåb, a baptism, or naming of a church-bell
 et Sölvlommeur, a silver pocket-watch
 en Skolelæsebog, a book of extracts, used in schools, for reading
 en Dameskrædderinde, a ladies' tailor, or mantle-maker
 et Kongebarn, a royal child.

II. Compounds may be formed of words belonging to different parts of speech; as for example:—

 et Frimærke, a postage stamp, from *fri*, free, *Mærke*, mark
 (*en*) *Lillefinger*, the little finger
 en Storherre, a magnate, the grand seignior
 (*en*) *Langelinie*, a long line
 femårig, five-yeared
 brunhåret, brown-haired
 en Mellemvej, an alternative, middle-way
 indelukket, locked in
 tjænstdygtig, capable of doing service.

III. In some cases the meaning of the compound differs from that conveyed when the different parts of the combined group are separated, or transposed; as for example:—

 en Blækflaske, an ink-bottle   *en Flaske Blæk*, a bottle of ink
 en Frugtkurv, an apple-basket   *en Kurv Frugt*, a basket filled with fruit
 en Vandkande, a water-can   *en Kande Vand*, a can full of water.

IV. A few compound words require that both parts should agree in number; as for example:—

 en Bondegård, a peasant-steading, farm, pl. *Böndergårde*
 et Barnebarn, a grandchild, pl. *Börnebörn*, grandchildren.

V. Many verbs, which are composed of adverbs or prepositions followed by another verb, admit of being expressed in the separate words of which the combination has been formed; as for example:—

at ihjelslå or *at slå ihjel*, to kill
at igennembore or *at bore igennem*, to penetrate, bore through
at afhugge or *at hugge af*, to cut off
at indelukke or *at lukke inde*, to lock in.

VI. In many cases the meaning of a compound verb is entirely different from that conveyed by the separation of the combined parts; as for example:—

at afstå, to concede
at udelukke, to exclude
at oversætte, to translate
at underholde, to maintain
at stå af, to dismount
at lukke ud, to let out
at sætte over, to cross over (water, etc.)
at holde under, to keep under.

VII. In some cases an *s* (the genitive singular), *n*, or *ns* is inserted between the parts of the compound; as for example:—

en Gadedörsnögle, a street-door key
en Skibskaptain, a ship's captain
en Hjærtensven, a heartily loved friend.

DIALOGUES.

Hvorledes ere Vejene nu?	How are the roads now?
De ere overordentlig smudsige.	They are excessively dirty.
Hvorledes var den Egn, gennem hvilken De passerede?	What was the country like through which you passed?
Meget klippefuld og bjærgrig.	Very rocky and mountainous.
Er Byen smuk?	Is the town handsome?
Gaderne ere godt brolagte; den förste Gade er meget smuk og förer lige ned til Havnen.	The streets are well paved; the principal street is very fine, and leads directly to the harbour.
Så De Havnen?	Did you see the harbour?
Ja! den er meget rummelig og besöges af alle Nationers Skibe.	Yes, I did; it is very roomy, and is frequented by ships of all nations.
Hvorledes kan De være så vel bekendt med disse Ting efter kun to Dages Ophold?	How can you know so much of all these things after only two days' stay?

Hr. B. har fört mig omkring i Byen og vist mig Alt hvad der var værdt at se.

Har De modtaget en Pakke, jeg sendte Dem fra Lyon?

Dersom De ikke allerede har fået den, vil De efter al Sandsynlighed få den imorgen eller iovermorgen.

Jeg beder Dem at hilse alle vore Kære på det Venligste.

Mr. B. has taken me about the town, and shown me everything worthy of notice.

Have you received a parcel I sent you from Lyon?

If you have not already received it, you will, in all probability, have it to-morrow or the day after to-morrow.

I beg you will give my kind remembrances to all our friends.

READING
to translate into English.

PEN OG BLÆKHUS.—(Continued.)

IV.

"Hvor tåbeligt,[1] om Buen og Violinen vilde hovmode[2] sig over deres Gerning![3] og det gör dog så tidt[4] vi Mennesker, Digteren, Kunstneren,[5] Opfinderen[6] i Videnskaben,[7] Feltherren;[8] vi hovmode os — og Alle ere vi dog kun Instrumenterne, Vor Herre spiller på; ham alene Æren![9] vi have Intet at hovmode os over!"

Ja, det skrev Digteren ned, skrev det som en Parabel, og kaldte den "Mesteren og Instrumenterne."

"Der fik De Deres, Madam!" sagde Pennen til Blækhuset, da de To igen vare ene. "De hörte ham vel læse op, hvad jeg havde skrevet ned!"

"Ja, hvad jeg gav Dem at skrive!" sagde Blækhuset. "Det var jo et Hib[10] til Dem for Deres Hovmod![11] at De ikke engang kan forstå, at man gör Nar[12] af Dem! jeg gav Dem et Hib lige fra mit Indvendige! jeg må dog kende min egen Malice!"

"Blækholderske!"[13] sagde Pennen.

"Skrivepind!"[14] sagde Blækhuset.

[1] foolish
[2] to pride oneself
[3] action
[4] often
[5] artist
[6] discoverer
[7] science
[8] commander
[9] honour
[10] thrust
[11] arrogance
[12] fool
[13] ink-holder
[14] writing-pin

Og Enhver af dem havde Bevidstheden[1] om at de havde svaret godt, og det er en behagelig[2] Bevidsthed at vide at man har svaret godt, det kan man sove[3] på, og de sov på det; men Digteren sov ikke! Tankerne[4] væeldede[5] frem, som Tonerne fra Violinen, trillende[6] som Perler, brusende som Stormen gennem Skoven; han fornam[7] sit eget Hjærte deri, han fornam Glimtet[8] fra den evige[9] Mester.

Ham alene Æren![10]

H. C. ANDERSEN.

THIRTY-SIXTH EXERCISE.

We must buy ourselves a bottle of ink, our ink-bottle is empty. The water-can is full, but to-morrow you must bring us a can of well-water. Can you give me a stamp for a letter to England? I have only three stamps, but the tailoress (dressmaker), Hansen, will give you several. The old peasant-man has his grandchildren in the ship with him. How many (peasant) farms does the Count own? He owns several, but his largest farm lies on the road between Copenhagen and Elsinore.

NAMES OF VARIOUS FAMILIAR PLANTS, ETC.

en *Plante*, a plant	en *Korsblomst*, a milk-wort
en *Rod*, a root	en *Geranium*, a geranium
en *Saft*, a juice	en *Sværdlilje*, an iris
en *Plantesaft*, a sap	en *Safran*, a crocus
en *Stængel*, a stalk	en *Sneklokke*, a snow-drop
en *Blomst*, a flower	en *Pinselilje*, a narcissus
et *Blad*, a leaf	en *Påskelilje*, a yellow daffodil
et *Træ*, a tree	en *Solsikke*, a sun-flower
en *Trætop*, a tree-top	en *Fruesko*, a lady's slipper
et *Frö*, a seed	en *Marie-Hånd* } an orchis
en *Fröskal*, a husk of seed	en *Fandens Hånd* }
en *Rose*, a rose	en *Brændenælde*, a nettle
en *Lilje*, a lily	(en) *Hamp*, hemp
en *Tulipan*, a tulip	en *Ener, Brisk, Bruse,* a juniper
en *Hyacinth*, a hyazinth	(en) *Enebærbrænderin*, gin
(en) *Reseda*, mignonette	en *Fyr,* (*Furu,* Norw.), a firtree

[1] assurance   [3] to sleep   [5] to pour   [7] to perceive   [9] eternal
[2] agreeable   [4] thought   [6] roll gently   [8] gleam   [10] honour.

(155)

en *Gran*, a pine
en *Sølvgran*, a white pine
et *Lærketræ*, a larch
et *Lindetræ*, a lime-tree
en *Birk*, a birch-tree
en *Dværgbirk* } a dwarf-
en *Fældrupe* (Norw.) } birch
en *Nøver*, a birch-bark
en *Ask* } an ash
et *Esketræ* }
en *Ol*, an alder
en *Eg* } an oak
et *Egetræ* }
en *Bøg* } a beech
en *Bøk* (Norw.) }
en *Elm* } an elm
et *Elmetræ* }
en *Vidje* }
en *Pil* } a willow
et *Piletræ* }

en *Asp* } an aspen
et *Æspetræ* }
en *Poppel*, a poplar
en *Hassel*, a hazel-bush
et *Morbærtræ*, a mulberry-tree
et *Figentræ*, a fig-tree
(en) *Humle*, hops
en *Kartoffel*, a potato
(en) *Ærter*, pl., peas
(en) *Bønner*, pl., beans
(en) *Spinat*, spinach
en *Rødbede*, a beet-root
en *Gulerod*, a carrot
en *Turnip*, a turnip
(en) *Syre* } sorrel
(en) *Bærgsyre* (Norw.) }
(en) *Endivie*, endive
(en) *Salat*, lettuce
en *Raddike*, a radish.

THIRTY-SEVENTH LESSON.

SYNTAX.

ON THE INDEFINITE ARTICLE (*det ubestemte Kendeord*).

The indefinite article *en, et* is simply the numeral "one" (*en, et*) spoken without accentuation of the *e*. The Old Northern had no indefinite article.

The indefinite article in Dano-Norwegian must agree with the noun which it precedes, as: *en Dreng, et Hus; en* being the form of the common gender to which *Dreng* belongs, and *et* the form of the neuter gender to which *Hus* belongs.

This article is sometimes used in the sense of "nearly," "almost," "about," carrying with it an idea of diminution, or indefiniteness; as for example:—

han bliver her en tre, fire Uger, he will stay here about three or four weeks.
min Ven gav mig en fem og tyve, tredive Böger, my friend gave me some twenty-five or thirty books.

Certain adjectives, as *sådan*, such, may be placed after as well as before the indefinite article, while *slig* and *mangen* must always be made to precede the article; as for example :—

> *sådan en Skole*, or *en sådan Skole*, such a school.
> *sådant et Skrin*, or *et sådant Skrin*, such a casket.
> *mangen en Gang*, many a time.
> *mangt et År*, many a year.
> *slig en Kone*, such a woman.
> *sligt et Sogn*, such a parish.

When an adjective is preceded by the adverbs *så*, *hvor*, *altfor*, or *for*, the indefinite article may, as in English, stand between the adjective and the noun; as for example :—

> *så smukt et Hus*, so fine a house.
> *hvor god en Ven!* how good a friend!
> *altfor sildig en Undskyldning*, too late an excuse.

The indefinite article must be repeated after *og*, and, when two or more nouns follow each other; as for example :—

> *en Pige og en Dreng*, a girl and a boy.

This repetition is not necessary with *eller*, or, unless the last-named word is of a different gender from those preceding it; as for example :—

> *en Pige, Kone eller Enke*, a girl, wife, or widow.
> *en Mand eller et Barn*, a man or a child.

In proverbs, axioms, or other tersely put sentences, the indefinite article may be dropped altogether when the noun is preceded by an adjective; as for example :—

> *Brændt Barn skyer Ild*, a burnt child dreads the fire.

The indefinite article is not used in Danish in characterising a profession, distinctive condition or designation; as for example :—

> *er han Kristen eller Jöde?* is he a Christian or a Jew?
> *Herr Madsen er Protestant, men hans Kone er Katholik*, Mr. Madsen is a Protestant, but his wife is a Catholic.
> *hvad er den Mands Sönner?* what are that man's sons?

den ældste er Jurist, den næste Billedhugger og den yngste Fabrikant,
the eldest is a lawyer, the next a sculptor, and the youngest a manufacturer.
min Tjæners Fader er Lysestöber, men hans Broder er Konditor, my servant's father is a chandler, but his brother is a confectioner.
er Deres Onkel Pebersvend? is your uncle a batchelor?
nej, han er Enkemand, no, he is a widower.

at *skamme sig*, to be ashamed
at *synes om*, to like
at *være ræd* (Norw.), to be afraid
at *bebo*, to inhabit
at *længes efter*, to long for
at *snige*, to creep
at *due*, to be worth, avail
det duer ikke, that will not do
at *skye*, to shun
at *være* (or at *göre sig*) *tilfreds*, to be contented
varsom, cautious
ussel (pl. *usle*), miserable, poor

en *Indfödt*, a native
en *Beboer*, an inhabitant
en *Bolig*, a dwelling
en *Gård*, a yard, court, farm
en *Klo*, pl. *Klöer*, claws, feet
et *Garn*, a thread, net
(en) *Fremtid*, time to come, future
et *Ordsprog*, a proverb
et *Hul* (pl. *Huller*), a hole
en *Farver*, a dyer
en *Murmester*, a master mason
en *Mur*, a wall

READING

to translate into English.

BARNET I GRAVEN.

I.

Der var Sorg[1] i Huset, der var Sorg i Hjærterne, det yngste Barn, en firårs Dreng, den eneste Sön, Forældrenes Glæde[2] og Fremtids Håb,[3] var död; to ældre Döttre havde de vel, den ældste skulde netop i dette År konfirmeres,[4] velsignede,[5] gode Piger begge To, men det mistede[6] Barn er altid det kæreste, og dette var den yngste og en Sön. Det var en tung Prövelse.[7] Söstrene sörgede som unge Hjærter sörge, grebne[8] især[9] ved Forældrenes Smerte, Faderen var nedböjet,[10] men Moderen overvældet[11] af Sorg. Nat og Dag havde hun gået om det syge Barn, plejet[12] det, löftet[13] og

[1] sorrow
[2] joy
[3] hope
[4] to confirm
[5] blessed
[6] lost
[7] heavy trial
[8] to seize
[9] especially
[10] to bow down
[11] to overpower
[12] to tend, nurse
[13] to lift

båret[1] det; det var en Del[2] af hende selv havde hun fölt og fornummet,[3] hun kunde ikke tænke sig at det var dödt, at det skulde lægges i Kiste[4] og gemmes[5] i Graven: Gud kunde ikke tage dette Barn fra hende, mente[6] hun, og da det dog skete[7] og var en Vished,[8] sagde hun i sin syge Smerte:

"Gud har ikke vidst det! han har hjærtelöse[9] Tjænere her på Jorden, de handle som de lyste,[10] de höre ikke en Moders Bönner."[11]

Hun slap[12] i sin Smerte Vor Herre, og da kom mörke Tanker,[13] Dödens Tanker, den evige Död,[14] at Mennesket blev Jord[15] i Jorden, og da Alt var forbi.[16] Ved sådan Tanke havde hun Intet at klamre[17] sig til, men sank i Fortvivlelsens[18] bundlöse[19] Intet.

I de tungeste[20] Timer kunde hun ikke græde mer; hun tænkte ikke på de unge Döttre hun havde, Mandens Tårer[21] faldt på hendes Pande,[22] hun så ikke op til ham; hendes Tanker vare hos det döde Barn, al hendes Liv og Leven[23] åndede[24] i at tilbagekalde sig hvert Minde[25] om Barnet, hvert af dets uskyldige[26] Barneord.

THIRTY-SEVENTH EXERCISE.

I.

I have never seen such a lovely rose! Such a flower is not to be had in every garden. Many a time have I wished myself in a house of my own. A clergyman should be ashamed of having such a parish; however good a house he may own, he ought not to rest till every peasant has something better than a miserable hole to

[1] to carry
[2] part
[3] to perceive
[4] coffin
[5] to hide
[6] to think
[7] to happen
[8] certainty
[9] heartless
[10] to like, list
[11] prayer
[12] to lose hold of
[13] thought
[14] everlasting death
[15] earth
[16] away, gone by
[17] to cling to
[18] despair
[19] bottomless
[20] heavy
[21] tear
[22] forehead
[23] living
[24] to breathe
[25] recollection
[26] innocent

live in (for his dwelling). What sort of animal is that? It may be a reindeer. I have never seen such an animal. Can you give me a dozen or a score of apples? I have not an apple in my shop, but if you would like a pear you may have it; here is one. I saw a child, a peasant woman, a soldier, a sailor, and a custom-house officer in the church. Is she a married woman or a widow? She is a widow, and one of her brothers is a widower. He will never be a good huntsman who fears every branch in the wood. A green Christmas makes a fat church-yard. A cat likes fish, but it will not wet its feet to get it. An honest man is soon known. It is a clever fish that can wriggle itself out of every net.

II.

Is he a tailor or a shoemaker? He is neither the one nor the other; he is a dyer, and the brother is a mason. The servant girl gave the beggar thirty or forty potatoes, a couple of onions, and ten or twelve plums. I should not like to have such a girl in my service. It is many a year since I have had such a dishonest servant in my house. I have many a time distrusted her, and in future I shall be more cautious, as the proverb says, "A burnt child dreads the fire." She says it was only once or twice she did anything of the kind, but such an excuse will not avail. How long will your uncle, the French merchant, stay in Copenhagen? Perhaps about four or five weeks. My brother is a Catholic, but my brother-in-law is a Jew. What a harsh parent that man has been to his young, motherless children! And what charming little girls he has! I have told him many a time that he ought to feel ashamed of letting his family live in such a wretched house.

THIRTY-EIGHTH LESSON.

ON THE DEFINITE ARTICLE (*det bestemte Kendeord*).

I. The substantive-article consists of the particles *en, et,* or *n, t,* pl. *ne, ene.*

As has already been shown, the modern Scandinavian tongues have retained the ancient Northern form of the definite article which admits of its amalgamation with the noun as a terminal appendage. It would seem that this form of the article originally represented the demonstrative pronoun "that," *hin, hint, hine* (*hinn, hin, hitt,* pl. *hinir, hinar, hin,* in Icelandic), which in accordance with the construction of the Northern languages followed the noun, and in process of time became amalgamated with it, losing the *h* for the sake of euphony, until the original Danish *Mand hin,* that man, passed into the modern *Manden,* the man.

Further changes have sprung up in regard to the mode of applying this terminal form of the article, which are similarly due to considerations of sound.

A. In cases where the noun ends in *e,* the substantive-article is simply indicated by the addition of *n* or *t*; as for example: *en Hede,* a heat, *Heden,* the heat; *et Æble,* an apple, *Æblet,* the apple.

B. Nouns whose plural ends in *e, r,* or *er,* take *ne* to mark the plural termination of the incorporated article; as for example: *Æbler,* apples, *Æblerne,* the apples.

C. Nouns which remain unchanged in the plural take *ene* to mark the addition of the substantive-article; as for example: *Mus,* mice, *Musene,* the mice.

D. The addition of the substantive-article to nouns ending in *el* or *en* may have the effect of eliminating the *e* which precedes the *l* or *n*; as for example:—

en Djævel, a devil, may be rendered *Djævelen* or *Djævlen*
et Lagen, a sheet　　　„　　„　*Lagenet* or *Lagnet.*

In the plural of such words the substantive-article is always appended to the abbreviated form, as :—

Djæv_lene, the devils   *Lag_nerne*, the sheets.

II. The adjective-article, *den, det*, pl. *de*.

This article is used in an independent form, where the noun is preceded by an adjective; as for example :—

den store Hval, the big whale
det runde Hjul, the round wheel
de stolte Hjorte, the proud stags.

According to some grammarians, this article may likewise be regarded as representing a demonstrative pronoun, differing from the substantive-article in having retained its independence as a distinct word, although, like the latter, it has lost the accentuated tone, which still characterises the Danish demonstrative *dén, dét, dé*.

In ordinary conversation *den, det, de* are often used instead of the affixes *en, et, ene*, where the noun is not qualified by an adjective; and in these cases they have the same sense as the English definite article, as for example :—

lad dog de Bøger ligge i Fred, do let the books rest in peace!
den Regn får ingen Ende, there is no end to the rain.
altid finder jeg det Bord stående ved Døren, I always find the table standing by the door.

at trænge til, to require	*et Skuespil*,* a play
at stå i Færd med, to be on the point	*et Lystspil*,* a comedy
	et Sørgespil,* a tragedy
at miste, to lose	*en Farce*, a farce
at spille, to play, act	*en Skueplads*, the stage
at forestille, to represent, act	*en Scene*, a scene, a stage
at stå til Tjæneste, to be at one's service	*en Rolle*, a part
	en Forfatter, an author
fortræffelig, admirable	*en Kummer, en Sorg*, a sorrow
hurtig, fast, quick	*en Bagtalelse*, a scandal, slander
lystig, merry, gay	*et Fingerbøl*,* a thimble
vittig, witty	*et Landsted*, a country-house
en Fjæder, a feather, spring	*en Hylde*, a shelf
et Klæde, a cloth	*en Æske*, a box, case
et Tørklæde, a handkerchief	*et Skab*, a cupboard
et Tøj, a stuff	*en Alen*, an ell, yard

* Here, as elsewhere in the present work, the asterisk indicates that the final consonant is doubled.

READING

to translate into English.

BARNET I GRAVEN.—(*Continued.*)

II.

Det var som om hun ikke kendte til Sövnen[1] mer, og alene den vilde være hendes bedste Ven, styrke[2] Legemet,[3] kalde Ro[4] i Sjælen; de fik hende til at lægge sig i Sengen, hun lå også stille som en Sovende.[5] En Nat, Manden lyttede[6] efter hendes Åndedrag[7] og troede for vist,[8] at hun fandt Hvile[9] og Lettelse,[10] han foldede[11] derfor sine Hænder, bad[12] og sov snart sundt og fast, mærkede ikke, at hun rejste sig,[13] kastede sine Klæder om sig og gik så stille ud af Huset, for at komme derhen hvor hendes Tanker Nat og Dag søgte, til Graven, der gemte hendes Barn. Hun gik gennem Husets Have, ud på Marken, hvor Stien[14] förte uden om Byen hen til Kirkegården; Ingen så hende, hun så Ingen.

Det var dejligt stjærneklart,[15] Luften[16] endnu så mild, det var först i September. Hun kom ind på Kirkegården, hen til den lille Grav, den var som en eneste stor Bouquet af Blomster, de duftede,[17] hun satte sig ned, böjede[18] sit Hoved imod Graven, som skulde hun gennem det tætte[19] Jordlag[20] kunne se sin lille Dreng, hvis Smil[21] hun så levende huskede;[22] det kærlige Udtryk[23] i Öjnene, selv på Sygelejet,[24] var jo aldrig til at glemme,[25] hvor talende havde der hans Blik været, når hun tog hans fine[26] Hånd, den han ikke selv mægtede[27] at löfte.[28]. Som hun havde siddet ved hans Seng sad hun nu ved hans Grav, men her havde Tårerne frit Löb,[29] de faldt på Graven.

[1] sleep
[2] to strengthen
[3] body
[4] quiet
[5] sleeper
[6] to listen
[7] drawing of breath
[8] for certain
[9] rest
[10] ease
[11] to fold
[12] to pray
[13] to get up
[14] path
[15] star-light
[16] air
[17] to give forth perfume
[18] to bend
[19] close, dense
[20] layer of earth
[21] smile
[22] to remember
[23] expression
[24] sick-bed
[25] to forget
[26] delicate
[27] to have power
[28] to lift
[29] course, run.

THIRTY-EIGHTH EXERCISE.

I.

When will the watch be ready? The watch requires to be cleaned; you must let it stay at the watchmaker's till the end of the week. Is the spring broken? No, it is not broken. Could you lend me a watch? I will lend you one. You are quite welcome to the watch which lies on the table. Does it go well? The French watch on the shelf in the cupboard goes very well, but the English watch in the case goes a little too fast. What is the price of the cloth? It costs 15 Kroner per ell. Where are the silk goods, the woollen stockings, the dress, the cloth, and the handkerchiefs? They are all here. Do you see the whale in the water? Is there really a whale so near the land? I have seen a whale in the ocean, but I did not think I should see the animal so close to the coast in this country. The girl has run away with the sheets of the bed. The sheets are on the bench in the garden. The cab standing at the door has lost one of its wheels.

II.

What piece do they give to-night at the theatre? The piece which is given to-night is "The School for Scandal," by Sheridan, the English writer. Is it a comedy or a tragedy? It is a very witty comedy in three acts. The last time we were at the theatre they gave a most wretched tragedy, and after that we saw a new farce in one act, translated from the French. What was the name of the farce? "The Widower's Trouble." The actress played the part of the widower's cousin admirably, but I preferred the actor who played the count's part in the first scene, which is laid in the interior of a grand English country-house, belonging to some rich nobleman.

THIRTY-NINTH LESSON.

ON THE ARTICLES (= Kendeord).

I. As in English, the definite article may be entirely dispensed with in Danish where the noun has a general sense; as for example:—

Rug er dyrere end Byg, rye is dearer than barley.
Kærlighed er Kristendommens Hoveddyd, love is the sovereign virtue of Christianity.

No article is required before a title or other distinctive appellation when this is followed by a personal noun; as for example:—

Kejser Vilhelm, the emperor William
Justitsråd Svendsen, the councillor Svendsen
Skrædder Hansen, the tailor Hansen.

In speaking of a special year, the article may be omitted, as also where definite periods of time, or names of places are expressed; as for example:—

År 1660 indførtes Enevoldsregeringen i Danmark, in the year 1660 absolute autocracy was introduced in Denmark.
sidste Gang jeg så Dem, the last time I saw you.
igår vare vi på Esromsø, we were on Esrom lake yesterday.

II. The definite article is used in Danish, contrary to English custom, where the noun expresses a general typical character or idea, or where it represents a species; as for example:—

Mennesket er dødeligt, man is mortal
Skæbnen var hende imod, fate was against her.

The definite article-affixes, *en*, *et*, pl. *ne*, *ene*, cannot be incorporated with the names of persons or places, which remain unaffected by case or by juxtaposition with other parts of speech, excepting when the grammatical construction requires that they should be put in the genitive case, when, as in English, they take the termination *s* or *es*; as for example:—

Jeg så Hansen, men Hansens Kone var ikke i Köbenhavn, I saw Hansen, but Hansen's wife was not in Copenhagen

Köbenhavn er Danmarks Hovedstad og Landets bedste Havneplads, Copenhagen is Denmark's capital, and the best haven in the kingdom.

III. Such names of countries, as *Tyrki, Tartari,* and others ending in *i,* take the final article-affix *et,* making *Tyrkiet, Tartariet,* on the ground that these have been derived from the names of the people, and must be regarded as the elliptical form of *Tyrkernes Land,* the land of the Turks; *Tartarernes Land,* the land of the Tartars.

It must be observed, however, that the termination *en,* which occurs in some names of countries, as for example in *Spanien* and *Italien,* is not the substantive-article incorporated with a verbal root, but an integral and inseparable part of the name itself.

IV. With some adjectives, as *hel,* whole, *alt,* all, the article-affix *en, et,* may be added to the noun, in which case the adjective is not preceded by the article; as for example:—

<blockquote>

hele Folket, the whole people
alt Kornet, all the corn.

</blockquote>

In the former case, the adjective article may also be used, as *det hele Folk,* but in the latter no such transposition can be made; *det alt Korn* being as inadmissible as "the all corn" would be in English.

at rase, to rage	*en Krig,* a war
at gå forbi, to pass by	*en Pligt,* a duty
at ödelægge, to lay waste	*et Kors,* a cross
öde, desolate	*en Fremgang,* an advance
at lide, to suffer	*en Umage,* a trouble, pains
at brænde af, to burn off	*en Födsel,* a birth
at föje sig, to submit	*en Födselsdag,* a birthday
at trække, to drag, pull	*en Træk,** a current of air
det trækker, there is a draught	(*et*) *Græs,** grass
grædselig, gruelig, horrible	*et Foder,* a fodder
umulig, impossible	(*et*) *Kreatur,* cattle.

READING

to translate into English.

BARNET I GRAVEN.—(*Continued.*)

III.

"Du vil ned til dit Barn!" sagde en Stemme tæt ved,[1] den lød[2] så klar, så dyb, den klang[3] ind i hendes Hjærte, hun så op, og der stod hos hende en Mand, hyllet[4] i en stor Sörgekappe[5] med Hætte[6] ned om Hovedet,[7] men hun så ind under den i hans Ansigt,[8] det var strængt, men dog så tillidsvækkende,[9] hans Öjne strålede[10] som var han i Ungdoms[11] År.

"Ned til mit Barn!" gentog[12] hun, og der lå en Fortvivlelsens[13] Bön[14] deri.

"Tör[15] Du fölge mig?" spurgte Skikkelsen. "Jeg er Döden!"

Og hun nikkede bekræftende;[16] da var det med Et, som om alle Stjærner ovenover lyste med Fuldmånens Glans,[17] hun så den brogede Farvepragt[18] i Blomsterne på Graven, Jorddækket[19] her gav blödt[20] og sagte[21] efter, som et svævende Klæde, hun sank, og Skikkelsen bredte[22] sin sorte Kappe om hende, det blev Nat, Dödens Nat, hun sank dybere end Gravspaden[23] trænger ned,[24] Kirkegården lå som et Tag[25] over hendes Hoved . . . .

Hun stod i en mægtig Hal,[26] der bredte sig stor og venlig; det var Skumring[27] rundt om, men foran hende, og i samme Nu,[28] tæt op til sit Hjærte, holdt hun sit Barn, det tilsmilede

[1] near by	[11] youth	[20] soft
[2] to sound	[12] to repeat	[21] gently
[3] to resound	[13] despair	[22] the figure spread
[4] wrapped	[14] prayer	[23] spade
[5] mourning cloak	[15] to dare	[24] to penetrate
[6] hood	[16] to nod affirmatively	[25] roof
[7] head	[17] brightness	[26] vast hall
[8] face	[18] variegated splendour of colour	[27] dusk
[9] to inspire confidence		[28] moment
[10] beam	[19] cover	

hende i en Skönhed,¹ större end nogensinde för;² hun udstödte³ et Skrig, dog hörligt⁴ blev det ikke, ti tæt ved, og derpå igen langt borte og atter⁵ nær, löd en svulmende,⁶ dejlig Musik, aldrig för havde så saligstemmende⁷ Toner⁸ nået⁹ til hendes Öre!

THIRTY-NINTH EXERCISE.

I.

Queen Victoria was in Germany a couple of years ago with her daughter, the Princess Beatrice. In the year 1870 the great war between the Germans and the French broke out, and the year afterwards King William of Prussia became emperor of Germany. Where there is war there is always trouble, sorrow, and suffering. Death passes no man by. What fate wills, man must submit to. A man has to perform many a painful duty. In these days a destructive war is raging in Turkey, between the Russians and Turks. When will there be an end to this horrible war? Virtue does not make its home in every house. I spoke yesterday to Count Moltke, who was travelling last year in Italy and Spain. but he did not go so far as Turkey.

II.

The whole country was in an uproar. The whole town is talking of Hansen's misfortune. All the grass in the fields has been burnt up by the sun, and will no longer serve as food for the cattle. Why do you not take the trouble to write better? I assure you that I take great pains. If you would take greater pains you would speak better English, but without taking trouble it is impossible to make any progress. Is your son a

¹ beauty
² ever before
³ uttered
⁴ audible
⁵ again
⁶ to swell
⁷ bliss-inspiring
⁸ tone
⁹ to reach.

captain? He is still a lieutenant, but after his next voyage he hopes to become a commander or first-lieutenant. Fate has always been against my friend, Holtman. Fortune will perhaps soon prove more friendly to him; at all events he must submit to his destiny whatever it may be.

FORTIETH LESSON.

ON NOUNS (= Navneord).

In the early form of Dano-Norwegian three distinct genders (male, female, and neuter) were recognised for nouns, and three different terminations were consequently used for the article, adjective, and pronoun, in order to bring the latter into accord with the noun to which each referred. Traces of this earlier form may still be met with in certain country dialects, although in the cultivated language of the Danes and Norwegians two genders only are now accepted: the *Fælleskön*, common gender, including words of male and female gender, and the *Intetkön*, neuter.

It is to be observed that some nouns have in the process of time undergone a change of gender, which in earlier ages was usually from the neuter to the common gender, although in more recent times the change has been in the opposite direction, as seen in the case of *et Sted*, a place, which was originally *en Sted*, and *et Bogstav*, a letter, which was *en Bogstav*. This explains why the Danes say *ingensteds*, nowhere, instead of *intetsteds*, and *efter Bogstaven*, according to the letter, instead of *efter Bogstavet*, for here the older form has lingered on in these familiar expressions, after the word itself has changed its gender. Some words are still passing through this period of change, as for example: *Slags*, kind, which good writers give indifferently *en Slags* and *et Slags*. The same indefiniteness exists in regard to *Helbred*, health; *Minut*, minute; *Punkt*, point, etc.

Except in the genitive, to which reference will be made in a subsequent lesson, the noun in modern Dano-Norwegian is not affected by case, remaining the same in the nominative, dative, objective, and vocative.

I. The noun (or pronoun, etc., representing it), when constituting the nominative (*Grundordet*), or subject, in the sentence, must always *precede the verb in a simple sentence, or in the primary clause of a compound sentence;* as for example: *Barnet sover længe,* the child sleeps long; *hvis Barnet sover, bliver jeg her,* if the child is sleeping, I will stay here.

II. The noun (or pronoun, etc., representing it), which constitutes the subject, *must follow the verb in the secondary part of the compound sentence;* as for example: *ifald min Ven ikke er hjemme, bliver jeg ikke længe borte,* in case my friend should not be at home, I shall not remain long away.

In conditional propositions, in the imperative, or in emphatic assertions, more especially when certain adverbs, as *aldrig, ofte, derefter,* are used, the nominative, or subject, must follow the verb; as for example:—

> *kunde Manden håbe at få en smuk Foræring, vilde han sikkert ikke glemme at komme tilbage,* if the man could hope to get a handsome present, he would certainly not forget to come back.
> *skynd Dem!* make haste!
> *aldrig forglemmer Kongen at vise sin Taknemlighed,* never will the king forget to show his gratitude.
> *ofte havde Dronningen i Sinde at modtage hende, omendskönt Konen ikke fortjænte en sådan Nåde,* again and again did the queen think of sending for her, although the woman did not deserve such a favour.

In questions of any kind, the nominative noun, or subject, follows the verb; as for example:—

> *ser De det Antal Mennesker?* do you see all those people?
> *husker han ikke Navnet?* does he not remember the name?

III. The dative (*middelbart Genstandsord*), of a noun, or its representative pronoun, may be expressed, either by its being made to follow the verb and precede the object; as for example: *jeg vil give Manden Bogen*, I will give the man the book ; or by the aid of a preposition, as for example : *jeg har i Sinde at give denne Bog til min Broder*, I intend to give this book to my brother.

As in English, nouns of time, space, quantity, value, etc., may be used in Danish in an objective or accusative sense, without any governing preposition ; as for example :—

han bliver her fjorten Dage, he will stay here a fortnight.
hun har rejst mange Mil, she has travelled many miles.
mit Barn er tre År gammelt, my child is three years old.
det vejer ti Lod, that weighs ten ounces.
jeg bruger min Paraply mange Gange om Sommeren, I use my umbrella many times in the summer.
hun har köbt fem Alen fransk Knipling, she has bought five ells of French lace.
det Rendyrskind koster fem og fyrretyve Kroner, that reindeer-skin costs forty-five crowns.

READING

to translate into English.

BARNET I GRAVEN.—(*Continued.*)

IV.

"Min söde Moder! min egen[1] Moder!" hörte hun sit Barn sige. Det var den kendte,[2] elskede Röst ;[3] og Kys[4] fulgte på Kys i uendelig Lyksalighed ;[5] og Barnet pegede[6] hen på det mörke Forhæng.[7]

"Så dejligt er der ikke oppe på Jorden ! ser Du, Moder! ser Du dem Allesammen ![8] det er Lyksalighed ! "

Men Moderen så Intet, dér hvor Barnet pegede, Intet, uden den sorte Nat ; hun så med jordiske Öjne, så ikke således som Barnet, det Gud[9] havde kaldt til sig, hun hörte Klangen,[10] Tonerne, men hun fornam[11] ikke Ordet,[12] det hun havde at tro.[13]

[1] own
[2] to know
[3] voice
[4] kiss
[5] bliss
[6] to point
[7] curtain
[8] all of them
[9] God
[10] sound
[11] to perceive, notice
[12] word
[13] to believe

"Nu kan jeg flyve,¹ Moder!" sagde Barnet, "flyve med alle de andre glade Börn lige derind ² til Gud! jeg vil det så gerne, men når Du græder, som Du nu græder, kan jeg ikke komme fra Dig, og jeg vilde så gerne! må jeg dog ikke nok! Du kommer jo derind til mig om ganske lidt,³ söde Moder!"

"O bliv, o bliv!" sagde hun, "kun et Öjeblik endnu! en eneste Gang endnu må jeg se på Dig, kysse Dig, holde Dig fast i mine Arme!"

Og hun kyssede og holdt fast. Da löd ⁴ hendes Navn ⁵ deroven fra; så klagende ⁶ kom disse Toner; hvad var det dog?

"Hörer Du!" sagde Barnet, "det er Fader, som kalder på Dig!"

Og atter, efter få Sekunder, löd dybe Suk,⁷ som fra Börn der græde.

"Det er mine Söstre!" sagde Barnet, "Moder, Du har jo ⁸ ikke glemt⁹ dem!"

FORTIETH EXERCISE.

I.

If it should be fine this evening I will go into the country. During the last three days the wind has been in all quarters, in the east, west, north, and south; but now it is blowing so strongly from the west that we are certain to have rain. If it should blow too hard I shall stay at home. If you could take the trouble to come again at seven o'clock you would certainly find the doctor. The children read to their mother every day, and never will they forget these happy times. The sculptor has been several years in Italy, but now he intends to come back to his own country. Why are you in such a hurry? Do you happen to be going to the theatre this evening? I am not going this evening

¹ to fly
² right in
³ in a little while
⁴ sounded
⁵ name
⁶ plaintively
⁷ sigh
⁸ surely
⁹ to forget.

because I must be in the office by nine o'clock. What shall I bring you from Paris? Whatever you bring me I shall accept with gratitude. I shall give her a China dinner-service as a present for her birthday, in case she happens to be in town at the time. How is she? Very ill, and she will never be better.

II.

Our garden is 250 feet long; how long is yours? This tree is 25 feet high. How many years is he to remain in England? They say he will remain about a couple of years longer. Does he often give his sister money? He hardly ever gives his sister anything; but he makes his brothers nice presents, notwithstanding that he seldom gives them money. He has travelled through many great countries, but yet he likes his own little native land the best. Do you remember how many instruments we heard at the concert? Was it 14 or 15? I cannot tell you so exactly what the number was, perhaps about 14 or 16.

FORTY-FIRST LESSON.

ON NOUNS (= Navneord).

Continued.

The genitive (*Ejeordet*) is the only case of the noun which is still marked in Danish by a change in the word; and, as in English, it may be expressed by the addition of *s* or *es*, or by the use of a preposition.

I. It may be accepted as an invariable rule that the genitive always precedes the word governing it; as for example:—

for Guds Skyld, for God's sake.

II. The genitive termination may be wholly dispensed with where the sense of quantity is conveyed by the noun governing the word; as for example:—

en *Mængde Mennesker*, a number (of) men.
en *Tønde Øl*, a ton (of) ale.

A similar ellipsis occurs in regard to the names of places; as for example:—

Odense By, the town (of) Odense.

Where the designation of a person or thing is derived from the name of a place, no such elliptical form is used, and the name is made to assume the form of an adjective, terminating in *er* for both genders and numbers; as for example:—

en *Hamborger Købmand*, a merchant of Hamburgh.
et *Londoner Hus*, a London-house.
to *Pariser Damer*, two ladies of Paris.

Where several words stand in apposition, it is only the last, as in English, which takes the genitive termination; as for example:—

den *forrige Kejser af Frankrig, Napoleon Bonapartes Grav var engang paa St. Helena*, the former emperor of France, Napoleon Buonaparte's grave was once at St. Helena.

III. The prepositions *af, til, på, i*, may all replace the genitive, and their respective modes of application constitute a very important element in the construction of good Danish. *Af* and *til* may often replace each other without detriment to style or sense; but the correct use of these prepositions, as well as of *på* and *i*, demands a careful attention to the conditions of the subjects; thus for instance we may find indifferently:—

Salomo, Davids Søn
Salomo, Søn af David } Solomon, the son of David.
Salomo, Søn til David

It will be observed, however, that in the following examples, the prepositions could not be transposed with equal accuracy:—

Husets Dör (*Dören til Huset*), the house-door
Husets Værelser (*Værelserne i Huset*), the rooms of the house
Dörens Haspe (*Haspen på Dören*), the door-latch.

IV. When a comparison is instituted between two objects, the word governing the genitive need not be repeated; as for example:—

Diamantens Værdi er større end Rubinens, the value of the diamond is higher than that of the ruby.
Dolkens Hæfte er smukkere end Sværdets, the handle of the dagger is handsomer than that of the sword.

V. In proper names the *es* of the genitive is now very often replaced by *'s ;* as for example: *Lars's Hest*, Lars's horse; *Judas's Pung*, Judas's purse. Some writers, however, still adhere to the older form, and write: *Larses, Judases*.

In words ending in *st, sk, sp ; es* is often used instead of *s*, for the sake of euphony; as for example: —

en Fiskes Öjne, instead of *en Fisks Öjne*, the eyes of a fish
en Bispes Tale ,, *en Bisps Tale*, a bishop's address.

The genitive of nouns, to which the substantive-article has been affixed, is formed both in the singular and plural by the addition of *s;* as for example: *Markens Grænse*, the boundary of the field; *Börnenes Legetöj*, the children's playthings.

In Old Northern the preposition *til* governed the genitive, and in conformity with this requirement, the noun following *til* continues in modern Dano-Norwegian to take *s*, wherever a general, and not a special meaning is conveyed; as for example: *at være til Sinds*, to have a mind; *at gå til Sengs*, to go to bed. When a special object is referred to, the genitive is not used; as for example: *lad Barnet gå hen til Sengen*, let the child go to the bed.

VI. Traces of the existence in Old Northern of different forms of declension for nouns, and various terminations of cases still linger in modern Dano-Norwegian, in such expressions as: *at hugge ned for Fode*, to cut down before one's feet;

ad Åre, up in years; *hvad er der på Færde?* what is the matter? *al Landsens Ulykke*, the misery of the whole country; *på Havsens Bund*, at the bottom of the sea; *af Hjærtens Lyst*, with heart-felt pleasure, etc. The termination of the three last examples is a survival of the Old Northern genitive of the neuter article *hins*.

READING

to translate into English.

BARNET I GRAVEN.—(Concluded.)

V.

Og hun huskede[1] de Tilbageblevne,[2] en Angst betog[3] hende, hun så frem for sig og altid svævede[4] Skikkelser[5] forbi, hun trode at kende Nogle, de svævede gennem Dødens Hal, hen mod det mörke Forhæng, og dér forsvandt[6] de.

"Moder, nu ringer Himmeriges[7] Klokker!" sagde Barnet. "Moder, nu står Solen op!"[8]

Og der strömmede[9] et overvældende[10] Lys mod hende; — Barnet var borte, og hun löftedes[11] — det blev koldt rundt om hende, hun hævede[12] sit Hoved og så, at hun lå på Kirkegården på sit Barns Grav; men Gud var i Drömmen[13] bleven en Stötte[14] for hendes Fod, et Lys for hendes Forstand,[15] hun böjede sine Knæ og bad:

"Tilgiv[16] mig, Herre min Gud! at jeg vilde holde en evig Sjæl[17] fra sin Flugt,[18] og at jeg kunde glemme mine Pligter mod de Levende, Du her gav mig!" Og ved disse Ord var det som om hendes Hjærte fandt Lettelse![19] Da bröd Solen frem,[20] en lille Fugl sang over hendes Hoved, og Kirkeklokkerne ringede til Morgensang. Der blev så helligt[21] rundt om, helligt som i hendes Hjærte!

[1] to remember
[2] left behind
[3] a fear seized
[4] float
[5] form
[6] to disappear
[7] kingdom of heaven
[8] to rise
[9] to stream
[10] to overpower
[11] to lift
[12] to lift, raise
[13] dream
[14] support
[15] sense
[16] to forgive
[17] soul
[18] flight
[19] relief
[20] to burst forth
[21] holy

hun kendte sin Gud, hun kendte sine Pligter, og i Længsel¹ skyndte² hun sig til Hjemmet. Hun böjede sig over Manden, hendes varme, inderlige³ Kys vækkede⁴ ham, og hun var stærk og mild som Hustruen kan være det, fra hende kom Fortröstningens Væld.⁵

"Guds Vilje⁶ er altid den bedste!"

Og Manden spurgte hende: "Hvorfra fik Du med Et denne Kraft,⁷ dette tröstende Sind?"⁸

Og hun kyssede ham og kyssede sine Börn:

"Jeg fik det fra Gud ved Barnet i Graven!"

H. C. ANDERSEN.

FORTY-FIRST EXERCISE.

I.

Is this boy your friend's son? Have you the book belonging to my brother's friend? No, I have not. Have you a bottle of mine in the carriage with you? I have a wine-bottle, but there is no wine in it; a London wine-merchant, whom we met in the town of Slagelse, had the last drop of the wine. The shoemaker is the son of the mason who built many of the houses in the town of Slesvig. There is no lock on this door; the carpenter must come and put a hasp on. A pane of glass is broken in the window, and now the draught comes right into the room. I was not calling your servant, but the nephew of your servant. He is not in the house; he may perhaps be sitting on the garden-seat, or he may be running about the fields. She has her own and her sister's thimble. Is it a silver or an ivory thimble? It it neither a silver nor an ivory thimble, but a gold thimble.

---

¹ longing   ⁴ to wake   ⁷ strength
² to hasten   ⁵ source of resignation   ⁸ consoling spirit.
³ hearty   ⁶ will

II.

Is it your umbrella that your servant brought me? No, my umbrella is standing in the corner of the green room in the hotel, and the one which my brother's servant brought you belongs to the doctor's daughter. Have you all you require? I have not all the papers that I shall want. The paper is all used (up). All the money is used. Has the coachman drunk a whole bottle of ale? No, he has only drunk half a bottle. It is my brother's fault that I came half an hour too late. Is the house built of granite or of Portland stone? I cannot tell you if the stone is granite or of some other kind. What is that hanging on the wall? It is an old Turkish dagger which was given me by an intimate friend.

FORTY-SECOND LESSON.

ADJECTIVES (Tillægsord).

I. As has already been shown, adjectives precede, and agree with, the noun to which they refer, and they follow both the indefinite article and the independent adjective-definite article; as for example:—

en god Soldat,   *den gode Soldat.*

A. Exceptions to the general rule, that an adjective must agree in number with the noun which it qualifies, are afforded by the plurals *få, alle, mange,* which may be used with a singular noun; as for example:—

han har kun få Mark i Lommen, he has only a few marks in his pocket.
tager fat alle Mand! take heed all ye men!
Klokken er mange, it is late (the clock is many [hours]).

II. In Danish, as in English, the adjective follows the

noun when it constitutes a surname, or distinctive appellation; as for example :—

Gorm den Gamle, Gorm the Old.
Kristian den Anden, Christian the Second.

III. Some adjectives, which express value, or obligation, follow the noun; as for example :—

han er mig mange Penge skyldig, he owes me a great deal of money.
De er den Ære værdig, you are worthy of the honour.

IV. *Begge*, both, and *al*, all, must precede the noun directly, without taking the independent adjective-article; as for example :—

begge Regenterne, both the reigning princes.
alt Byttet, all the booty.
alt Forrådet, all the stores.

V. Numerals immediately precede the noun, and those of the ordinal numbers which are declinable must agree in number and gender with the noun; as for example :—

Damen har tabt tre Öre, the lady has lost three öre.
jeg mödte ham på anden Sal, I met him on the second floor.
han tog den förste Lejlighed at öve sig i Udtalen, he took the first opportunity of perfecting (exercising) himself in the pronunciation.
han behöver ikke at skrive mere end en Stil, he need not write more than one exercise.
förste Torsdag i næste Måned skulle nogle af Sultanens oprörske Undersåtter lide Döden, the first Thursday of next month some of the Sultan's rebellious subjects will be put to death.

VI. In speaking of large combinations, a singular noun may sometimes be employed with the plural numeral; as for example :—

Generalen faldt ind i Landet med femten tusinde Mand, the general invaded the country with fifteen thousand men.

VII. *Megen, anden, egen, liden* undergo no change when preceded by the adjective-article *den*; as for example :—

den liden Dåd han udförte! the small achievement that he performed!
den megen Regn vi havde igår, the quantity of rain we had yesterday.

A. In the neuter these adjectives drop the *n*, and take *t*, to agree with the noun; as for example:—

det lidet Godt hun bestilte, the little good she did.
mit eget Hus er mit Slot, my own house is my castle.

VIII. The adjective *hel*, all, whole, in combination with a numeral, conveys a difference of meaning in accordance with its place in the sentence; as for example:—

ti hele År, ten complete years.
hele ti År, all the ten years.

IX. As the ordinary terminations of adjectives have already been given, it is only necessary here to draw attention to certain differences of meaning, which are conveyed by these affixes; thus for example:—

agtig and *lig* express resemblance to, or affinity with, an object, and may generally be rendered in English by the particle "ish," as *sortagtig*, blackish; *syrlig*, sourish;

bar (derived from *at bære*, to bear) corresponds to the English "ful," "able;" as *frugtbar*, fruitful; *ærbar*, honourable;

som conveys a sense of action, while *lig*, when joined to a word referring to properties of the mind, implies a possible rather than an existing action; as for example: *tænksom*, thoughtful, meditating; *tænkelig*, conceivable; *følsom*, feeling; *følelig*, perceptible.

READING

to translate into English.

Extract from H. C. Andersen's Tale "Dejlig."

"Rom gad jeg nok se!"[1] sagde hun, "det må være en yndig[2] By med alle de mange Fremmede, som komme der, beskriv[3] os nu Rom! hvorledes ser der nu ud idet man kommer ind ad Porten?"[4]

[1] Rome I should so much like to see, [2] charming, [3] to describe, [4] gate.

"Det er ikke let at beskrive!" sagde den unge Billedhugger.[1] "Der er en stor Plads;[2] midt på den står en Obelisk, som er fire tusind År gammel!"

"En Organist!" udbröd[3] Fruen, hun havde aldrig för hört Ordet Obelisk; Nogle vare nær ved at le,[4] Billedhuggeren med, men det Smil[5] som kom, gled hen i Beskuelse,[6] thi han så tæt[7] ved Fruen et Par store havblå[8] Öjne, det var Datteren af hende, der talte, og når man har en sådan Datter, kan man ikke være enfoldig![9] Moderen var et ösende[10] Spörgsmåls Væld,[11] Datteren Vældets Skönheds Najade,[12] der hörte til.[13] Hvor var hun dejlig! hun var Noget for en Billedhugger at se på, men ikke tale med, og hun talte Intet, idetmindste[14] meget lidt.

"Har Paven[15] en stor Familje?" spurgte Fruen.

Og den unge Mand svarede, som Spörgsmålet bedre kunde have været stillet:[16] "Nej, han er ikke af stor Familje!"

"Det mener[17] jeg ikke!" sagde Fruen; jeg mener, har han Kone og Börn?"

"Paven tör[18] ikke gifte[19] sig!" svarede han.

"Det holder jeg ikke af!"[20] sagde Fruen.

Klögtigere[21] kunde hun vel have spurgt og talt, men om hun ikke havde spurgt og talt, som hun gjorde det, mon da vel[22] Datteren således havde heldt sig op til[23] hendes Skulder[24] og sét med dette næsten rörende[25] Smil?

Og Hr. Alfred talte, talte om Italiens Farvepragt,[26] de blånende[27] Bjærge, det blå Middelhav,[28] Sydens Blå, en Dejlighed,[29] som man i Norden kun fandt overtruffen[30] i den nordiske Kvindes[31] blå Öjne. Og det blev her sagt med

[1] sculptor
[2] square
[3] to exclaim
[4] to laugh
[5] smile
[6] gave place to a look of attention
[7] close to
[8] sea-blue
[9] silly
[10] to pour forth
[11] questioning spring
[12] Naïd
[13] to listen
[14] at least
[15] the pope
[16] to put
[17] to mean
[18] to dare
[19] to marry
[20] *at holde af*, to like
[21] more cleverly
[22] would then
[23] *holde sig op til*, to lean oneself against
[24] shoulder
[25] touching
[26] splendour of colour
[27] blue-tinted
[28] Mediterranean
[29] beauty
[30] exceeded
[31] woman

Hentydning,[1] men hun som skulde forstå[2] det, hun lod sig ikke mærke med[3] at hun forstod det; og det var jo nu også dejligt!

"Italien!" sukkede[4] Nogle, "rejse!" sukkede Andre. "Dejlig! Dejlig!"

FORTY-SECOND EXERCISE.

I.

What is the little girl doing? She is writing her French exercise. Is it a difficult exercise? Yes, the exercise is rather difficult; but she has been learning French a whole year. Has she learnt to speak English? Not yet, and next year she is going to England with her old aunt, therefore she will certainly have many excellent opportunities of acquiring a good accent without giving herself much trouble. Charles the First of England, who was the grandson of Frederick the Second of Denmark, was beheaded by his rebellious subjects. It is more than two centuries since that unfortunate event occurred. This king had two sons who became sovereigns, viz.: Charles the Second and James the Second. I only want one or two pairs of gloves, and in case you have not got the gloves at hand it is not worth while to fetch them. How much money do I owe you?

II.

I met two strange ladies on the first floor. They were not really strangers, because they live on the third floor; but during all the ten years that I have lived in the house I have never once seen them. How much money do you want? At this moment I have only very little money in my pocket, but still I may be

---

[1] special meaning [2] to understand, [3] she gave no sign, [4] to sigh.

able to give you a few marks. All I want is a few öre. Have you read the German papers to-day? It is said that a general with some 5,000 or 6,000 men has made an incursion into the country, and secured possession of a large booty in money and stores, and taken a number of prisoners. The soldiers are all efficient and well-trained men.

Names of Animals, etc.

en Hund, a dog
en Hvalp, a puppy
en Kat,* a cat
en Kattekilling, a kitten
en Mus, a mouse
en Rotte, a rat
en Vandrotte, a water-rat
et Egern, a squirrel
en Væsel, a weasel
en Grævling, a badger
en Mår, a marten
en Jærv (Norw.) } a glutton
en Fjældfras (Norw.) }
en Björn, a bear
en Los,* a lynx
en Hermelin, a stoat
en Rén } a reindeer
et Rensdyr }
en Smile (Norw.), a doe of reindeer
en Sæl, a seal
en Hval, a whale
en Hvalros,* a walrus
en Stör, a sturgeon
en Laks, a salmon
en Torsk, a cod
en Örred } a trout
en Örret (Norw.) }
en Forelle, a trout
en Sild, a herring
en Rödspætte, a plaice
en Flynder, a flounder
en Pigvarre, a turbot
en Östers, an oyster
en Hummer, a lobster

en Krabbe, a crab
en Reje, a shrimp
(store Rejer, prawns)
en Flodkrebs, a cray-fish
en Elg, an elk
en Elgko, a female elk
en Hjort, a stag, reddeer
en Hind, a hind
et Dådyr, a fallow deer
en Odder, an otter
en Bæver, a beaver
en Ræv, a fox
en Ulv, a wolf
en Hare, a hare
en Kanin, a rabbit
et Får, a sheep
en Ged, a goat
en Ko, a cow
en Kalv, a calf
en Tyr, a bull
en Okse, an ox
en Hest, a horse
en Hoppe, a mare
et Föl,* a foal
en Gris, a pig
en Fasan, a pheasant
en Århane (Norw.), black cock
en Agerhöne, a partridge
en Tjur (Norw.), a capercailzie
en Rype, a ptarmigan
en Edderfugl, an eiderduck
en Örn, an eagle
en Hönsehög, a goosehawk
en Stork, a stork
en Svane, a swan

en *Svale,* a swallow
en *Stær,* a starling
en *Krage,* a crow
en *Ravn,* a raven
en *Spurv,* a sparrow
en *Lærke,* a lark

en *Drossel (Droslen),* a thrush
en *Sortdrossel,* a blackbird
en *Digesvale,* a martin
en *Finke,* a finch
en *Skade,* a magpie
en *Nattergal,* a nightingale.

FORTY-THIRD LESSON.

ON PRONOUNS (*Stedord*).

Pronouns more than any other parts of speech have retained traces of the various modes of declension which characterised the Old Northern, since they alone have distinctive terminations to mark different cases, as for example: Nom., *jeg,* I; Acc., *mig,* me; Nom., *vi,* we; Acc., *os,* us. (*See* Fourteenth Lesson).

I. As already shown, *De,* you (obj., *Dem*) is the pronoun ordinarily used in addressing another person; *Du* being limited to special grades of relationship or intimacy, and *I* to numbers. *I* is, however, occasionally still used in addressing one individual, in which case, as when *De,* you, is employed, the verb, adjective, etc., which it governs, must be in the singular; as for example: *Er De syg?* are you ill? *hvor gammel er I?* how old are you?

II. *Han* and *hun* were at one time in use when servants or inferiors were addressed, but this mode of address is being rapidly superseded by the more courteous *De.*

Han and *hun* are used in referring to persons, whilst *den* and *det* are used in speaking of animals (excepting perhaps domesticated animals, or household pets). Amongst the lower classes *han* and *hun* are occasionally employed to indicate inanimate objects of all kinds. *Hannem* and *dennem* are found in poetry for *ham* and *dem.*

III. *Eders, jeres*, and *deres* have nearly superseded the older *jer, jert, jere*, your; *der, dert, dere*, their; while *vores*, although regarded by Grammarians as incorrect, is also used in ordinary speech in the place of *vor, vort, vore*, our.

De, they, cannot be used, as in English, in a general sense; and in such sentences as "they say" it is necessary to employ the pronoun *man*, as *man siger*, instead of *de sige;* the same meaning may, however, be conveyed by using a noun, as for example: *Folk sige*, people say.

IV. The relative *hvilken* may be used instead of *som* or *der*, when the pronoun occurs parenthetically as a secondary, rather than as an essentially necessary reference to the preceding noun; as for example:—

> gode Æbler, hvilke man lettere kan have i Norden end i Syden, er en nyttig Frugt, good apples, which are more common in the North than in the South, are useful fruits.

Hvilken, in consequence of its various terminations, admits of being used with precision where *som* or *der* might leave room for doubt; as for example:—

> Hensyn til min Konge og mit Fædreland, hvilket jeg elsker höjst af alle, skal i denne Sag bestemme mig, consideration for my king and my country, which I love above all things, shall determine my conduct in this matter.

Som and *der* refer directly to the person or thing named in the first clause of the sentence; as for example:—

> giv mig den Bog, som ligger dér, give me the book that lies there.
> jeg så Manden, som blev bankerot for et Par År siden, I saw the man, who became a bankrupt a few years ago.
> det er vist ikke Officeren, der gik i fransk Tjæneste, this is surely not the officer who went into the French service.

The relative pronoun may be omitted when it is governed by a verb or a preposition; as for example:—

> Koen, dér ligger, the cow that lies there.
> dér står Drengen, jeg gav Bogen, there stands the boy to whom I gave the book.
> Huset, jeg bygger, the house I am building.

Although a pronoun, as a rule, must agree in gender and number with the noun which it represents, an exception is very generally made in respect to nouns whose grammatical gender is at variance with the natural gender of the individuals or objects which the nouns indicate; thus for example:—

Mennesket slog sig, da han faldt, the man struck himself when he fell.
Fruentimmeret viste Heltemod, da hun forsvarede sig, the woman showed valour when she defended herself.

at beundre, to admire
at tilstå, to confess
at forsikre, to assure
at tage på, to put on, wear
at styrke, to strengthen
at påtage, to assume
at komme sig, to recover
at bygge, to build
at fornærme, to affront

at Bryllup,* a wedding
en Klædedragt, an attire
en Disk, a shop-counter
et Pus, a dear little creature
en Styrke, a strength
en Fare, a danger
farlig, dangerous
hurtig, quick
fornuftig, sensible.

READING
to translate into English.

LEANDERS TÅRN.¹

Det såkaldte "Leanders Tårn" står på en Klippe² i Strædet,³ ikke langt fra den asiatiske Kyst. — Det er let at skönne,⁴ at Tårnet med Uret bærer dette Navn; Leander gjorde jo ikke sit Mesterstykke⁵ i Bosporus, men i Hellespont. — I det græske Kejserdömmes⁶ Dage tjente Tårnet til Fæste⁷ for den ene Ende af den store Kæde,⁸ hvormed man spærrede Indløbet⁹ til Konstantinopels Havn,¹⁰ det gyldne Horn, når fjendtlige¹¹ Fläder truede¹² Staden. Dens anden Ende var fæstet i Serailodden.¹³ Tyrkerne kalde Tårnet "Kis-Kulessi," d. e. Jomfrutårnet,¹⁴ efter følgende Sagn.¹⁵

[1] tower
[2] cliff
[3] straits
[4] to perceive
[5] master-piece, feat
[6] empire
[7] fastening,
[8] chain
[9] closed the entrance
[10] haven
[11] hostile
[12] threatened
[13] point of land by the Seraglio
[14] the tower of the maiden
[15] tradition

"Sultan Mohammed havde en sjælden[1] smuk Datter, hvem en Zigöinerinde[2] havde spået,[3] at hun skulde dö af et Ormestik.[4] For at ingen Orm skulde komme hende nær, lod Sultanen hende bo i en Kiosk, som han havde ladet bygge på denne Klippe. Da Schahen af Persiens Sön engang kom til Konstantinopel, hörte han den smukke Mehar-Schegid omtale,[5] og blev forelsket[6] i hende. Han sendte hende en betydningsfuld[7] Blomsterbuket,[8] der skulde sige hende, hvad han fölte. Men iblandt Roserne og Hyacinterne var ulykkeligvis en Orm skjult.[9] Den stak[10] Prindsessen i Hånden, da hun tog Buketten, og da Ingen var at formå til[11] at udsuge[12] Giften,[13] var den visse[14] Död forhånden.[15] Schahen af Persiens Sön fik det at vide,[16] ilede[17] over til hende i en Båd, og sugede Giften ud af hendes Hånd. Sultanen gav ham derpå Mehar-Schegid til Hustru."[18]

FORTY-THIRD EXERCISE.

I.

A man often hears what he does not like. They say in town that the prince is going to be married. One should never talk too much about oneself. As you come into the village you see the church and the churchyard, which lie on your left, whilst the clergyman's house, which is near Mr. Svendsen's farm, is seen on the right hand. Is that the woman who was talking to your husband yesterday on the road by the sea? No, it was not she; the person who talked to my husband was an older woman. When it was first reported that the king of Italy was dangerously ill, I heard that his daughter,

[1] unusually
[2] gipsy
[3] to foretell
[4] snake's bite
[5] to be talked of
[6] in love with
[7] full of meaning
[8] bouquet
[9] to hide
[10] to bite
[11] *at formå til*, to induce
[12] to suck out
[13] poison
[14] certain
[15] at hand
[16] to know
[17] to hasten
[18] wife

the queen of Portugal, and her sister, who lives in Paris, had been telegraphed to, to come to Rome with all haste. It was hoped that the danger was past; but people said that the king was much depressed, and did not himself think that he would recover. Is the house in the wood yours? No, that is the house my brother-in-law built two years ago.

II.

Which of these hats will you wear to-day? Not any one of them, the old one which I wore yesterday looks so remarkably well. What kind of lace do you wish for? I do not like those that you have on the counter; I prefer the French lace that lies on the shelf. Do you know my sister's little child who was here at Christmas? She is such a sensible little creature. How old is the child? She is about three years old. Is it the custom in England for a woman to take such a thing upon herself? I think not, but at any rate she could not do it in Denmark. That person who is sitting on the red chair is very much admired; but for my part I must confess that I admire his clothing more than his person. Have you anything against the man who has married my niece? No, I am quite indifferent to him. Hast thou seen my dog; is it not here? The dog lying there is not mine. It is not conceivable that he should owe his tailor so much money; he says that he will take the first opportunity of paying his tradesmen with the little that he has remaining of the fortune which his father left him some years ago.

FORTY-FOURTH LESSON.

ON PRONOUNS (*Stedord*).
(*Continued.*)

I. The reflective pronoun *sig*, and the possessive pronouns *sin*, *sit*, *sine* referred originally to plurals as well as to singulars, but the tendency of later times has been to limit their use to the third person singular; *dem* and *deres* being employed when more than one person is referred to; as for example:—

de beklagede dem over deres Skæbne, they lamented (themselves) over their fate.
de tog deres Hatte og gik, they took their hats and went.

It must be observed, however, that the use of *dem* and *deres*, instead of the characteristic *sig* and *sin* in the plural, is almost entirely limited to the Danes, who have forsaken a vernacular form in favour of a German mode of speech, while the Norwegians and Swedes still adhere to the original usage of these pronouns.

The difference between *sin* and *hans* has already been elsewhere sufficiently explained (*see* Thirteenth Lesson), and we need, therefore, here only draw attention to the fact, that although it may be accepted as a general proposition that the former pronoun refers to the subject in the sentence, it must be borne in mind that practically it is made to refer to the *nearest* preceding noun; as for example:—

hans Herre befalede ham at tage sine Sager og gå, his master ordered him to take away his things and go.
hun hörte Faderens Formaning til sine Börn, she heard the father's admonition to his children.
Moderen roste sin Sön, fordi han var flittig, the mother praised her (own) son, because he was diligent.
enhver söger for sines Vel, each one tries to provide for his own welfare.
hun overlod sig til sine Tanker, she gave herself up to her thoughts.

II. As has already been stated, the pronoun *man* can only be used as a nominative or subject; where an objective or other case is required, *En* must be used; as for example :—

Ens eget er dog det bedste, one's own is nevertheless the best.

III. The demonstrative pronouns *denne* and *hin* answer in some respects to the English "this one" and "that one;" the former indicating something last-named or nearest, while the latter refers to something first-named, or more remote; as for example :—

Pompejus og Cæsar havde mange Tilhængere i Rom, hin af Adelen, denne af Almuen, Pompey and Cæsar had many adherents in Rome, the former among the nobles, the latter among the lower classes.

IV. The interrogative pronouns *hvo, hvem, hvad,* when used as the subjects of an objective or secondary clause in the sentence, are generally followed by a relative in Danish; as for example :—

jeg véd ikke hvem der har gjort det, I do not know who has done it.
ser De, hvad det har at sige? do you see what that means?

Hvo (*hvem*) is also used in a demonstrative sense, as :—

hvo som elsker sit Fædreland, he who (whoever) loves his country.

Hvad is often used in the sense of an adjective, as for example :—

hvad for Efterretninger har De? what (kind of) news have you?
til hvad for en Pris er det? how much (at what price) is it?

It is also used interjectionally, as :—

hvad for en Lykke! what happiness!

V. Some Danish grammarians include the cardinal and ordinal numbers generally under the head of pronouns, although they consider the words "a hundred," "a thousand," etc., as nouns; as for example :—

et Hundrede, pl. *Hundreder,* a hundred
et Tusinde, pl. *Tusinder,* a thousand
en Million, pl. *Millioner,* a million
en Billion, pl. *Billioner,* a billion.

Hundrede and *tusinde*, when used before a noun as simple numerals remain unchanged; as for example:—

ni hundrede Mennesker, nine hundred people
fem tusinde Sømænd, five thousand seamen.

The Danish system of counting between 50 and 100 in half-twenties can advance no good claim in favour of its continuance. The old Northmen followed the simpler and more rational method of counting by tens, as is still done by the Swedes and Norwegians, who say *treti*, 30, *firti*, 40, *femti*, 50, *seksti*, 60, instead of using the clumsy Danish forms of *tredive*, *fyrretyve*, *halvtredsindstyve*, *tredsindstyve*, etc. The O. N. meaning of *sind* is "times"; consequently, the etymological meaning of *halvtredsindstyve*, fifty, is half on to three times twenty, while *halvfemsindstyve*, ninety, means half on to five times twenty. For convenience sake, the word *sindstyve* is frequently dropped in ordinary speech when the numeral is not followed by a noun; as for example:—

de vare halvtreds, there were fifty of them
han er to og firs, he is eighty-two.

But where a noun comes after the number, the entire word must be written; as for example:—

der var halvtredsindstyve Mennesker i Salen, there were fifty people in the room.
hun er næsten firsindstyve År gammel, she is nearly eighty years old.

READING.

To translate into English.

BRYLLUP I TYRKIET.

Bryllupsforberedelserne[1] optage[2] en Tid af åtte til ti Dage, og ende enten Mandag eller Fredag Aften. På den næstsidste Dag drager Bruden i offentlig[3] Procession til Badet.[4] I Spidsen gå nogle Musikanter[5] med Hoboer[6] og Trommer;[7]

[1] wedding preparations
[2] occupy
[3] public
[4] bath
[5] musician
[6] hautboys
[7] drums

efter dem gå Mænd, som bære Badelinned,¹ Flasker med Rosenvand, hvormed de bestænke² de Forbigående,³ Kar⁴ med brændende Aloetræ⁵ og andre vellugtende⁶ Substanser. En Mand bærer en Læderflaske⁷ med Vand, ifald Nogen af Fölget⁸ skulde overfaldes⁹ af Törst.¹⁰ Så komme Brudens gifte¹¹ Slægtninge og Venner; derpå en Skare¹² unge Piger, der bære hvide Schawl, og endelig Bruden under en Baldakin,¹³ båret¹⁴ af fire Mænd. Et stort rödt Kaschmirsschawl er kastet over hende, så man hverken kan se Kronen¹⁵ på hendes Hoved eller den rige Klædedragt og de mange Smykker.¹⁶ Blot et eller to ere fæstede udenpå Schawlet. I varmt Vejr vifter¹⁷ en gammel Kone, som går baglænds,¹⁸ Bruden med en Vifte af sorte Strudsfjædre.¹⁹ Processionen slutter²⁰ med nogle Musikanter. — I den varme Årstid finder den ofte Sted om Aftenen, efterat Solen er gået ned. Isåfald²¹ bære unge Brudepiger og Andre Lamper, som de Tid efter anden fylde²² med Olie.²³ Processionen går i Reglen²⁴ Brudgommen imöde,²⁵ når han kommer fra Badet, og fölger ham ind i Bryllupshuset, hvis Dör lukkes, og hvor Gæsterne iföres²⁶ Bryllupsklæder. Man mindes her Lignelsen²⁷ om de ti Jomfruer, som gik Brudgommen imöde, og Lignelsen om Bryllupsklæderne. På den sidste Dag går Bruden i lignende²⁸ Procession til Brudgommens Hus, medens Brudgommen går i Procession til Moskeen²⁹ for at forrette sin Aftenbön,³⁰ hvorfra han vender tilbage³¹ til Bryllupshuset. Hans Procession standser ofte på Vejen, hvor han modtager mange Lykönskninger³² af sine Venner.

P. BLOM.

1 linen
2 to sprinkle
3 passers by
4 vessel
5 aloes
6 sweet smelling
7 leather-bottle
8 attendants
9 to overcome
10 thirst
11 married
12 band
13 canopy
14 to carry
15 crown
16 ornaments
17 to fan
18 backwards
19 ostrich feathers
20 to close
21 in that case
22 to fill
23 oil
24 as a rule
25 to meet the bridegroom
26 to be clothed with
27 reminded of the parable
28 similar
29 mosque
30 perform his devotions
31 to return
32 congratulations

FORTY-FOURTH EXERCISE.

I.

Who is with your father? The man who sells his gloves so cheap is with him. Which of the ladies is in my sisters' room? There is no one with them excepting their servant. Where has your nephew come from? He has come from our cousin in England, and as soon as he returns from his sea-voyage he is to enter his uncle's counting-house. Who has my little boy's copy-book? Has your brother got it? He has only his own? but I do not know if this writing paper is your son's or his own. Those men give themselves no trouble. There were nearly three hundred soldiers at the station, each with his sword and rifle. To whom do the cattle on this field belong? They belong to our cousin, the squire (owner of estate), but the animals on yonder field belong to the miller. Has your cousin no more cows than these four? He has several more on his farm near Rensborg. The peasant says the horses are his; but I thought they were yours. The horses are not mine, but my neighbour's. He who wears the shoe knows best where it pinches. Some slept in the carriage, others gave themselves up to their silent thoughts.

II.

What news have you of your brother-in-law? I have not had particularly good news, as you will see from these letters. Is your sister with her husband in the country? No, she is still with her daughter in Ribe; but as soon as she learns with what a dangerous illness her husband has been attacked, she will immediately return. May my daughter take your umbrella to her uncle? Why does she not take your own instead of borrowing mine?

Mino is good for nothing; it fell from our carriage yesterday and was driven over, and now we cannot use it any longer. Have you heard of the misfortune that happened to-day? A man fell from his horse in one of the narrowest of our streets, the horse darted off, and the man, who was much shaken (*röstet*), has been taken to a hospital. Do you know for how much (at what price) I might buy a handsome carriage and a pair of strong horses? Perhaps for about two hundred and fifty, or three hundred pounds. That is a hundred more than I wish to pay.

FORTY-FIFTH LESSON.

ON VERBS (*Udsagnsord*).

I. The present of the indicative (*Nutiden af den fremsættende Måde*) has a wider application than the same tense in English, and is used:—

A. To express, as in English, what usually happens at a definite period; as for example:—

Drengen går hver Dag i Skole, the boy goes every day to school.

B. In the place of the past tense, in descriptive narration; as for example:—

imedens han talte, hörte hun på ham, og löber så hen og anklager ham, whilst he was speaking, she listened to him, and ran and denounced him.

C. In the place of the future and conditional, in which respect it constitutes a marked characteristic of the language; as for example:—

jeg rejser næste år, I shall travel next year.
går hun med, bliver jeg hjemme, if she should go too, I shall remain at home.

II. The imperfect, or past tense, (*Datiden*) is used:—

A. To express a past period of indefinite date or limitation, and is employed in historical narration; as for example:—

> *Napoleon opsvang sig til Frankrigs Kejser*, Napoleon raised himself to be emperor of France.
> *jeg læste, da han kom*, I was reading when he came.

B. In an optative, conditional sense; as:—

> *gik det blot godt!* if it only would go well!
> *handlede De efter mit Råd, kunde det endelig blive godt*, if you would act by my advice, it might in the end go well.
> *jeg gik ud i Aften, hvis jeg vidste det blev godt Vejr*, I would go out this evening, if I knew that it would be fine (weather).

III. The future tense (*Fremtiden*) is often expressed by the help of the auxiliary (*Hjælpeordet*) *blive*, as well as by that of *skulle* and *ville*; as for example:—

> *om det ikke holder op, bliver jeg gal*, if that does not cease, I shall go mad.
> *i År bliver hun ikke gift*, she will not be married this year

Skal and *vil* are not used precisely as their English representatives "shall" and "will," since the first implies, in Danish, an obligation or intention on the part of the agent, while the second expresses futurity without any action of the will; as for example:—

> *Jeg spörger om De skal rejse*, I am asking whether you are going to travel (must travel).
> *jeg tror at jeg vil være altfor træt*, I think that I shall be too tired.
> *jeg håber at De vil göre det*, I hope that you will do it.
> *det skal jeg nok*, yes, that I will.
> *kommer De imorgen? ja, jeg skal nok komme*, are you coming to-morrow? yes, I shall certainly come.
> *Posten vil idag næppe komme i rette Tid*, the post will hardly arrive at the proper time to-day.

Here it will be seen that *vil* is used where the action depends upon something foreign to, or apart from the subject, while *skal* is employed where the action, will, or determination refers to, or emanates from the subject.

READING.

To translate into English.

SAMFUNDETS STÖTTER, Skuespil i fire Akter, af HENRIK IBSEN.
("The Props [Supports] of Society," a drama in four acts, by Henry Ibsen.)

SCENE I.

Fuldmægtig[1] KRAP.—Nå, er det Dem, som banker.[2]
Skibsbygger[3] AUNE.—Konsulen[4] har havt Bud[5] efter mig.
Fuldmægtig KRAP.—Har så; men kan ikke modtage[6] Dem; har overdraget[7] til mig at . . .
Skibsbygger AUNE.—Til Dem? Jeg vilde nok helst—[8]
Fuldmægtig KRAP.—Overdraget til mig at sige Dem det. De må holde op[9] med disse Lördags.ore Irag[10] for Arbejderne.[11]
Skibsbygger AUNE.—Så? Jeg tænkte dog, jeg måtte bruge[12] min Frihed[13]—
Fuldmægtig KRAP.—De må ikke bruge Deres Frihed til at göre Folkene ubrugelige[14] i Arbejdstiden. Sidste Lördag har De talt om den Skade,[15] Arbejderne skal have af vore nye Maskiner,[16] og af den nye Arbejdsmåde[17] på Værftet.[18] Hvorfor gör De det?
Skibsbygger AUNE.—Det gör jeg for at stötte[19] Samfundet.[20]
Fuldmægtig KRAP.—Det var mærkeligt! Konsulen siger, at det er Samfundsoplösende.[21]
Skibsbygger AUNE.—Mit Samfund er ikke Konsulens Samfund, Herr Fuldmægtig! som Formand[22] i Arbejdersamfundet må jeg—
Fuldmægtig KRAP.—De er först og fremst[23] Formand på Konsulens Værft. De har först og fremst at göre Deres Skyldighed[24] imod det Samfund, som kaldes Konsul Bermiks Firma,[25] for det er *det* vi alle sammen leve af.—Ja, nu véd De hvad Konsulen havde at sige Dem.

[1] head-clerk or director
[2] knock
[3] ship-builder
[4] the consul
[5] message
[6] receive
[7] commissioned
[8] rather
[9] cease
[10] addresses
[11] workmen
[12] use
[13] leisure
[14] useless
[15] injury
[16] machines
[17] mode of working
[18] ship-building yard
[19] support
[20] society
[21] dissolution of the social fabric (society)
[22] foreman, president
[23] first and foremost
[24] duty
[25] firm

Skibsbygger AUNE.—Konsulen vilde ikke have sagt det på *den* Måde! men jeg skönner¹ nok hvem jeg har at takke for dette her. Det er den fordömte amerikanske Havarist.² De Folk vil, at Arbejdet skal gå som de er vant³ til det derovre, og det—

Fuldmægtig KRAP.—Ja, ja, ja, jeg kan ikke indlade⁴ mig på Vidtlöftigheder.⁵ Nu kender De Konsulens Mening;⁶ altså basta!⁷ vil De så gå ned på Værftet igen; det kan vist behöves;⁸ jeg kommer selv derned om lidt.

FORTY-FIFTH EXERCISE.

I.

My son goes to the office every morning at nine. I will not suffer him to make such a noise (*Stöj*, c.g.). Are you going to town to-day? No, I am not going to-day, because I have not been very well since I returned from my last voyage. When are your friends going out hunting? They are going as soon as my uncle arrives. I heard that your uncle had come last Thursday. He did come on that day, but he went away again, and now we do not know at what time we may expect him. If he does not come at the appointed time my friend will go without him. Yesterday I saw a large number of birds at the farm in Frederiksdal. What kind of birds did you see? We saw storks sitting on the gable, a swan which was swimming in the pond, and several little birds, as larks, finches, swallows, sand-martens, and thrushes twittering in chorus.

---

[1] perceive
[2] confounded ship-wrecked American
[3] accustomed
[4] enter into
[5] longwinded dissertations
[6] meaning
[7] enough
[8] certainly be necessary

II.

Has your aunt praised you (ye)? She praised us because we had been diligent this week. We shall not sell our horses if our son comes back from the East-Indies. When do you expect him? Oh! if we only knew when to expect him! But his coming home depends upon the war, if that should cease, he will probably come this year, but if the war should be prolonged, it is impossible to say when we may hope to see him again. Would you oblige me by changing (at bytte) a sovereign? I shall be very glad to do so. Would you like to have English shillings or Danish marks? Many thanks (I thank you), I prefer Danish money. Mrs. Paulsen said that you were going to travel next summer; is it true? Yes, it is; I am going (intend to go) to France next August.

FORTY-SIXTH LESSON.

ON THE AUXILIARY VERBS, etc. *(Hjælpeverberne, o.s.v.)*

I. The auxiliary (*Hjælpeordet*) at få, to get, when joined to a participle past, was at one time generally used in the Scandinavian languages to express the sense of "shall have;" as for example:—

 når jeg får spist, when I shall have dined.

The use of få in this sense has, however, been almost wholly superseded in Danish by that of *have*. In either case the adverb used in combination with the verb indicates the distinct period of time which is to be expressed; thus: *når*, when, while: implies a sense of definite futurity; *da*, when: implies a sense of definite past; as for example:—

 da han havde spist gik han i Byen, when he had dined, he went into town.

II. Two or more auxiliaries may be added to the governing verb, as may be seen from the following sentences:—

hun har villet gå, she had wished (intended) to go.
han skal have sagt, he shall (is reported to) have said.
det skal være skrevet, it is said to have been written.
det skal have været besluttet, it is said to have been resolved.
det skal være blevet gjort, it is said to have been done.

The English auxiliaries "have," "be," "do," etc., when used with a present participle, are often replaced in Danish by various other modes of construction, as may be seen from the following sentences:—

hun er færdig med at spille, she has done playing.
Manden var red at sove, the man was sleeping.
Konen skrev ikke igår, the woman was not writing yesterday.
han er i Færd med at rejse, he is in the act of (on the point of) travelling.

III. Participles (*Tillægsformerne*) may be used as adjectives, in which case they must agree, like these, in gender and number with the noun to which they refer; as for example:—

den brölende Löve, the roaring lion
en indbunden Bog, a bound book
et bundet Dyr, a chained animal
de fangne Soldater, the captured soldiers.

In some cases these participles may be used adverbially, as for example:—

han kom ridende, he came riding
hun sidder fangen, she is (sits) imprisoned.

The present participle in English is frequently best rendered in Dano-Norwegian by the reiterated use of the present indicative; as for example:—

hun sidder og læser, she is reading
han står og taler, he is speaking.

IV. Although the rule, that the verb should agree in number and person with the noun to which it refers, is accepted in Dano-Norwegian, as in other languages, it is evident, that a decided tendency to reduce both numbers of the verb to the singular form is apparent, even amongst the best educated Danes and Norwegians; thus, for example, most persons will be heard to say *vi har* instead of *vi have*, *de er* instead of *de ere*. This substitution of the singular of the present tense of the indicative for the plural is perhaps most prevalent in regard to the auxiliaries, but it is not limited to these verbs.

The impersonals *det er*, it is, *det var*, it was, *hvor er*, where is, *der er*, there is, etc., remain unchanged whether the subject to which they refer is plural or singular; as for example:—

hvor er Manden? where is the man?
der er nogle Piger, there are some girls.

---

at være indtagen, to be taken with
at beslutte, to determine
at indsætte, to instal
at erhverve, to acquire
at udnævne, to nominate
at trampe, to stamp, trample
at fare afsted, to rush away
at være i Færd med, to be on the point
at besöge, to visit
at vente, to wait
at forlade, to leave
at forlade sig på En, to trust to one

et Dampskib, a steamboat
et Kompagni, a company
en Plads, a place, situation
en Forretning, a business
en Sag, a case, matter
sagkyndig, conversant with a subject
(en) Erfarenhed, experience, skil
en Kontorist, a clerk in a counting-house
(en) Gallop, a gallop
en Hestehov, a horse's hoof.

READING.

To translate into English.

Uddrag af "Tilfjælds i Ferierne, eller Jæger- og Fiskerliv i Höjfjældene," af J. A. Friis.

(Extract from "On the Fjelds in the Holidays, or the Life of the Huntsman) and Fisherman on the high Fjelds," by J. A. Friis.)

Det er ofte komisk[1] at se mangen Fluefisker[2] kaste sin Flue[3] hen på Steder[4] i en Höl[5] eller Dele af Elv, hvor den Erfarne[6] ikke vil væde en Töm,[7] og igen undlade[8] at pröve der, hvor Fisken netop helst plejer[9] at stå.

Det Hele går på Slump.[10]

[1] comical
[2] fly-fisher
[3] fly
[4] places
[5] a hole (Norw.)
[6] expert
[7] line (Norw.)
[8] omit
[9] to be accustomed
[10] hap-hazard

I Reglen er det altid bedst at fiske ovenfra nedover, af den gode Grund,[1] at de största Fisk, som för sagt, stå överst oppe i Hölene.

Man nærmer sig altså Hölen med den Forudsætning,[2] at Fisken ikke er blind, men at man bliver sét af denne. Kan man derfor allerede ovenfra Hölen have "længet Tömmen"[3] således, at man med en Gang kan göre et smukt Kast[4] ned i den överste Del af samme, uden at komme lige[5] ned til den, eller i en Afstand[6] af 8—10 Alen, er det bedst.

Det har oftere hændt[7] mig, at jeg netop i den alleröverste Del af en Höl, tæt[8] inde ved Land, på ganske grundet[9] Vand, ved förste Kast med Fluen, efter formelig[10] at have luret mig ned[11] enten bag Træer eller en stor Sten, har fået en större Fisk, end jeg senere har sét ned over hele Hölen. Havde man gået i Syne[12] af denne lige ned til Stranden og begyndt med at göre, som sædvanligt, nogle Småkast[13] for at få Tömmen lang, vilde man ikke blot have skræmt[14] den, men også andre fra sin Plads, og i Elve, hvor der ofte fiskes med Flue, gjort den så sky,[15] at de på en lang Stund[16] ikke vilde vove[17] at hoppe.[18]

FORTY-SIXTH EXERCISE.

I.

I am bound to tell you that I am not able (in a position) to pay you the money which I owe you. Perhaps when you obtain the situation which the head-clerk, Mr. Thorlingen, promised you in the steam-boat company's office, you will be able to pay me some of the money which you owe me. That I will, with the greatest pleasure; but I ought to tell you, it is said that

[1] reason
[2] assumption
[3] run out the line
[4] throw
[5] quite
[6] distance
[7] happened to
[8] close to
[9] shallow
[10] almost
[11] laid in wait
[12] in sight
[13] short throws
[14] frightened
[15] timid
[16] a long time
[17] venture
[18] rise

the director of the company has resolved, that no clerk is in future to be nominated to a place in the office, who has not acquired some experience in business-transactions of a similar character to these. I was in the act of going out when he came running towards me with a letter in his hand, which had just arrived from my wife in Sweden. The peasant was working in his field when a troop of cavalry came tearing across the (farm) place, trampling under the hoofs of their horses everything that lay in the way, as they dashed off in full gallop.

II.

His brother is more prepossessing than he is, but yet he ought not to take so much upon himself in his relations with (in regard to) his family. The consul was sitting writing while I was with him. It seems to me he ought not to have been writing while a friend was calling on him (paying him a visit). I do not know how the consul could write while his secretary, Mr. Lang, was standing at the table and talking the whole time. I had to wait a whole hour before I could speak to the consul, and since I left him I have been writing for three hours. You must be tired after having done so much. Mr. Samuelsen is a very expert fisherman; he has often succeeded (it has often happened to him) in getting a large salmon the first time he threw his line into the water. I have no experience in fishing, and I do not think I have ever thrown (wetted) a line. What kind of flies do you use when you fish in Esrom lake? I use small silver-white flies when I fish in shallow water close to land.

FORTY-SEVENTH LESSON.

ON ADVERBS, etc. (Biord o.s.v.)

I. Some adverbs are used in Danish as adjectives; as for example:—

en særdeles Tildragelse, a peculiar occurrence
hun har anvendt temmelig Flid, she has shown tolerable industry.

II. Adverbs may be transposed and fused into verbs; as for example:—

Manden som er her
den herværende Mand } the man who is here

III. The adverbs *ja* and *jo*, yes, cannot be indifferently used, thus:—

A. *Ja* is used in answer to a question which is affirmative; as for example:—

er De her? ja! are you here? yes!

It may also be employed as an exclamation, or interjection; as for example:—

han bad mig, ja, bønfaldt mig endog med Tårer derom, he begged me, nay, implored me even with tears.

B. *Jo* is used in answer to a question which involves a doubt, or implies a denial; as for example:—

er De ikke dér? jo! are you not there? yes!

It is also used to give emphasis to a negative proposition, and, in some cases, as an ironical interjection; as for example:—

du var jo ikke her för...jo, jeg var, thou wast not here before... yes, I was.
jo, det var smukt! oh! that was grand!

Jo...jo, jo...desto are used as comparative or relative conjunctions; as for example:—

jo længere, jo værre, the longer the worse
jo mer han eftertænkte sin Forfatning, desto mer blev han bestyrket i sit Forsæt, the more he reflected on his condition, the more he was confirmed in his resolution.

IV. Some adverbs and conjunctions require to stand in a certain correlation to each other; as for example:—

ligesā...som, as...as
ikke alene...men endnu, ...endog } not only...but
ej blot...men ogsaa
dels...dels, partly...partly.

han er ligesā stor som jeg, he is just as tall as I am.
hun er ikke alene uskyldig, men fortjener endog Belönning, she is not only innocent, but she even deserves recompense.

at le, to laugh	en Karakter, a character
at regere, to rule	en Bagtaler, fem. -ske, a slanderer
at besörge, to care for	en Bekandt, acquaintance
at anskaffe, to procure	et Bekændtskab, an acquaintance-
at indrette, to prepare	ship
at föje sig, to submit	(et) Sylletöj, sweetmeats
at snakke, to chatter	en Agurk, a cucumber
at spise, to eat, dine	en Agurkesalat, sliced cucumber
at löbe, to run	en Ed like, vinegar
at sylte, to pickle, preserve	(en) Mad, food, meal
dum, stupid	Aftensmad, supper
sulten, hungry	hvor som helst, anywhere
törstig, thirsty	hvad som helst, whatever
snaksom, talkative	fuldkommen, quite, perfectly
omkring, round about	en Fogtning, a tight
en Lærer, -inde, teacher	en Gartner, a gardener.
en Skyld, a fault	

READING.

To translate into English.

Extract from the Christiania Daily Paper "MORGENBLADET."

In this extract the spelling has been left as in the original. The student will observe that the double a is used instead of å, and that i is used instead of j in such words as Öjeblik, while, on the other hand, j is inserted in igjen (igen), etc., where the modern system of orthography has discarded it as useless.

Fra Throndhjem 15de Decbr.—Der er afgaaet et Par Dampskibe til Levanger med Födemidler [1] osv.,[2] ved hvilken Leilighed flere Privatmænd, hvoriblandt specielt nævnes [3] DHrr. Jenssen & Ko., Jenssen & Sönner og H. T. Jenssen,

[1] provisions
[2] et cetera (in words: og sā videre)
[3] amongst whom are specially named

Konsul Lundgreen m. fl.,[1] skal have vist megen Gavmildhed,[2] der kommer vel med og er et godt Exempel. Den nedsatte Komite,[3] som skal indsamle Bidrag,[4] har inddelt[5] Byen i Distrikter, i hvilke Listerne cirkulere.[6]

Vi henstiller[7] til dem, som indkjöbe Julegaver til den forestaaende Fest,[8] at betænke, hvilke kjærkomne Julegaver[9] der vil kunne gives til de mange virkelig nödlidende[10] i vor Nærhed, hvoraf mange, om de end hjælpes noget i Öieblikket, dog ere blevne blottede for sin Smule höist fornödne Lösöre.[11] Hr. Sogneprest Pienes Opraab indeholder[12] en levende og talende Beskrivelse over Nöden.

Iaften Kl. 8 sendtes Dampskibet "Nea" til Levanger med mange Fornödenhedsartikler[13] samt 1660 Kroner fra Indsamlingskomiteen.[14] Her viser sig overhovedet megen Deltagelse[15] og Villighed til at hjælpe.

Den Tanke hörer vi dukke op[16] paa mange Kanter,[17] om det er rimeligt,[18] at man, efterat Levanger By, af Störrelse omtrent 1000 Indbyggere[19] ialt, er opbrændt saa godt som totalt,—bör indlade sig paa at före den op igjen[20] paa dens gamle Sted, hvor den, efter længe at have været i Tilbagegang,[21] end mere synes at mangle Betingelsen for Trivsel,[22] naar Svensketrafiken[23] ved Jernbanen föres ganske forbi Stedet. Hvis der for Alvor[24] skulde blive Spörgsmaal[25] om at slöife[26] Byen, maatte der vel hertil banes Adgang[27] ved et Forlig med Brandforsikringsindretningen om, at Erstatnings-

[1] *med flere*, with others
[2] liberality
[3] the committee appointed
[4] collect contributions
[5] divided
[6] lists are sent round
[7] propose
[8] coming festival
[9] welcome Christmas gifts
[10] suffering want
[11] stripped of their trifle of much needed belongings
[12] the parish-minister Piene's appeal contains
[13] necessary articles
[14] collecting committee
[15] very great sympathy
[16] come to the surface
[17] sides
[18] reasonable
[19] inhabitants
[20] undertake to raise it up again
[21] decline, decay
[22] requirements for prosperity
[23] Swedish traffic
[24] seriously
[25] question
[26] raze
[27] opening made

summen¹ blev at yde uden Forpligtelse til at gjenopføre Bygningerne.² Hertil vilde maaske udkræves³ ialfald kgl. Resol.⁴ om ikke en Storthingsbeslutning.⁵

FORTY-SEVENTH EXERCISE.

I.

You have not seen the soldiers who have come back, have you? Yes, I have, I saw them as they were coming back from their last engagement. The reigning prince is not beloved by his subjects, and the longer he reigns the less he accommodates himself to their wishes. It is not only on account of her being so talkative that we care so little for her visits, but also on account of her being at the same time the greatest slanderer of our acquaintance. The boy is not only idle, but he is stupid, and I think that his sister is just as idle and still more stupid. That is a pretty character to give the children of one's best friend. You may laugh if you will, but it is quite true. It may perhaps not be the parents' fault that the children are stupid; that may be due to (come from) nature, but it certainly is their fault that the children are idle, partly because they let them run about when and as (how) they like, and partly because they give themselves no trouble to procure them efficient teachers and governesses.

II.

The gardener has not yet brought us flowers from the garden, but he will soon bring some. Is the garden far from here? Not at all (quite the contrary), it is

[1] towards an arrangement with the fire insurance company that the compensation-money
[2] payable without obligation to re-erect the buildings
[3] require
[4] royal decree
[5] resolution of the Storthing

close to the house. My son has been in the garden from this morning until now, and he is both hungry and tired. You must tell the servant to get the supper ready as soon as possible, so that the young gentleman may get something to eat. If the servant should ask what he is to bring, only tell him to bring whatever there happens to be at hand : cold meat, ham, tongue, cheese, cucumber, preserves ; the more things the better. The servant says he will attend to what you say (do all that you require) as soon as he can.

FORTY-EIGHTH LESSON.

ON PREPOSITIONS (*Forholdsord*).

I. Some prepositions admit of being placed after, instead of before the words which they govern, and thus lose their predominant characteristic; as for example, in sentences of the following kind :—

han gik mig forbi, he went past (by) me.
Dem var det ikke han talte om, it was not you of whom he spoke.
det var mig som hun gav det til, it was to me she gave it.
den Bekymring kunne vi være foruden, that consideration need not trouble us.
luk Dören op, open the door.
luk ikke Dören i (til), do not shut the door.
der er Skuffen hvor jeg lagde det i, there is the drawer in which I laid it.
der ligger Bunken hvor jeg tog det af, there lies the heap from which I took it.
tag Deres Kåbe på, put on your cloak.

The following prepositions do not admit of this mode of transposition, but must always precede the words which they govern :—

foran, before
bag, behind
ifölge, according to
næst, next to
ovenfor, above
indenfor, within

nedenfor, below
henimod, towards
samt, together with
ved Siden af, by the side of
uden, without.

II. Prepositions in Danish generally govern the ablative, or perhaps more correctly speaking, the dative, since the language scarcely admits of a definite distinction between these two cases. But where we have to indicate a movement from one spot to another, or a transition from one condition to another, the preposition governs the accusative.

The distinction between rest and motion is, however, most frequently shown in Danish by the help of an adverb placed before the preposition; as for example:—

at gå ind i Stuen, to go into the room.
at gå inde i Stuen, to walk about in the room.
at flytte et Træ ned (ud, ind, hen, om) i Haven, to move a tree down (into, from one place to another) in the garden.
at flytte et Træ i Haven, to move a tree in the garden.

Fra and *i*, in the same manner as *til*, require to be followed by a genitive in certain relations of place and time; as for example:—

at gå fra Bords, to leave the table.
vi vare der i Mandags, we were there on (last) monday.

Ad and *af*, which through a careless mode of pronunciation, may be made to sound very nearly alike, ought to be carefully distinguished, the former meaning "on," "towards," and the latter "off," "away," as will be seen in the following examples:—

han gik ad Skoven til, he went towards the wood.
han gik af Vejen, he went off the road.

---

at betyde, to signify
at gøre Nar, to make a fool
at spille, to act, play
at hilse, to greet
at volde, to cause
at gribe, to seize
at straffe, to punish
at skrække, to frighten

en Amtmand, a magistrate
en Fortræd, a vexation
et Fængsel, a prison
en Gield, a debt
en Frihed, a liberty
et Oprör, an uproar, riot
en Straf, a punishment
en Skræk, a terror
en Mening, an opinion.

READING.

To translate into English.

Uddrag af "De tre nordiske Rigers Historie," af C. F. ALLEN.
(Extract from " The History of the three Northern Kingdoms by C. F. Allen.)

Christiern[1] den Anden ankom til Nederlandene[2] sidst i Juli 1524 og forblev[3] her til den 13 Marts 1526, da han vendte tilbage til Tydskland. I Nederlandene traf han sin Ægtefælle,[4] som omtrent en Måned tidligere havde begivet sig herhid[5] til sin Faster[6] Margrete, og sine Börn, som under Forældrenes Ophold[7] i Tydskland havde været overgivne til Margretes Varetægt.[8] Christiern den Anden nåede[9] Nederlandene, som vi vide, ikke uden at have været udsat[10] for Fare[11] for sit Liv eller sin Frihed, og en hel Hær[12] af Sorger og Bekymringer, som havde forfulgt[13] ham i Tydskland, fulgte med ham til Nederlandene. Han var nedböiet,[14] men ikke knækket;[15] thi al hans Hu[16] og Tragten[17] gik fremdeles[18] ud på at finde Midler[19] til sine Rigers Gjenerobring,[20] eller i det Mindste til at skade[21] sine Fjender så meget som muligt: derpå pönsede[22] han både ved Dag og ved Nat. Foruden de övrige Tryk,[23] hvorunder han led,[24] forbittredes[25] ham Opholdet i Nederlandene ved det uvenlige Sind, han altid mödte[26] hos Regentinde Margrete. Hun havde Intet tilovers for ham[27] fra den Tid, han var regerende Konge, da han i de sidste Aar, sköndt[28] ikke uden gyldig Grund,[29] var optrådt fjendtlig[30] mod Nederlandene; og hendes Stemning[31] imod ham forbedredes ikke, da han kom

[1] Christian
[2] Netherlands
[3] remained
[4] consort
[5] hither
[6] father's sister
[7] sojourn
[8] guardianship
[9] reached
[10] exposed
[11] danger
[12] army, array
[13] pursued
[14] bowed down
[15] crushed
[16] desire
[17] aim
[18] moreover
[19] means
[20] kingdom's reconquering
[21] injure
[22] ponder
[23] besides the other difficulties
[24] suffered
[25] embittered
[26] encountered
[27] she had borne him no good will
[28] although
[29] valid grounds
[30] shown himself hostile
[31] disposition

som Flygtning,¹ fordreven fra sine Riger, krævede² Hjælp og manede om Betalingen af sit Tilgodehavende,³ men især⁴ var hun bleven opfyldt af Bitterhed mod ham, da han var gået over til den lutherske Vranglære,⁵ og ikke blot det, men havde, som hun sagde, forført⁶ sin Dronning, Kejserens Söster, til det Samme, og derved sat en Plet⁷ på det kejserlige⁸ Huses Ære.

FORTY-EIGHTH EXERCISE.

I.

Who are you talking to? I am talking to the peasant-woman's little boy. Where is the little boy going (to)? He is going into town to sell his mother's chickens. My brother has come from home, and he says the town is in an uproar. What is the reason of it? In his opinion it is not an affair of any consequence; but at the same time it must be admitted that the men in authority whom he spoke to were all in a state of terror, and were intending to have the soldiers brought into the town. According to my brother's opinion some strangers had been making fools of these gentlemen, most of whom are (up in years) elderly. What did he wear? He wore his black coat. Were you at the theatre last Thursday? No, I was not there. It is said that the actress, Mrs. Petersen, has killed herself with a dagger. When did this occur? Her death must have happened within an hour after she came home from the theatre, where she acted that evening in the new tragedy. What has become of the Swedish lady who was here in the summer? I do not at all know where she has gone.

¹ fugitive
² sought for
³ importuned her for payment of what was due
⁴ especially
⁵ Lutheran heresy
⁶ misled
⁷ a stain
⁸ imperial

II.

Be so good as to go into the room, you will find the lady and her children there. There is the man who caused me that annoyance; I will have nothing more to do with him. I know the man of whom you are speaking, he sat next to me last evening; but as soon as I knew who he was I got up, and went from him without taking any notice of him. As you may believe, there is no friendship between him and me. Where does the watchmaker live from whom you bought your watch? I do not know his address, it was not to me he gave his address. The man of whom you are speaking is in prison for debt. When will the poor fellow come out? That I cannot tell you, but according to what (as) I hear, the woman is afraid that her husband will never be set free; but I believe she need have no such apprehension; the man will most likely come out of prison when the usual time of punishment expires.

List of Geographical and Other Terms.

(en) Natur, nature
en Grund, a ground, land
et Land, a land, country
en Sö, a sea
et Hav, an ocean
en Flod ⎱ a river
en Elv (Norw.) ⎰
en Flod, a flood-tide
en Ebbe, an ebb, low tide
(det) Store Bælt, the Great Belt
Bælterne, the Belts
Öresundet, the Sound
Österlandet, the East
Östersöen, the Baltic
Vesterharet, the Atlantic
Fastlandet, the Continent
en Ö, an island
et Bjærg, a mountain
en Dal, a valley
en Halvö, a peninsula
et Forbjærg, a promontory
et Höjland, a highland
Höjlandene i Skotland, the Highlands
Nederlandene, the Netherlands
(et) Danmark, Denmark
(et) Slesvig, Slesvig
(et) Jylland, Jutland
en Jyde, a Jutlander
jydsk, jutish
(et) Köbenhavn, Copenhagen
köbenhavnsk, of Copenhagen
(et) Helsingör, Elsinore
(et) Kattegat, the Cattegat
en Bugt, a bay
en Indsö, a lake

en *Å*, a rivulet
en *Klint*, a cliff
en *Bæk*,* a stream, little river
en *Bredde*, a longitude
en *Breddegrad*, a degree of longitude
en *Höjde*, a latitude
en *Höjdegrad*, a degree of latitude
en *Bro*, a bridge
en *Havn*, a port, haven
et *Landingssted*, a landing place
et *Værft*, a wharf
en *Kanal*, a canal
en *Told*, custom, duty
et *Toldhus*, a custom-house
en *Strand*, a strand
en *Krig*, a war
en *Orlogsflåde*, a fleet of men-of-war

et *Orlogsskib*, a line of battle ship
en *Båd*, a boat
et *Bådleje*, berth for a boat
Bådlejen, the boat-hire
et *Bådskur*, a boat-shed
en *Åre*, an oar
et *Ror*, a rudder
at *lystre Roret*, to obey (answer) the helm
at *ro*, to row
et *Sejl*, a sail
et *Anker*, an anchor
et *Tovværk*, ropes, lines
et *Flag*, a flag
en *Flagstang*, a flagstaff
en *Vimpel*, a pennant
en *Kanon*, a cannon
en *Kanonkugle*, a cannon ball
en *Fæstning*, a fortress
en *Vold*, a rampart.

FORTY-NINTH LESSON.

ON SOME PREPOSITIONS

Forholdsord).

I. Some prepositions have the effect of making the noun with which they are combined, take a final *e* when the compound word is used adverbially; as for example: *ilive*, alive; *itide*, in time; *tildöde*, to death; *tilskamme*, for shame's sake; *medrette*, in justice.

The final *e* is retained even when the preposition and noun are decomposed into distinct words; as for example: *ad Åre*, years to come; *til Skamme*; *i Tide*, etc.

In this form we have either a survival of an otherwise extinct Northern dative in *e*, or a modification of the known Icelandic dative terminations *i* and *u*.

II. According to some grammarians, the final *s* in nouns, governed by such prepositions as *ad* and *i*, is used either elliptically, or for purposes of euphony, rather than to show that the preposition governs the genitive directly. This assumed elliptical character of the *s* is also shown in the case of *hos*; as for example: *hos Generalens*, which may be assumed to mean *hos Generalens Familje*, with the General's family.

The following examples illustrate the distinctive meanings conveyed by the prepositions *i*, *på*, *om*, *ad*, and *til*, when used with nouns indicative of periods of time. Thus, while *i*, in conjunction with a noun in the genitive (or a noun having the termination *es* or *s*), always refers to a past period, *i* with a noun in the accusative, without the termination *s*, may imply the present, like *om*, or the future, like *på*. *Ad* and *til* are used in a special, but somewhat arbitrary manner, as will be seen below:—

i Mandags, on (last) Monday	*på Söndag*, on (next) Sunday
i Sommers, last summer	*om Morgenen*, in the morning
i Morges, this recently past morning	*Morgendags*, to-morrow's
i Morgen, to-morrow	*om Tirsdagen*, on Tuesdays
i Dag, to-day	*i År*, this year
om Dagen, in the day-time	*ad Åre*, years to come
i Går Aftes, last evening	*idag om et År*, this day twelvemonth
i Aften, this evening	
i Nat, to-night, last night	*til Års*, in years
om Natten, at night	*År for År*, year by year
til Natten, for the night	*engang om Året*, once a year.

The word *Nat* affords an exception to the rule, that the noun following the preposition *i* must end in *s*, when a past period of time is indicated. Thus, for instance, we say *i Nat*, and never *i Nats*, to indicate the preceding night, and consequently the difference between *i Nat*, *this* night, and *i Nat*, *last* night, can only be shown by the general meaning of the context, as in the following examples:—

i Nat kunde jeg ikke sove, I could not sleep last night.
i Nat går jeg tidlig til Sengs, to-night I shall go early to bed.

The difference of meaning between *på* and *om*, when used

before the names of the days of the week, will be seen by the following examples :—

kommer han måske på Söndag? will he be likely to come on Sunday? *nej! om Söndagen rejser han bestemt ikke,* no! on the Sunday (on Sundays) he will certainly not travel.

Om answers to the English *on, in, about,* when a slightly indefinite sense is to be expressed ; as for example :—

vi vænte vor Fader om fjorten Dage, we expect our father in about a fortnight.
min Söster var her om Morgenen, my sister was here in the morning

at synge, to sing	*en Ild,* a fire
at besöge, to visit	*en Ildlös* ⎱ a conflagration
at lande, to land	*en Ildebrand* ⎰
at være nödt til, to be obliged to	*en Flamme,* a flame
at beholde, to keep	*en Balle,* a ball, bale
at færdes (dep.), to travel	(*en*) *Bomuld,* cotton
at befærdes, to be frequented	*Bomuldsgarn,* cotton yarn
at fortære, to consume	(*en*) *Jord,* earth
at forlade, to leave	*jordisk,* earthly
at ligne, to be like	*underjordisk,* subterranean
lige, just, like	*forskellig,* different
iligemåde, in the same manner	*sildig,* sent, late
ligefrem, right onwards	*en Sædvane,* a custom
en Bogholder, a bookkeeper	*sædvanlig,* usual.

READING.

To translate into English.

Uddrag af "De tre nordiske Rigers Historie," af C. F. ALLEN.

(Extract from "The History of the three Northern Kingdoms," by C. F. Allen).

Samtidige tillægge[1] Christian III et ualmindeligt[2] smukt Ydre[3] og en Ynde[4] i Væsen og Fremtræden,[5] der gjorde, at han ligesom ved en Naturens Gave vandt[6] Alle, med hvem han kom i Berörelse.[7] Til Lærer eller som det kaldtes Tugtemester[8] fik han, da han gik i sit 15de Ar, Wolf

[1] contemporaries
[2] uncommon
[3] exterior
[4] grace
[5] in carriage and appearance
[6] to win
[7] contact
[8] tutor

Utenhoff, der siden blev Kong Frederiks höjt betroede Kanstler;[1] Johan Rantzau blev nogle År efter hans Hofmester.[2] Christian synes i sin Ungdom at have havt et glad og let Hjærte og Noget af en Spögefugl[3] i sig. Det viser den bekændte Historie om hans Ophold[4] på Rigsdagen[5] i Worms 1521, hvor han ledsaget[6] af Johan Rantzau var tilstæde[7] og hörte Luther forsvare sin Sag[8] for Kejseren og Tydsklands Fyrster[9] og Herrer. En Dag hörte han en Munk[10] af Gråbrödreordenen prædike[11] i Slotskirken. Prædikanten[12] talte med stor Salvelse[13] og var meget hæftig i sine Lader og Fagter,[14] så han snart hævede sig til sin hele Höjde, snart sank så dybt ned, at han næsten blev borte for Tilhörerne.[15] Ved den sidste Bevægelse hændte det sig, at Enden af det Reb,[16] som Gråbrödrene pleje at bære om Livet, faldt ned i en Sprække,[17] der tilfældigvis var på Bunden af Prædikestolen. Hertug Christian, som bemærkede det, greb hurtigt Rebet og slog en Knude[18] derpå. Det Råb af Skræk, som Munken udstödte,[19] da han mærkede, han ikke kunde rejse sig,[20] frembragte först nogen Uro og Forvirring[21] blandt de Forsamlede;[22] men da man mærkede, hvorledes det hang sammen, blev der en almindelig Munterhed.[23] Kejseren, som var tilstæde, slog ind i Spögen[24] og sagde, " den unge Herre bliver næppe Munkene god."[25]

[1] trusted chancellor
[2] master of the household
[3] wag
[4] sojourn
[5] diet
[6] accompanied
[7] present
[8] defend his cause
[9] princes
[10] monk
[11] preach
[12] preacher
[13] unction
[14] movements
[15] audience, hearers
[16] rope
[17] slit
[18] tied a knot
[19] uttered
[20] raise himself
[21] confusion
[22] assembled
[23] general merriment
[24] took part in (fell into) the joke
[25] "the young prince is not likely to prove himself a friend to the monks."

FORTY-NINTH EXERCISE.

I.

She sings from early morning till late in the evening. My son goes out in the country on a Saturday, as soon as he is able to leave the office. What does he do on a Sunday? On the Sundays he generally dines at his grandfather's, but he sometimes makes a little excursion by water. Can I keep the book, which I borrowed last Sunday from your daughter, till this evening? You may keep it till the day after to-morrow, if you like. Thank you, then I will bring it on Thursday. Do you know that there was a fire this evening? No, I have been all day in the country at the clergyman's, and I have only this moment come into town. Was it a large fire, and was any one injured? It was a frightful fire; Hansen's private house and both his warehouses with seven hundred bales of cotton were entirely consumed by the flames; but, as far as I know, there was no one injured.

II.

The first time we went to England we landed towards evening on a summer's day. Did you remain all the time in London, or in any one of the provincial towns? We remained only about a fortnight in London, but you would hardly believe (it is almost incredible) how much we managed to see in that short time. It is impossible in such an enormous place to get on very far on foot, the distances between the different parts of the town are too great; one is obliged to drive, or, at all events to go by the underground-railway, which runs right under the principal and most frequented streets. I think it must be dreadful to travel on such a railway; I would rather go above the ground than under it.

FIFTIETH LESSON.

ON THE USE OF CERTAIN PREPOSITIONS AND CONJUNCTIONS.

I. The words *af, efter, for, med, om, over, til, ved* are frequently found in Danish governing an infinitive preceded by the conjunction *at*, and used as a gerund; as for example:—

> *jeg er ked af at höre den Mand tale*, I am tired of hearing that man talk.
> *efter at göre sig megen Umage, önsker man at få Tak*, after taking so much pains, one wishes to be thanked.
> *han kom ikke for at undskylde sig*, he did not come to exculpate himself.
> *Bonden var ved at arbejde, da jeg så ham*, the peasant was working when I saw him.
> *hun var hjærtelig glad over at se ham*, she was heartily glad to see him.
> *her er ingen Plads til at sidde på*, there is no place here to sit on.

II. In simple sentences not modified by any secondary clause, or where the subject is not indicated, some prepositions, as *om, til, over*, may be dispensed with; thus we may say, either: *der er ingen Plads at sidde på*, or: *der er ingen Plads til at sidde på*; but the preposition is imperatively required whenever the subject is expressed, as: *han havde Möje med at vende sig om*, he had a difficulty in turning round.

When the infinitive is used in apposition to a noun, no preposition precedes it; as for example:—

> *den gode Skik at stå tidligt op*, the good habit of getting up early.

---

at *spörge efter*, to enquire for
at *indbyde*, to invite
at *foretage*, to undertake
at *forsyne*, to provide
at *vide*, to know
at *lave*, to prepare, make
at *läse*, to fasten, lock
at *söge*, to seek
at *tabe*, to lose

at *mistænke*, to distrust
på...nær, excepting
langt fra, far from
et *Spörgsmål*, a question
en *Pröve*, a trial, rehearsal
et *Beslag*, a requisition
at *lægge Beslag på Ens Tid*, to engross one's time
en *Udsigt*, a prospect.

en *Grund*, a ground, reason
en *Frokost*, a breakfast
en *Top*,* a top, summit
   netop, precisely
et *Bud*, a message, messenger

(et) *Befindende*, state, condition
en *Tilstand*, a condition
en *Efterretning*, news, information
et *Universitet*, a university.

READING.

To translate into English.

Uddrag af "De tre nordiske Rigers Historie," af C. F. ALLEN.
(Extract from "The History of the three Northern Kingdoms," by C. F. Allen).

Staden[1] Lier, hvor Christiern den Anden, sköndt med en lang Afbrydelse[2] fra 1526—28, da han var i Tydskland, havde sit Ophold lige til 1531, fåer af en Forfatter[3] der ved Midten af samme Århundrede forfattede[4] en Beskrivelse af Nederlandene (L. Guicciardini) det Skudsmål,[5] at det i Sandhed er en god og behagelig lille By, hvis Indbyggere[6] ere godmodige, sindige,[7] höflige og omgængelige.[8] Den ligger, som sagt, ved Åen[9] Nethe, der står i Forbindelse med Schelde, så at ved Höjvande ikke ganske små Skibe kunne komme op til Byen. Den er rundtomkring omgivet[10] af et frugtbart, af mange Aløb[11] gennemskåret[12] Sletteland[13] med dansk Præg[14] og Tone. Den kunde således minde[15] de Danske, som Skæbnen her havde henkastet, om Næstved med Susåen eller en anden sjællandsk By med lignende Omgivelser,[16] og, når ikke Andet havde været i Vejen, vilde have kunnet føle sig hjemlige og vel her blandt en Befolkning,[17] der var så venlig og omgængelig. Sproget kunde ikke göre store Vanskeligheder,[18] da Indbyggerne den Gang talte flamsk,[19] hvilket Tungemål[20] de endnu til vore Dage

[1] town
[2] although with a long interval
[3] author
[4] wrote
[5] character (*lit.*: object aimed at)
[6] inhabitants
[7] orderly
[8] courteous and sociable (*Omgang*, intercourse)
[9] small stream
[10] surrounded
[11] rivulets, water-runs
[12] intersected
[13] flat-lands
[14] character
[15] remind
[16] surroundings
[17] population
[18] difficulties
[19] Flemish
[20] mother-tongue

jo mere jo bedre, the more the better.

jo oftere jeg ser hende, jo mer holder jeg af hende, the oftener I see her, the more I like her.

jo mere han eftertænkte sin Forfatning — de få Venner han havde, og de mange Fjender der bestræbte sig for at tilintetgöre hans Lykke — desto mere blev han bestyrket i sit Forsæt, the more he considered his circumstances—the few friends he had, and the many enemies who endeavoured to destroy his happiness—the more he was confirmed in his resolution.

III. After correlative, or compound, conjunctions, the predicate may in ordinary conversation be omitted at the close of the secondary part of the sentence; as for example:—

han er lige så flittig som du (er), he is just as diligent as you are.
han er ikke alene flink i Norsk, men også i Tysk, he is not alone expert (well-versed) in Norwegian, but also in German.

IV. The repetition, or omission, of prepositions and copulative conjugations depends very much, as in English, upon the nature of the sentence, the repeated use of the preposition giving force or emphasis; as for example:—

Fuglene sang i Haverne, i Skovene, på Træerne, på Hegnene, overalt, the birds were singing in the gardens, in the woods, on the trees, on the hedges, everywhere.

at *anfalde,* to attack
at *stöde op til,* to be next, to approach
at *nedstöde,* to knock down
at *indeholde,* to contain
at *anrette,* to cause, prepare
at *tænde,* to kindle
at *straffe,* to punish
at *adoptere,* to adopt
at *bestå af,* to consist in
at *stride,* to contend
at *trættes,* to dispute
at *erstatte,* to compensate
at *give ud,* to expend
at *angå,* to concern
at *modsige,* to contradict
at *opnå,* to obtain, attain

(en) *Prygl,* a beating
dygtig Prygl, a sound thrashing
en *Landevej,* a highroad
(en) *Fraværelse,* absence
en *Ulykke, Skade,* a mischief
en *Straf,** a punishment
en *Anstrængelse,* labour, effort
en *Ærgrelse,* a vexation
en *Kriger,* a warrior
en *Skribent,* a writer
en *Lue,* a flame
en *Bagatel,** a trifle
en *Eftersporgsel,* an investigation
et *Forår,* spring
gerrig, avaricious
nödvendig, necessary

READING.

To translate into English.

Uddrag af "Tilfjælds," af J. A. FRIIS.

Der var en Ridder[1] i Valders, som i lang Tid havde ligget i Strid[2] med Sandboridderen.[3] Engang som Sandboridderen ikke var hjemme, tog Valdersridderen Lejligheden iagt,[4] kom med sine Svende[5] over Fjældet ned til Sandbo og afbrændte Gården. Ejeren,[6] som straks efter kom hjem, samlede öjeblikkelig en Del Folk og satte efter Valdersen.[7] Denne havde om Natten taget Kvarter[8] på en Sæter, som hedder[9] Fuglesæteren,[10] og udstillet Vagter[11] rundt omkring. Sandboridderen og hans Folk red[12] hele Natten gennem, og da han mod Dagningen[13] nærmede sig Sæteren, lod han sine Folk afhugge[14] små Birketræer[15] og holde disse foran[16] sig og Hestene. I Begyndelsen mærkede Vagterne ikke Uråd,[17] men da de tilslut[18] tydeligt syntes, at Birkeskoven bevægede sig og kom nærmere, gjorde de Anskrig.[19] Dog nu var det for silde. Sandboingerne faldt over Valderserne og huggede dem ned, så samtlige[20] bleve på Valpladsen[21] så nær som[22] Valdersridderen selv og hans Våbendrager.[23] Disse undkom[24] tilhest og troede sig allerede reddede,[25] da de pludselig stödte[26] på Elven Sjoa, som med ubændig[27] Vildhed styrter[28] sig skummende[29] ned mellem bratte[30] Klippevægge.[31] Fortvivlet[32] standser Valdersridderen ved en Klöft, som tværs-

[1] knight
[2] strife
[3] the knight of Sandbo
[4] *at tage Lejligheden i Agt*, to take advantage of the opportunity
[5] serving men
[6] owner
[7] pursued the Valders knight
[8] quarters
[9] is called
[10] the Bird Sæter
[11] posted guards
[12] rode
[13] daybreak
[14] hew off
[15] birch
[16] before
[17] danger
[18] *tilslut* (Norw.), at length; (*til Slutning*, in the end)
[19] *göre Anskrig*, give the alarm
[20] one and all
[21] field of battle
[22] excepting
[23] page, weapon bearer
[24] escaped
[25] saved
[26] came upon
[27] irrepressible
[28] dash
[29] foaming
[30] steep
[31] rocky walls
[32] in despair

over[1] vistnok[2] ikke er mere end 3 Alen bred, men Stranden på modsatte[3] Side er höj og Klippevægen aldeles glat.[4] Dog de forfölgende[5] Fjender give ham intet Valg,[6] han hopper af Hesten, sætter i fuld Rustning[7] tilsprangs[8] over Gabet[9] og er så heldig at få Fodfæste[10] på den modsatte Side af dette Svælg,[11] som endnu den Dag i Dag[12] hedder "Ridderspranget." Våbendrageren springer efter, men tumler[13] tilbage igen og styrter redningslös[14] i Afgrunden[15] til Skræk og Advarsel[16] for Enhver, der vilde forsöge Spranget.[17] Valdersridderen undkom, men måtte senere afstå[18] Hejmdalsvandet til Gjæslingerne,[19] og det har siden i 700 Åar tilhört Gården Sandbo, indtil det, Skam at fortælle,[20] for nogle Åar siden blev solgt til en Engelskmand for en Spotpris[21] af så eller så mange Hundrede Speciedaler.[22]

FIFTY-FIRST EXERCISE.

I.

If I am too late for the boat, I need not remain here. If he wishes to discover it, I will give him all the necessary directions. The warrior does battle with his sword, the writer with his pen. Will you take a seat here by the side of my wife and myself? He is a Frenchman by birth, but an American by adoption. They are only contending about a trifle, and not about anything important. If the boy should do that again, he will certainly get a sound thrashing. We came back over land and sea, mountains and rivers, and now we shall probably never make a long journey again. The more money an avaricious man

[1] right across
[2] certainly
[3] opposite
[4] smooth
[5] pursuing
[6] choice
[7] armour
[8] to make a spring (Norw.)
[9] chasm
[10] foot-hold
[11] chasm
[12] to this day
[13] to fall
[14] without chance of saving
[15] abyss
[16] warning
[17] leap (Norw.)
[18] give up
[19] (the name of a family)
[20] shame to say
[21] dead bargain
[22] specie dollars

acquires, the less he spends. The more enquiries the lawyer made in reference to the stranger, who was attacked and ill-treated on the highroad near the royal castle at Birkelund last spring, the more contradictory was the information that he obtained concerning the man.

II.

How that man has travelled! Why, he has been in England, in Scotland, in America, in France, in Spain, and in many other countries. I wish I could travel far and wide, as he has done. And he, perhaps, wishes that he had a happy home and dear children, as you have. I should not like to have so few friends as he has.

Sir Isaac Newton had a little dog which he called "Diamond." One day when Sir Isaac was called into an adjoining room, Diamond remained behind, and when he returned after only a few minutes absence, he had the vexation to see that some papers containing the almost completed work of many years' labour were in flames, owing to Diamond having knocked over a lighted candle. The loss was irreparable, but without punishing the dog, he only exclaimed: "Oh! Diamond! Diamond! you little know what mischief you have done!"

FIFTY-SECOND LESSON.

ON THE USE OF CERTAIN CONJUNCTIONS (*Bindeord*).

I. Some verbs, as *at håbe*, to hope; *at tro*, to believe; *at tænke*, to think; *at forstå*, to understand; *at magte*, to be able; *at ønske*, to wish; *at bede*, to entreat, etc., may take another verb as an object, in which case the latter must be put in the infinitive, and be preceded by the conjunction *at*; as for example:—

jeg håber at se Dig, I shall hope to see ye.
han forstår at spille på Klaver, he knows how to play the piano.

II. The conjunction *at* is not used before the infinitive, when the preceding and governing verb belongs either to the group of the auxiliaries, or to verbs of perception; as for example:—

jeg tör ikke göre det, I dare not do it.
han burde gå, he ought to go.
vi hörte ham sige det, we heard him say it.
de så hende give ham Bogen, they saw her give him the book.

III. Although, in Danish, the general rule is recognised, that the verb "to be," or any other verb in a similar sense, should have the same case after as before it, an exception is made when the verb may be considered to be used as an impersonal; as for example:—

det var mig, it was I.
er det dig? is it thou?
ja, det er mig, yes, it is I.

Through custom, more than on any sound grammatical grounds, the Danes have been led to accept as an established rule, that the objective case should always be used after the verb "to be" in such sentences as the following:—

hvis du var mig vilde du ikke göre det, if you were me you would not do it.

---

at glemme, to forget
at banke, to knock
at være på Færde, to be about, to happen
hvad er der på Færde? what is the matter?
at rette sig, to conform to
at vinde, to win
at tabe } to lose
at miste }
at værge, to defend
passende, suitable

at stå op, to get up
at sy, to sew
taus, silent
et Råd, an advice
Tierne (pl.), tens
en Dame, the queen (in games)
en Makker, a partner (at cards)
et Kort, a card
et Es,* an ace
et Spil,* a game
en Verden, a world
en Rænke, a machination.

READING

to translate into English.

Uddrag af " To Tidsaldre," af Forfatteren til " En Hverdagshistorie."

(Extract from "Two Ages," by the author of "An Every-day Story.")

Ved Juletid[1] havde han det snilde Indfald[2] at bringe den lille Charles en hel Kurv fuld af Julegaver.[3] Det barnlige Sind er næsten altid taknemmeligt.[4] Den glade Dreng klyngede[5] sig med Hjærtelighed til den milde Giver, der opstillede[6] ham Huse, Træer, Soldater o. s. v. for at vise ham Brugen[7] af de forskellige Herligheder,[8] forklarede[9] ham Billeder[10] og især anviste[11] ham nogle små Spil og spillede dem med ham til en Pröve.[12] Dette var meget forstandigt beregnet[13] på at trække[14] Tiden ud. Charles jublede,[15] og med moderlig og bedstemoderlig Interesse toge begge Fruentimmerne Del i deres Yndlings[16] Glæde og Taknemmelighed.[17] Det var Juledag. Den foregående[18] Aften var i det simple Hus bleven festligholdt[19] efter ringe Lejlighed.[20] Et lille Juletræ stod endnu i Stuen. Man oppyntede[21] det påny[22] med friske[23] Æbler, Kager og Lys, som man tændte[24] til Ære for den store Tilvæxt[25] af Julegaver. Baronen hjalp ved dette Arbejde. De to gamle Husvenner kom imidlertid[26] også og bragte deres lille Skærv.[27] De fölte ingen synderlig[28] Fornöjelse ved at træffe[29] den uventede,[30] fornemme Gjæst, der også på sin Side önskede dem til

[1] Christmas-time	[11] showed	[21] decorated
[2] ingenious idea	[12] by way of trial	[22] again
[3] Christmas presents	[13] sensibly calculated	[23] fresh
[4] grateful	[14] draw out	[24] to light
[5] clung	[15] rejoiced	[25] addition
[6] set up	[16] darling	[26] in the meanwhile
[7] the use	[17] gratitude	[27] mite
[8] glorious things	[18] preceding	[28] special
[9] explained	[19] celebrated	[29] meet
[10] pictures	[20] humble means	[30] unexpected

Bloksbjerg.¹ Men Husets Damer havde et så skönt Talent til at göre Honneurs,² forenet³ med en så god Tone, at Enhver snart fandt sig på sin Plads. Baronen viste imidlertid de Nysankomne⁴ al Artighed,⁵ og de godmodige ældre Mænd kom snart i deres gamle Folder.⁶ Damerne bade Baronen at tage tiltakke⁷ hos dem, man satte sig om det tarvelige,⁸ men nette Bord i det bedste Lune,⁹ og tilbragte¹⁰ en Aften, der forekom¹¹ Enhver som et lyst Punkt¹² i Vinterens mörke¹³ Tid.

FIFTY-SECOND EXERCISE.

I.

Is it you, Mr. Svendsen, knocking at the door? Yes, it is I, if you will only let me come in, I will soon tell you what is the matter. Do you wish to speak to my father? No, I am not wanting to speak to him, but my nephew is, and he hopes to be able to see him as soon as possible. I do not know how that can be managed, because my father was not to get up to-day. I wish he could see your nephew, but I heard him say that he was far too unwell to be able to receive visits to-day. I hope to find him better the next time I call upon you; and I must say, if I were he, I would remain in bed a few days longer. I do not think he will do so, but I will, at all events, beg him to follow your advice.

II.

You ought to have won your game, as you had all the tens, kings, and queens, and three aces. I did think that we should have won the game, as my partner and I

[1] "wished them at Jericho"
[2] the honours
[3] combined
[4] newly arrived
[5] civility
[6] grooves, folds
[7] be content with, make the best of
[8] humble
[9] temper
[10] spent
[11] appeared to
[12] point
[13] dark

had the best cards between us. Was it you, who saw him fall? No (it was not I), I saw him run away, but I did not see him fall. If he fell, it must have been after I lost sight of him. When my husband has to write in the evening, I dare not speak; I must sit silent at my sewing. We were obliged to wait three hours before we could see him; his servant did not know when he would be at home. Wheresoever I may go in the world, whether South, East, or West, I shall never forget my old home in the North. If I were in your place, I would never again go to that scoundrel, and I hope at all events that you will know how to defend yourself against his machinations. Your mother ought not to allow you to do it. It is an improper thing which should not be permitted

FIFTY-THIRD LESSON.

ON THE USE OF SOME OF THE AUXILIARIES.

I. The auxiliary *at have*, to have, may be omitted in Danish after the auxiliaries *burde, turde, kunne, ville, skulle, maätte*, when it indicates a past perfect, as for example:—

jeg kunde gjort det, I could (have) done it.
han burde været hjemme, he ought to (have) been at home.

The verb *at få* is often used by Norwegians, but scarcely ever by Danes, in the place of the auxiliary *at have*: as for example:—

når jeg får læst vil jeg gå ud, when I have (shall have) done reading, I will go out.

II. The verbs *få, have, lade* admit of the verb which they govern being used in the active infinitive, as in English; as for example:—

jeg fik Lov til at gå, I got leave to go.
han har meget at bestille, he has a great deal to do.
hun lader Barnet gå, she lets the child go.

In some cases, however, the Danes employ the active infinitive after the above auxiliaries in a manner not admissible in English; as for example:—

min Broder lader et Hus bygge, my brother is having a house built.

III. The infinitive of verbs, whether active or passive, admits of being used in the sense of a nominative or objective noun; as for example:—

at elske sit Barn er en Moders største Pligt, to love her child is a mother's highest duty.
vi erhverve os vor Næstes Agtelse ved at være redelige, we gain the esteem of our neighbour by being upright.
at agtes er noget som Enhver skulde stræbe efter, to be esteemed is what every one should strive after.

The following examples will show the great similarity between English and Danish in regard to certain modes of using the infinitive:—

her er Plads nok til at stå, here is room enough to stand.
hun er god at arbejde for, she is good to work for.
det er vanskeligt at skrive om, that is a difficult thing to write about.
han er let at overtale, he is easy to persuade (talk over).
jeg har Intet at klage over, I have nothing to complain of.
det er ikke værd at græde for, it is not worth crying for.

---

at have i Sinde, to intend
at forlade sig på, to trust to
at spadsere, to take walks
at bedrage, to deceive
at indbilde sig, to imagine
at omgås, to associate with
at benægte, to deny
at afgøre, to settle
at ærgre sig, to worry oneself
at blande sig i, to meddle with
det er til ingen Nytte, it is of no use

behagelig, pleasant
et Løfte, a promise
en Næste, (*Nabo*) a neighbour
(*et*) *Velbehag*, pleasantness
et Anliggende, an affair, business
et Bud, a command, commandment
en Nægtelse, a denial
(*en*) *Fornuft*, sense
fornuftig, sensible.

(229)

READING
to translate into English.

Uddrag af " Fra Østerland " (From the East), af P. Blom.

Ramazan er Mohammedanernes Fastemåned.¹ Den er en Efterabelse ² af de Kristnes ³ Fastetid, kun med den Forskel,⁴ at man for Dagens Forsagelser ⁵ tager₆ sig rigeligt betalt i Nattens Forlystelser.⁶ Den falder i Årets* niende Måned. Mohamed valgte ⁷ denne Måned til Fastemåned, fordi den Almægtige,⁸ som han sagde, havde forkyndt ⁹ ham hans Sendelse ¹⁰ på den niende Dag i denne Måned og Dagen derefter åbenbaret ¹¹ ham Koranens første Kapitel.¹² I hele denne Måned, i hvilken det er befalet Profetens Tilhængere ¹³ at faste hver Dag fra Dagbrækningen ¹⁴ til Solnedgang,¹⁵ skulle de afholde ¹⁶ sig fra at spise, drikke, ryge, og snuse Tobak,¹⁷ og fra at lugte på Essenser.¹⁸ Syge, Soldater i Krig og lidende Kvinder ¹⁹ göre en Undtagelse ²⁰ herfra; men man forventer,²¹ at de indhente det Forsömte ²² i en anden Måned. —

Blandt de forskellige Overtrædelser,²³ som göre den daglige Faste ugyldig,²⁴ og som må afsones ²⁵ med overordentlig ²⁶ Bön og overordentlige Spegelser,²⁷ er Bagtalelse.²⁸

* Det mohammedanske År deles i 12 Månemåneder,²⁹ hvoraf seks indeholde tredive, og seks ni og tyve Dage. Således har Året 354 Dage, hvilket gör en Forskel af elleve Dage mellem vort og det mohammedanske. De mohammedanske Fester komme selvfölgelig ³⁰ hvert År elleve Dage senere ³¹ end det foregående.³²

¹ fasting month
² imitation, after-aping
³ Christians
⁴ difference
⁵ deprivations
⁶ amusements
⁷ chose
⁸ Almighty
⁹ announced
¹⁰ mission
¹¹ revealed
¹² chapter
¹³ enjoined upon the prophet's adherents
¹⁴ daybreak
¹⁵ sunset
¹⁶ abstain
¹⁷ take snuff, (snuff tobacco)
¹⁸ smell, inhale perfumes or essences
¹⁹ women
²⁰ exception
²¹ expect
²² atone for that which has been omitted
²³ transgressions
²⁴ invalid
²⁵ be atoned for
²⁶ extraordinary
²⁷ penance
²⁸ slander
²⁹ lunar months
³⁰ consequently
³¹ later
³² previous

Den daglige Fastes Begyndelse og Ende angives i Konstantinopel ved vældige Kanonskud[1] fra Batterierne ved Bosporus og det gyldne Horn. Når Ramazan falder i Sommertiden, er Fasten ofte såre pinlig.[2] Ikke at tale om, at det også er meget slemt for Tyrkerne at måtte undvære[3] Tobak, da de i Regelen ere Slaver[4] af den skadelige Tobaksrygning.[5] — Man indtager det förste Måltid[6] straks efter Solnedgang og det sidste henimod Morgenen, da Fasten må være begyndt 20 Minutter för Bönnen i Dagbrækningen. Natten tilbringes af de Fornemme og Rige enten hjemme eller tilvogns, og af den lavere[7] Klasse og de Fattige i Kaffehusene, på Gaderne og de offentlige Pladse.[8] I Kaffehusene, hvoraf der gives en stor Mængde, musiceres,[9] drikkes Kaffe og Scherbet, ryges Tobak og fortælles Nyheder[10] og Historier.[11]

FIFTY-THIRD EXERCISE.

I.

He ought to have taken the trouble to come to my house to-day. She should have trusted to her brother's promises. My master should have been here at ten o'clock to give me and my sisters our music lesson. We are wanting to go out for a walk, but now we are obliged to remain at home until we have played with him. To love God above all things, and one's neighbour as one self is the first (highest) commandment of Christianity. We shall secure God's approval if we are (by being) virtuous. The Swedish merchant is not so easily deceived (cheated). My cousin asks me about something of which it is somewhat difficult to speak. It is not at all agreeable to live with a person, who allows himself to be persuaded that he has a great deal to complain of. I am intending to let my little children learn dancing.

[1] loud firing of cannon
[2] sorely trying
[3] dispense with
[4] slaves
[5] tobacco smoking
[6] meal
[7] lower
[8] public places, squares
[9] there is music
[10] news
[11] tales

Is it true that your father is buying a pair of black horses and a handsome carriage? It is of no use for you to hurry; you will come too late to see the comedy. Do you imagine that her denial of her words has anything to do with the matter? The cause pending between her and me does not so easily admit of being decided.

II.

People often worry themselves when they ought not. Such a sensible person (lady) as you are, ought never to have worried yourself as you did yesterday. That is easily said, but no one knows where the shoe pinches, but he who wears it. Charles, have you done writing your French exercises? You ought to have written it this morning. Do not interfere in my affairs; I beg you will attend to your own concerns. I shall have my exercise written in good time; and if I do not, it is all the same to me. Who is upstairs? Where is Anna? —is it she, who is in the garden?—it is Charles. Is it he?—It is we—are you coming up to us? Was that you (thou)? Yes; it was I!

FIFTY-FOURTH LESSON.

ON THE USE OF THE PARTICIPLES (*Tillægsformerne*).

I. The present and past participles of most Danish verbs may be used in the sense of adjectives; as for example:—

en *indbunden Bog*, a bound book (a book that has been bound).
et *fundet Ærme*, a found sleeve (a sleeve that has been found.
en *sörgende Enke*, a sorrowing widow.
den *overfyldte Vogn*, the filled (over-full) carriage.
de *brugte Penne*, the used-up pens.

A. When the present participle (*den handlende Tillægsform i Nutiden*) is used elliptically as a noun, it takes an s, to mark the genitive case; as for example:—

den Lidendes Tilstand, the suffering person's condition.
en Rejsendes Bagage, a travelling person's luggage.

B. This participle, which has been derived from the O.N. participle present in *andi,* corresponds in its varied modes of application both with the Latin active participle present in *ans, ens,* and the Latin future participle in *andus, endus;* as for example :—

jeg har ikke set ham i indeværende Måned, I have not seen him in the present month.
har I e Lyst til at høre den derover holdende Tale? do you wish to hear the speech which is to be made concerning it?

The use of the participle present as a gerund is not admissible in Dano-Norwegian, which requires some other mode of construction; as for example :—

on going up the hill, I..., *da jeg gik op ad Højen...*
after listening to her singing, they..., *efter at de havde hört på hende medens hun sang...*
in thinking over it, he..., *da han tænkte derpå...*
by scolding her, *ved at skænde på hende.*

---

at udnærne, to nominate
at lide, to like, suffer
at afskedige, to discharge
at angre, beklage, to regret
at hente, to fetch
at redvare, to last
at skure, rense, to scour, clean
at ödelægge, to waste
at tilfredsstille, to satisfy
at levere, to deliver, give out
at söge, to seek
at fordærve, to spoil
gid han var her! would that he were here!
et Tæppe, a carpet

(en) Post, the post, mail
et Postbud, a letter carrier
et Posthus, a post office
tilværende, present, existing
langvarende, long-lasting
en Forgænger, a predecessor
en Landsby, a village
en Straf,* Plage, a scourge
nödtrængende, needy
en Ödeland, a spendthrift
ankommende, arriving
(en) Tören, delay
en Direktör, a director
langsomt arbejdende, dilatory
et Uheld, an accident.

READING

to translate into English.

Uddrag af " Tremasteren *Fremtiden*,"[1] af JONAS LIE.

VRAGET.[2]

Det var en af de forfærdelige[3] Novemberstorme i 1807, der siden stod som et Mærkeår i mangen gammel Sjömands Ungdomsminde,[4] at Tremasteren " Fremtiden " en snetyk Vinterdag lå og drev som mastelöst Vrag udenfor Finmarkens Kyst. Skandseklædningen[5] var brækket ind, og Tremasteren lå nu halv fyldt af Vand over til den ene Side.

Skibet tilhörte en af de köbenhavnske Kompagnier, der endnu ejede Faktorier[6] i Varangerfjorden, og var bestemt[7] for Köllefjord. Udenfor Trondhjemsleden[8] var det bleven overfaldet af en pålands Storm, der tvang[9] dem til at sætte ud til Sjöes,[10] og i flere Dögn[11] havde Havet gået om Tremasteren med Skumbjærge[12] og Bråt jævnhöje med Salingen.[13] Nede i Sjögangen[14] lå det med fire grönne Bölgemure[15] om sig og en Stump[16] uvejrsgrå Himmel som Tag,[17] indtil Bölgeryggen[18] atter[19] löftede dem op til den gamle trösteslöse Udsigt over Stillingen.[20] Skipperen var en Nat bleven slået af Bommen,[21] han lå bevidstlös[22] og droges med Döden,[23] og Fartöjet[24] var, — værgelöst[25] og uden Styring,[26] som det lå med det knagende Tömmerværk i Rullingerne,[27] — sprunget Læk[28] på flere Steder.

[1] three-master "The Future"
[2] the wreck
[3] frightful
[4] seaman's reminiscence of the days of his youth
[5] bulwarks
[6] owned factories
[7] bound
[8] const-side
[9] compelled
[10] Sö (Norw.), sea
[11] days and nights
[12] mountains of foam
[13] surging, noisy waves level with the cross trees of the masts
[14] swell of the sea
[15] wave-walls
[16] small piece
[17] roof
[18] crests of the waves
[19] again
[20] prospect before them
[21] beam, yard
[22] unconscious
[23] to be in the last agony
[24] the vessel
[25] defenceless
[26] guidance
[27] creaking timbers in the breakers
[28] leak

Den fjærde Dag, da Vejret havde bedaget[1] sig en Smule,[2] og man troede at have Sigte[3] af Land, havde Mandskabet, der indså,[4] at det ikke længer magtede[5] at holde det gående med Pumperne, resolveret at bjærge[6] Livet i Storbåden for, om muligt, at nå ind etsteds[7] på Kysten. Den syge Skipper var allerede bragt ned i den, og tilbage ombord[8] var kun hans Hustru med det lille Barn — hun havde endnu ikke kunnet overvinde[9] sin Ængstelighed[10] for den farlige Nedstigning,[11] — da en truende Bræksjö[12] tvang dem, som vare nede i Båden, til at sætte fra.[13]

FIFTY-FOURTH EXERCISE.

I.

I could have done it if I had only known that my father wished me to have done it. He has been going about for a long time seeking a wife, but he has not yet found one. Mrs. Falsen gave me her son's letter to read, and I certainly ought to have read it on the spot (immediately). Have you the full basket or the empty one in the carriage?—The empty one. It is only the whim of an invalid (suffering person). While she was travelling she longed so much for her native land, but now that she has been able to return, it seems as if she regretted returning. You must make haste or you will not see your niece. The present clergyman at Orderup is a very dear friend of mine, and his predecessor (the one before him) was in like manner a dearly loved friend of my father's. There was lately a destructive illness in this village; but it was fortunately not a long-lasting scourge. Do you know the brewer Anderson, my new neighbour?—No! but I hear that he is a wasteful and at the same time needy man.

[1] cleared
[2] little bit
[3] sight
[4] perceived
[5] have power
[6] resolved to save
[7] some place
[8] onboard
[9] overcome
[10] fear
[11] dangerous descent
[12] threatening high-sea
[13] to put off

II.

If you let that full cup fall, you will spoil the newly cleaned carpet with the coffee as it pours out. Has the servant fetched the letters from the post that has just come in? He says that the long-expected post has not come in yet. A person whom he met on the way told him that at the post office they knew no satisfactory cause for this unusual and somewhat alarming delay in the delivery of the day's letters. I trust no accident has happened to the train which is due. How do you like (what do you think of) our lately appointed post-director Svane? I do not like him much, but still I like him rather better than Blom, who was discharged because he was an inefficient, slow man.

Names of Minerals, etc.

en *Diamant*, a diamond
en *Smaragd*, an emerald
en *Rubin*, a ruby
en *Ametist*, an amethyst
en *Beryl*, a beryl
en *Granat*, a garnet
en *Ædelsten*, a precious stone
en *Juvel*, a jewel
et *Juvelsmykke*, a set of jewels
en *Perle*, a pearl, bead
(en) *Koral*, coral
(et) *Rav*, amber
en *Ravspids* (*Pibespids af Rav*), an amber mouth-piece of a pipe
et *Mineral*, a mineral
et *Metal*, a metal
(et) *Jern*, iron
(et) *Kobber*, copper
(en) *Messing*, brass
(en) *Bronse*, bronze
(et) *Marmor*, marble
(en) *Alabast*, alabaster
(en) *Malm*, ore
en *Sten*, a stone

(et) *Ler*, *Lerjord*, clay
(en) *Skifer*, slate
en *Skifertavle*, a slate (to write on)
et *Skifertag*, a slate-roof
et *Skiferbrud*, a slate quarry
(en) *Kalk*, lime
et *Brud*, a quarry
en *Grube*, a pit
en *Ovn*, a kiln
(en) *Kul* * (*Stenkul*), coal
Trækul * } charcoal
Krudtkul * }
(et) *Bly*, lead
et *Lod*,* a lead (nautical)
en *Blyant*, a pencil
(et) *Stål*, steel
en *Stålpen*,* a steelpen
(en) *Svovl*, sulphur
en *Svovlkilde*, a sulphur-spring
en *Svovlstikke*, a sulphur-match
(et) *Salt*, salt
(et) *Kogsalt*, common salt
en *Saltsø*, a salt-lake
(et) *Saltvand*, (salt) sea-water

(236)

(et) *Glas*,* glass
en *Rude*, a pane
(et) *Sand*, sand
(en) *Sanddyne*, downs
en *Sandgrav*, a sandpit
en *Sandslette*, a sandy plain
et *Sandur*, an hour-glass
(en) *Sandsten*, sandstone
(en) *Granit*, granite
en *Mine*, a mine
en *Minebygger*, a miner
en *Minegang*, gallery of a mine
en *Minetragt*, a funnel, shaft of a mine

et *Mineralrige*, a mineral kingdom
en *Mineralog*, a mineralogist
en *Syre*, an acid
en *Gas*,* a gas
en *Gasmåler*, a gasometer
et *Pulver*, a powder
(et) *Stöv*, dust
(et) *Krudt*, powder, gunpowder
en *Krudtdamp*, a smoke of powder
en *Krudtladning*, a charge of powder
en *Krudttrende*, a train of gunpowder.

FIFTY-FIFTH LESSON.

ON THE DIFFERENT FORMS OF VERBS.

Some Danish grammarians designate the first and second regular conjugations of verbs as *åbne*, open, or *svage*, weak, while they include the irregular verbs under the head of *lukte*, closed, or *stærke*, strong. This distinction, which was observed in O.N., and is still maintained in German, is based on the conception that a word which admits of being changed by mere alteration of its more unessential constituents, without external aid through composition, or the addition of syllables, possesses a certain innate strength, which is wanting in verbal roots, that can only be varied by the addition of foreign elements.

I. The weak (*svage*) mode of inflection, to which belong the two so-called regular conjugations (in *ede*, *et*, and *te*, *t*), includes the larger number of imported or foreign roots.

A. It would appear, that in the earlier forms of modern Dano-Norwegian, these two modes of conjugation were used **indifferently**, or, in other words, that both were included in one group; hence we may assume that the present distinctive characteristics of the first and second conjugations have become established through usage only, or from considerations of euphony, emphasis, or other requirements of speech.

Many verbs still admit of being conjugated according to either form; as for example:—

at bröle	brölede	or brölte,	to bellow
at ile	ilede	„ ilte,	to hasten
at lyne	lynede	„ lynte,	to lighten
at nævne	nævnede	„ nævnte,	to name
at öse	ösede	„ öste,	to bale, draw water
at prale	pralede	„ pralte,	to boast
at ramme	rammede	„ ramte,	to hit
at spöge	spögede	„ spögte,	to haunt, joke
at tale	talede	„ talte,	to talk.

II. Where the verb can be used both in a transitive and an intransitive sense, it usually follows the regular (weak) mode of inflection in the former case, and the irregular (strong) mode of inflection in the latter; as for example:—

han hængte Kjolen op, he hung up the coat.
Frugten hang pa Træet, the fruit hung on the tree.
hun brækkede Benet, she broke her leg.
Grenen brak, the bough broke.

III. Modern Dano-Norwegian is deviating more and more widely from the O.N. in disregarding distinctions of number in verbs, and using the singular form for all persons; as for example: jeg, or vi red, instead of vi ride. The O.N. termination t is still used in poetry for the second person, as du vilt. More frequently, however, st, which is rarely found in O.N. is employed in poetry.

The Old Northern termination st had originally no reference to the second person singular, but was a mere corruption of sk contracted from sik (sig), one self, himself, which still survives in the s of the passive form of Dano-Norwegian verbs, as for example: at höre, to hear; at höres, to be heard, make one self heard.

READING

to translate into English.

ET FJÆLDVAND.

Jeg sad en Aften i en liden Båd
på et af disse dybe, stille Vande,
der ligge, som et Öje blankt[1] af Gråd,[2]
imellem Norges Fjælde. Let og varm
stod Aftenhimlen om de mörke Strande,
og sænkte sig i Söens klare Barm,[3]
så Båden syntes let ophængt[4] at svæve[5]
mid[6] i et Lufthav, hvor der ej[7] var Bund,[8]
men lige dybt foroven og forneden,
som Jordens Kugle[9] mid i Evigheden.[10]
Dödstilhed hvilte[11] over Sö og Lund.[12]
Der fandtes ej en Fugl, som vilde leve,
som vilde synge her en Aftenstund.[13]
Ingen romantisk Klang[14] om Fjældet drog[15]
på klare Vinger, som i Tyrols Dale; —
den norske Fjældegn[16] ejer[17] ingen Tale
undtagen Ensomhedens[18] stille Sprog.
De tause[19] Rorsfolk dypped Åren blot,
og lydlöst[20] i de kolde, klare Vover.[21]
Jeg smelted[22] hen i denne Stilhed södt;
det var som om min Sjæl[23] gled sagte[24] over,
og tabte sig i inderlig Forening[25]
med Fjældnaturens dybe, dunkle Mening.[26]

A. Munch.

[1] polished
[2] weeping
[3] bosom
[4] suspended
[5] float
[6] midst
[7] not, never
[8] bottom
[9] sphere, ball
[10] eternity
[11] rested
[12] grove
[13] one evening hour
[14] sound
[15] to pass, wander
[16] Fjælds' district, spot
[17] owns
[18] excepting solitude's
[19] silent
[20] soundless
[21] billows (poet.)
[22] to melt away
[23] soul
[24] softly
[25] inmost union
[26] meaning, significance

FIFTY-FIFTH EXERCISE.

LETTER.

I.

Paris, *6th September,* 1877.

Dear Robert.

In consequence¹ of the general stagnation² of trade here, and owing to some very considerable losses³ which my father has recently had (suffered), I have determined to seek a situation, and provide for myself. As I know how many acquaintances you (thou) have in London, it has occurred to me that you would be likely to hear⁴ of something that might suit me.

You know that I have always kept my father's books,⁵ and that I must, therefore, have acquired a good deal of useful information.⁶ I have also been studying⁷ English during the last two years, and have made considerable progress.⁸ I should be extremely glad if it were possible for me to get a situation in an English house of business (Counting House). I should, of course, prefer one which has business relations with France (has a French correspondence), as I should be able to undertake⁹ a French correspondence.

I have not yet spoken to my father of my intentions¹⁰ as I am well aware (know) that he would like to keep me at home. I should not, however, be much missed,¹¹ as my brother Richard can take my place. When you write, be good enough to address your letter

---

¹ som en Følge
² Standsning i Tab
⁴ få Kundskab
⁵ at føre Bøger, *to keep books, book-keeping*
⁶ Kundskaber
⁷ lagt mig efter
⁸ Fremgang
⁹ overtage
¹⁰ Forehavende
¹¹ savnet

to me *Poste Restante*, as I do not wish my father to know anything of this correspondence,[1] until I have secured a situation.

Believe me

Yours most truly,[2]

. . . . .

NOTE.

II.

Mr. Campbell begs that Mr. Green will not give himself the trouble of coming to him to-morrow, as he is going into the country. Mr. Campbell will be happy to see Mr. Green, at any time most convenient[3] to himself, the day after to-morrow.

Thursdag morning.

[1] Brevveksling, *interchange of letters*
[2] hengivne, *(devoted)*; oprigtige, *sincere*
[3] belejligt

FIFTY-SIXTH LESSON.

ON THE IRREGULAR VERBS (*Uregelrette Udsagnsord*).

The strong (*stærke*) mode of inflection includes all the Danish irregular verbs, and to this more ancient class, which still numbers upwards of 100 verbs, belong almost all the simple verbal roots in the language. Modern Dano-Norwegian manifests a tendency to incorporate some of these verbs into one or other of its two recognised regular conjugations, as may be seen in many words, which are in a transition stage, and admit of being used in the past of the indicative in two distinct forms; as for example:—

at briste, bristede (brast). to burst
at gale, galede (gol), to crow
at grave, gravede (grov), to dig
at veje, vejede (vog), to weigh
at væve, vævede (vov), to weave.

The irregularities of the Dano-Norwegian verbs admit in most instances of being reduced to some definite method, and may generally be referred to one or other of the following groups:—

I. Verbs which retain the same radical vowel in all their parts, and do not take any terminal letters to mark the past tense; as for example: *faldt, falden,* from *at falde,* to fall.

II. Verbs which change the radical vowel in the past tense only; as for example: *gik,* from *at gå,* to go.

III. Verbs which change the radical vowel both in the past tense and in the participle past; as for example: *bandt, bunden,* from *at binde,* to bind.

These distinctive differences have led grammarians to arrange irregular verbs in several classes, such as the following; which, although not sufficiently comprehensive to include every aberrant verbal form, will be found of great use for the comparison of the prominent differences and affinities between Danish and English irregular verbs.

1st CLASS.

Verbs which retain the radical vowel of the infinitive in all their parts:—

INFINITIVE.	PAST.	ACTIVE PAST PARTICIPLE.	PASSIVE PARTICIPLE.
at græde, to weep	græd	har grædt	
at hedde, to be called	hed	har hedt	
at holde, to hold	holdt	har holdt	er holdt, ere holdte
at hugge, to hew	hug or huggede	har hugget	er huggen, t, ere hugne
at komme, to come	kom		er kommen, ere komne
at løbe, to run	løb	har løbet	er løben, ere løbne
at sove, to sleep	sov	har sovet	

A. *Holden* is used as an adjective in the following manner: *en holden Mand,* a man well to do, a man of substance; *hel og holden,* safe and sound.

R

B. *At holde* is used in the following manner: *det vil holde hårdt*, it will be difficult (hard work); *Vognen hólder for Dören*, the carriage is at the door; *at holde op*, to hold up, leave off; *at holde af*, to care for, to like; *at holde en Avis*, to take in a paper.

READING

to translate into English.

KONG[1] KRISTIAN.

(*Words sung to the Danish National Anthem.*)

Kong Kristian stod ved höjen Mast
    I Rög[2] og Damp.
Hans Værge[3] hamrede[4] så fast,
At Gothens Hjælm og Hjærne[5] brast,[6]
Da sank hvert fjendtligt Spejl[7] og Mast
    I Rög og Damp.
Fly,[8] skreg de, hver som flygte kan,
Hvo står mod Danmarks Kristian
    I Kamp?

Niels Juel[9] gav Agt på Stormens Brag,[10]
    Nu er det Tid!
Han hejsede[11] sit röde Flag,
Og slog på Fjenden Slag i Slag;[12]
Da skreg de höjt blandt Stormens Brag:
    "Nu er det Tid!"
Fly, skreg de, hver, som véd et Skjul,[13]
Hvo kan bestå[14] mod Danmarks Juel
    I Strid?[15]

[1] King
[2] smoke
[3] weapon
[4] to hammer
[5] the Goths' (Swedes') helms and heads
[6] burst
[7] stern of ship
[8] to flee
[9] "Niels Juel," a Danish naval hero
[10] crash
[11] hoist
[12] blow for blow
[13] hiding-place
[14] exist, stand
[15] strife

O, Nordhav,[1] Glimt [2] af Vessel [3] bröd [4]
　　Din tykke Sky;
Da tyede [5] Kiemper til dit Sköd,[6]
Thi med ham lynte Skrœk og Död,
Fra Valen [7] hörtes Vrål,[8] som bröd
　　Din tykke Sky.
Fra Danmark lyner Tordenskjold; [9]
Hver give sig i Himlens Vold,[10]
　　Og fly!

Du Danskes [11] Vej til Ros [12] og Magt,
　　Sortladne [13] Hav!
Modtag din Ven, som uforsagt [14]
Tör möde Faren med Foragt,[15]
Og kæk [16] som du, mod Stormens Magt,
　　Sortladne Hav!
Og rask igennem Sang og Spil [17]
Og Kamp og Sejer [18] för [19] mig til
　　Min Grav!

　　　　　　　　　　　　EWALD.

[1] German Ocean (*lit.*, Northern Ocean)
[2] gleam
[3] "Vessel," a great Danish naval commander, generally known under his title, Tordenskj ld.
[4] broke, pierced
[5] sought refuge
[6] lap
[7] battle-ground
[8] roar
[9] *see* 3
[10] submit to heaven's power
[11] the Danes
[12] praise
[13] blackish
[14] undaunted
[15] contempt
[16] bold
[17] sport
[18] victory
[19] lead

FIFTY-SIXTH EXERCISE.

LETTER.

I.

Thursday Morning.

My dear Charles,
　　　　We are proposing [1] to represent [2] an English play during the holidays,[3] and need your help.

[1] ere ifœrd med,
[2] bringe istand,
[3] Ferien.

We have not yet decided upon any piece, because we do not know how many of our friends will help us. I have written to all those among my friends who are acquainted with [1] English, and a general meeting [2] is to be held at my house next Thursday evening. You must, of course,[3] not fail us, and if you have any friend who is half as clever [4] as you are, we should be delighted to see him,[5] and for your sake he will receive a hearty welcome.

We are sufficiently well provided [6] with ladies, for my own sisters and both the Miss Bang's have kindly [7] offered their services. You know how clever and persevering [8] they are, and, therefore, you will not doubt that they will do us great credit; I wish you would bring your catalogue of English plays with you to help [9] us in making our choice [10] (of a piece), as we propose to have [11] our first rehearsal [12] next week, if possible. There is no time to lose.[13] We are anxious that the whole thing should go off as well as possible, [14] and we, therefore, also intend to put our musical friends under requisition.[15] Oblige me by doing the same by yours, and believe me always [16]

Yours very truly,
. . . . .

(In haste.) [17]

[1] have noget Kendskab	[7] velvillig	[12] Pröve
[2] Generalforsamling	[8] udholdende	[13] spilde (to waste)
[3] selvfölgelig	[9] være behjælpelig	[14] gentilt *
[4] flink	[10] Valg	[15] lægge Beslag på
[5] se ham	[11] holde	[16] Levvel
[6] forsyne		[17] I Hast

* The Danes use the word *gentilt* for " in good keeping," " successfully," " suitably," and pronounce the word as the French *gentil*, with *t* added to it.

NOTE.[1]

II.

ROSENLUND, THE STRAND ROAD.

Mr. & Mrs. Palmblad present their compliments [2] to Mr. & Mrs. Young, and request the pleasure [3] of their company [4] to dinner on Thursday, the 24th inst., at 7 p. m.

June 3rd, 1877.

[1] Billet
[2] Hilsen
[3] Ære (Fornöjelse)
[4] Nærværelse

FIFTY-SEVENTH LESSON.

ON THE DISTINCTIVE CHARACTERISTICS OF THE IRREGULAR VERBS.

(Continued.)

2nd CLASS.

Verbs which change the long radical *i* of the infinitive into long *e* in the past tense and the past participle:—

INFINITIVE.	PAST.	ACTIVE PAST PARTICIPLE.	PASSIVE PARTICIPLE.
at blive, *to remain*	blev		er bleven, t, ere blevne
at drive, *to drive, urge*	drev	har drevet	er dreven, t, ere drevne
at glide, *to glide*	gled	har gledet	er gleden, ere gledne
at gnide, *to rub*	gned	har gnedet	er gneden, ere gnedne
at gribe, *to seize*	greb	har grebet	er greben, ere grebne
at knibe, *to pinch*	kneb	har knebet	er kneben, ere knebne
at pibe, *to pipe, whistle*	peb	har pebet	
at rive, *to tear*	rev	har revet	er reven, ere revne
at skrige, *to cry*	skreg	har skreget	er skregen, ere skregne
at skrive, *to write*	skrev	har skrevet	er skreven, ere skrevne
at stige, *to mount*	steg		er stegen, ere stegne
at stride, *to strive, contend*	stred	har stredet	er stredet, stridt ere stredne, stridte
at vige, *to give way*	veg		er vegen, t, ere vegne
at vride, *to wring*	vred	har vredet	er vreden, ere vredne.

3rd CLASS.

Verbs in which the radical long *i* is changed to *e* only in the past tense :—

INFINITIVE.	PAST.	ACTIVE PAST PARTICIPLE.	PASSIVE PARTICIPLE.
at bide, *to bite*	bed	har bidt	er bidt, ere bidte
at lide, *to suffer*	led	har lidt	er lidt, ere lidte
at slide, *to drudge, wear out*	sled	har slidt	er slidt, ere slidte
at smide (Norw.), *to forge*	smed	har smidt	er smidt, ere smidte.

4th CLASS.

Verbs in which the radical short *i* and *y* are changed to *a* in the past tense, and to *u* in the participles :—

INFINITIVE.	PAST.	ACTIVE PAST PARTICIPLE.	PASSIVE PARTICIPLE.
at binde, *to bind*	bandt	har bundet	er bunden, t, ere bundne
at drikke, *to drink*	drak	har drukket	er drukken, t, ere drukne
at finde, *to find*	fandt	har fundet	er funden, t, ere fundne
at spinde, *to spin*	spandt	har spundet	er spunden, t, ere spundne
at springe, *to spring*	sprang	har sprunget	er sprungen, t, ere sprungne
at synge, *to sing*	sang	har sunget	er sungen, t, ere sungne.

The verb, *pibe*, can only be used in the past participle in combination with some preposition or conjunction, as for example: *Stykket er pebet ud*, the piece has been hissed. *At stige* can only be used in the past when conjoined with a preposition, as for example: *han er steget op på Bjærget*, he has ascended (up) the mountain.

READING

to translate into English.

GAMLE NORGE.

Der ligger et Land mod den evige Sne,
i Revnerne [1] kun er der Vårliv [2] at se.
Men Havet går til med Historie-Dön, (*Norw.*) [3]
og elsket er Landet som Mor [4] af Sön.

[1] crevices
[2] spring-life
[3] the ocean moves with the swell of its history
[4] Moder (mother)

Hun¹ tog os i Fanget,² dengang vi var små,
og gav os sin Saga³ med Billeder⁴ på.
Vi læste, så Öjet blev stort og vådt;
da smilte den Gamle og nikked⁵ blot.

Vi sprang ned til Fjorden og stirrede⁶ mod
den askegrå⁷ Bautasten,⁸ gammel den stod;
hun stod der end ældre, så Ingenting;
men stensatte Hauger⁹ lå rundt i Ring.

Hun tog os ved Hånden, og Fölge hun gav¹⁰
bort derfra til Kirken så stille og lav,¹¹
hvor Fædrene ydmygt¹² har böjet¹³ Knæ,
og mild'lig hun sagde: gör I som de!

Hun strödde¹⁴ sin Sne over fjældbratte Li,¹⁵
böd så sine Gutter¹⁶ at stå den på Ski.¹⁷
Hun knuste¹⁸ med Stormhånd det Nordhavs Spejl,¹⁹
böd så sine Gutter at hejse Sejl.²⁰

Hun satte de vakreste Jenter²¹ i Rad²²
at fölge vor Idræt²³ med Smil og med Kvad,²⁴
og selv sad hun höjt i sin Sagastol
og Måneskinskåben²⁵ op under Pol.

Da lösned²⁶ Begejstringens²⁷ rullende Form,²⁸
da döbtes vi af hendes mægtige Ånd,²⁹
da stod over Fjældet et Syn³⁰ i Glöd,³¹
der siden os maner³² indtil vor Död.

B. BJÖRNSON.

¹ "Gamle Norge"
² in her arms
³ Saga (myth)
⁴ pictures, illustrations
⁵ nodded (approval)
⁶ looked earnestly
⁷ ash-gray
⁸ memorial stones over graves of old Northmen
⁹ stone-planted mounds (Norw.)
¹⁰ give an escort
¹¹ low
¹² humbly
¹³ bent
¹⁴ strewed
¹⁵ steep Fjæld slope
¹⁶ boys, sons (Norw.)
¹⁷ cross it on snow-shoes
¹⁸ crush
¹⁹ mirrow
²⁰ hoist sail
²¹ maidens (Norw.)
²² in a row
²³ actions
²⁴ song
²⁵ the moonlight cloak
²⁶ was loosened
²⁷ inspiration
²⁸ flowing numbers
²⁹ spirit
³⁰ vision
³¹ in glowing flames
³² appeal to, conjure

FIFTY-SEVENTH EXERCISE.

LETTER.

To Messrs. A. & B.

COPENHAGEN, *May 6th*, 1877.

Gentlemen,

Having heard [1] that you require a clerk,[2] able to conduct [3] your French and English correspondence,[4] I take the liberty of offering [5] you my services. A long experience [6] in a first class firm [7] has made me thoroughly conversant with business matters,[8] and I flatter [9] myself that I am thoroughly competent to carry on [10] your foreign [11] correspondence. I have the most unexceptionable [12] references, and can give security [13] to any amount.[14] If you should desire to have further [15] information (in regard to me), you will perhaps do me the honour of sending [16] me a few lines.

I have the honour, Gentlemen, to remain,

Your obedient servant,[17]

. . . . . .

NOTES.

I.

Friday, Morning.

If Mr. Nutt should have a few minutes to spare [18] to-morrow morning, he would greatly oblige Mr. Smith, if he would come to him about ten o'clock. Mr. Smith hopes to see Mr. Nutt at that hour, when he will explain the reason [19] why he makes this request.[20]

[1] bragt i Erfaring
[2] Kommis
[3] forestå
[4] Korrespondance
[5] tilbyde
[6] Övelse
[7] anset Hus's Kontoir
[8] Handelsanliggender
[9] smigre
[10] före
[11] udenlandsk
[12] udmærket
[13] stille Sikkerhed
[14] Beløb
[15] yderlig
[16] Godhed at beære
[17] höjagtelsesfuld, ærbödigst
[18] tilovers
[19] forklare Grunden
[20] Anmodning

II.

Mr. & Mrs. Wilson request[1] the honour of Mr. & Mrs. Sörensen's Company on Saturday evening at 8 o'clock to meet[2] a few friends.

No. 4, HIGH STREET.

Thursday afternoon.

III.

GROVE LANE, 1st *February*, 1878.

Mrs. Bell requests the pleasure of the Misses Dale's company at a small party on Monday evening the 3rd instant.[3]

IV.

The Misses Dale have the honour of accepting Mrs. Bell's polite invitation[4] for the 3rd instant.

V.

The Misses Dale regret extremely that an earlier engagement[5] prevents[6] their accepting Mrs. Bell's kind[7] invitation for the 3rd instant.

VI.

LONDON, *March* 3rd, 1878.

Gentlemen,

We have received[8] your circular[9] of the 4th instant, and beg to inform you that we shall be happy to open an account[10] with your firm.

We are,

Yours obediently,

. . . . . .

---

[1] udbede sig
[2] ville træffe
[3] d. M. (denne Måned)
[4] Indbydelse
[5] Forpligtelse
[6] forhindre
[7] forekommende
[8] modtage
[9] Cirkulære
[10] knytte en Forbindelse

FIFTY-EIGHTH LESSON.

ON THE IRREGULAR VERBS.
(Continued.)

5th CLASS.

Verbs which change the radical vowel *e* or *æ* of the infinitive to *a* in the past tense:—

INFINITIVE.	PAST.	ACTIVE PAST PARTICIPLE.	PASSIVE PARTICIPLE.
at bede, *to bid, beg*	bad	har bedet	er bedt, ere bedte
at gælde, *to avail, be worth*	gjaldt	har gældt	
at hænge, *to hang* (intr.)	hang	} har hængt	er hængt, ere hængte
at hænge, *to hang* (tr.)	hængte		
at knække, *to crack*	knak	har knækket	er knækket, ere knækkede
at kvæde, *to sing*	kvad	har kvædet	er kvædet, ere kvædede
at smække, *to taste*	smak *or* smækkede	har smækket	er smækket, ere smækkede
at være, *to be*	var	har været	

6th CLASS.

Verbs which change the short *æ* of the infinitive to short *a* in the past tense, and to *u* in the participles; and the long *æ* of the infinitive to long *a* in the past tense, and to *å* in the participles:—

INFINITIVE.	PAST.	ACTIVE PAST PARTICIPLE.	PASSIVE PARTICIPLE.
at brække, *to break*	brak	har brukket	er brukken, t, ere brukne
at bære, *to bear*	bar	har båret	er båren, ere bårne
at hjælpe, *to help*	hjalp	har hjulpet	er hjulpen, t, ere hjulpne
at stjæle, *to steal*	stjal	har stjålet	er stjålen, t, ere stjålne
at træffe, *to hit, meet*	traf	har truffet	er truffen, t, ere trufne.

7th CLASS.

Verbs which change the long *y* of the infinitive into long *ö* in the past, and into long *u* or *ö* in the participles, although the latter occasionally retain the long *y* :—

INFINITIVE.	PAST.	ACTIVE PAST PARTICIPLE.	PASSIVE PARTICIPLE.
at bryde, *to care about*	bröd	har brudt	er brudt, ere brudte
at gyde, *to pour*	göd	har gydt	er gydt, ere gydne
at lyde, *to sound*	löd	har lydt	er lydt, ere lydte
at skyde, *to shoot*	sköd	har skudt	er skudt, ere skudne.

8th CLASS.

Verbs which change the *a* of the infinitive into long *o* in the past tense :—

INFINITIVE.	PAST.	ACTIVE PAST PARTICIPLE.	PASSIVE PARTICIPLE.
at erfare, *to experience*	erfor	har erfaret	er erfaret, ere erfarede
at jage, *to chase*	jog or jagede	har jaget	er jagen, t, ere jagne
at slå, *to slay*	slog	har slået	er slået (slagen).

9th CLASS.

Verbs which change the *i* of the infinitive into *a* in the past tense :—

INFINITIVE.	PAST.	ACTIVE PAST PARTICIPLE.	PASSIVE PARTICIPLE.
at give, *to give*	gav	har givet	er given, t, ere givne
at klinge, *to resound*	klang	har klinget	
at sidde, *to sit*	sad	har siddet	
at tie, *to be silent*	tav or taug	har tiet	

10th CLASS.

Verbs which take *o* or *ä* in the past tense, while they retain the radical vowel of the infinitive in the participles :—

INFINITIVE.	PAST.	ACTIVE PAST PARTICIPLE.	PASSIVE PARTICIPLE.
at le, *to laugh*	lo	har let	
at ligge, *to lie (down)*	lå	har ligget	
at se, *to see*	så	har set	er set, ere sete
at æde, *to eat (of animals)*	åd	har ædt	er ædt, ere ædte.

READING

to translate into English.

GURRE.

Hvor Nilen vander Ægypterens Jord
i Afrikas brændende Lande,
der mödtes to Fugle, de kom fra Nord,
de talte om Danmarks Strande:
"O! husker du Sjölund,[1] den deilige Ö,
hvor de vilde Skovduer kurre,[2]
de duftende Böge, den stille Sö,
husker du Gurre?"[3]
"Ja, der jeg bygged en Sommerdag;"
— så talte den lille Svale; —
"jeg havde min Rede[4] ved Bondens Tag,
jeg hörte ham synge og tale:
Jeg tror, der er skönnest i Danmark!"

Ved Gurresö[5] lå Kong Valdemars Borg,
den så ham med Tovelille,[6]
den kændte hans Lykke, den kændte hans Sorg.
— Ak,[7] Tröstens Harpe[8] hang stille!
Hans Glæde blev skrinlagt[9] bag Kirkens Mur,
hvor de vilde Skovduer kurre;
— om Tovelille sang Guds Natur
deiligst i Gurre!
Der havde de vandret hver lönlig Sti[10]
Naturen blev her til hende;
hun kunde ei gå en Blomst forbi,
den sagde: "kan du mig kænde?"
— Jeg tror, der er skönnest i Danmark!

[1] rememberest thou Seeland
[2] wood-pigeons coo
[3] Gurre: a country palace occupied by King Valdemar
[4] nest
[5] lake of Gurre
[6] the name of Valdemar's mistress
[7] alas!
[8] harp
[9] enshrined
[10] secluded way

Ved Gurresö holdt Kong Valdemar Jagt,
smukt Hornet löd gennem Skoven:
den stod i sin rigeste Sommerpragt,
og Stjærnerne funkled¹ foroven;
da råbte Kongen så lystelig,²
hvor de vilde Skovduer kurre:
"Lad Gud beholde sit Himmerig,³
har jeg kun Gurre!"
— Det er så deilig en Sommerdag,
men deiligst i Nattens Stille,
naar Stjærnerne blinke og Droslens Slag⁴
fortæller om Tovelille!
Jeg tror, der er skønnest i Danmark!

H. C. ANDERSEN.

¹ sparkled,   ² merrily,   ³ Kingdom of Heaven,   ⁴ thrush's note.

FIFTY-EIGTH EXERCISE.

I.

A person¹ petitioned² Frederick the Second to give him an office. The king asked him where he was born. "I was born in Berlin," he answered. "Off with you then!³" said the monarch, "no Berliners are worth anything!" "I beg pardon, Your Majesty," answered the candidate, "there are some good Berliners, and I know of two." "Who are these two?" enquired the king: "the first," answered the candidate, "is Your Majesty, and I am the second." The king could not forbear laughing at this answer, and granted⁵ the petition.⁶

¹ Kandidat   ³ så gå blot   ⁵ bevilligte
² ansögte   ⁴ bare sig for   ⁶ Andragende

II.
LADY MONTAGUE IN TURKEY.

I went to see the Sultana,[1] and was led into a large room with a sofa the whole length of it covered [2] with blue velvet,[3] embroidered with silver, with cushions [4] of the same. Her dress was something so surprisingly [5] rich, that I cannot forbear describing it (to you). She wore a vest [6] called *donalma,* which differs from a *caftan* in having longer sleeves.[7] It was of purple cloth, straight [8] to her shape,[9] and set on each side down to her feet and round the sleeves, with beautiful pearls.[10] This dress was tied at the waist with two large tassels [11] of smaller pearls, and embroidered round the arms with large diamonds.[12]

Her chemise [13] was fastened with a great diamond; her girdle,[14] as broad as the broadest English ribbon, entirely covered with diamonds. Round her neck she wore three chains which reached to her knees; one of large pearls, at the bottom of which hung a fine, coloured emerald [15] as big as an egg; another consisting of two hundred large emeralds of the most lively green; and another of small emeralds perfectly round. But her ear-rings eclipsed [16] all the rest.[17] They were two diamonds shaped [18] exactly like pears, as large as a big hazelnut.[19]

(*To be continued.*[20])

[1] Sultaninden
[2] betrukken (*trække,* to draw over)
[3] et Fløjel
[4] en Pude
[5] forbavsende
[6] et Klædebon
[7] et Ærme
[8] sluttet
[9] et Liv
[10] en Perle
[11] en Kvast
[12] en Diamant
[13] en Chemise
[14] et Bælte
[15] en Smaragd
[16] fordunklede
[17] Øvrige
[18] af Form
[19] Hasselnød
[20] fortsættes

FIFTY-NINTH LESSON.

ON PASSIVE AND DEPONENT VERBS.

Passive and deponent verbs are distinguished by the following characters:—

I. The passive (*Lideformen*) of verbs requires:—

A. That all persons of both numbers in the simple tenses shall have the letter *s* added to the active form (*Handlende Form*) of the corresponding parts of the verb; as for example:—

Active: *jeg bringer, vi bringe,* I bring, we bring.
Passive: *jeg bringes, vi bringes,* I am brought, we are brought.
Active: *han bragte, de bragte,* he brought, they brought.
Passive: *han bragtes, de bragtes,* he was brought, they were brought.

B. That the compound tenses shall be conjugated with the auxiliaries *at være* or *at blive*; as for example:—

jeg er bragt, han bliver bragt, I am brought, they are brought.
han var bragt, de bleve bragte, she was brought, they were brought.

II. The Deponent (*Genvirkende Form*) requires:—

A. That the participle past shall always end in *ts*, which is a survival of the O.N. *sk* or *sik*, reflective pronoun *sig*: as for example:—

det har lykkets mig, I have been lucky.
de havde skændts, they had wrangled.

B. That the compound tenses shall be conjugated with the auxiliary *at have*; as for example:—

jeg har bluets, I am ashamed.
det havde synts, it had appeared.
han har længts, he has longed.

The tendency in modern Dano-Norwegian is to disregard these distinctions, and to allow the more genuine Northern forms of the deponents to be merged in those of the passive verbs, whose softer terminations are rapidly superseding the characteristic *ts* of the O.N.

III. Active verbs may, as a rule, be made to assume a passive form; as for example:—

vi slå, we strike.   *vi slås*, we fight.

IV. Neuter verbs do not admit of a passive form.

V. The reciprocal action expressed in some deponents may be rendered by using the active form of the verb with a reciprocal pronoun, such as *hinanden* or *hverandre*; as for example:—

de se hinanden i Spejlet, they see each other in the glass.
Hundene bide hverandre i Benet, the dogs bite each other in the leg.

A. The repetition of the pronoun in the accusative case gives, as in English, a *reflective*, and not a reciprocal, meaning; as for example:—

vi se os i Spejlet, we see ourselves in the glass.
Hundene bide dem i Benet, the dogs bite themselves in the leg.

VI. A difference of meaning is conveyed; whether we use a deponent verb, or an active verb with a reciprocal pronoun; as for example:—

vi ses i Aften på Komedien } we shall meet to-night
vi se hinanden i Aften på Komedien } at the theatre.

By the former mode of construction we convey the meaning that we shall meet in close proximity, either in the same box, etc.; while by the latter we simply imply that we shall both be present on that evening in some part or other of the theatre, but not necessarily at the same part. Thus, again in the case of the expressions *de slås*, *de slå hinanden*, the first would convey the meaning that they—two people—were fighting, and the latter that they—some persons—were striking one another. The deponent thus expresses some inner or more proximate relation, while the active verb, with the pronoun, expresses an extraneous, or more general relation.

READING

to translate into English.

"NÅR DU VIL PÅ FJELDESTI."[1]

Når du vil på Fjældesti
og skal Nisten snöre,[2]
læg så ikke mere i,
end du let kan före.
Drag ei med dig Dalens Tvang[3]
i de grönne Lier,
skyl den i en freidig[4] Sang
ned ad Fjældets Sider.

Fugle hilser dig fra Gren,
Bygdesnakket viger,[5]
Luften bliver mere ren,
höjere du stiger.
Fyld dit glade Bryst og syng,
og små Barneminder
nikke vil blandt Busk og Lyng[6]
frem med röde Kinder.

Standser, lytter du engang,
vil du få at höre
Ensomhedens store Sang
bruse[7] til dit Öre.
Straks en Fjældbæk risler kvikt,[8]
straks en Småsten ruller,
föres hid din glemte Pligt
med en Verdens Bulder.[9]

Bæv,[10] men bed, du bange Sjæl,
mellem dine Minder!
Gak så frem: den bedre Del
du på Toppen finder.
Der som for går Jesus Krist,
Elias og Moses;
ser du dem, skal ganske vist
Farten[11] evig roses.[12]

B. BJÖRNSON.

[1] mountain-path
[2] buckle on a knapsack
[3] restraint
[4] pour it forth in a fearless
[5] town-chatter departs (vanishes)
[6] heather
[7] sound
[8] trickles merrily (quickly)
[9] crash
[10] tremble
[11] excursion
[12] be praised

FIFTY-NINTH EXERCISE.

LADY MONTAGUE IN TURKEY.—(Continued.)

Round her *kalpac* she had four strings[1] of pearl, the whitest and most perfect in the world, fastened[2] with two roses, consisting of a large ruby[3] for the middle stone, and round them twenty drops of pure[4] diamonds to each. Besides this, her head-dress[5] was covered with pins[6] of emeralds and diamonds. She wore large diamond bracelets, and on her fingers she had five rings, the largest I ever saw in my life. It must be left to[7] jewellers to compute the value of those things; but according to the estimation[8] of jewels in our part of the world, her whole dress must be worth a hundred thousand pounds sterling.

She gave me a dinner of fifty dishes of meat, which, after their fashion,[9] were placed on the table but one at a time, which was extremely tedious.[10] But the magnificence of her table answered very well to that of her dress. The knives were of gold, and the hafts[11] set with diamonds. But the piece of luxury[12] which grieved my eyes was the table cloth[13] and napkins,[14] which were all gauze,[15] embroidered with silk and gold, in the finest manner, in natural flowers. The sherbet, which is the liquor they drink at meals, was served in china bowls,[16] with covers[17] of massive gold. After dinner, water was brought in gold basins, and towels of the same kind as the napkins; and coffee was served in china cups with gold saucers.[18]

[1] en Snor
[2] sammenhæftet
[3] en Rubin
[4] rene
[5] en Hovedpynt
[6] en Nål
[7] det tilkommer
[8] en Vurdering
[9] en Skik
[10] kedsommelig
[11] et Skaft
[12] en Luksusgenstand
[13] en Dug
[14] en Serviette
[15] en Gase
[16] Porcellainsskål
[17] et Låg
[18] en Underkop

SIXTIETH LESSON.

ON THE USE OF THE AUXILIARIES "AT VÆRE" AND "AT HAVE."

I. The auxiliary *at have*, to have, should be used:—

A. In the compound tenses of all deponents; as for example:—

    han har altid nöjets med lidt, he was always satisfied with a little.

B. In cases where a persistent action, or permanent condition, is implied; as for example:—

    han har længe giet omkring i Haven, he has been walking for a long time about the garden.
    han har boet mange Ar i Huset, he has lived for many years in the house.

C. In the narration of events which imply action on the part of, or in regard to the subject; as for example:—

    der harde nær skét Mord i mit Hus, murder had nearly happened in my house.

II. The auxiliary *at være*, to be, should be used:—

A. To indicate a change of action or condition; as for example:—

    han er kommen ind i Huset, he has come into the house.
    han er kört ud på Landet, he has driven out into the country.

B. To express a temporary condition or action; as for example:—

    når er han falden ned? when did he fall down?
    han er kommen ridende, he came on horseback.

C. The auxiliary *at være* is used with verbs of motion: as for example:—

    de ere komne, they have come.
    det er gået på det bedste, it went off admirably.

The auxiliary *at have* was formerly in general use in the conjugation of all intransitive verbs in Danish, as it still is in Swedish, and in the ordinary speech of the Norwegians. A tendency has, however, been gaining ground in modern Danish to discard it for the auxiliary *at være*, which, in accordance with German usage, is now frequently employed as a simple auxiliary, without reference to action or condition.

It should, however, be borne in mind, that this practice is wholly at variance with the spirit of the O.N., which restricted the use of *at være* to cases, in which no direct agency was implied on the part of the subject, and where a condition rather than an action was to be expressed; while *have* carried with it a sense of direct action, or independence on the part of the subject.

READING

to translate into English

JEG GIK MIG UD EN SOMMERDAG.

Jeg gik mig ud en Sommerdag at höre
Fuglesang, som Hjærtet monne röre,[1]
i de dybe Dale,
blandt de Nattergale,
blandt de andre Fugle små, som tale.

Den allermindste Fugl af dem, der vare,
sang fra Træet ned i Toner klare,
i de dybe Dale
blandt de Nattergale,
blandt de andre Fugle små, som tale.

Den sang: "Mens[2] Ungersvenden[3] går så ene,
længes En imellem Löv[4] og Grene,
i de dybe Dale,
blandt de Nattergale,
blandt de andre Fugle små, som tale.

[1] might move   [2] while   [3] young man (swain)   [4] foliage

Hen under Løvet gå de lune [1] Vinde,
der du skal din Hjærtenskjære finde,
i de dybe Dale,
blandt de Nattergale,
blandt de andre Fugle små, som tale."

Hav Tak, du lille Fugl, for du har sjunget!
ellers var mit Bryst af Længsel [2] sprunget,
i de dybe Dale,
blandt de Nattergale,
blandt de andre Fugle små, som tale.

Hav Tak, du lille Fugl, der sang med Ære,
stillede min Længsel og Begjære, [3]
i de dybe Dale,
blandt de Nattergale,
blandt de andre Fugle små, som tale.

Af større Ve [4] kan Verden ikke trænges, [5]
end at skilles, [6] når man såre længes,
i de dybe Dale,
blandt de Nattergale,
blandt de andre Fugle små, som tale.

En større Fryd [7] kan Verden ikke bære,
end at samles med sin Hjærtenskjære,
i de dybe Dale,
blandt de Nattergale,
blandt de andre Fugle små, som tale.

— Da nu min Hjærtenskjæreste var funden,
sang og blomstrede det rundt i Lunden, [8]
både dybe Dale,
og de Nattergale,
og de andre Fugle små, som tale.

H. Hertz.

[1] genial
[2] longing
[3] desire
[4] anguish (woe)
[5] suffer
[6] part
[7] joy
[8] grove

SIXTIETH EXERCISE.

LETTER.

Marseilles, *May* 10*th*, 1878.

My dear Sister,

When I last wrote to you, I was on the point of setting off for Marseilles, where I arrived the day before yesterday. I did not find the journey so agreeable as that from Paris to Lyons. The roads are excessively dusty, and the country rocky and mountainous; the weather, however, is very fine though somewhat hot.

I have already paid several visits, and seen a great part of the town, which I like very much, particularly that called *the new town;* the streets are very clean and well paved ; the principal one is elegant, and leads directly to the port, which is very capacious, and frequented by ships of all nations.

You will, perhaps, ask how I can be so well acquainted with these things two days after my arrival. I will tell you. Our friend Mr. H. has been kind enough to act as my guide, and to describe to me everything worthy of notice. He has also asked me to dine with his family, at his country-house, on Sunday.

You do not say, in your last letter, whether you have received a little parcel I sent you from Lyons ; do not fail to let me know in your next. If I continue to like Marseilles, I shall stay some time ; therefore your next letter will, in all probability, find me still here. Pray, send me all the news you can, and give my kind remembrances to our dear friends.

Believe me always, dear Anna,
Your Affectionate Sister.

SIXTY-FIRST LESSON.

ON THE USE OF THE POTENTIAL MOOD, etc.

I. The use of the optative or potential mood (*den önskende Måde*) is limited to solemn appeals, adjurations, or conventional expressions; as for example:—

Vor Herre være os nådig! the Lord have mercy on us!
Kongen leve! long live the king!
Gud bevare! Goodness! God preserve us!

II. Where an optative, or conditional sense is to be expressed in ordinary conversation, defective expletives, such as *gid*, and *mon*, or *bare*, are used to convey this meaning; as for example:—

gid jeg må komme godt fra det! if I only may come well out of that!
mon han skulde være blevet syg? could he have fallen ill?
bare han kommer! if only he would come!

A. *Gid*, used in this form, is supposed to be an abbreviation of the full exclamation *Gud give!* may God grant! and it is probable that the defective verb *at gide*, to prevail upon one self, may be identified with the more common form *gid*.

B. *Mon* (*monstro*, Norw.) is accepted in Dano-Norwegian as an adverb, meaning "whether," "if," etc., and it may generally be translated as "I wonder whether," "if," etc. There is, however, a definite auxiliary *at monne*, which admits of being translated as do, did, may, might; as for example:—

hun ser hvordan det monne lade, she is seeing how it may turn out.

This is the derivative of the O.N. auxiliary *munu*, will, would. The use of *at monne* in Danish is now, however, nearly limited to poetry, although *mon*, as an expletive, retains its full force in the language.

C. *Bare* is an adverb, meaning "only," "merely," etc.

III. The irregular verb *at lade*, to let, may be used exactly as in English in the sense of an auxiliary; as for example:—

lad ham være! let him be!

and like the other auxiliaries *ville, skulle, måtte, kunne, turde, burde*, it precedes the infinitive of the governing verb, without the intervention of the conjunction *at*, to; as for example:—

han lod hende stå, he let her stand.
det lader sig ikke sige, that cannot be said.

READING.

To translate into English.

TONEN.—(*Af* "*Arne.*")

I Skogen[1] Smågutten[2] gik Dagen lang,
    gik Dagen lang;
der havde han hört slig en underlig Sang,
    underlig Sang.

Gutten en Flöite[3] af Selje[4] skar,
    af Selje skar, —
og pröved, om Tonen derinde var,
    derinde var.

Tonen, den hvisked og nævnte sig,
    og nævnte sig;
men bedst som han lytted, den löb sin Vej,
    den löb sin Vej.

Tit, når han sov, den til ham smög,[5]
    den til ham smög,
og over hans Pande med Elskov strög,[6]
    med Elskov strög.

Vilde den fange og vågned brat,[7]
    og vågned brat;
men Tonen hang fast i den blege[8] Nat,
    den blege Nat.

[1] wood (Norw.)
[2] small boy (Norw.)
[3] flute
[4] willow
[5] crept
[6] touch (stroke)
[7] suddenly
[8] pallid

"Herre, min Gud, tag mig derind,
    tag mig derind ;
thi Tonen har fåt mit hele Sind,[1]
    mit hele Sind !"

Herren, han svared : "Den er din Ven,
    den er din Ven,
skjønt aldrig en Time du ejer [2] den,
    du ejer den.

Alle de andre dog lidt forslår,[3]
    dog lidt forslår,
mod denne, du søger, men aldrig når,[4]
    — aldrig når !"

B. BJÖRNSON.

SIXTY-FIRST EXERCISE.

LETTER.

LYONS, *June 3rd*, 1878.

Dear Sir,

An opportunity of going to London has just presented itself to me. As you have been there several times, and are, no doubt, acquainted with the different modes of travelling and living there, I take the liberty of applying to you for information, and a little advice on these subjects.

I intend to be as economical as possible, but at the same time to see all I can. I shall stay, perhaps, six weeks or two months, and should like to know in what part of the town it would be most advantageous for me to stay Perhaps you could also give me an idea how much the journey would cost me, and whether I had better procure English money before I leave home. I should like to take a few trifling presents for some friends to whom I am recommended, and shall feel much

---

[1] mind, heart   [2] own   [3] avail, suffice   [4] attain

obliged if you will tell me what you think would prove most acceptable. I intend to set off in about a week, and I shall therefore feel especially grateful to you, if you will kindly give me a prompt reply to my enquiries.

I am, yours faithfully,

. . . . .

SIXTY-SECOND LESSON.

ON THE POSITION OF WORDS IN A SENTENCE, etc.

I. The arrangement, or position of words in a sentence depends very much in Danish, as in English, upon the idea to be expressed, and the prominence to be given to certain parts of the sentence. As a general grammatical rule it may, however, be observed that where the predicate is an active transitive verb, the *personal object* must precede the *thing-object* (Dan., *Ting-Objekt*); as for example :—

min Fader har igår lovet mig en Bog til Foræring, my father promised me a book yesterday.

II. In passive verbs, used in their compound tenses, the personal object is often placed between the auxiliary and the participle; as for example :—

Brevet blev mig sendt, the letter was sent to me.
det blev ham sagt, it was told him.

Notwithstanding the generally absolute rule that the verb must agree in number with its subject, the Danes, as has already been stated, habitually disregard the plural after *vi*, we, *de*, they, in ordinary conversation, as for example :—

vi har ikke i Sinde, we are not disposed.
de er ikke her, they are not here.

In composition, however, and even in speaking, where it is desired to give emphasis to the words spoken, this neglect of the plural is not considered admissible.

III. In a primary simple sentence the subject precedes the predicate; as:—

Ferskener ere en fortræffelig Frugt, peaches are an excellent fruit.

EXCEPTIONS to this rule are afforded in Danish:—

A. In interrogative sentences, unless the pronouns *hvo, hvem*, who, what, *hvad, hvilken*, which, are used, as for example:—

skriver han? is he writing?
but: *hvem skriver?* who is writing?

B. In optative, conditional sentences; as for example:—

gjorde Du blot dette! if thou wouldst only do that!
havde jeg skrevet ham et Brev, var min Fader vist bleven vred, if I had written him a letter, my father would certainly have been angry.

C. In all secondary clauses, and wherever an adverb, conjunction, or other part of speech, besides the nominative noun, is brought prominently forward in a sentence; as for example:—

var han min Ven, så hjalp han mig i min Nød, if he were my friend, he would help me in my need.
gör du blot dette, er jeg tilfreds, if only you will do this, I shall be contended.
desårsag kan jeg ikke agte Dem, for that reason I cannot esteem you.

IV. In reflective verbs governing an accusative, the verb must always stand, as in English, between the pronouns; as for example:—

jeg bader mig, I bathe myself.
vi skynde os, we are hurrying ourselves.
I understå Jer, you dare.

V. In an expanded sentence (*udvidet Sætning*), where a verb is used in a compound tense, the adverb, or other word qualifying the verb, generally requires to be placed between the auxiliary and the verb; as for example:—

jeg har ofte sét Deres Mand, I have often seen your husband.

READING
to translate into English.

BERGMANDEN.[1]

Bergvæg,[2] brist med Drön og Brag[3]
for mit tunge Hammerslag!
Nedad må jeg Vejen bryde,
til jeg hörer Malmen[4] lyde.

Dybt i Fjældets öde Nat
vinker mig den rige Skat,[5] —
Diamant og Ædelstene
mellem Guldets röde Grene.

Og i Dybet er der Fred, —
Fred og Örk[6] fra Evighed; —
bryd mig Vejen, tunge Hammer,
til det Dulgtes[7] Hjærtekammer!

Engang sad som Gut jeg glad
under Himlens Stjernerad,[8]
trådte Vårens[9] Blomsterveje,
havde Barnefred i Eje.

Men jeg glemte Dagens Pragt
i den midnatsmörke Schakt,[10]
glemte Liens Sus[11] og Sange
i min Grubes Tempelgange.[12]

Dengang först jeg steg herind,
tænkte jeg med skyldfrit Sind:
Dybets Ander skal mig råde[13]
Livets endelöse Gåde.[14]

[1] miner
[2] rocky wall
[3] din and crash
[4] ore
[5] treasure
[6] a desert
[7] concealed
[8] rows of stars
[9] the spring
[10] shaft
[11] revel
[12] aisles
[13] solve
[14] riddle

End har ingen Ånd mig lært,
hvad mig tykkedes så sært;[1]
end er ingen Stråle runden,
som kan lyse op fra Grunden.

Har jeg fejlet?[2] Förer ej
Frem til Klarhed denne Vej?
Lyset blinder jo mit Öje,
hvis jeg söger i det Höje.

Nej, i Dybet maa jeg ned;
Der er Fred fra Evighed.
Bryd mig Vejen, tunge Hammer,
til det Dulgtes Hjærtekammer! —

Hammerslag på Hammerslag
indtil Livets sidste Dag,
Ingen Morgenstråle skinner;
ingen Håbets Sol oprinder.[3]

H. IBSEN.

[1] seemed so strange   [2] err   [3] rise

SIXTY-SECOND EXERCISE.

LETTER.

LONDON, *April 4th*, 1878.

Gentlemen,

Having this day formed[1] a mercantile establishment,[2] under the firm[3] of Blain Brothers, we take the liberty of waiting upon you with our circular[4] and of requesting the favour of your orders.[5] We flatter ourselves that our general knowledge of business, and our extensive connections,[6] will offer peculiar advantages[7] to our correspondents; and by a strict attention

[1] etableret   [4] Cirkulære   [6] udstrakte Forbindelser
[2] Handelsforretning   [5] at beværes med Deres Ordrer   [7] specielle Fordele
[3] Firma

to their interest, we shall endeavour to merit their confidence. We beg to refer you for further particulars, regarding our newly-established firm, to Messrs. Blain & Thornton, of London.

We have the honour to be,

Your obedient servants,

JOHN & ANDREW BLAIN.

Mr. and Mrs. A. beg the favour of Mr. F.'s company to play a friendly rubber with them this evening.

Wednesday, 11 *a.m.*

Mr. F. presents his best compliments to Mr. and Mrs. A., and is extremely sorry he cannot have the pleasure of accepting their friendly invitation, as he is confined to his room by a severe cold.

Mr. P. begs to inform Mr. J. that he has returned from his excursion, and will be glad to resume his lessons. Mr. P. hopes to see Mr. J. on Wednesday next at 10 a.m. as usual.

Monday evening.

SIXTY-THIRD LESSON.

ON THE APPOSITION OF WORDS.

I. When two nouns are placed in appellative or designative apposition to each other, the special follows the more general appellation, while the latter takes the definite substantive-article; as for example:—

> *Hunden Hektor*, the dog Hector.
> *Byen Bergen*, the town of Bergen.
> *Forbjærget Nordkap*, the promontory of Northcape.

II. In descriptive apposition the distinctive characteristic precedes the general designation; as in:—

> *Nordkap*, Northcape.
> *Dampbaad*, steamboat.

III. In titular or other designations used as cognomina, the words stand in simple apposition without the article; as for example:—

> *Dronning Margrete*, Queen Margaret.
> *Valdemar Sejr*, Valdemar the Conqueror.

A. Titles ending in *e* lose the final *e* when used before the patronymics or personal names to which they belong; as for example: *Kong Kristian, Fyrst Reuss, Grev Solmers, Herr Als, Fru Smidt, Madam Olsen*, instead of *Konge, Fyrste*, etc. An exception to this rule is, however, afforded by those feminine designations which end in *inde* and *esse*: as for example: *Admiralinde Rothe, Baronesse Falsen*. When the designation "Mr." is to be used for more than one individual in the sense of "Gentlemen," "Messrs.," it is written *DHrr*.

IV. As a rule, the names applied to places, or periods of time, are usually placed in simple apposition with the nouns which they designate; as for example:—

Kristiania Fjord, Christiania Fjord.
Stavanger By, the town of Stavanger.
Bornholm Ö, the island of Bornholm.
St. Hans Aften, St. John's eve.
Juli Måned, the month of July.
Tirsdag Morgen, **Tuesday morning.**

This rule is occasionally set aside for the sake of euphony as for example:—

Drammens Fjord, **Drammen Fjord.**
St. Birgits Dag, Saint Bridget's day.

READING

to translate into English.

I.

MED EN VANDLILJE.

Se, min bedste, hvad jeg bringer;
Blomsten med de hvide Vinger.
På de stille Strömme båren
svam den drömmetung [1] i Våren.[2]

Vil du den til Hjemmet fæste,
fæst den på dit Bryst, min bedste;
bag dens Blade da sig dölge [3]
vil en dyb og stille Bölge.[4]

Vogt [5] dig, Barn, for Tjernets [6] Strömme;
farligt, farligt der at drömme!
Nökken [7] lader som han sover;—
Liljer leger ovenover.

Barn, din Barm [8] er Tjernets Strömme.
Farligt, farligt der at drömme;— —
Liljer leger ovenover;—
Nökken lader som han sover.

H. IBSEN.

[1] dream-weighted
[2] the spring
[3] conceal
[4] billow
[5] take heed
[6] mountain-tarn
[7] water-sprite (Norw.)
[8] bosom

II.

LÆNGSEL.[1]

Jeg kunde slet ikke sove
for Nattergalens Röst,[2]
som fra de dunkle Skove
sig trængte [3] til mit Bryst.
Jeg åbnede Vinduet stille,
og stirred [4] i Mulmet [5] hen,
og lod hver Elskovstrille [6]
mig synge om dig igjen.

Et Posthorn i det Fjærne,[7]
et Suk [8] af Nattens Vind,
et Glimt af en ensom Stjærne
vakte mit stille Sind;
dit Billed sagte hensvæved [9]
paa Nattens Baggrund huldt; [10]
mit Hjærte sitred og bæved [11]
længsel- og smertefuldt.

Min Tanke jeg dig sendte,
jeg sendte dig mit Blik;
ak, hvor mit Hjærte brændte,
at intet Svar jeg fik!
kun Pust [12] af Nattevinden,
fra Grenen hist et Vink,
den kolde Dugg [13] fra Linden,
og Stjærnens kolde Blink.

Du tænker vel, jeg har glemt dig?
men tro mig, om du kan,
jeg har i Hjærtet gæmt [14] dig,
og skal over Gravens Rand,[15]

[1] Longing
[2] voice
[3] penetrated
[4] gazed
[5] gloom
[6] love-cadence
[7] distance
[8] sigh
[9] softly floated
[10] calm, gentle
[11] vibrate and tremble
[12] breath
[13] dew
[14] hidden
[15] margin

trods Dödens bitre Kulde,
hinsides Livets Kyst
bære dit Navn, det hulde,
prentet [1] dybt i mit Bryst.

C. WINTHER.

[1] engraven.

SIXTY-THIRD EXERCISE.

There sat the young woman half snowed-down, her eyes closed in death [1] while the child had still life in it. The mother held it as before in her arms [2] under her cloak, holding it moreover [3] round its body with her folded and now stiffened hands.

Isack took it carefully [4] up between his large rough [5] hands, and stood for a while, apparently embarrassed [6] what to do with the child he had found. [7] He looked about him with an irresolute [8] air, but as it was obvious that there was no help to be expected from any one else, he seated himself carefully on the deck with his burden [9] still in his hands. Then with a good deal of trouble [10] he drew off one of his heavy sea boots, put [11] the child down into it, and carried it in that way by the straps, [12] hobbling [13] upon his one stocking-foot over the sloping [14] deck to the side [15] where the boat was lying.

Then he stepped carefully down with his burden in his hands, laid the sea-boot in the hold [16] at the stern of the boat, [17] with his coarse cloth jacket [18] over it, and remained sitting in expectation [19] of the coming of the other two men.

[1] brustne Öjne
[2] Favn
[3] fremdeles
[4] varsomt
[5] barkede
[6] öjensynlig forlegen
[7] sit Fund
[8] rådvild
[9] Byrde
[10] Besvær
[11] puttede
[12] efter Stroppene (Norw.)
[13] linkende
[14] skrå
[15] Ræling
[16] Rum
[17] Agtertoft
[18] Vadmels Kufte
[19] på Vænt (Norw.)

APPENDIX.

EXAMPLES OF THE USE OF DANISH PREPOSITIONS.

Vi gik opad Bjærget.	We went up the mountain.
Lad os gå ovenpå.	Let us go upstairs.
En Mand med sin Kone.	A man with his wife.
Han har et Hus med Have til.	He has a house with a garden.
Han leverede mig Bogen tilbage med mange Taksigelser.	He returned me the book with many thanks.
Jeg vil ikke have Noget at göre med Dem.	I will not have anything to do with you.
Han blev forbauset over (slået ved) dette Svar.	He was struck with this answer.
Han dræbte sig med en Dolk.	He stabbed himself with a dagger.
Jeg skriver med en Stålpen.	I write with a steel-pen.
Indenfor Murene.	Within the walls.
Det står ikke i min Magt.	It is not in my power.
Vi ere ikke ti Mile fra Stedet.	We are not ten miles from the place.
De må være her inden en Time.	You must be here within an hour.
Hvad er Livet uden en Ven?	What is life without a friend?
Han finder Noget at udsætte derpå.	He finds something to object to in it.
På min Risico.	At my risk.
På min Befaling.	At my command.
Hvad hedder det på Engelsk?	What is that called in English?
Svar på mit Spörgsmål.	Answer my question.
At være vred på Nogen.	To be angry with one.
Det er klart af den hellige Skrift.	It is clear from Scripture.
Af Had. Af Overbevisning.	From hatred. From conviction.
At tabe af Sigte.	To lose sight of.

Der var Ingen uden disse to.	There was nobody besides these two.
Jeg har ingen Penge hos mig.	I have no money about me.
De ere ved Bordet.	They are at table.
At være ved Hånden.	To be at hand.
Ved hans Afrejse.	At his departure.
Ved alle Lejligheder.	On all occasions.
Under Dödsstraf.	On pain of death.
At stå i Gunst hos En.	To be in favour with one.
Han er ret hendes Yndling.	He is a great favourite of hers.
Indtil dette Öjeblik.	Till this moment.
En Mand mellem 30 og 40 År.	A man from thirty to forty years of age.
Fra Top til Tå.	From top to toe.
Det var henimod Aften.	It was towards evening.
At være ifærd med Noget.	To be about a thing.
I Slaget ved Hastings.	At the battle of Hastings.
Efter Skik og Brug.	According to usage.
At se efter; söge efter.	To look for.
Med et Ord.	In one word.
At handle med Noget.	To deal in something.
Med gyldne Bogstaver.	In letters of gold.
At klæde sig på Moden.	To dress in the fashion.
Ifölge (overensstemmende med) Deres Befaling.	According to your orders.
At sælge alenvis; efter Vægt.	To sell by the yard; by weight.
Efter min Mening.	In my opinion.
Ved Bordet.	At table.
Det er ude med ham.	It is all over with him.
At sove under åben Himmel.	To sleep in the open air.
På den Betingelse.	On condition.
Det fölger af sig selv.	That is a matter of course.
Selvfölgelig; naturligvis.	Of course.
Han blev greben of Skræk.	He was seized with terror.
Han bor i Paris.	He lives in Paris.
Han er ikke hjemme.	He is not at home.
På samme Tid.	At the same time.
At tage Mål til en Dragt.	To take measure for a dress.
At tage til Kone.	To take to wife.
At sidde godt til Hest.	To sit well on horseback.
Daphne blev forvandlet til et Laurbærtræ.	Daphne was transformed into a laurel tree.

Jeg synes meget godt om den unge Mand.	I am very much pleased with the young man.
Jeg har hört det af forskellige Personer.	I have heard it from several persons.
Jeg kommer hjemmefra.	I come from home.
Maleriet hænger på Væggen.	The picture hangs against the wall.
Der er Nogen ved Dören.	There is somebody at the door.
Ved Enden af Året.	At the end of the year.
Jeg kender ham på Talen.	I know him by his speech.
Han hindrede mig i at skrive.	He hindered me from writing.
Tingen i og for sig selv.	The thing of itself.
Hvad er Grunden dertil?	What is the reason of it?
London ligger ved Themsen.	London lies on the Thames.
Vi have nu i atte Dage ikke været udenfor Dören.	We have not been out of doors this week.
Han var placeret udenfor Linierne.	He was placed without the lines.
De kom uden nogen Indbydelse.	They came without any invitation.

DANISH IDIOMS IN COMMON USE.

Jeg har ikke Råd til det.	I cannot afford it.
At være rask til Fods.	To be a quick walker.
Det er rav galt.	It is sheer nonsense.
Rede Penge.	Ready money.
Göre sig til Regel at…	To make it a rule to…
Det ser ud til Sne, Vind, o.s.v.	It looks like snow, wind, etc.
At rejse.	To raise; to travel.
At rejse Vildt.	To start game.
At rejse en Trætte.	To stir up strife.
En Storm rejser sig.	A storm is rising.
At skrive rent.	To make a copy.
Den rene Mathematik.	Pure Mathematics.
Den rene Sandhed.	The plain truth.
Der var sådant et Rend efter Aviserne.	There was such a run on the papers.

At udlåne Penge på Rente.	To put money out at interest.
Rentekammeret.	The exchequer.
Rentefod.	Rate of interest.
Reserve-Vogn; Hest, o.s.v.	Spare carriage; horse, etc.
At komme tilpas.	To come in the nick of time.
Han har Ret.	He is right.
Ret Dem efter mig.	Guide yourself by me.
Vær De kun rolig.	Make yourself easy; be quiet.
At skulke af Skole.	To shirk school.
Skudår.	Leap year.
På Skud.	Within gunshot.
At trække på Skuldrene.	To shrug one's shoulders.
At sætte sit Segl under....	To put one's seal to....
At træffe En hjemme.	To find a person in; at home.
Denne Maler træffer godt.	That painter hits off a likeness well.
At lære (kunne) Noget udenad.	To learn (to know) anything by heart.
At göre store Öjne.	To be astonished.
At få et blåt Öje.	To get a black eye.
Det er ham en Torn i Öjet.	It is an eyesore to him.
Under fire Öjne.	Between ourselves, confidentially.
Efter Vægt.	By weight.
At lægge Vægt på.	To lay stress on; attach importance to...
Jeg er ham ikke voksen.	I am not equal to him.
At være stærk i Mathematiken, o.s.v.	To be well versed (strong) in mathematics, etc.
Hvad fattes Dem?	What ails you?
Jeg tager Fejl.	I am mistaken.
Hvad fejler Dem?	What ails you?
Den fine Verden.	The fashionable world.
Vi sés nok igen.	We shall meet again.
Hun véd det på Fingrene.	She has it at her fingers' ends.
Den flade Hånd.	The palm of the hand.
At have Fluer i Hovedet.	To have a bee in your bonnet; a screw loose.
For stedse.	For ever.
Gud forbarme sig!	Good Gracious!
Det er forbi med ham.	It is all over with him.
Jeg forgår af Kulde, Sult, o.s.v.	I am perishing of cold, hunger, etc.
At bringe i Forslag.	To propose; make a motion in Parliament.

At forsömme en Musik-, Fransk (o.s.v.) Time.	To miss a music, (French, etc.) lesson.
Trække frisk Luft.	To get fresh air, an airing.
At være fuld.	To be drunk.
At föje sig i.	To accommodate oneself to.
At föle sig.	To have a good opinion of oneself.
At före Kården, Pennen, o.s.v.	To wield the sword, pen, etc.
Skibet gik under.	The ship went down.
Dören står på Klem.	The door stands ajar.
Blive gal.	To go mad.
Gammelt Bröd.	Stale bread.
Han gik alt Ködets Gang.	He went the way of all flesh.
At have sin Gang i et Hus.	To have the run of a house.
Gråt (Kardus) Papir.	Brown paper.
Det er alt for grovt (galt).	That is too bad.
At slå En gul og blå.	To beat one black and blue.
At komme i Gæld.	To run into debt.
At göre sin Bön.	To say one's prayers.
Indskrive sig som Medlem, o.s.v.	To enter oneself as a member, etc.
At begrave, stede til Jorden.	To bury.
Jordemoder.	Midwife.
At vidne imod Nogen.	To give evidence against any one.
Det vidner om stor Flid.	That indicates great industry.
Det vil bekomme Dem vel.	That will do you good.
Det bekom ham ilde.	He came off badly.
At tage Benene på Nakken.	To take to one's heels.
At vide god Besked med.	To be well-acquainted with anything, (posted up), be up to.
At have at bestille med.	To have to do with.
Hvad skal det betyde?	What is the meaning of that?
At se flau ud.	To look sheepish.
Jeg er ganske flau.	I feel quite faint.
Den blinde Makker (i Whist).	Dummy (at Whist).
En blind Dör (Vindue), o.s.v.	A false door (window), etc.
At före til Bogs.	To make an entry; to book.
Skyde Bom; at bomme.	To miss the mark.
En Bov; et Bovstykke.	The shoulder of an animal.
Bringe; Bringestykke.	Breast of an animal.
Han bryder sig ikke om det.	He does not care about it.
Selskabet bröd tidlig op.	The company broke up early.
At sende Bud efter En.	To send for any one.

De ti Bud.	The Ten Commandments.
Byrd, Byrdsadel, Byrdsbrev.	Birth, nobility by birth, certificate of birth.
At have trådt sine Börnesko.	To be past childhood, (trodden out one's child-shoes).
På anden Hånd.	At second hand.
Han er ikke et Hår bedre end Broderen.	There is not a pin to choose between him and his brother; he is not a whit better than his brother.
På et hængende Hår.	Within a hair's breadth.
At hakke på.	To cavil at.
Over Hals og Hoved.	In desperate haste.
Slutte en Handel.	To strike a bargain.
At drive Handel med Ost, Speseri, Sko, o.s.v.	To trade in cheese, spices, shoes, etc.
Hartkorn.	"Hartkorn," the Danish standard of land-tax.
Denne Gård står höjt i Hartkorn.	This farm is rated high.
Havblik; havareret.	Dead calm; damaged by seawater.
Her og Hisset.	Here and hereafter (this world and the next.)
Ligge for Döden.	Be at death's door.
At drages med Döden.	To be in the last agonies of death.
At få Hjemlov.	To get a furlough.
Hundedage; Hundevagt.	Dogdays; middle watch at sea.
At före et stort Hus.	To live in great style.
At holde Hus.	To make a racket.
At drikke Ens Skål.	To drink to one; drink one's health.
At fordrive Tiden.	To while away the time.
At drive Spot (Spög) med En.	To ridicule, make fun of.
At være Dus med En.	To say thou (as between most intimate friends).
Dövstum; Dövstummeanstalt.	Deaf-and-dumb; institution for..
Hvidetirsdag; Langfredag.	Shrove Tuesday; Good Friday.
Hvirvel, Hvirvelben; Hvirveldyr.	Vertebra; vertebrate animals.
At fægte med Hælene.	To take to one's heels.
At hæve Pengene på en Anvisning.	To cash a cheque.
En höj Sö. En höj Mand.	A heavy sea. A tall man.
Ved höjlys Dag; höjmælet.	In broad daylight; loud-tongued.
Höjtidsdragt; Höjild.	Festive dress; bonfire.
Jeg har en Höne at plukke med Dem.	I have a crow to pick with you.

At höre for noget.	To be blamed for something.
At höre pa En.	To listen to a person.
At höre med; höre sammen.	To belong to, be one with.
Dögnets Smag, Dögn (24 hours).	Fashion of the moment.
Döguliv.	A trivial, ephemeral life.
Et egent Menneske.	An eccentric person.
Ej alene; ej engang.	Not only, not even.
En sölle Mand.	A poor, silly fellow.
At stå Fadder til et Barn.	Stand godfather to a child.
Fuddersladder.	Gossip.
Det er ikke i mit Fag.	It is out of my line.
Kjolen falder, (sidder), ikke godt i Ryggen.	The dress (the coat) does not fit well in the back.
At falde om.	To fall down.
Det kunde aldrig have faldet mig ind.	That never would have occurred to me.
Hvorledes er det fat med ham?	What is the matter with him?
Kan jeg få fat på hende?	Can I find (get hold of) her?
At holde Bryllup.	To be married.
At stå Brud.	To go through the marriage ceremony (in speaking of a woman).
At gifte sig.	To marry; to be married.
At vie.	To perform the marriage ceremony.
Brud; Brudgom.	Bride; bridegroom.
Kæreste; Forlovede.	Engaged man, or woman.
Hvedebrödsdage.[1]	Honeymoon.
At önske En til Lykke.	To congratulate one.
At önske Lykke på Rejsen.	To wish one a pleasant journey.
Han er Faderen op ad Dage.	He is the very image of his father.
Hun gav ham en Kurv.	She refused (rejected him).
At samle Affald i en Have.	To gather windfalls.
At rette Maden an.	To serve up a meal.
Lad mig være! Slip mig!	Leave me alone! Let me go!
At dyrke Videnskaberne.	To devote oneself to science.
At dyrke Gud.	To worship God.
At have Sans for Musik, (Poesi).	To have a taste for music, (poetry).

[1] "Wheaten-bread days," in reference probably to the time when wheaten bread was used only at special festivities, rye and barley being the cereals in ordinary use in Scandinavian bread-stuff, till a comparatively recent period.

At lege med en Dukke.	To play with a doll.
At lege med Börn, som et Barn.	To play (with children), as a child.
At lege.	To play at games, etc., where no skill or special effort is required.
Spille på Klaver, Flöjte, o.s.v.	To play on the piano, flute, etc.
At spille Skak, Biljard, Kort, o.s.v.	To play on instruments or at games of skill, as chess, billiards, cards, etc.
At have en Skrue lös.	To have a screw loose.
Han er for længe siden död og borte (begraven).	He has long been dead and gone.
At holde Jul.	To keep Christmas.
Jævnårig.	Contemporary; the same age.
At brænde Kaffe.	To roast coffee
At lægge i Kakkelovnen.	To light (make) a fire in the stove.
Kammerfrue; Kammerfröken.	Lady of honour; maid of honour.
Kammerherre; Kammerjunker.	Chamberlain; gentleman in waiting.
Drikke, (löbe), om Kap.	To drink, (run a race), for a wager.
Jeg kan ikke blive klog derpå.	I cannot make it out.
Det klæder Dem ilde.	That is unbecoming in (to) you.
Tiden er for knap.	There is not time.
Jeg finder det koldt.	I think it is cold.
Han kommer sig godt.	He is improving.
Det kommer an på, om han er der.	That depends upon whether he is there.
Hun er kommen sig af sin Sygdom.	She has recovered from her illness.
At fatte sig kort.	To be brief.
At være i Kost hos En.	To board with any one.
Så lang han var.	At full length.
Langt ud på Natten.	Far on in the night.
Han er rent af Lave.	He is quite out of his mind.
At lave Mad.	To cook, prepare food.
At le i Skægget.	To laugh in one's sleeve (beard).
Et lyst Hoved.	A clear head.
Jeg har Lyst til.	I am inclined to.
Hvad De lyster.	Whatever you like.
Det ligger mig på Læberne.	It is on the tip of my tongue.
At læse sin Lektie op.	To say one's lesson.
Lyset löber.	The candle drips (runs).
Jeg har aldrig sét Magen.	I never saw anything like

Majgrevinden; Majstang.	The May-queen; Maypole.
At finde sin Mand.	To find one's equal.
Vil De være med?	Will you go too?
At lade sig nöje.	To be content.
Et Kort over Danmark.	A map of Denmark.
Pak Dig!	Be off with you!
Pas Dem selv!	Mind your own business!
Passiar.	Nonsense.
At være Pebersvend.	To be a bachelor.
En Peberkage.	Gingerbread.
Et Pennehus.	Pen-case.
Et Persontog.	A passenger train.
Han er i Perlehumör.	He is in the best of tempers.
Småpenge.	Small change.
At skære en Pen.	To make (mend) a pen.
At tage Patent på.	To take out a patent.
Regnen pisker på Ruderne.	The rain is beating on the windows
En Pladsmand (Norw.).	A cotter; small farmer.
En Plejefader (Moder), o.s.v.	A foster father (mother), etc.
En Plejeskole.	A charity school.
At praje et Skib.	To hail a ship.
Med omgående Post.	By return of post.
Post Frimærke.	Postage stamp.
Postpenge.	Postage.
Barnet begynder at sanse.	The child begins to take notice.
En Sansekage.	A box on the ear.
Mellem os sagt.	Between ourselves.
Det er sagtens ikke sandt!	That is surely not true!
Drengen er splittergal.	The boy is stark mad.
Det er lutter Sniksnak.	It is sheer nonsense.
Det er pære engelsk.	That is ultra English.
Hun taler ram lavtysk.	She speaks genuine Low German.
Han radbrækker det engelske Sprog.	He murders the Queen's English.
At lære på Ramse.	To learn by rote.
At ransage (Ran, robbery).	To ransack.
At sidde överst i Klassen.	To be at the head of the class.
At sidde överst ved Bordet.	To sit at the head of the table.
At rende En omkuld.	To run over, upset one.
At råbe Navnene op.	To call out the names.
At slå til Ridder.	To create (dub) a knight.
Ridder af Hosebåndet.	Knight of the Garter.

At komme til Roret.	To come into power.
Rigsdag.	The diet (Parliament).
Rigsdagsmand.	Member of Parliament.
Sangværk.	Chime of bells.
At slå Rynker i Panden.	To knit the brows.
At rage i Ilden.	To stir the fire.
At rage sig.	To shave.
At ride en Hest til.	To break in a horse.
Skibet rider Stormen af.	The ship is riding out the storm.
At sejle i rum Sö.	To sail in an open sea.
At före noget til Regning.	To put down to one's account.
At have en Rus.	To be intoxicated.
At sove Rusen ud.	To sleep one self sober.
At blive rört af Slag.	To have a stroke (paralysis).
De må se ind til mig.	You must come and see me.
Se efter Börnene!	Look after the children!
Han bor på anden Sal til Gaden.	He lives on the second floor to the front.
At stå i lys Lue.	To be in flames.
At stå på Grund.	To be aground.
Hvorledes står det til?	What are the rights of it?
Hun sætter meget på Stads.	She spends much on finery.
At tælle Stemmerne.	To count the votes.
En Stiftsdame.	A lady belonging to an asylum, or endowed lay-convent.
En Stiftskirke.	A cathedral.
Bunden Stil.	Verse.
Ubunden Stil.	Prose.
At stille et Ur.	To set a watch.
At stille Kaution.	To give security.
En Stipendiat.	An exhibitioner, bursar.
At sætte et Stævne.	To make an appointment with one.
At stöde i en Trompet.	To blow a trumpet.
Det suser for mine Ören.	My ears are tingling
Et ægte Geni.	A true-born genius.
Mine övrige Dage.	The rest of my days.
Enden på Bogen.	The end of the book.
At knytte Næven.	To clench one's fist.
At se nöje til.	To look narrowly into.
At lade sig nöje.	To be content with.
At dreje Nöglen om to Gange.	To double-lock the door.

For ingen Pris.	Not on any account.
En Pris Tobak.	A pinch of snuff.
At puste Lyset ud.	To blow out the candle.
At pröve et Par Sko.	To try on a pair of shoes.
At nedgrave sit Pund.	To hide one's talent.
At ägte med sin Tid.	To make the most of one's time.
Der blev pebet.	The people hissed.
Ondt Vejr.	Bad, hard weather.
At byde En til Dans.	To ask one to dance.
At byde En Go Imorgen.	To wish one good morning.
At falde sine Venner til Byrde.	To become a burden to one's friends.
At föje sig efter Loven.	To conform to the law.
At fæste Tjenestefolk.	To engage servants.
At blive forlovet.	To be engaged (betrothed).
At love sig ud.	To make an engagement.
At være ilde til Mode.	To be uneasy, uncomfortable.
At være ved godt Mod.	To be of good heart, at ease.
Glædelig Jul!	Merry Christmas!
Lykkeligt Nytår!	Happy New Year!

ABBREVIATIONS OF COMMON OCCURRENCE.

d. Å., dette År.	This year.
d. M., denne Måned.	The present month, "instant."
f. M., forrige Måned.	Last month.
f. T., for Tiden.	For the time being.
s., se.	See.
l., læs.	Read.
smlg., sammenligne	} Compare.
jvfr., jævnför	
ff., följgende.	As follows.
o. s. fr., og så fremdeles	} Et cetera, and so on.
o. s. v., og så videre	
o. dsl., og deslige.	The same.
d. v. s., det vil sige	} That is to say.
d. e., o:, det er	
Udg., Udgave, Udgiver.	Edition, editor (publisher).
Bd., Bind.	Volume.
Kpt., Kapitel.	Chapter.
S., Side.	Page.
No., Nummer.	Number.
Anm., Anmærkning.	Observation.
Tlg., Tillæg.	Supplement.
Bl., Blad.	Plate, leaf.
Dl., Daler.	Dollar.
Rdl., Rigsdaler.	Rixdollar.
Kr., Krone.	Crown.
Ö., Öre.	Öre ($\frac{1}{100}$ Crown).
Mk., ℳ, Mark.	Mark.
Sk., β, Skilling.	Skilling.
Hs. Maj., Hans Majestæt.	His Majesty.
Hds. Maj., Hendes Majestæt.	Her Majesty.
K. H., Kongelige Höjhed.	Royal Highness.
Hr., Herr.	Sir, Mr.
F., Fru.	Madame, Mrs.
Frk., Fröken	} Miss.
Jmf., Jomfru	

APPENDIX II.

THE ALPHABET.

	CALLED.	PRONOUNCED.
A	Ah	like *a* in far, barn, rather.
B	Bey	like English *b*.
C	Sey	like English *k* before a, o, u; like *s* before e, i, in words of foreign origin.
D	Dey	like English *d* at the beginning of words; like *th* in the middle[1] or at the end of a word, as *beder*, beg, as in bather; *lad*, let, as in lath.
E	Aye	when long or close, like *a* in baby; when short or open, like *e* in bell.
F	Eff	like English *f*.
G	Ghey	hard, like *g* in go, gain.
H	Haw[2]	like English *h* aspirated, except before *j* and *v*, when it is not sounded.
I	Ee	when long, like *e* in eel; when short, like *i* in bit.
J	Yodth	like *y* in yellow.
K	Kaw	like English *k*. (In Sweden, and some parts of Norway, *k* before *j* or certain vowels, has the sound of *ch*.)
L	Ell	like English *l*.
M	Em	like English *m*.

[1] The Norwegians do not give so strongly marked a *th* sound to the *d* in the middle, and at the end of words as the Danes.

[2] The Scandinavian tongues have retained the old Northern combination of *hv* in pronouns and other words which we write in English with *wh*; thus, for example, the Dano-Norwegian forms *hvo*, *hvem*, *hvad*, *hvis* (Icelandic *hvar*, *hveim*, *hvat*, *hvess*) answer to the English who, whom, what, whose. In these combinations the *h* is not aspirated.

	CALLED.	PRONOUNCED.
N	En	like English n.
O	O	when long or close, like o in fore; when short or open, like o in for.
P	Pey	like English p.
Q	Coo	like English k, and qu.
R	Er	like English r in its weak sound.
S	Ess	like English hard s.
T	Tay	like English t.
U	Oo	when long or close, like oo in school, cool; when short or open, like u in fulsome.
V	Vay	like v in veil, and w in scowl.
Y	U (French)	when long, like French u in dure, futaie; when short, like French u in dur, nul.
Å å	Awe	like aw in awful. This is written **aa** in all works printed before the beginning of this century, and is still much used in this double form by printers and writers.
Æ æ	Eh	when long, like a in ale; when short, like e in net.
Ö ö	(Eu French)	when long or close, like French eu in seule; when short or open, like French eu in peut.

Till recently it has been customary to distinguish these two sounds by distinct characters, as ø and ö, the former having been used to denote the sound of French eu fermé, in peu, as Øre, ear; while the latter was reserved for words having the sound of French eu ouvert, in veuve, as Örn, eagle.[1]

---

[1] It seems to be nearly as difficult for native-born Scandinavians, as for foreigners, to appreciate any greater difference of sound between these two letters than between various sounds of one and the same vowel under different positions in regard to other letters; and hence there is a general and very widely spreading tendency perceptible amongst writers of the present day to use only one sign—the ö—for all modifications of the Danish eu sound. The mixed Danish, Swedish, and Norwegian Commission, which met at Stockholm in 1869, to decide upon the system of orthography to be followed in the three countries, was opposed to the rejection of two distinct types for these sounds. It was, however, unanimous in its opinion "that if only one sign were to be retained in Dano-Norwegian, it should be the Ö ö instead of the Ø ø, the former having more affinity with the sign in use in Swedish."

ON THE USE OF THE LETTERS.

In accordance with the requirements of modern Dano-Norwegian orthography, the letters *c*, *q*, *w*, *x*, and *z* should be wholly expelled from the alphabet, or, if admitted, should be regarded as mere alien characters, admissible only where a foreign word cannot be accurately represented without their aid.

C occurs in Old Northern, or Icelandic MSS., but it is in the character of a foreign letter; *k* expresses in the vernacular all the hard sounds of this letter, and *s* its softer sounds, while *kv* represents the sound of *qu* or the *qv* of the later Scandinavian peoples.

W occurs only in foreign names of places or persons, and is not a Scandinavian letter.

The sounds of *x* and *z* were in Old Northern rendered by the use of *ks*, and by *s* or *ts*.

Modern orthography has reverted to these ancient usages, and words derived from foreign sources, or others in which these letters were formerly used, are now written as follows: *en Kandidat*, a candidate; *en Kvinde*, a woman; *et Eksempel*, an example; *at sitre* (*zittre*), to tremble.

D is not pronounced after *l*, *n*, *r*, as *Guld*, gold (*gul*), *Land*, land (*lann*), *Ord*, word (*ore*).

Final *e* is always pronounced in Danish like the French *e* in *de*, *le*, as *en Have*, a garden (*hav'e*).

Ej has the sound of *i* in "idle," as *Vej*, way (*vie*), *stejl*, steep (*stile*).

G often loses its distinctive sounds when preceded by a vowel, as *Negl*, finger-nail (*nile*); *Nögle*, key (*noyl'e*); *jeg*, I (*yei*); *Steg*, roast (*sty*); *Leg*, play (*lie*). It must be observed, that in the last two words (but never in *jeg*, which is invariably pronounced *yei*), and in many others in which *g* is preceded, either in a monosyllable or dissyllable by *e*, the *g* may be sounded where emphasis is to be given, as in poetry, etc. Thus *meget*, much, may in ordinary parlance be called *meyet*, or in more impressive appeals *meyget;* at *lege*, to play, may similarly be pronounced *at ley'e* or *at layg'e*.[1] *Vogn*, carriage, is always pronounced *voun*, but *Sogn*, parish, may be sounded with or without the distinct *g*.

J has the sound of *i* in the middle and at the end of words, when preceded by *e*, as *at eje*, to own (*eye'e*); *Vej*, way (*vie*). When preceded by *ö* it becomes *oye*, as *Öjne*, eyes (*oyn'e*).

Modern orthography rejects *j* after *k*, where it has no distinctive sound, as in *kjær*, dear; *Kjöbenhavn*, Copenhagen, etc.; and these words are now written: *kær*, *Köbenhavn*, etc.

Sk in words such as *et Skud*, a shot, has the sound of *sy*, or *sch* in "school." It must be borne in mind, however, that this remark applies to the language spoken by Danes, rather than to that heard in Norway. In the latter country *sk* has often the sound of *sh*, as among Swedes; thus the word *Skyds* (conveyance by carriages and horses) is pronounced by Norwegians as *Shyts*: *en Skilling* (a small coin) as *en Shilling*, etc.

V has somewhat of the sound of English *w*, when preceded by *a, e, i*, as *tavs*, silent (*towes*); *Evropa*, Europe (*eweropa*); *Tvivl*, doubt (*tweew'el*).

The letter *å* which has been substituted in the modern spelling of Dano-Norwegian for double *a* (*aa*) has long been used by the Swedes, and is to be found in Danish and Norwegian MSS. of the 14th century.

Its restoration to the written language of the people has met with the approval of all the best writers of Denmark and Norway, but this character may nevertheless be said still to lack a fixed place in the alphabet. Thus, while in some dictionaries it is made to precede the single ordinary *a*, in others it follows *y*. The sound of the letter *å* (Engl. *aw*) very nearly approximates to that of short, or open Danish *o*, as in *koge*, to cook.

Æ, which may be compared to English *e* in "verse," " terse," resembles open Danish *e*, in such words as: *Herre*, master, gentleman.

---

[1] The Norwegians are more careful than the Danes to give the sound of *g* to words such as *Leg*, *Steg*, etc.

ON ACCENTUATION.

Attempts have often been made by native writers to reduce the pronunciation of the Danish vowels to definite rules of accentuation, and various methods have been suggested for the arrangement of the vowel-accents (*Tonehold*, *Tonefald*) under definite groups of sounds. However important and valuable such systems may be, there is none, as far as we know, that can lay claim to any special authority among native-born Danes, or as being adapted to afford much practical help to the foreign student.[1]

The following general rules may, however, be accepted as aids towards the pronunciation of Danish words.

I. In words of genuine Northern origin, the accent (*Tonehold*) falls on the first radical syllable, as: *be**ty**delig*, considerable; *Ubetydelighed*, insignificance; *kongelig*, kingly; *forglemmelig*, forgettable; *uforglemmelig*, not to be forgotten.

II. In words of foreign origin, the accent generally falls on the last syllable, as: *Telegram*, telegram; *Karakter*, character; *Natur*, nature; *Inspektör*, inspector.

III. In compound words the accent is generally laid on the syllable which indicates the special character of the compound, or the predominant idea associated with it, as: *Spisesal*, dining-room (*at spise*, to dine; *Sal*, room); *Kirkegård*, churchyard (*Kirke*, church; *Gård*, yard, court).

IV. In compound names of places, the syllable which expresses the predominant character of the spot generally receives the accent, as: *Kristiansborg*, the castle of Christian; *Köbenhavn*, Copenhagen (the merchants' haven); *Fredensborg*, the castle of *peace* (that palace having been built to commemorate a peace).

---

[1] The advanced student in Danish, who is desirous of enlarging his knowledge of the mode in which the question of the vowel-accents is treated by native philologists, may with advantage consult a paper entitled "Det danske Sprogs Tonelag," by L. L. Hommel, in the *Tidsskrift for Philologi og Pædagogik*, Kjöbenhavn, 1868-69.

V. The vowels *e, o, i, u,* and *y* usually receive the accent, or in other words, maintain their close sound in monosyllables, as: *at l***e**, to laugh; *en B***y**, a town; or in the first syllable of a dissyllable; as: *rolig,* quiet; *Frihed,* freedom.

VI. Where a syllable ends in one or more consonants, the accent is seldom strongly marked, as: *Kongen,* the king; *fandt,* found; in some words, however, the vowel has a marked accent, as: **O***rd,* word; *N*o*rd,* north.

VII. Words of foreign origin ending in *e* mute are pronounced in accordance with the rules of the language to which they belong, the *e* not being sounded, as: *en* **Sc***ene,* a scene; *en Façade,* often written *Fassad,* etc.

ON THE DIVISION OF SYLLABLES.

The following may be accepted as general rules:—

I. A consonant standing between two vowels should be joined to the latter of the two, as: *at ma-le,* to paint; *en Va-ne,* a custom.

II. When two consonants stand between two vowels, they must be separated, as: *Læs-ning,* reading; *flit-tig,* industrious.

An exception to this rule is afforded by some words in which the second consonant is *r*, as: *at er-o-bre,* to conquer; but where the *r* is preceded by *g* or *v*, the two consecutive consonants are generally separated, as: *at flag-re,* to flutter, flicker; *Hav-re,* oats.

III. *Sk* and *st* usually remain inseparable, and form one syllable with the vowel, which they precede, as: *at hu-ske,* to remember; *He-ste,* horses.

IV. Vowels that combine with one another, or with *j*, to form one sound, do not admit of separation, as: *nöj-e,* exact; *Vej-e,* ways.

V. Where vowels do not coalesce with one another, or with *j*, they form separate syllables, as: *u-e-gentlig*, inappropriate; at *be-ja-e*, to confirm by an affirmative.

SPELLING AND MODE OF WRITING.

A complete revolution in spelling and in writing has, as already remarked, been in operation in Denmark and in Norway since the year 1869. As the question of the causes which led to this movement has already been considered in the Introduction to the present work, where attention was drawn to the numerous advantages presented by the new over the older system of spelling, we need here only recapitulate in a general form the main objects aimed at by the originators of the movement, and the most important orthographical changes which the system was intended to effect.

These changes were:—

I. To reject all foreign elements from the spelling of Dano-Norwegian, and to bring the latter back to the forms of the Old Northern, as far as existing conditions would allow of such a reversion.

II. To establish greater uniformity in the spelling of Swedish and Dano-Norwegian, in order to facilitate the comprehension of the literature of Scandinavia by all its three peoples.

III. The rejection of all the superfluous letters, together with a more exact determination of the vowel-sounds.

IV. The adoption of Latin characters in the place of the Gothic or German letters, which had previously been almost universally employed both in writing and printing; and the rejection of capitals for the initials of nouns.

The following examples, which are given with the view of exhibiting some of the most characteristic differences between the two modes of spelling will be found to indicate the leading features of the principles of conciseness and simplicity on which the modern system is based.

OLD FORM.—Drengen saae ham slaae Faaret med smaae graae Steene.
NEW FORM.—Drengen så ham slå Fåret med små grå Stene.
The boy saw him strike the sheep with little gray stones.

Hun har et blaaet Baand paa Haanden.
Hun har et blåt Bånd på Hånden.
She has a blue band on her hand.

Kongen faaer ikke Armeeen paa Beenene.
Kongen får ikke Armeen paa Benene.
The king will not be able to raise the army.

Beenaaren er saaret.	Viin.	Viinaand.
Benåren er såret.	Vin.	Vinånd.
The vein of the leg is wounded.	Wine.	Spirits of wine.

Hver Viismand har ikke Viisdomsaanden.
Hver Vismand har ikke Visdomsånden.
Every wiseacre has not the spirit of wisdom.

Min kjere Ven kommer snart igjen til Kjøbenhavn.
Min kære Ven kommer snart igen til Köbenhavn.
My dear friend will come soon again to Copenhagen.

Hun har forskjellige Fugle paa Gaarden i Aar.
Hun har forskellige Fugle på Gården i År.
She has different kinds of birds on the farm this year.

Qvæget faaer strax dets Qvældsmad.
Kvæget får straks dets Kvældsmad.
The cattle will immediately get their evening meal.

Qvindens Characteer.	Det qvidbrende Chor.
Kvindens Karaktér.	Det kviddrende Kor.
Woman's character.	The twittering chorus.

Min Cammerat og Collega Hansen er Commandant.
Min Kammerat og Kollega Hansen er Kommandant.
My comrade and colleague, Hansen, is a commandant.

Commandeuren gaaer paa Comedie i Aften.
Kommandören gär på Komedie i Aften.
The commodore is going to the theatre this evening.

Redacteuren er Cabinetssecretair, men ikke Cancellist.
Redaktören er Kabinetssekreter, men ikke Kansellist.
The editor is a private secretary, but not a clerk in a government office.

Seer De Huusets Façade?	Viinen er suur.
Ser De Husets Fasád?	Vinen er sur.
Do you see the front of the house?	The wine is sour.

Kjödet er i Kjökkenet.	At kjöre.	Kjön.
Ködet er i Kökkenet.	At köre.	Kön.
The meat is in the kitchen.	To drive.	Sex.

Mit Uhr og min Kjæde ere hos Uhrmageren.
Mit Ur og min Kæde ere hos Urmageren.
My watch and my chain are at the watchmaker's.

Vexelviis.	At voxe.	Væxt.
Vekselvis.	At vokse.	Vækst.
Alternately.	To grow.	Growth.
Guulbruun.	At guulne.	Huul.
Gulbrun.	At gulne.	Hul.
Yellow-brown.	To turn yellow.	Hollow.
Zobel.	At zittre.	Wilhelm.
Sobel.	At sitre.	Vilhelm.
Sable.	To tremble.	William.

APPENDIX III.

RECAPITULATION OF GRAMMATICAL RULES

ETYMOLOGY (*Formlære*).

Two genders are recognised in Danish, viz.: the common gender, *Fælleskön* (*fælles*, common; *Kön*, sex); and the neuter gender, *Intetkön* (*intet*, nothing; *Kön*, sex).

All nouns belong to one or other of these genders.

Articles, adjectives, and pronouns must agree in gender and number with the noun to which they refer.

There are three articles in Danish: the indefinite article, *det ubestemte Kendeord*; and the definite article, *det bestemte Kendeord*, which is used under two distinct forms, viz: as an affix, when it is known as "the substantive's article," and as an independent word, when it is known as "the adjective's article."

THE INDEFINITE ARTICLE (*det ubestemte Kendeord*).

The indefinite article is: *en*, a, common gender; *et*, a, neuter gender.

I. The indefinite article, *en*, *et*, precedes the noun directly; as *en Mand*, a man; *et Barn*, a child.

II. Where the noun is qualified by an adjective, the indefinite article precedes the adjective directly, as: *en god Mand*, a good man; *et godt Barn*, a good child.

EXCEPTIONS to this rule are afforded, as in English, by the use of certain adjectives, adverbs, etc., which in most instances are the same in both languages, as : *mangen en Gang*, many a time ; *sådant et Barn!* such a child ! *for god en Mand*, too good a man ; *hvor stor en Ære*, how great an honour.

III. The indefinite article is omitted before titles, designations of profession, business, etc., or other characteristic specifications, as : *han er General*, he is a general ; *er han Præst eller Jurist?* is he a clergyman or a lawyer ? *er hun Protestant eller Katholik?* is she a Protestant or a Catholic ?

IV. The indefinite article may be used to express an approximative quantity, in the sense of "about," "nearly," as : *jeg så en tyve, tredive Mand*, I saw about twenty or thirty men.

The Old Northern had no indefinite article. The *en, et*, used in the modern Scandinavian tongues are simply adaptations of the numeral *én, ét*, one, without the accentuation of the vowel by which the latter are distinguished.

THE DEFINITE ARTICLES (*de bestemte Kendeord*).

The two forms of the Danish definite article are :—

1. The affix ...*en*, ...*et* (or ...*n*, ...*t*) pl. ...*ene* (or ...*ne*).

2. The independent article, *den, det ;* pl., *de*.

I. The former, which is known as the substantive's article, is added to, and incorporated with the word, which it directly defines, as :—

c.g. *Mand*, man ; *Manden*, the man ; *Mænd*, men ; *Mændene*, the men.
n.g. *Barn*, child ; *Barnet*, the child ; *Börn*, children ; *Börnene*, the children.

Here the affixes ...*en*, ...*et*, ...*ene*, are used because the nouns end in a consonant ; but where the noun ends in an *e*, this vowel is dropped in the affix, as :—

c.g. *Kone*, woman ; *Konen*, the woman ; *Koner*, women ; *Konerne*, the women.
n.g. *Værelse*, room ; *Værelset*, the room ; *Værelser*, rooms ; *Værelserne*, the rooms.

This form of the definite article is the representative of the Old Northern demonstrative pronoun *hinn, hitt;* pl. neuter, *hin*, that; which was originally made to follow in an independent form the noun to which it referred. In process of time the *h* was dropped, and the remaining *inn* (or *in*), *itt*, etc., of the pronoun was amalgamated with the noun which it indicated; the original, *Madr-hinn, Dyr hitt*, of the Old Northern becoming finally changed in modern Danish into *Manden*, the man ; *Dyret*, the animal.

II. The second, or independent form of the definite article —c.g., *den* ; n.g., *det;* pl., *de*, the—is used to precede the adjective which qualifies the noun, as :—

 den gode Mand, the good man   *det gode Barn*, the good child,
pl. *de gode Mænd*, the good men   *de gode Börn*, the good children.

This article is an adaptation of the demonstrative pronoun, *dén, dét, dé*, this, that, these, those; without the accentuation of the *e*.

THE NOUN (*Navneord*).

All nouns belong either to the common gender (*Fælleskön*), or the neuter gender (*Intetkön*).

In the older forms of the Scandinavian language there were three genders, the masculine, feminine, and neuter ; but in process of time, words belonging to the two former fell under one common gender, while the original sexual differences in the terminations of articles and adjectives, etc., disappeared from the language spoken by the educated classes, although some traces of these triple distinctions of sex may still be met with in rural dialects.

I. As a general rule, nouns which indicate individual beings belong to the common gender, as :—*en Dreng*, a boy ; *en Pige*, a girl ; *en Fader*, a father ; *en Moder*, a mother ; *en Læser*, a reader ; *en Student*, a student; *en Ko*, a cow ; *en Tyr*, a bull ; *en Fugl*, a bird ; *en Fisk*, a fish..

Exceptions to this rule are :—*et Mandfolk*, a male ; *et Fruen-*

timmer, a woman (Germ. *Frauenzimmer*); and numerous words which indicate a class as well as an individual, as :— *et Folk*, a people ; *et Barn*, a child ; *et Menneske*, a person ; *et Dyr*, an animal.

A. A distinctive feminine meaning is conveyed by the addition to the noun of such terminations as *inde*, *ske*, as : *en Sangerinde*, a female singer (masc. *Sanger*); *en Forförerske*, a temptress (masc. *Forförer*).

B. In some instances, distinctions of sex are expressed by the use of a characteristic noun or pronoun, as : *en Bondemand*, a peasant ; *en Bondekone*, a peasant woman (*Bonde*, peasant) ; *en Hankat*, Tom-cat ; *en Hunkat*, a female cat (*Kat*, cat ; *han*, he ; *hun*, she).

C. The feminine of national designations is formed by the addition of *inde* where the noun consists of two or more syllables, as : *en Englænder*, an Englishman ; *en Englænderinde*, an Englishwoman ; *en Russer*, a Russian ; *en Russerinde*, a Russian woman. Where the designative noun consists of only one syllable, as *en Dansk*, a Dane, it may imply a person of either gender, or the distinctive feminine must be otherwise conveyed, as : *en dansk Dame*, a Danish lady ; *en dansk Pige*, a Danish girl.

II. To the common gender belong the names of most trees and flowers, as : *en Bög*, a beech ; *en Rose*, a rose. (The word *Træ*, tree, is, however, of the neuter gender.)

III. To the common gender belong numerous words expressive of quality or character, ending in *e*, *de*, *dom*, *hed*, *skab*, as : *en Varme*, a warmth ; *en Höjde*, a height ; *en Barndom*, a childhood ; *en Dumhed*, a stupidity ; *en Ondskab*, a badness.

IV. Also various nouns expressive of action, derived from verbs, and ending in *en*, *else*, *ing*, *st*, *t*, as : *en Löben*, a running ; *en Læsning*, a reading ; *en Opfindelse*, a discovery ; *en Fangst*, a capture ; *en Vækst*, a growth.

To the neuter gender belong :—

1. The names of countries, metals, and letters, as :

England, England; *Tyrkiet*, Turkey; *Guld*, gold; *Sölv*, silver; *et A*, an A; *et B*, a B.

II. Many words derived from foreign sources, which end in *at, et, eri, ti*, as: *et Kvadrat*, a square; *et Kabinet*, a cabinet; *et Krammeri (Skramleri)*, lumber; *et Politi*, police.

III. Many nouns of one syllable formed from verbs by dropping the final *e* of the infinitive, as: *et Skrig*, a cry (*at skrige*, to cry); *et Digt*, a poem (*at digte*, to compose poetry).

REMARKS.—The gender of nouns has in some instances been changed in the course of time, this change having originally been more general from the neuter to the common gender, as: *en Sommer*, a summer; *en Vin*, a wine, etc., which in the older forms of the language were neuters. In later times the change has been more frequently in the opposite direction, as: *et Sted* (formerly *en Sted*), a place; *et Bogstav* (formerly *en Bogstav*), a letter of the alphabet. This earlier form of gender is still to be traced in certain compound and other words, as: *ingensteds*, nowhere; *efter Bogstaven*, according to the letter.

Some words may be said to be still passing through this process of change; as: *Slags*, kind; *Helbred*, health; *Minut*, minute; *Punkt*, point; which occur with either gender.

Some words have different meanings according to the different gender to which they belong, as: *en Bord*, a border; *et Bord*, a table.

(For a list of such words, see *p.* 123, *Twenty-ninth Lesson*).

Compound words follow the gender of the last word of the group, as: *en Landmand*, a countryman, farmer; *et Bögetræ*, a beech-tree.

Nouns may be classed under three heads:—

I. Those which form their plural by the addition of *e* to the singular, as: *et Hus*, a house, pl. *Huse*.

REMARK.—The words belonging to this class were originally nearly all of the masculine gender, but it now includes a large number of neuters.

(301)

For a full list of words ending in *e* in the plural, *see pp.* 111—113, *Twenty-sixth Lesson*, where words, which double the final consonant in inflection, are marked by an asterisk, as : *en Ryg*, a back, pl. *Rygge*.

II. Those which form their plural by the addition of *er* to the singular, as : *en Sö*, a sea, pl. *Söer*.

To this class, which is the most numerous, belong words of foreign origin, and more especially those which are derived from Latin or Greek, as : *et Fotografi*, a photograph ; *et Telegram*, a telegram ; *en Kandidat*, a candidate.

This class may also be said generally to include nouns ending in *hed*, and *skab*, and many in *ing*, as : *en Menighed*, a community ; *en Egenskab*, a property ; *et Venskab*, a friendship ; *en Mening*, an opinion.

(For a list of words belonging to this class, see *pp.* 116—117, *Twenty-seventh Lesson*).

III. Those which remain the same in the plural as in the singular, as : *et År*, a year ; *ti År*, ten years.

REMARK.—The majority of words in this class belong to the neuter gender.

(For a list of words belonging to this class, see *pp.* 119—120, *Twenty-eighth Lesson*).

THE DECLINATION OF NOUNS (*Navneordets Böjning*).

I. As in English, nouns are not modified by any case, except the genitive, which is formed by the addition of *s*, or *es*, according to the termination of the word ; as for example :—

SINGULAR.—Nom., Dat., Obj.

et *Skib*, a ship,   *Skibet*, the ship,   *det store Skib*, the large ship.
en *Ko*, a cow,   *Koen*, the cow,   *den store Ko*, the large cow.

Genitive.

et *Skibs*, of a ship,   *Skibets*, of the ship,   *det store Skibs*, of the large ship.
en *Koes*, of a cow,   *Koens*, of the cow,   *den store Koes*, of the large cow.

PLURAL.—Nom., Dat., Obj.

Skibe, ships,   *Skibene*, the ships,   *de store Skibe*, the large ships.
Köer, cows,   *Köerne*, the cows,   *de store Köer*, the large cows.

Genitive.

Skibes, of ships, *Skibenes*, of the ships, *de store Skibes*, of the large ships.
Köers, of cows, *Köernes*, of the cows, *de store Köers*, of the large cows.

The genitive *es* occurs as a rule in words ending in any vowel but *e;* as *en Bro*, a bridge, gen. *Broes;* and in *y*, *s* or *sk;* as for example: *en By*, a town, gen. *Byes; en Tjavs*, a rag, gen. *Tjavses; en Laks*, a salmon, gen. *Lakses*.

II. After proper names ending in *s*, *'s* is sometimes used instead of *es*, as *Lars's Hest*, the horse of Lars; *Judas's Pung*, Judas's purse.

III. Where several words are used to indicate the noun standing in the genitive, it is only the last, as in English, which takes the *s*, as: *Kongen af Danmarks Börn*, the king of Denmark's children.

IV. As in English, the genitive case may be indicated by the use of the preposition *of* (Danish *af, til*) ; as : *Melken af Koen*, the milk of the cow ; *hun er Söster til Soldaten*, she is the sister of the soldier.

V. The genitive always precedes the word governing it, as : *for Guds Skyld*, for God's sake.

VI. The genitive of nouns, to which the substantive-article has been affixed, is formed both in the singular and plural by the addition of *s;* as for example : *Markens Grænse*, the boundary of the field ; *Börnenes Legetöj*, the children's playthings.

VII. The genitive termination may be wholly dispensed with, where the sense of quantity is conveyed by the noun governing the word ; as for example :—

> *en Mængde Mennesker*, a number of men
> *et Pund Köd*, a pound of meat
> *en Hob Penge*, a heap of money.

A similar ellipsis may occur in regard to the names of places ; as for example :—

> *Odense By*, the town (of) Odense.

Where the designation of a person or thing is derived from the name of a place, no such elliptical form is used, and the name is made to assume the form of an adjective, terminating in *er* for both genders and numbers; as for example:—

en *Hamborger Købmand*, a merchant of Hamburg
et *Londoner Hus*, a London-house
to *Pariser Damer*, two ladies of Paris.

ON ADJECTIVES (*Tillægsord*).

I. Adjectives retain their abstract form when they stand between the indefinite article *en*, a C.G., and the noun which they qualify, as for example:—

en *god Dreng*, a good boy
en *smuk Pige*, a pretty girl.

But when an adjective stands between the indefinite article *et*, a N.G., and the noun which it qualifies, it takes a *t* at the end of the word (except in cases to which reference will be made), as for example:—

et *godt Barn*, a good child
et *smukt Bånd*, a pretty ribbon.

EXCEPTIONS.—This rule is not followed where the adjective ends in *e, o, es, s, sk, t, u, y*, as for example:—

et *bange Dyr*, a timid animal
et *tro Hjerte*, a true (faithful) heart
et *stakkels Fruentimmer*, a poor (miserable) woman
et *norsk Ord*, a Norwegian word
et *let Arbejde*, a light labour
et *ædru Menneske*, a sober person
et *bly Barn*, a shy child.

II. Adjectives are made to end in *e*:—

1. When they stand between the definite, independent article, *den, det, de*, and the noun which they qualify, as: *den gode Broder*, the good brother; *det store Træ*, the large tree; *de gode Marker*, the good fields.

2. When they are used as representative nouns, and are preceded by the definite, independent article, *den, det, de*, as: *den Gode*, the good person; *de Gode*, the good persons; *det Slette*, the bad thing.

3. When they are used as plural representative nouns, without being preceded by an article, as: *Rige*, rich (people); *Kære*, dear (ones).

III. Adjectives follow the same rules, in regard to cases, as nouns, undergoing no change except in the genitive, where they take *es* or *s*, according to the terminal letter of the word; as for example:—

<table>
<tr><td colspan="2">Singular.</td><td colspan="2">Plural.</td></tr>
<tr><td>Nom.—</td><td>*en Rig*, a rich man</td><td>Nom.—</td><td>*Rige*, rich men</td></tr>
<tr><td>Gen.—</td><td>*en Rigs*, of a rich man.</td><td>Gen.—</td><td>*Riges*, of rich men.</td></tr>
<tr><td>Nom.—</td><td>*den Gode*, the good man</td><td>Nom.—</td><td>*de Gode*, the good men</td></tr>
<tr><td>Gen.—</td><td>*den Godes*, of the good man.</td><td>Gen.—</td><td>*de Godes*, of the good men.</td></tr>
</table>

IV. The adjective follows the noun, instead of preceding it, when it constitutes a surname, or distinctive appellation; as:

Karl den Store, Charles the Great
Gorm den Gamle, Gorm the Old
Kristian den Anden, Christian the Second.

V. Some adjectives, which express value, or obligation, follow the noun; as:—

han er mig mange Penge skyldig, he owes me a great deal of money
De er den Ære værdig, you are worthy of the honour.

REMARKS.—Exceptions to the general rule, that an adjective must agree in number with the noun which it qualifies, are afforded by the plurals *alle*, *mange*, which may be used with a singular noun; as:—

tager fat alle Mand! take heed all ye men!
Klokken er mange, it is late (the clock is many [hours]).

The adjective *hel*, all, whole, in combination with a numeral, conveys a difference of meaning in accordance with its place in the sentence; as:—

ti hele År, ten complete years
hele ti År, as much as ten years.

VI. Adjectives ending in *el*, *en*, or *er*, lose the *e* before *l*, *n*, *r*, when they are preceded by the definite, independent article *den*, *det*, *de*, or when they are used as nouns. Thus for example:—

ædel, noble,   changes to ædle,   den ædle Mand, the noble man
moden, ripe,   ,,   modne,   den modne Pære, the ripe pear
mayer, meager, thin, ,,   mayre,   den mayre Hest, the thin horse.

VII. Adjectives of one syllable, or those in which the last syllable is short, double the final consonant; as:—

slem } had { slemme
slet }   { slette.
tör, dry, törre

fornem, distinguished, fornemme
let, light, easy, lette.
krum, crooked, krumme.

VIII. In regard to the terminations of adjectives, the following may be accepted as general rules:—

1. That *agtig* and *lig* express resemblance to, or affinity with an object, and may generally be rendered in English by the particle "ish," as *sortagtig*, blackish; *syrlig*, sourish;

2. That *bar* (derived from *at bære*, to bear) corresponds to the English "ful," "able;" as *frugtbar*, fruitful; *ærbar*, honourable;

3. That *som* conveys a sense of action, while *lig*, when joined to a word referring to properties of the mind, implies a possible rather than an existing action; as: *tænksom*, thoughtful, meditating; *tænkelig*, conceivable; *fölsom*, feeling; *fölelig*, perceptible.

ON THE COMPARISON OF ADJECTIVES
(*Tillægsordenes Gradforhöjelse*).

I. In Dano-Norwegian the comparative of the adjective is formed by adding *ere* to the positive, except when the word ends in *e*, in which case it takes only *re*; while the superlative is formed by adding *est* to the positive, except when the word ends in *e*, *ig*, or *som*, in which cases it takes only *st*, as for example:—

Positive.	Comparative.	Superlative.
blöd, soft	blödere	blödest
grov, coarse	grovere	grovest
stille, quiet	stillere	stillest
gruelig, horrible	grueligere	grueligst
virksom, active	virksommere	virksomst

X

REMARK.—It will be observed that in the last example the *m* is doubled in the comparative. This is done because the last syllable *som* in *virksom* is unaccentuated, and the doubling of the final consonant is required in the comparative and superlative of words consisting of one short, unaccentuated syllable, as for example :—

grön, green	*grönnere*	*grönnest*
tör, dry	*törrere*	*törrest*
let, light (easy)	*lettere*	*lettest*
smuk, pretty	*smukkere*	*smukkest*.

II. Adjectives ending in *el*, *en*, *er*, drop the *e* in the comparative and superlative, as for example :—

ædel, noble	*æd_lere*	*æd_lest*
doven, idle	*dov_nere*	*dov_nest*
sikker, certain	*sik_rere*	*sik_rest*.

III. As in English, the comparative and superlative may be expressed by the adverbs *mér*, *mere*, more; and *mest*, most; as for example :—

våd, wet	*mere våd*	*mest våd*
fattig, poor	*mere fattig*	*mest fattig*.

The use of *mér* or *mere*, and *mest* is imperative :—

1. For adjectives, derived from the participles of verbs.

2. For adjectives, compounded of another adjective and a noun.

3. For adjectives, ending in unaccentuated *et*, *ed*, *s*, *sk* ; as :

ophidset, excited	*mere ophidset*	*mest ophidset*
skævbenet, crooked-legged	*mere skævbenet*	*mest skævbenet*
fremmed, strange	*mere fremmed*	*mest fremmed*
fælles, mutual, common	*mere fælles*	*mest fælles*
malerisk, picturesque	*mere malerisk*	*mest malerisk*.

IV. The comparative and superlative of the diminutive degree are expressed by *mindre*, less, and *mindst*, least.

V. The superlative may be made additionally forcible by the use of the word *aller*, all, most of all, as for example: *det allergrönneste Træ*, the greenest tree of all.

VI. *End*, than, is used as in English to characterise a comparative; as for example :—

min Pære er södere end hendes, my pear is sweeter than hers.
hun er mindre ophidset end min Broder, she is less excited than my brother.

Many adjectives form their comparative degrees irregularly, as: *god,* good, *bedre,* better, *bedst,* best.

REMARK.—For a list of such adjectives, and the changes to which they are subjected, see *p.* 43, *Twelfth Lesson.* For defective adjectives, see *p.* 44, same Lesson.

The Danish Cardinal Numbers are:—

én	1	*elleve*	11	*tredive*	30
to	2	*tolv*	12	*fyrretyve*	40
tre	3	*tretten*	13	*halvtreds,* or *halvtredsindstyve*	50
fire	4	*fjorten*	14	*tredsindstyve*	60
fem	5	*femten*	15	*halvfjerds,* or *halvfjærdsindstyve*	70
seks	6	*seksten*	16	*firsindstyve*	80
syv	7	*sytten*	17	*halvfems,* or *halvfemsindstyve*	90
åtte (otte)	8	*atten*	18	*hundrede (et Hundrede)*	100
ni	9	*nitten*	19	*tusinde (et Tusinde)*	1000
ti	10	*tyve*	20	*en Million*	1,000,000

Up to one hundred the lesser numeral precedes the greater; after one hundred it follows it, as for example: *én og tyve, to og tredive, tre og fyrretyve,* 21, 32, 43; *hundrede og én, tusinde og to,* 101, 1002.

REMARK.—For an explanation of the differences between the Danish and Norwegian modes of numeration, see *p.* 190, *Forty-Fourth Lesson.*

The Danish Ordinal Numbers are:—

den förste	1st	*den ellevte*	11th	*den tredivte*	30th
„ *anden*	2nd	„ *tolvte*	12th	„ *fyrretyvende*	40th
„ *tredje*	3rd	„ *trettende*	13th	„ *halvtredsindstyvende*	50th
„ *fjerde*	4th	„ *fjortende*	14th	„ *tredsindstyvende*	60th
„ *femte*	5th	„ *femtende*	15th	„ *halvfjærdsindstyvende*	70th
„ *sjætte*	6th	„ *sekstende*	16th	„ *firsindstyvende*	80th
„ *syvende*	7th	„ *syttende*	17th	„ *halvfemsindstyvende*	90th
„ *åttende*	8th	„ *attende*	18th	„ *hundrede*	100th
„ *niende*	9th	„ *nittende*	19th	„ *tusinde*	1000th
„ *tiende*	10th	„ *tyvende*	20th		

I. The only ordinal number which is modified by gender is *anden,* which makes *andet* in the neuter.

II. As in English, it is only the second of two composite numbers that is declined, as for example: *den én og tyvende,* the one and twentieth ; *den syv og tredivte*, the seven and thirtieth.

III. Numerals immediately precede the noun; and those of the ordinal numbers which are declinable must agree in number and gender with the noun ; as for example :—

Damen har tabt tre Öre, the lady has lost three öre.
jeg mödte ham på anden Sal, I met him on the second floor.
han tog den förste Lejlighed at öve sig i Udtalen, he took the first opportunity of perfecting (exercising) himself in the pronunciation.

IV. In speaking of large combinations, a singular noun may sometimes be employed with the plural numeral; as for example :—

Generalen faldt ind i Landet med femten tusinde Mand, the general invaded the country with fifteen thousand men.

REMARK.—For terms of quantity, and the manner in which these are made to precede the noun to which they refer, without the intervention of a preposition (as : *et Glas Vand*, a glass of water), *see pp.* 36—37, *Tenth Lesson*.

ON ADVERBS (*Biord*).

We pass directly from adjectives to adverbs, in order the better to draw attention to the close association which exists between these two parts of speech, as may be seen in the following groups.

I. Some adverbs are identical with adjectives, especially where the latter end in *s*, *ig*, etc., as : *fælles*, mutual, mutually ; *indvortes*, internal, internally ; *evig*, eternal, eternally ; *rigtig*, right, rightly :

II. Some adverbs are identical with the neuter singular of adjectives, as : *smukt*, prettily (C.G. *smuk*) ; *vildt*, wildly (C.G. *vild*) ; *tyndt*, thinly (C.G. *tynd*) ; *godt*, well (C.G. *god*) ; *klogt*, cleverly (C.G. *klog*) :

III. Some adverbs are formed from nouns, or adjectives, by the addition of certain affixes, viz., *vis* (Engl. "wise"), *ledes*, etc., as : *stykkevis*, piecewise ; *lykkeligvis*, happily ;

sandsynligris, probably; *anderledes*, otherwise; *ligeledes*, likewise; *således*, suchwise.

IV. Some adverbs of time are formed by adding *lig* (identical with English "ly") to the noun from which they are derived, as for example: *årlig*, yearly; *daglig*, daily; *ugentlig*, weekly.

Many adverbs of time and place are formed, however, by prefixing a preposition to the noun which they indicate, as for example: *iår*, this year; *tilårs*, in years; *ifjor*, last year; *imorgen*, to-morrow, etc.; *underrejs*, underway, on the way; *tilsøs*, by sea.

REMARK.—It must be observed that, in accordance with the rules of modern spelling, these words should be written separately, as: *i Fjor*, *under Vejs*, etc.

For a list of irregular adverbs, and certain words used adverbially, see p. 70, *Seventeenth Lesson*.

COMPARISON OF ADVERBS.

(*Biordenes Gradforhöjelse.*)

Danish adverbs admit, like adjectives, of various modes of comparison:—

I. By dropping the final *t*, and taking *ere* or *re* in the comparative, and *est* or *st* in the superlative, as for example:—

POSITIVE.	COMPARATIVE.	SUPERLATIVE.
klogt, cleverly	klogere	klogest
slemt, badly	slemmere	slemmest
morsomt, amusingly	morsommere	morsomst
nydeligt, charmingly	nydeligere	nydeligst
ofte, often	oftere	oftest.

The comparative and superlative are the same in adverbs as in adjectives, where the former have been derived from the latter; as: *klogt* from *klog*, *slemt* from *slem*, etc.

For the manner in which some adverbs form their comparative and superlative, see p. 74, *Eighteenth Lesson*.

II. Some adverbs of place indicate motion towards a spot, by the absence of a terminal *e;* and repose at a spot, by the addition of an *e;* as for example :—

at *gå ud*, to go out   at *være ude*, to be out
at *gå hjem*, to go home   at *være hjemme*, to be at home
at *gå op ad Trappen*, to go up the stairs
at *være oppe på Bjærget*, to be up on the mountain.

Thus it will be observed that a condition of rest is expressed by the addition of *e*.

III. Some adverbs are formed by the addition of an *s* to an adjective, and sometimes to a noun, and are in such cases generally used in combination with a preposition; as :—

tværs, på tværs, across, from *tvær*, cross
til Sengs, to bed,   ,,   *en Seng*, a bed.

ON PRONOUNS. (*Stedord*.)

The Danish personal pronouns (*Personlige Stedord*) are: sing. *jeg*, I; pl. *vi*, we; sing. *du*, thou; pl. *I*, ye; sing. *han*, he, *hun*, she, *det*, it; pl. *de*, they.

For the manner in which these and the possessive pronouns are declined, see p. 51, *Thirteenth Lesson*.

REMARK.—It must be observed that *jeg*, I, is written with a small initial letter, unless when it begins a sentence; *du*, thou, is used, as in German, among near relatives and friends, in prayer, etc.; *I*, ye, is used in addressing numbers; *han*, he, and *hun*, she, are still employed in rural districts in addressing an individual of inferior rank; *de*, they, written with a capital *D*, as *De*, is used with the verb in the singular in the sense of "you" in addressing one individual, as: *Har De Deres Hat med Dem?* have you your hat with you?

The possessive pronouns (*Ejestedord*), as will be seen by referring to *p*. 51, are inflected, and must be made to agree in gender and number with the noun, as: *min Fader*, my father; *dit Barn*, thy child; *vore Venner*, our friends.

For the distinctive differences between the pronouns *hans*, his, and *sin*, his own, see p. 52, *Thirteenth Lesson*; and p. 188, *Forty-fourth Lesson*.

The demonstrative pronouns (*Påpegende Stedord*) are:—

Singular.		Plural.	Singular.		Plural.
COMMON G.	NEUTER G.		COMMON G.	NEUTER G.	
den, that	det	de	slig, such	sligt	slige
denne, this	dette	disse	sådan, such	sådant	sådanne
hin, that	hint	hine	samme, same	samme	samme.

Selv, pl. *selve*, self, admits, as in English, of being added to pronouns for the sake of emphasis or distinction; as, for example: *jeg selv*, I myself; *selvsamme Mand*, the self-same man.

Begge, both, is used directly before the numeral *to*, two; as *begge to*, both of them.

A. The demonstrative pronouns *den*, *det*, *de* are, in point of fact, the component parts of the independent definite (adjective) article used as pronouns, and distinguished, when thus employed, by a special intonation of the *e*, as *dēt Bord*, that table; *dēn Stol er min*, that chair is mine.

B. *Hin, hint, hine*, that, those, used in opposition to *denne, dette, disse*, this, these, are similarly mere adaptations of the Old Northern independent definite article.

C. *Slig, slige*, such, are used very much the same in Danish as in English. In the singular, *slig* must precede the indefinite article, as *slig en Mand*, such a man; in the plural, *slige* precedes the substantive directly; as, for example, *slige Koner*, such women.

D. *Sådan, sådant, sådanne*, such, may be used both before and after the indefinite article; as, for example, *en sådan Mand, sådan en Mand*, such a man.

E. *Samme*, same, is the defective form of an Old Northern demonstrative pronoun, and is used very much as its English equivalent; as, for example, *den selv samme Mand*, the self-same man; *den samme Aften*, the same evening.

The Relative Pronouns (*Henvisende Stedord*) are:—

	Singular.		Plural.
	COMMON GENDER.	NEUTER GENDER.	
Nom., Acc.,	hvilken, which	hvilket	hvilke
,, ,,	som, which, that	som	som
only used in Nom.,	der, which, that	der	der.

I. *Hvem*, objective of *hvo*, who; is used instead of *hvilken*, when the relative applies to a *person*.

II. *Hvad*, *hvad for en*, what; is used instead of *hvilket*, where the relative is taken in a general sense, and refers exclusively to a neuter singular.

III. *Hvis*, whose, which; is used as the genitive of all the above given demonstrative pronouns.

These three last are used as interrogative pronouns, see p. 60, *Fifteenth Lesson*; where, and at p. 61, the indefinite and irregular pronouns will be found, together with explanations of the manner in which they are respectively used. *See* also pp. 188, 189.

VERBS. (*Udsagnsord*.)

The auxiliaries, *at have*, to have; *at være*, to be; *at blive*, to become; *at skulle*, shall; *at ville*, will; *at måtte*, may; *at få*, to get, are all used in the conjugation of verbs.

For complete paradigms of the verbs at *have*, and at *være*, see pp. 23—25, *Appendix* to *Sixth Lesson;* for those of *at skulle*, and *at ville*, see pp. 49, 50, *Appendix* to *Twelfth Lesson*.

At skulle and *at ville* serve to express the future tenses; as do also *at blive* and *at få*.

Remarks.—The auxiliary *at have* is used (1) in the compound tenses of active verbs, as: *jeg har elsket*, I have loved; (2) in the conjugation of all deponents, as: *han har nöjets med lidt*, he was satisfied with little. The auxiliary *at være* is used (1) with neuter verbs, as: *han er bleven*, he has become; (2) with verbs of motion, as: *hun er kommen*, she has come.

At være and *at blive* are also used in the conjugation of passive verbs.

Skal and *vil* (present indicatives of *at skulle* and *at ville*) are not used precisely as their English representatives "shall" and "will," since the first implies, in Danish, an obligation or intention on the part of the agent, while the second expresses futurity without any action of the will; as for example:—

>*Jeg spörger om De skal rejse,* I am asking whether you are going to travel (will travel).
>*jeg tror at jeg vil være altfor træt,* I think that I shall be too tired.

REGULAR VERBS. (*Regelrette Udsagnsord.*)

Danish regular verbs admit of being grouped under two heads:—

I. Those which take *ede* in the past tense of the indicative, and *et* in the past participle, as *at elske,* to love.

II. Those which take *te* in the past tense of the indicative, and *t* in the past participle, as *at tænke,* to think.

For paradigms of these two modes of conjugation see pp. 64—66, *Sixteenth Lesson;* and for examples of verbs conjugated in accordance with these two typical forms, see p. 78, *Appendix* to *Eighteenth Lesson.*

Some verbs admit of being conjugated according to both forms, see p. 79.

PASSIVE VERBS. (*Lideformen.*)

The passive is formed by adding *s* to the infinitive and the simple tenses of the active form of the verb, both in the singular and plural; as: *at elske,* to love; *at elskes,* to be loved; *jeg elsker,* I love; *jeg elskes,* I am loved; *vi elskede,* we loved; *vi elskedes,* we were loved.

REMARKS.—In the present indicative, as will be observed, the final *r* of the singular is changed into an *s;* as: *han elsker* becomes *han elskes,* he is loved. The *s* of the passive is the representative of the reflective pronoun *sig,* self.

For a paradigm of the passive forms of the regular verbs *at elske,* to love (Conjugation I.), and *at tænke,* to think (Conjugation II.), *see* p. 89, *Twenty-first Lesson;* and for the manner in which the passive may be rendered by the help of *at være* and *at blive,* and its impersonals may be formed, *see* the same Lesson, p. 88.

REMARKS.—Neuter verbs cannot be put in a passive form. Passive verbs cannot be conjugated with the auxiliary *at have,* to have, but must, as already observed, take *at være,* to be; while certain tenses may be formed by the help of *at blive, at få,* etc., *see p.* 88.

DEPONENT VERBS. (*Genvirkende Formen.*)

Deponents, or passive verbs having an active sense, require to be conjugated with the verb *at have,* to have, while they take *ts* in the participle past; as: *det har lykkets mig* (*at lykkes,* to succeed, be lucky), I have succeeded.

The reciprocal action expressed in some deponents may be rendered by using the active form of the verb with a reciprocal pronoun, such as *hinanden* or *hverandre*; as for example:—

de se hinanden i Spejlet, they see each other in the glass.
de gör hverandre stor Skade, they do each other great injury.

REMARK.—The repetition of the pronoun in the accusative case gives, as in English, *a reflective,* and not a reciprocal meaning; as for example:—

vi se os i Spejlet, we see ourselves in the glass.
de gör dem stor Skade, they do themselves great injury.

For the difference of meaning conveyed by the use of a deponent, or of an active verb with a reciprocal pronoun, as:—

vi ses i Aften på Komedien } we shall meet to-night at the
vi se hinanden i Aften på Komedien } theatre,

see p. 256, *Fifty-ninth Lesson.*

IRREGULAR VERBS. (*Uregelrette Udsagnsord.*)

The irregularities of Danish verbs admit, to some extent, of being reduced to definite rules, and to be classed under distinct heads, as in the following:—

I. Verbs which retain the same radical vowel in all their parts, and which do not take any terminal letters to mark the past; as for example: *faldt, falden*, from *at falde*, to fall.

II. Verbs which change the radical vowel in the past only; as for example: *gik*, from *at gå*, to go.

III. Verbs which change the radical vowel both in the past tense and in the participle past; as for example: *bandt, bunden*, from *at binde*, to bind.

These three groups admit of being subdivided into various lesser groups, or classes, as will be seen by the following examples:—

1st CLASS.

Verbs which retain the radical vowel of the infinitive in all their parts:—

INFINITIVE.	PAST.	ACTIVE PAST PARTICIPLE.	PASSIVE PARTICIPLE.
at græde, *to weep*	græd	har grædt	
at hedde, *to be called*	hed	har hedt	
at holde, *to hold*	holdt	har holdt	er holdt, ere holdte
at hugge, *to hew*	hug, or huggede	har hugget	er huggen, t, ere hugne
at komme, *to come*	kom		er kommen, ere komne
at løbe, *to run*	løb	har løbet	er løben, ere løbne
at sove, *to sleep*	sov	har sovet	

2nd CLASS.

Verbs which change the long radical *i* of the infinitive into long *e* in the past tense and the past participle:—

INFINITIVE.	PAST.	ACTIVE PAST PARTICIPLE.	PASSIVE PARTICIPLE.
at blive, *to remain*	blev		er bleven, blevet, ere blevne
at drive, *to drive, urge*	drev	har drevet	er dreven, t, ere drevne
at glide, *to slide*	gled	har gledet	er gleden, t, ere gledne
at gnide, *to rub*	gned	har gnedet	er gneden, t, ere gnedne
at gribe, *to seize*	greb	har grebet	er greben, t, ere grebne
at knibe, *to pinch*	kneb	har knebet	er kneben, t, ere knebne
at pibe, *to pipe, whistle*	peb	har pebet	
at ride, *to ride*	red	har redet	er reden, t, ere redne
at rive, *to tear*	rev	har revet	er reven, t, ere revne
at skride, *to step, advance*	skred	har skredet	er skreden, t, ere skredne
at skrige, *to cry*	skreg	har skreget	er skregen, t, ere skregne
at skrive, *to write*	skrev	har skrevet	er skreven, t, ere skrevne
at stige, *to mount*	steg		er stegen, t, ere stegne
at stride, *to strive, contend*	stred	har stredet	er stredet, stridt, ere stredne, stridte
at svide, *to scorch*	sved	har svedet	er sveden, t, ere svedne
at vige, *to give way*	veg		er vegen, t, ere vegne
at vride, *to wring*	vred	har vredet	er vreden, t, ere vredne

3rd CLASS.

Verbs in which the radical long *i* is changed to *e* only in the past tense:—

at bide, *to bide*	bed	har bidt	er bidt, ere bidte
at lide, *to suffer*	led	har lidt	er lidt, ere lidte
at slide, *to drudge, wear out*	sled	har slidt	er slidt, ere slidte
at smide, *to forge*	smed	har smidt	er smidt, ere smidte
at trine, *to tread*	tren	har trinet	er trint, ere trinte.

4th CLASS.

Verbs in which the radical short *i* and *y* are changed to *a* in the past tense, and to *u* in the participles:—

at binde, *to bind*	bandt	har bundet	er bunden, t, ere bundne
at briste, *to burst*	brast		er brusten, t, *or* bristet, ere brustne
at drikke, *to drink*	drak	har drukket	er drukken, t, ere drukne
at finde, *to find*	fandt	har fundet	er funden, t, ere fundne
at rinde, *to run, flow*	randt	har rundet	er runden, t, ere rundne
at slippe, *to slip*	slap	har sluppet	er sluppen, t, ere sluppe
at spinde, *to spin*	spandt	har spundet	er spunden, t, ere spundne
at springe, *to spring*	sprang	har sprunget	er sprungen, t, ere sprungne
at svinde, *to vanish*	svandt		er svunden, t, ere svundne
at svinge, *to swing*	svang	har svunget	er svungen, t, ere svungne
at synge, *to sing*	sang	har sunget	er sungen, t, ere sungne

5th CLASS.

Verbs which change the radical vowel *e* or *æ* of the infinitive to *a* in the past tense:—

INFINITIVE.	PAST.	ACTIVE PAST PARTICIPLE.	PASSIVE PARTICIPLE.
at bede, *to bid, beg*	bad	har bedet	er bedt, ere bedte
at gælde, *to avail, be worth*	gjaldt	har gieldt	
at længe, *to hang* (intr.)	hang	har hængt	er hængt, ere hængte
at hænge, *to hang* (tr.)	hængte	har hængt	
at knække, *to crack*	knak	har knækket	er knakket, ere knækkede
at kvæde, *to sing*	kvad	har kvædet	er kvædet, ere kvædede
at skælve, *to tremble*	skjalv or skælvede	har skælvet	
at smække, *to smack*	smak or smækkede	har smækket	er smækket, ere smækkede
at være, *to be*	var	har været	

6th CLASS.

Verbs which change the short *æ* of the infinitive to short *a* in the past tense, and to *u* in the participles; and the long *æ* of the infinitive to long *a* in the past tense, and to *å* in the participles:—

INFINITIVE.	PAST.	ACTIVE PAST PARTICIPLE.	PASSIVE PARTICIPLE.
at brække, *to break*	brak	har brukket	er brukken, t, ere brukne
at bære, *to bear*	bar	har båret	er båren, t, ere bårne
at hjælpe, *to help*	hjalp	har hjulpet	er hjulpen, t, ere hjulpne
at skære, *to cut, score*	skar	har skåret	er skåren, t, ere skårne
at sprække, *to crack*	sprak or sprækkede	har sprukket	er sprukken, t, ere sprukne
at stjæle, *to steal*	stjal	har stjålet	er stjålen, t, ere stjålne
at træffe, *to hit, meet*	traf	har truffet	er truffen, t, ere trufne
at trække, *to draw, pull*	trak	har trukket	er trukken, t, ere trukne

(318)

7th CLASS.

Verbs which change the long *y* of the infinitive into long *ö* in the past, and into long *u* or *ö* in the participles, although the latter occasionally retain the long *y* :—

INFINITIVE.	PAST.	ACTIVE PAST PARTICIPLE.	PASSIVE PARTICIPLE.
at bryde, *to break*	bröd	har brudt	er brudt, ere brudte
at byde, *to order, offer*	böd	har budt	er buden, t, ere budne
at flyde, *to flow*	flöd	har flydt	er flydt, ere flydte
at flyve, *to fly*	flöj	har flöjet	er flöjen, t, ere flöjne
at fortryde, *to repent*	fortröd	har fortrudt	er fortrudt, ere fortrudte
at fyge, *to rush*	fög or fygede	har föget or fyget	
at gyde, *to pour*	göd	har gydt	er gydt
at gyse, *to shudder*	gös	har gyst	
at krybe, *to creep*	kröb	har kröbet	er kröben, t, ere kröbne
at lyde, *to sound*	löd	har lydt	er lydt, ere lydte
at lyve, *to tell a lie*	löj	har löjet	
at nyde, *to enjoy*	nöd	har nydt	er nydt, ere nydte
at nyse, *to sneeze*	nös	har nyst	
at ryge, *to smoke*	rög	har röget	er röget, ere rögede
at skyde, *to shoot*	sköd	har skudt	er skudt, ere skudte
at snyde, *to cheat, blow one's nose*	snöd	har snydt	er snydt, ere snydte
at stryge, *to stroke, to iron linen*	strög	har ströget	er strögen, t, ere strögne.

8th CLASS.

Verbs which change the *a* of the infinitive into long *o* in the past tense :—

INFINITIVE.	PAST.	ACTIVE PAST PARTICIPLE.	PASSIVE PARTICIPLE.
at drage, *to drag, draw*	drog	har draget	er dragen, t, ere dragne
at erfare, *to experience*	erfor	har erfaret	er erfaret, ere erfarede
at fare, *to drive*	fór	har faret	er faret, ere farede
at grave, *to dig*	grov or gravede	har gravet	er gravet, ere gravne
at jage, *to chase*	jog or jagede	har jaget	er jagen, t, ere jagne
at lade, *to let be, to load*	lod	har ladet	
at slå, *to slay*	slog	har slået	er slået (slagen)
at stå, *to stand*	stod	har stået	
at tage, *to take*	tog	har taget	er tagen, t, ere tagne.

(319)

9th CLASS.

Verbs which change the *i* of the infinitive into *a* in the past tense:—

INFINITIVE.	PAST.	ACTIVE PAST PARTICIPLE.	PASSIVE PARTICIPLE.
at gide, *to like*	gad	har gidt	
at give, *to give*	gav	har givet	er given, t, ere givne
at klinge, *to resound*	klang	har klinget	
at sidde, *to sit*	sad	har siddet	
at stinke, *to stink*	stank	har stinket	
at tie, *to be silent*	tav *or* taug	har tiet	

10th CLASS.

Verbs which take *o* or *å* in the past tense, while they retain the radical vowel of the infinitive in the participles:—

INFINITIVE.	PAST.	ACTIVE PAST PARTICIPLE.	PASSIVE PARTICIPLE.
at le, *to laugh*	lo	har lét	
at ligge, *to lie (down)*	lå	har ligget	
at se, *to see*	så	har sét	er sét, ere sete
at æde, *to eat (of animals)*	åd	har ædt	er ædt, ere ædte
at sværge, *to swear*	svor	har svoret	er svoren, t, ere svorne.

Some verbs are both etymologically and grammatically irregular; of these the principal are the auxiliaries; as:—

INDICATIVE.		PARTICIPLE.	INFINITIVE.	
PRESENT.	PAST.	PAST.		
Sing.	Sing. and Plur.			
jeg	jeg, vi			
er	var, vare	været	at være	*to be*
har	havde	haft	at have	*to have*
kan	kunde	kunnet	at kunne	*to be able, can*
må	måtte	måttet	at måtte	*to be allowed, may*
skal	skulde	skullet	at skulle	*to be obliged, shall*
vil	vilde	villet	at ville	*to be willing, will.*

Besides these, the following verbs are similarly irregular:—

bör	burde	burdet	at burde	*to be obliged, ought*
dör	döde	(er) död	at dö	*to die*
gör	gjorde	gjort	at göre	*to do, make*
tör	turde	turdet	at turde	*to dare, ought*
ved	vidste	vidst	at vide	*to know.*

I. Verbs are distinguished as being *open*, or "*weak*," or *closed* or "*strong*." Under the former head are included verbs belonging to the two regular forms of conjugation, while under the latter, which is the more numerous, and more genuinely Northern in its character, are comprised all the irregular verbs. (*See p.* 236, *Fifty-Fifth Lesson.*)

II. Some verbs admit of being conjugated in accordance both with the "weak" (regular) and the "strong" (irregular) mode of inflection, but this is generally where the verb can be used both in a transitive and an intransitive sense. In such cases the transitive is expressed by the regular, and the intransitive by the irregular form; as: *han brækkede Armen*, he broke his arm; *Grenen brak*, the bough broke.

III. Some intransitive verbs may acquire a transitive sense by a change in the radical vowel of the word; as:—

at brage, to crack	*at brække*, to break
at falde, to fall	*at fælde*, to fell
at fare, to go, drive	*at füre*, to lead
at knage, to creak	*at knække*, to crack
at ligge, to lie	*at lægge*, to lay
at ryge, to smoke	*at röge*, to smoke (meat, etc.)
at sidde, to sit	*at sætte*, to set.

IV. Reflective verbs must be followed by an objective pronoun; as: *jeg bader mig*, I bathe myself (me).

V. Impersonals may be derived from active, neuter, or passive verbs; as: *det blaser*, it blows; *der går han*, there he goes; *her köres ikke*, no one may drive here, *lit.*, here is not to be driven. (*See p.* 88, *Twenty-First Lesson.*)

ON THE MOODS AND TENSES OF VERBS.

(*Udsagnsordenes Måder og Tider.*)

I. The present indicative is used in a future and conditional, as well as in a present sense; as:—

imorgen rejser han, he is going to leave to-morrow.
rejser han, så går jeg med, if he should leave, I shall go also.

II. The past tense is used to express a period of indefinite time, answering often to the English compound imperfect, and also in a conditional or potential sense; as:—

jeg læste da han kom, I was reading when he came.
gik hun blot bort! if only she would go away!

III. The future tenses, as already observed, are formed by the help of *at skulle*, shall, implying obligation; *at ville*, will, implying merely futurity; *at blive*, to become, and *at få*, to get; as:—

jeg skal nok komme imorgen, I shall certainly come to-morrow.
jeg vil straks göre det, I will do it immediately.
om det ikke holder op, bliver jeg gal, if that does not cease, I shall go mad.
när jeg får skrevet, when I shall have written.

It must be observed that the use of *at få*, in this sense, is nearly, if not quite, obsolete among Danes, although still prevalent among Norwegians.

IV. The use of the optative or potential mood is limited to solemn appeals or conventional expressions; as:—

Vor Herre vere os nådig! the Lord have mercy on us!
Kongen leve! long live the king!
Gud beware! Goodness! God preserve us!

Where an optative, or conditional sense is to be expressed in ordinary conversation, defective expletives, such as *gid*, and *mon*, or *bare*, are used to convey this meaning; as:—

gid jeg må komme godt fra det! if I only may come well out of that!
mon han skulde vere blevet syg? could he have fallen ill?
bare han kommer! if only he would come!

(*See p.* 263, *Sixty-First Lesson.*)

V. Participles (*Tillægsformer*) may be used as adjectives, in which case they must agree, like these, in gender and number with the noun to which they refer; as for example:—

en brölende Löve, a roaring lion
en indbunden Bog, a bound book
et bundet Dyr, a chained animal.

In some cases these participles may be used adverbially, as for example:—

han kom ridende, he came riding
hun sidder fangen, she is (sits) imprisoned.

When the present participle is used elliptically as a noun, it takes an *s* to mark the genitive case; as:—

den Lidendes Tilstand, the suffering person's condition.
en Rejsendes Baggage, a travelling person's luggage.

The use of the participle-present as a gerund is not admissible in Danish, which requires some other mode of construction; as for example:—

on going up the hill, I..., *da jeg gik op ad Höjen*...
after listening to her singing, they..., *efter at de havde hört på hende medens hun sang*...

VI. The infinitive of verbs, whether active or passive, admits of being used in the sense of a nominative or objective noun; as for example:—

at elske sit Barn er en Moders störste Pligt, to love her child is a mother's highest duty.
vi erhverve os vor Næstes Agtelse ved at være redelige, we gain the esteem of our neighbours by being upright.
at agtes er noget som Enhver skulde stræbe efter, to be esteemed is what every one should strive after.

PREPOSITIONS. (*Forholdsord.*)

I. Prepositions in Danish admit of being grouped under two heads:—

As primary and simple.

ad, to, at
af, of, from
bag, behind ⎫ (implying surroundings
blandt, among ⎭ of the same kind)
efter, after
for, for, before (space)
fra, from
för, before (time)
gennem, through
hos,* at the house of, with
i, inde i, inden i, in
mellem, between, in the midst (implying different surroundings)

med, with
mod, against
om, about
over, over
på, on
samt, together with
siden, beside
til, to
trods, in spite of
uden, without
under, under
ved, by, at near.

* For remarks on the use of *hos*, see p. 20, *Sixth Lesson*.

As compound.

bagefter, after
bagved, behind
foran, before, beyond
formedelst, by means of
iblandt, amongst
igennem, through

imellem, between
imod, against
istedetfor, instead of
omkring, round about
ovenpå, on the top of
udenfor, outside of.

The difference between *blandt* and *mellem* will be seen in the following example : *Klinten vokser mellem Stene blandt Hveden*, the corn-cockle grows in the midst of stones among the wheat.

II. Some prepositions have the effect of making the noun, with which they are combined, take a final *e* when the compound word is used adverbially : as for example : *ilive*, alive ; *itide*, in time ; *tildøde*, to death ; *tilskamme*, for shame's sake ; *medrette*, in justice.

The final *e* is retained even when the preposition and noun are decomposed into distinct words ; as for example : *til Åre*, in years ; *til Skamme* ; *i Tide*, etc. (See *p.* 118, *Thirty-Fifth Lesson.*)

III. *Til*, to, *fra*, from, when followed by a noun in the genitive, convey a sense of motion ; as : *at gå til Sengs*, to go to bed ; *at gå fra Bords*, to leave the table.

IV. Differences in respect to periods of time admit of being indicated by the use of *i*, *på*, and *om* : the first implying the past, where the noun takes final *s* ; the second the future ; and the third some recurring period ; as : *jeg var der i Tirsdags* ; *jeg skal dér igen på Torsdag, men jeg er dér ellers altid om Søndagen*, I was there on Tuesday, I shall be there again on Thursday, but I am otherwise always there on Sundays.

På, when used before the names of the days of the week, always conveys a sense of futurity ; as :—

han kommer måske på Søndag, he may possibly come on Sunday.
men jeg tror heller at han gør Rejsen hertil på Mandag, but I rather think that he will come here next Monday.

Om answers to the English "on," "in," "about," when a slightly indefinite sense is conveyed; as for example:—

vi vænte vor Fader om fjorten Dage, we expect our father in about a fortnight.
min Söster var her om Morgenen, my sister was here in the morning

V. The prepositions *af, for, om, over, til, ved* frequently govern an infinitive preceded by *at*, and used as a gerund; as:—

jeg er ked af at höre den Mand tale, I am tired of hearing that man talk.
ham kom ikke for at undskylde sig, he did not come to exculpate himself.
jeg bryder mig ikke om at se ham, I do not care about seeing him.
Bonden var ved at arbejde da jeg så ham, the peasant was working when I saw him.
hun var hjærteligt glad over at se ham, she was heartily glad to see him.
her er ingen Plads til at sidde på, there is no place here to sit on.

REMARK.—When the infinitive is used in apposition with a noun, no preposition precedes it; as for example:—

den gode Vane at stå tidlig op, the good habit of getting up early.

VI. Some prepositions admit of being placed after instead of before the words which they govern, and thus lose their predominant characteristic; as for example:—

han gik mig forbi, he went past (by) me.
Dem var det ikke han talte om, it was not you of whom he spoke.
det var mig som hun gav det til, it was to me she gave it.
luk Dören op, open the door.
luk ikke Dören i (til), do not shut the door.

For a list of prepositions which do not admit of such transposition, see p. 206, *Forty-Eight Lesson*.

VII. *Ad*, on, towards, at, to, by; and *af*, off, from, of, although occasionally confounded, are generally marked by distinctive meanings; as:—

han gik ad Skoven til, he went towards the wood.
han gik af Vejen, he went off the road.

For the special mode of using some of he Danish prepositions, see APPENDIX I., *p.* 275.

(325)

CONJUNCTIONS. (*Bindeord.*)

The following are the principal Danish conjunctions:—

I.—COPULATIVE CONJUNCTIONS.

at, that
både...og, both ...and
da, as, since (past time)
dernæst, in the next place
dersom, in case that, if
fordi, because
hvis, if, in case that
ifald, in case

når, when, if (present and fut. time)
og, ogsi, and, also
om, if
så, so, therefore
samt, together with
siden, since
som, as
såvel...som, as well...as

II.—COMPOUND AND OTHER CONJUNCTIONS.

alligevel, notwithstanding
efterdi, since
eftersom, whereas, in accordance with
eller, ellers, or, otherwise
end, than
enddog, although
for at, in order that
hverken...eller, neither...nor

ligesom, as
men, såmen, but, indeed
nok så mange, ever so many
nok så snart, ever so soon
skönlt (endskönt)
om endskönt } notwithstanding
så godt som, as good as, as well as
uagtet, notwithstanding.

REMARK.—*At*, to, is used to indicate the infinitive of the verb, as in English.

1. Adverbs and prepositions are frequently used in the sense of conjunctions; as:

> *han købte mange Ting, nemlig Knive, Sakse, o.s.v.*, he bought many things, as knives, scissors, etc.
> *jo større Besværlighed, jo større Ære*, the greater the difficulty, the greater the honour.

(*See p.* 219, *Fifty-First Lesson.*)

2. The conjunctions *at*, that; *hvis, ifald*, in case, if; *når*, when; *dersom, if*, in case, may be omitted, when the second co-ordinate part of a compound sentence expresses the main idea; as for example:

> *jeg så (at) han faldt*, I saw that he fell.
> *vidste jeg det (dersom jeg vidste det), spurgte jeg ikke derom*, had I known it (if I had known it), I should not have asked about it.

INTERJECTIONS. (*Udråbsord.*)

Danish interjections are either derived from the imperative of verbs, or are mere ejaculatory, or imitative sounds; as: *Ti!* hush! from *at tie,* to keep silence; *Hej!* Ho! *Puf!* Pop!

ON THE FORMATION OF WORDS.

(*Orddannelse.*)

I. Nouns (*Navneord*), as has already been stated, frequently end in *de, dom, e, hed, me, skab,* and it is by the addition of one or other of these terminal affixes to an adjective, that a large class of nouns is formed; as :—

en *Dybde,* a depth, from *dyb,* deep.
en *Plathed,* a flatness ,, *plat,* flat.
en *Troskab,* a fidelity ,, *tro,* faithful.

For additional examples of this mode of formation, and for the distinctive differences of meaning attached to the various affixes, see *pp.* 131, 132, *Thirty-First Lesson.*

1. Many nouns are formed by the addition of *en, ing, ning, else, sel,* to verbs; as :—

en *Tænken,* a mode of thought, from *at tænke,* to think.
en *Længsel,* a longing ,, *at længes,* to long for.

REMARK.—The terminations *ing, ning,* generally indicate actions, but occasionally they are used for personal nouns, as: *en Olding,* an old man; *en Hedning,* a heathen. The same is the case with regard to *else,* as: *et Spøgelse,* a ghost, although this affix usually implies a property or mental action. (See *p.* 15, *Fifth Lesson,* and *p.* 131, *Thirty-First Lesson.*)

II. Most adjectives (*Tillægsord*) end in *agtig, ig, lig, tig, som, bar, et, sk,* or *isk.*

(327)

REMARKS.—*Agtig* generally implies direct resemblance or approximation, as : *tyragtig*, thief-like ; *storagtig*, grand.

Sk, isk, usually indicate the nationality of an individual or thing, as : *dansk*, Danish ; *præussisk*, Prussian ; but the termination *sk* in ordinary adjectives is often associated with words conveying a disparaging meaning, as : *spodsk*, derisive ; *lumsk*, deceitful.

For fuller definitions of the terminations of adjectives, see p. 139, *Thirty-Third Lesson*.

III. Adverbs (*Biord*), as has already been observed, are formed from adjectives, or are identical with them. Grammarians are undecided, and some of the best writers are even at variance with one another, and not determined in their own practice, as to whether any distinction should be made between adverbs and adjectives, where the latter end in *lig*. Thus, while some would write : *det kan umuligt blive farligt*, that cannot possibly be dangerous, others might write : *det kan ikke mulig blive farlig*.

IV. Verbs (*Udsagnsord*) derive great nicety of definition by means of the different particles in which they end, or by a change in their radical vowel, as :—

    at flage, to deck with flags   *at kvæde*, to chant
    at flagre, to flap, flicker   *at kvidre*, to chirp.

1. The German affixes *be* and *er* convey an intensified reflective or psychical meaning to the original verb ; as :—

    at tænke, to think   *at fare*, to move on
    at betænke, to consider   *at erfare*, to learn by experience.

2. The affixes *mis, und, van*, generally imply a negation, or deficiency, as :—

    at forstå, to understand   *at gå*, to go
    at misforstå, to misunderstand   *at undgå*, to evade.

(*See p. 143, Thirty-Fourth Lesson.*)

V. It may be observed, in regard to certain prepositions (*Forholdsord*) and conjunctions (*Bindeord*), and also with reference to some adverbs, that the differences in their terminations, which convey different meanings, are due to the survival of the different forms of inflection, which characterised the original Old Northern noun, or adjective, from which they have been derived.

Thus, for instance, in such words as *hjem*, *hjemme*, we trace the original distinction of cases in the terminal *e*, which represents the Old Northern dative in *i*, while the absence of any affix, or the termination *n*, similarly indicates the accusative; accordingly, we have: *hjem* (*at gå hjem*, to go home, acc.), *hjemme* (*at være hjemme*, to be at home, dat.).

The same indication of original distinctions of case are similarly observable in such prepositions, as: *op*, *oppe*, up; *ind*, *inde*, *inden*, in; *ud*, *ude*, *uden*, out. Here, as has already been noticed, the *e* implies rest (dat. and abl.), while its absence, or the addition of *n*, implies motion (acc.).

COMPOSITION OF WORDS.

(*Ordsammensætning*.)

I. The main rule to be observed in the formation of compound words, is that the last member of the verbal group should indicate the part of speech to which the compound word belongs, and should express its main character. Where the compound is a noun, the whole must follow the gender and number of this last member of the group, as: *et Rødvinglas*, a claret-glass; *Guldpenge* (pl.), gold money.

II. The combined words may be joined without undergoing any change, as: *et Ølglas*, a beer, or ale-glass; or they may undergo certain alterations, by taking a terminal *e*, *n*, or *ns*, or by dropping a final letter. This is either simply for the sake of euphony, or more frequently in accordance with some earlier mode of inflection, to which the words had conformed in O.N.; as: *Gudelære* (*Gud*, god; *Lære*, doctrine), mythology; *Barnepige*, nursemaid; *Øjenslyst*, lust of the eye; *hjærtensgod*, amiable; *Kvindfolk*, womankind.

III. Some compounds have in the course of time lost the distinctive features of their several parts, as in the expletives *hillemænd! sømænd!* which were originally *o, hellige Mænd!* oh, ye Saints! *så sandt, hjælpe mig de hellige Mænd!* it is true, so help me the Saints!

IV. Some compounds can only be interpreted by a reference to the Old Northern, as: *Davre*, breakfast; *Nadvere*, supper (*den hellige Nadver*, the Lord's supper); the O.N. being *dagverðr, nattverðr*, (*dag*, day; *natt*, night; *verðr*, a meal): *örkeslös*, idle (*yrkja*, O.N., work; *lauss*, loose, free).

V. Some compounds are perverted renderings of German words (more especially of low German), as: *Bommesi*, fustian (Ger., *Baumseide*); *Slobrok*, dressing gown (Ger., *Schlafrock*).

For further notice of compound words, see pp. 150-152, *Thirty-Sixth Lesson*.

CONSTRUCTION OF SENTENCES.

(*Sætningsbygning.*)

1. The nominative, or subject (*Grundord*) usually precedes the predicate (*Omsagn*), as: *Hun den løber hurtig*, the dog runs quickly; but in a secondary sentence, or in asking a question, the nominative follows the verb, as: *da jeg var i Skoven, löb Hunden endnu*, when I was in the wood the dog was still running; *löb Hunden i Skoven?* was the dog running in the wood?

1. The verb, or predicate, must agree in person and number with the nominative; as: *han går og trækker Slæden efter sig*, he goes and drags the sledge after him; *Hans, Niels og Anders vare i den samme Vogn*, John, Niels, and Andrew were in the same carriage.

REMARK.—In addressing an individual the plural personal pronoun *de*, they (written with a capital *D*, as *De, Dem, Deres*) is used with a singular verb; as: *er De syg?* are you ill? *De har tabt Deres Stok*, you have lost your stick.

2. Where an adjective is used as a predicate it must agree in gender and number with the subject; as: *Stolen er bred, men ikke höj*, the chair is broad, but not high; *Huset er bredt, men ikke höjt*, the house is wide, but not high; *Trapperne vaskes rene*, the stairs will be washed clean.

II. Where two nouns come together, the one of which denotes possession in regard to the other, the first, as in English, is put in the possessive, or genitive case (*Ejendomsforhold, Ejeord*), as: *det er ikke Mandens Skyld*, it is not the man's fault. Where two or more nouns are included in the same possessive sense, it is only the last which takes the distinctive mark of the genitive; as: *på min Moder og min Kones Vegne*, on behalf of my mother and my wife.

For a further definition of the use of the genitive, *see pp.* 172-175, *Forty-First Lesson.*

III. The object (*Genstand*) follows the subject and its verb directly, in a simple sentence: as: *han skriver et langt Brev*, he is writing a long letter; *de spise lækkert Smörrebröd*, they are eating delicious bread and butter (sandwiches). Some adjectives require that the objective noun should precede them; as: *han er den Ting magtig*, he is competent to do that.

1. Nouns of time, space, measure, value, and cost, may be used in the objective case without a preposition after neuter verbs, as: *han blev her fjorten Dage*, he stayed here a fortnight; *han er kommen mange Mil*, he has come many miles; *Kanden vejer ti Lod*, the can weighs ten ounces.

2. The verbs *at være* and *at blive* take the accusative after them, when used impersonally; as: *det er mig*, it is I; *det bliver Dem*, it will be you.

3. These verbs, as well as *at hedde, at kaldes*, to be called, when used as the predicate to the subject, are followed directly by a nominative without an article; as: *han er Köbmand*, he is a merchant; *hun hedder Louise*, she is called Louise. Where an adjective is used to designate the individual, it is preceded by the independent adjective article, and has the character of a proper noun in apposition to the subject; as: *Karl kaldtes den Store*, Charles was called the Great.

IV. The dative (*middelbare Gienstand, Hensynsord*) precedes the objective, as in English, when expressed directly, as: *han gav Drengen en Skilling*, he gave the boy a skilling. But where it is expressed by a preposition, its place in a sentence changes, as: *han gav en Skilling til Drengen*, he gave a skilling to the boy.

V. When the subject is represented by a personal pronoun (*Stedord*), the latter in all respects follows the rules by which the noun would have been governed, as: *han slog sig da han faldt*, he struck himself when he fell.

REMARK.—The third person plural "they," *de*, cannot be used in an impersonal sense as "they say," "they think;" the Danish mode of construction requiring that a noun, or the indefinite pronoun *man*, one, should be used before the verb, as: *Folk fortælle*, people relate; *man siger*, one says.

1. The objective case of the personal pronoun is used in some instances in a possessive sense; as: *det er en Ven af mig*, it is a friend of mine.

2. The interrogative and relative pronouns *hvo, hvem*, who, whom; *hvad*, what; require to be followed by another relative pronoun (*der, som*), when used as the subjects of the secondary clause in a sentence; as: *jeg ved ikke, hvo der har gjort det*, I do not know who has done it. The relative pronoun is not required, however, where the adverbs *her*, here, *der*, there, may be made to precede the verb; as: *jeg ved hvo her er*, I know who is here.

The use of the second relative is optional where the verb is preceded by an adverb, as: *hvo gjerne arbejder, fortjener vel sit Bröd*, he who works willingly, well earns his bread.

When *hvad for* is used in the place of *hvilket*, which, what, it immediately precedes the noun to which it refers, and may be employed before plurals, as well as singulars; as: *hvad for Efterretninger bringer han?* what tidings does he bring?

3. *Hinanden*, each other, *hverandre*, one another; can only be used reflectively and objectively, and must follow the verb

that is governed by the subject which they reflect; as: *to Venner bör hjælpe hinanden*, two friends should help each other.

For a definition of the distinctive uses of the possessive pronouns *sin, sit, sine,* and *hans, hendes, deres, see p.* 52, *Thirteenth Lesson,* and for the use of the pronouns generally, *see pp.* 183-185, *Forty-Third Lesson,* and *pp.* 188, 189, *Forty-Fourth Lesson.*

VI. The verb (*Udsagnsord*) ought to agree with its subject in person and number, and follow it in a simple sentence, as :—

min Broder og min Söster ere ikke i dette Værelse, my brother and my sister are not in this room.

In interrogatives, as already remarked, the verb precedes its subject, as :—

er min Broder i dette Værelse? is my brother in this room?
kommer De? are you coming?

REMARK.—In common parlance and familiar correspondence, and even occasionally in composition, the verb is used in the singular, irrespective of its subject, as :—

vi var der i Går, we were there yesterday.
de taler meget höjt, they speak very loudly.
har vi ikke Ret? are we not in the right?

(*See p.* 198, *Forty-Sixth Lesson*).

1. When an infinitive, or an entire clause of a sentence constitutes the subject, the latter is considered as a singular, and the verb is made to agree with it; as :—

at dö for sit Fædreland er herligt, it is noble to die for one's Fatherland.
at de faldt var bedröveligt, it was sad that they should have fallen.

2. Some of the auxiliaries, as *ville, skulle, måtte, kunne, turde, burde*, take an infinitive directly as the object of the sentence, without *at*, to, as :—

jeg turde ikke se ham, I did not dare to see him.

3. Some verbs of sensation, or feeling, take an infinitive as the object of the sentence, but only when preceded by *at*, to, as:—

> *han håber at finde hende*, he hopes to find her.

4. Some verbs of sense, command, etc., and the defective verb *at lade*, to let, may be followed by an entire sentence having an infinitive with an objective case, as:—

> *hun så ham løbe hen til Konen*, she saw him run towards the woman.
> *jeg lader dig ikke gå på Vandet i Dag*, I will not allow you to go on the water to-day.

At lade, when followed by an accusative and an active infinitive sometimes conveys to the latter a passive sense, as:—

> *min Fader lader et Hus bygge*, my father is having a house built.

5. Every active verb may, by the help of a preposition, be converted into a passive; as: *Soldaten slog Drengen*, the soldier struck the boy; *Drengen sloges (blev slået) af Soldaten*, the boy was beaten by the soldier.

Conversely, by dropping the preposition, and converting the objective into a nominate case, a passive can be turned into an active form, as: *Landet erobredes af Fjenden*, the country was conquered by the enemy, which may be rendered *Fjenden erobrede Landet*.

Where the verb has no direct object, and is used in an intransitive, neuter sense, the passive can only be employed in an impersonal form, as: *der skrives af mig*, there is writing done by me (*jeg skriver*, I write).

6. In addition to the active and passive form, the Danish has a deponent form of the verb (*Gencirkende Form*) which in most respects is identical with the Latin deponent.

7. The indicative mood is very generally employed, both in active and deponent verbs, in the place of the optative or

subjunctive, whose use is practically limited to certain exclamations, or invocations, as :—

> *Gud tröste dig!* may God comfort thee!
> *Dronningen leve!* long live the queen!

The present tense (*Nutiden*, indicative) is used, as already shown, to express both that which is passing at the moment, and that which usually occurs at a definite time, as : *Drengen går hver Dag i Skole*, the boy goes every day to school. It may also be used for the imperfect, or past, in historical or descriptive narrative, as : *Cæsar kommer, ser og sejrer*, Cæsar came, saw, and conquered ; and it is used as a future tense, when the precise period of time is indicated by the other parts of the sentence, as : *jeg rejser næste År til Amerika*, I shall go next year to America.

The past tense (*Datiden*) is used to indicate a past period, whose precise limitation is undefined ; as :—

> *Generalen ödelagde Landet*, the general laid waste the country.
> *jeg skrev, da han kom*, I was writing when he came.

It also is used as a conditional, and as a second future; as :—

> *handlede De efter mit Råd, kunde det endnu blive godt*, if you had acted in accordance with my advice, all might still go well.
> *jeg gik ud i Aften, hvis jeg vidste det blev godt Vejr*, I would go out this evening, if I knew that it would be fine.

The perfect is used to express a completed past ; as :—

> *jeg har læst Bogen, kender altså dens Indhold*, I have read the book, and therefore I know the contents.

The pluperfect is used when reference is made to something that had passed when some other past event was yet in operation ; as :—

> *jeg var gået, da han kom*, I had gone when he came.

The present future (*Fremtiden*) is used when a future is spoken of, which may follow something present ; as :—

> *jeg håber at du vil göre det*, I hope that you will do it.

The imperfect future (*Förfremtiden*) is used where a future is spoken of, which has reference to a past period; as:—

jeg önskede at han vilde komme, I wished that he would come.

8. The imperative (*Bydende Måde*) is used in the active and deponent form of verbs (but not in the passive); as:—

giv mig Kniven, give me the knife.
blues over din Frækhed! blush for thy audacity!

9. Where participles (*Tillægsformerne*) are used as adjectives, they must be made to accord, like the latter, with their subject; as: *Bogen er skreven : en skreven Bog*, the book is written; a written book; *Bogstavet er skrevet ; et skrevet Bogstav*, the letter (of the alphabet) is written; a written letter; *Bogstaverne ere skrevne : de skrevne Bogstaver*, the letters are written; the written letters; *en bidende Vind*, a biting wind. The same conformity is required where the participles are used in their genuine verbal character; as: *Bogstavet er blevet skrevet*, the letter has been written.

The present participle may be made to take the place of a relative pronoun, as *den hjemkommende Mand*, the man who is coming home.

REMARK.—On the other hand, the present participle cannot be used, as in English, as a gerund, or in the sense of an ablative absolute, which must be otherwise rendered : as: thinking that he was there, I went to the house, *da jeg troede han var der, gik jeg hen til Huset*.

V. The negative *ikke*, not: admits of a more extended application in Danish than in English, since it may elliptically be made to replace the verb; as: *De kommer, ikke sandt?* you are coming, are you not? (*sandt*, true); *ikke andet?* is there nothing else?

REMARK.—It must be observed that in statements, or questions, involving a negative, the adverb *jo*, yes, must be employed as an affirmation : while *ja*, yes, is required where no negation is expressed, or implied; as: *han er vel ikke syg?* he is surely not ill; *jo, han er syg*, yes, he is; *er han syg? ja, han er syg*.

The determination of the right place in a sentence for the negative, *ikke*, presents considerable difficulty, which can only be completely overcome by an extended knowledge of the writings of the best authors; it may, however, be accepted as a general rule:—

(1) That in simple sentences of negation, having reference to a question. or preceding statement, the negative should stand last; as :—

fordærver han sine Börn ? nej, han fordærver dem ikke, does he spoil his children? no, he does not spoil them.
véd De det? do you know?
jeg véd det ikke, I do not know.

(2) The negative *ikke* should, if possible, stand next to the verb to which it refers; as :—

de Fleste ere glade ved ikke at behöve at ændse Börnene i et Hus, most persons are glad not to be forced to notice the children of a household.
den Enkelte, der virkelig elsker Börn, behöve Forældrene ikke at frygte, parents need not have any fear of the one individual who may chance to have a real love for children.

VI. Although prepositions (*Forholdsord*) generally may be said to govern an accusative, or dative, several, as has already been observed, (*see p.* 148, *Thirty-Fifth Lesson*), govern a genitive; as :—

mine Börn gå til Sengs Klokken ni, my children go to bed at nine o'clock.

1. Certain adverbs of time and place, composed of a preposition and another part of speech, admit of being dissolved into their several parts, in which case the preposition may be put at the end of the sentence; as:—

der er Skuffen hvor jeg lagde det i, there is the drawer in which I laid it.
her er Bordet jeg tog Bogen af, there is the table from which I took the book.

This post-position of some prepositions is frequent after the relative pronoun *som* ; as :—

hvor er Manden, som jeg gav det til? where is the man to whom I gave it?

For a list of prepositions which do not admit of such a transposition, see p. 206, *Forty-Eighth Lesson*.

2. The conjunctions *at*, that; *när*, when; *hvis*, *i Fald*, *dersom*, if, in case; *altsä*, consequently, therefore; may be omitted, as :—

jeg sä han faldt, I saw he fell.

gjorde du det, var det mig kært, if you would do that, it would be most agreeable to me (*ifald du gjorde det, sä var det mig kært*).

www.ingramcontent.com/pod-product-compliance
Lightning Source LLC
Chambersburg PA
CBHW031430230426
43668CB00007B/485